PEOPLE AND
PUBLIC ADMINISTRATION

PEOPLE AND
PUBLIC ADMINISTRATION
Case Studies and Perspectives

Phillip E. Present
California State University, Northridge

PALISADES PUBLISHERS   Pacific Palisades, California 90272

Library of Congress Catalog Card Number: 78-70260
International Standard Book Number: 0-913530-13-1

Palisades Publishers
P.o. Box 744
Pacific Palisades, California 90272

Printed in the United States of America

Contents

TOPIC ONE
PUBLIC ADMINISTRATION:
ITS CHARACTERISTICS AND CHALLENGES

TOPIC TWO
THE INDIVIDUAL IN ADMINISTRATION:
ETHICAL CHOICES

TOPIC THREE
THE INDIVIDUAL AND THE ORGANIZATION

TOPIC FOUR
THE INDIVIDUAL IN THE
PUBLIC PERSONNEL PROCESS

TOPIC FIVE
THE ADMINISTRATOR
AS DECISION AND POLICYMAKER

TOPIC SIX
BUDGETS AND PROGRAM EVALUATION:
ON THE ROAD TO ACCOUNTABILITY

Preface

Public policies and the people who administer them are a pervasive influence in modern life. Few citizens can escape their effects. Conversely, public administrators cannot ignore for long the pressure brought to bear upon them and their programs by people both inside and outside the bureaucracy. This book highlights these important elements and shows the interaction of people, organizations, and programs and their effects in public administration.

In thinking about any public organization, including the most depersonalized, complex, and unresponsive one imaginable—and that may describe precisely the one in which you currently are being educated or employed—what needs to be remembered is that the bureaucracy is largely the sum total of the people who work for it and those who influence it from the outside. Individuals associated with an organization, singly and collectively, contribute to the character of the bureaucracy. Even if two organizations have the same structure, they will not be identical in procedures or nature because of the differences in the personalities of the employees within the organization and the people outside toward whom the policy is directed.

It is this human perspective and influence on public administration which is the theme of this book. Two general purposes are intended to be served by the Topic Introductions and the selections. First, they should alert the readers to the importance of the attitudes, values, and behaviors of individuals in the administration of government. These personal qualities influence and sometimes determine what public agencies do. The cases illustrate that public administration does not function in a neat, mechanical, and sterile environment, but that it is an ongoing process of conflict and resolution which is based upon individual and group perceptions of problems, values, and power.

A second objective of this book is to give a clearer picture of what public administrators actually do in their work. This is not to restate what they are supposed to do, but rather to illustrate how the individuals' responses determine what they do. Examples of people at all levels within an agency are given. This perspective on public administration is especially useful for students who have had no administrative experience and who have little idea of the demands, frustrations, responsibilities, and rewards in administration.

A deficiency in most other public administration casebooks and readers has been their lack of a unifying theme. If there is any particular emphasis at all—rather than simply a collection of articles about administration—it is on the amorphous topic of the "administrative system." Many instructors have come to realize that unless there is a more specific and concrete focus on the people who are administrators, students get only the vaguest notion about the real factors that influence public administration.

Another feature of this book is that its selections are not drawn solely from academic journals. Many come from the type of periodicals that students are likely to read even if they take no other course in public administration. Several of the cases are written by professional journalists and political writers whose lively style enhances the drama of the administrative event being analyzed. Yet their writing does not neglect the salient points needed by students to understand the significance of the issue. Some of the other contributions in this book are written by working administrators or by the people affected by them, thereby bringing a very personal perspective to the subject. With a few exceptions, each case is about actual people and events, and illustrates the fact that these occurrences happen more often than most administrators would want to admit.

Even though the human aspects of public administration are emphasized, it is essential for students not to underestimate the importance of also knowing administrative skills and techniques. Some of these are discussed in the Topic Introductions, as a degree of balance is required between them and the human factors. Just as interesting "war stories" (cases) without a theoretical setting may not tell us much about general administrative processes, so a great deal about "principles and theory" without the test of reality does little to help a working administrator. To enable a student to test the principles that are being studied, some realistic examples of the types of problems faced by public administrators are presented. Together, these principles and practices should round out a student's views of public administration.

Phillip E. Present

An Overview

This book was designed to be read primarily in consecutive order because the Topic Introductions often refer to materials and selections previously presented. There has been an attempt to build each Topic upon the preceding one to show a continuity and relationship among these six major issue-areas in public administration. It is suggested, therefore, that students keep in mind the general theme and the two objectives of the book touched upon in the Preface and the specific issues found in the Topic Introductions to see how these are constantly appearing in the selections.

Topic One sets out some concepts pertinent to the study and practice of public administration. A discussion is presented about the special characteristics of governmental administration, the importance of accountability, what administrators do, and some broad principles of public administration in practice.

In Topic Two, the focus is on some very real and difficult ethical choices that confront administrators and the manner in which several people have met these challenges. Because ethical values do not exist in a vacuum but are a product of many factors, a brief examination is made of the political cultures which influence individual administrative behavior.

Topic Three looks at the relationship of individuals to formal and informal organizations. Some of the questions considered are why organizations are formed, what kinds of structural models are adopted, what are the relationships between individual motivations and organizational structures, and what are the key elements in reorganization.

Topic Four on personnel administration examines more closely the individual within the organization. Because of the controversial and emotionally-charged nature of such issues as civil service regulations and affirmative action, personnel administrators face individual conflicts and pressures in their efforts to make the personnel process more human while at the same time trying to satisfy rigid governmental rules. Much of this Topic deals with attempts to reconcile two or more defensible, yet conflicting, administrative goals.

Topic Five concentrates on the administrator as decisionmaker. The various ways that decisions can be made and the importance of individuals in the process are analyzed. The five selections illustrate the influence of organizations, ethics, and politics upon the individual administrator in the decisionmaking process.

Topic Six traces the development of the use of budgets by public administrators. The linkage of budgets, program evaluation, and administrative accountability is shown, along with the specific role that individual administrators serve in each of these functional areas. The book closes, therefore, as it began—with an emphasis on public administrators, their special responsibilities, and their need to be aware of the human elements in the administrative process.

Topic One

Public Administration: Its Characteristics and Challenges

Introduction

Administration, or the process by which resources and techniques are coordinated to formulate, implement, and manage policy decisions, is an ancient human activity. Written records of some of the earliest societies show that people were organized formally to attain certain objectives such as building monuments, aqueducts, and cities, or to conduct commerce or war. One of the first written accounts of a public administrator is in the *Bible*, where Joseph was given responsibility for the planning and distribution of the food supply for Egypt. Down through the ages, the basic administrative functions of planning, decisionmaking, coordinating, directing, supervising, staffing, budgeting, and evaluating have remained fairly constant.

What has changed tremendously, however, has been the size of administrative activities in terms of resources used and people affected. The types of techniques employed to achieve these administrative functions have been modified. As a result, administration over the past generation has become a highly specialized academic field and profession which today shows few signs of becoming any less complex.

As large-scale business and governmental organizations have become the rule rather than the exception, two important consequences have developed. First, these entities and the people working in them no longer are perceived in human or personal terms. From time to time we may be rudely or pleasantly reminded that these organizations are staffed by people, but for the most part such organizations are viewed in impersonal ways. Similarly, employees within these organizations often lose the human perspective on either their own particular administrative role or on the relationship of their agency to other people and organizations.

The second consequence stemming from complex organizations is the lack of accountability both within these bureaucracies and between these organizations and the public. In its simplest form, the principle of administrative accountability means that individuals will be held responsible for their organizational actions. Under this doctrine, it is possible for people in a particular organization and the public to know who made certain administrative decisions or who performed particular administrative procedures and under what authority.

The issues covered so far are well illustrated in Selection 1, "The Pornography of Everyday Life." Warren Bennis cites several examples there which show that administrators in large organizations often build "shields against any inclination to think of the human and social consequences" of their actions. Instead, these people prefer to measure their performance in the organization in terms of "efficiency." Their concern is to carry out administrative tasks and not to think about the effect or results of their work on others or even themselves.

Bennis asks a fundamental administrative question that has implications for all of society: Is there something inherent in large organizations which causes individuals, when acting on behalf of their organization, to be able and willing to shun personal responsibilities for their actions? If the reader's answer is Yes, then what realistically can be done within organizations to correct this? If the answer is No (organizations do not adversely affect human personality), how else can one account for this type of behavior and what would rectify it?

As Bennis and others have suggested, solutions advocating simple or symbolic answers do not deal effectively with the issue. Similarly, readers of this book should be cautioned also that the approach contained here—emphasizing the importance of people in the administrative process—should not be confused with a "down with technocracy" view. Instead, an assumption of this book is that people need and want many services, products, and activities, which can only be delivered widely and inexpensively because of the existence of some highly technical and complex organizations. In short, bureaucracy involves a trade-off: a sense of employee impersonality in an organization in exchange for mass application of expertise. The administrative challenge is to reconcile these two forces to the benefit of both the individual and the organization.

Public Administration Defined

What is public administration and what do public administrators actually do? For every person with the title "administrator" there will be a different answer to both questions, although there should also be some common ground for agreement. The definition for "administration" given at the beginning of this Introduction could be applied to public administration if the word "public" were placed in front of the words "resources" and "policy." Another writer defines public administration as "the accomplishment of politically determined objectives."[1] A more lengthy definition says public administration is "all processes, organizations, and individuals (the latter acting in official positions and roles) associated with carrying out laws and other rules adopted or issued by legislatures, executives and courts."[2]

These two definitions convey the impression that public administrators always respond to public decisions after they have already been made. In fact, and as will be seen in several of the selections, public administrators are instrumental in the formulation of the issue as well as the decision, thereby assuming more than a passive role in public policy. Public administrators, therefore, whether they are active or inactive (that is, refusing to act) are always exerting some effect on public policy questions at all stages of the policy process. Administration is not separate from politics but an integral part of the entire political process.

Unfortunately for students and administrators alike, public administration is not like chemistry where the precise mixture of prescribed chemicals produces predictable results. There are some rules, some do's and don't's in administration, but not to the extent found in the natural sciences. Administrators might be likened more to great chefs than chemists. A chef will start with the basic ingredients and have a fairly precise idea of the proper proportions. But the really outstanding recipe requires more than just the basic foodstuffs and measured amounts. It results from experience in knowing how to acquire the finest ingredients and then in blending, balancing, and bringing out certain flavors. Finally, the chef understands how to present the product in a pleasant setting. Successful administrators work in a comparable manner. They do not always act the same way because the problems they face are not identical. Yet, they have a feel for knowing what special techniques are needed in a given situation instead of always using the same formulas regardless of the circumstances. It must be remembered, however, that basic technical skills are essential as well as knowing how to employ them in the human situation.

The case study "The Seven Secrets of the Metroliner's Success" (Selection 2) focuses on what its author contends are essential ingredients for a successful program. The key is based on individuals and their own sense of administration, meaning their ability to coordinate people and resources. Whether these administrative skills can be learned or are inherent is an important question that is widely debated among administrators and educators. The case illustrates, nevertheless, the myriad tasks, responsibilities, and obstacles which public administrators encounter and with which they must contend.

Unique Characteristics of Public (Governmental) Administration

The term "administration" can be used without any designation between public (meaning governmental) and private (meaning business or nonprofit). Some administrators, educators, and graduate schools insist on the generic nature of administration and see little or no purpose in separating the term into categories. It is said that there are commonly accepted practices—some use the term principles—which all administrators employ regardless of their setting. For example, planning, personnel staffing, and budgeting take place at both General Motors and the U.S. Department of Housing and Urban Development, and the same effective management techniques can be applied to both agencies. Moreover, variables in administration such as organizational goals, size, and technology can be as useful in describing and explaining differences in administration and organizations as a public-private distinction.

Other writers, however, including this one, without denying the existence of similar administrative practices or the influence of many other factors, believe that there are certain distinctive and even unique attributes of public administration which private administration does not have. The reason for this is that public administration is a part of government and shares government's characteristics. It is this relationship to government, therefore, that gives public administration its special essence. It is not the administration by itself that is so distinctive; it is the governmental content and influence on the administration that distinguishes it. An understanding of government begins to explain the nature and practice of public administration.

Government has always been considered a unique form of social organization. Aristotle and the ancient Greeks viewed government as the instrument through which a person literally became civilized and could develop his or her full potential as a human being. Modern writers characterize government as having a monopoly on the legitimate use of force (Max Weber) and as the organization which establishes and enforces the "rules of the game" on all individuals and groups (David Truman and Robert Dahl). Both the ancients and moderns regard government as set apart because it provides the necessary preconditions for basic human needs of security, respect, and those values which can only be provided through collective action.

Although the responsibilities which people assign to government vary from time to time, they flow from the basic need of people to regulate and order their relationships with one another. The freedoms of speech, press, and assembly guaranteed by the First Amendment to the U.S. Constitution, for example, have little value without an agreed-upon means of ensuring them for each citizen and of resolving conflicts among them. For instance, do the American Nazis have the right to hold a rally and march where and when they want? It is to government—the courts in this situation—that we assign the responsibility for deciding among several conflicting rights. We authorize government to use force, if necessary, to enforce the rules we establish. People tolerate the use of force, however, only if they believe that it serves the best interest of them all. In this sense, governmental acts have a moral dimension. Citizens give government the right to command only so long as government acts fairly and serves the values of those governed. Most people do not have similar expectations of other secular organizations. Government is different and the differences permeate every aspect of governmental activity, especially public administration.

There are five significant attributes of public administration which flow from the fact that it does partake of governmental characteristics. These in turn create the conditions and setting in which public administrators must function.

1. Governmental structures are complex and fragmented. The American governmental system (or the U.S. Constitution, if one prefers) has certain structural characteristics which reflect concerns about the abuse of power and which affect governmental administration. Federalism and the separation of powers greatly influence the practice of public administration. Federalism is the basic political framework of the United States. It is a distribution of power between two or more levels of government, and in the case of the United States, it outlines the political and administrative relationships between the national (federal) and state governments. Specifically, federalism is a structural arrangement "whereby: (1) the same territory and people are governed by two levels of government, both of which derive their authority from the people and both of which share some functions and exercise other functions autonomously of each other; (2) the existence of each level is protected from the other; and (3) each may exert leverage on the other."[3] Much of American history, beginning with the Federalists and Anti-Federalists, has been a struggle over defining the precise boundaries and limits in the relationship between the national and state governments. Except in those few areas where the Constitution assigns exclusive jurisdiction, the unanswered questions have been: Which level of government should have administrative responsibilities for governmental policies? What role should each level of government play in administering programs? In seeking answers, the national and state governments over the years have generally been "flexible, fluid and pragmatic, ever changing and adjusting with shifts in power loci and public attitudes" and not highly doctrinaire.[4]

Federalism has had several consequences for public administration. First, it has caused competition between and among agencies and administrators on both levels of government. Sometimes this competition has led to cooperation; other times it has resulted in fierce conflict and suspicion. Second, federalism has offered the opportunity for administrators to experiment with programs and management techniques. Because of so many governmental jurisdictions within the federal structure, it has afforded administrators a chance to try programs on a limited basis and under more controlled conditions. Many federal programs currently in existence, for example, owe their origins to state administrators who first implemented them. Third, federalism has enabled a greater number of citizens direct access to the policymaking process. With the wide range of federal-state programs and their increased requirement for citizen participation, more people are involved in policy formulation and evaluation than ever before. This has had both positive and negative consequences for accountability. On one hand, active citizens are in a position to know about administrators and to make judgments on their performances. This has made public employees conscious of being responsible for what they do. On the other hand, too many citizens involved in the administrative process can actually obscure administrative accountability. Administrators can shift some of their functions to citizen groups, thereby absolving themselves of responsibilities and negating some of the advantages of citizen participation.

A second structural influence on public administration is separation of powers. This is a distribution of power among or between branches of government on the same level of government. Because the United States has this type of government at the national, state, and to a lesser extent at the local level, public administration is affected. Regardless of the level of government, struggles arise among the executive, legislative, and judicial branches over policymaking, implementation, and evaluation. All three branches have responsibilities pertaining to administrative agencies; however, the lines of authority often are not clear. Conflicts then occur over the question of where the legislative function ends and the executive function begins with respect to an agency. For example, the present debate at the national level over so-called "legislative vetoes" illustrates how struggles arise between Congress and the President over the control of public policy. In cases such as this, the courts often become involved in the attempt to define the functions and powers of the other two branches.

Another related consequence of separation of powers pertains to organizational change. Public organizations often must seek both executive and legislative approval before making any fundamental alterations in their goals or structure. This is a time-consuming process for administrators and full of political obstacles. As a result of separation of powers, the most effective administrators are those who can walk a narrow line between the executive and legislative branches and still maintain a degree of their own independence.

Federalism and separation of powers lead almost inevitably to another characteristic of American politics—fragmentation. There are a great many governmental jurisdictions with overlapping geographical boundaries, especially at the local level. Each has its own limited authority and decisionmaking responsibilities, which create insufficient cohesiveness and integrated effort in solving common problems. As a result of this fragmentation, administrators often cannot deliver certain levels of services to people because they lack sufficient authority to deal with problems that exceed their particular jurisdictions.

Fragmentation is not necessarily undesirable. To many people, it represents the democratic ideal of local government. Fragmented jurisdictions can provide many access points to the decisionmaking process. Above all, it can be a protection against the abuse of centralized power. Whatever the merits, if any, of fragmentation, it, along with federalism and separation of powers, tests daily the skills of thousands of public administrators as they work within these structural arrangements.

2. Accountability in the administrative process. The second attribute of public administration derived from its relationship to governmental characteristics is accountability. The concept of accountability and its relation to individual behavior is a theme in many selections throughout this book. At the beginning of this Introduction, accountability was defined in terms of individuals being held responsible for their adminstrative actions. The term also implies that there will be some kind of external control or standard by which administrative action can be regulated or judged.

This notion of performance standards is certainly not new. Almost 4,000 years ago in Babylonia, the Hammurabi Code stated that a builder must pay with his own life if a building he constructed should fall on his client. Today there is increasing effort to find ways of holding people, particularly governmental employees, responsible for what they do in public life, although few would advocate going as far as the penalty in Babylonia. There are many practical and theoretical obstacles in applying accountability at the working level, yet that should not be used as an excuse for failing to make accountability an inherent part of public service employment.

Accountability is not unique to government. People should expect that business organizations will act in a responsible manner, and that their employees will be liable for acts detrimental to the public. At the very least we would expect them to produce a safe product. Of course, this does not always happen. The question then becomes, Does government have a responsibility to protect its citizens? Economist Milton Friedman and others believe that the economic marketplace can police and regulate those who act irresponsibly, and thereby eliminate the need for government in this area. Others believe that such mechanisms are insufficient, and that government must perform a regulatory role to some degree although the extent is subject to considerable debate. When governmental administrators are given this role, therefore, they acquire special obligations because they are being entrusted with fiduciary responsibilities on behalf of the public. This is the "moral dimension" of public administration discussed earlier that places additional burdens upon those individuals occupying positions in governmental administration.

A recent case illustrates the lack of accountability and performance standards that we have in the governmental administrative process. Jack Anderson and Les Whitten in their syndicated column of December 18, 1977, wrote about a building problem in Newark, New Jersey. Several warnings were given to the U.S. Department of Housing and Urban Development (HUD) that sections of the 24-story Weequahic Park Plaza building were about to fall. Outside consulting reports and even HUD's own engineers all confirmed what local officials had been saying to the federal government. HUD refused to take corrective action. Then, as predicted, portions of the seventh floor collapsed to the street below. It happened after midnight and no one was hurt. The next morning some emergency repairs were begun, but then the crews were suddenly pulled off the job. Apparently, HUD reasoned that if it made the repairs, this agency would be admitting responsibility. At the time of the Anderson-Whitten article, the citizens of Newark were not only attempting to get federal officials to fix the building, but even to admit that it existed.

Without knowing more details, it is impossible and unfair to place blame. What is certain, however, is that particular individuals were responsible for ensuring that a public building was safe. Yet it was not possible to identify them or to get them to fulfill their administrative duties in a competent manner. Unfortunately, this is not an unusual example, as similar situations can be found almost daily.

3. Interest group influences. A third characteristic of public administration attributable to government is interest group activity in the administrative process. At all levels as well as in and out of organizations we find group influence. At their best, interest groups fulfill the Madisonian model of competing groups guaranteeing the survival of the democratic process because of changes in their relative strength. In the past decade, there have been more groups representing views not previously expressed in the administrative process. Not all interest group activity, however, is necessarily beneficial to everyone. Interest groups, including those of public employees, can lead to parochialism and an emphasis on organizational survival. The relationships among organizations, therefore, can become ones of conflict instead of competition. It is possible for some groups to thwart administrative action taken without their approval. At the same time, the proliferation of interest groups tends to diffuse each group's influence.

Democratic government must encourage and provide the means for people and groups to participate in the decisionmaking process if the government is to remain democratic in practice. Interest groups are an effective way to do this. Democratic government must also deliver expected services and, to do this, policy decisions must be made and carried out. This process requires group compromise and a give-and-take attitude on the part of the participants. Because public administrators are often at the same time members of various interest groups as well as subject to them, they are likely to manifest special pressures and conflicts in the course of their administrative duties.

4. Ambiguous and imprecise organizational goals. The fourth significant quality of public administration is the existence of many goals which are not clearly defined and precise, especially in the public service and social welfare areas. This results from the multiplicity of groups competing in the political process, the bargaining and compromising process in which goals are determined, and the fragmented structure of the political system.

In addition, it is not unusual to find competing agencies with conflicting goals dealing with the same issue. The classic example for years at the national level has been the issue of tobacco. The Department of Health, Education and Welfare warns against the use of tobacco while Congress and the Department of Agriculture encourage farmers to grow the crop and assist in overseas sales.

The lack of precisely defined goals and the conflict among organizational subgoals have consequences for public administrators because they make planning, implementation, and evaluation of governmental programs difficult. An administrator without a clear understanding of the purpose of a goal may select an inadequate means to reach that goal. Further, the administrator may not be able to determine if the goal has been achieved because it was so vague in content.

It should be noted that not all governmental goals are imprecise. Some are very specific. The effort, however, to make governmental goals unequivocable becomes complicated by the very characteristics and constraints of the governmental system already described in this section.

5. *Civil service regulations.* The fifth attribute of public administration stemming from governmental characteristics is the multitude of civil service regulations under which personnel actions must be taken. A range of benefits and problems results from this extensive system of regulating employees in public organizations. Since parts of Topics Three and Four are devoted to a discussion of personnel procedures and their implications for organizations, the subject will not be developed here. It is sufficient to stress that public employees are in a trade-off situation under civil service. When compared to their counterparts in the private sector, public employees have certain advantages in their working conditions such as greater job security, higher total compensation (salary and fringe benefits) at the entry and middle levels, more predictable paths to promotion, and higher pension benefits. In exchange for these, public employees have more restrictions on rapid promotions (time-in-grade is a usual obstacle); they may have fewer opportunities to demonstrate their initiative in a freewheeling manner because of legal constraints; and top-level administrators will receive less compensation than comparable management levels outside of the civil service. These working conditions have implications for public administration and administrators. As a consequence, civil service regulations can create attitudes in public employees of indifference and smugness toward their jobs and the public which run counter to the highest standards of public service and accountability.

In summary, the features which distinguish public administration— structural arrangements, accountability, interest groups, imprecise goals, and civil service regulations—all can lead easily to administrative duplication, waste, ineffectiveness, and a lack of responsibility. This is not inevitable and certainly these negative descriptions do not fit all governmental agencies or employees. Yet there is always the possibility that the influence of the five features will be negative on public administration. The challenge to the conscientious public administrator is to make them work to the public's benefit and not to become overwhelmed by these factors. It is precisely that opportunity which can make public administration both an exciting and rewarding profession.

Public Administration in Practice

With this background on some of the important features of public administration, it is useful at this point to examine two cases which illustrate many of these points in practice.

The case study on overhauling the New York City welfare agency (Selection 3) contrasts working in government and private organizations. As Arthur Spiegel describes the situation, it was "an almost foreign culture" for those people coming from industry and getting their first encounter with the world of civil service. The experiences of the private sector people in the case indicate why it is sometimes very difficult for successful business executives to achieve the same outstanding results in high-level governmental administration. A number of business people, such as George Romney and Robert McNamara, have been frustrated in their efforts to deal with administration in Washington.

Many employees of the NYC welfare agency felt they were being invaded by outsiders, and adjustments by both groups were required. This case study highlights some striking differences in perspectives between the public and private administrators concerning organizational goals, management techniques and philosophies, approaches to problem-solving, and policy evaluation. Many of these differences are conditioned by the influences of the governmental system.

The Spiegel study might lead some readers to jump to the conclusion that the only prescription for improving public administration is more business administration. The case study by Max Ways on Watergate (Selection 4), however, should provide a cautionary note. In this case we see a number of managerial mistakes made by people who had come from the business world and who were expected to apply their previous business experience. In addition to their inability to put into practice some fundamental managerial principles, the other major problem was their lack of understanding and sensitivity to the meaning of the democratic procedures within which administration was to take place. With the notable exception of the President, most of the White House personnel had had very little experience in government although, sadly enough, several were lawyers who had been exposed to basic constitutional law. Previous governmental administrative service certainly does not guarantee honesty, but neither should the goal of efficiency and "business-like management" overshadow the importance of democratic values.

The final selection in Topic One is optimistic in tone. It suggests that there are practical answers to some of the difficult questions raised in this Introduction and the other selections in this Topic. The personality profile of William Coleman (Selection 5), the former U.S. Secretary of Transportation, reveals that not all administrators are necessarily engulfed by the administrative forces they encounter, nor are they unwilling to be accountable for their public actions.

Notes

1. Marshall E. Dimock and Gladys O. Dimock, *Public Administration* (New York: Holt, Rinehart and Winston, 1969), p. 3.

2. George J. Gordon, *Public Administration in America* (New York: St. Martin's Press, 1978), p. 8.

3. Parris N. Glendening and Mavis M. Reeves, *Pragmatic Federalism* (Pacific Palisades, Calif: Palisades Publishers, 1977), p. 7.

4. *Ibid.*, p. 8.

1

The Pornography of Everyday Life

Warren Bennis

When the Pentagon Papers were published, what disturbed me more than the deceits, the counter-deceits, the moral numbness and ethical short-circuiting of our leaders, was the pornography of it all. The hubris of those men, thousands of miles away, making life-and-death decisions for others, manipulating the most modern tools of technology, using game theory with models so abstract they could reproduce one another in one joyless, scream-less parthenogenetic act. But not once, these men, not once could they experience the epiphany of childbirth—or the smell of burning flesh.

I thought of pornography because that, also, is distance from reality, from direct experience. Actors in porn films are not real people making love, but appendages of sexual organs engaged in mechanical acts. These appendages are so without personalities or identifiable social characteristics that, as one movie critic pointed out, they are more about physical engineering than love—so many pistons and valves. Loveless sex. Distant, remote, calculated, vicarious.

The "war room" at the Pentagon is as distant from the reality of war as downtown Boston's so-called "combat zone," the festooned, free area for porno sales, is from the reality of sex.

In those now yellowing Papers, we see Secretary of Defense Robert S. McNamara busying himself with minutiae of war planning because lists of numbers and cost estimates have a distracting if illusory moral neutrality.

Toward the end of his tenure, he stops questioning the military or political significance of sending 206,000 more troops into Indochina, into a war he now knew could not be won and concentrates, instead, on the logistical problems of getting them there. That's administration. And as he fulfilled the require-ments of efficiency and effectivenes, during his own final days, his wife reports that he began to grind his teeth—every night—while tossing fitfully.

Albert Speer elevated the promises of Hitler's "technocracy" to a point where these promises quickly became shields against any inclination to think of the human and social consequences of his actions. The challenges, the deadlines, the deadly routines of the Third Reich—as of the Defense Depart-ment, or any large bureaucracy—become tasks to be performed, power to be exercised, problems to be solved, monuments to be designed (or demolished).

Is it the nature of large-scale organizations to make it possible for an

Warren Bennis is a former president of the University of Cincinnati.

ethical person such as a McNamara—or unethical Watergaters—to work toward an ultimately immoral end—without an immediate sense of personal
responsibility or guilt? Bureaucracies are, by definition, systems of increased
differentiation and specialization, and thus the ultimate morality of bureaucracy is the amorality of segmented acts.

Coming home:

On the first real day of spring, two beautiful trees in the infancy of bloom
are chopped down to make more room for cars to turn down a campus
driveway. Everybody is outraged. Students pack into my office to tell me about
it. A few are hysterical and crying. I leave my office and walk over to the little
grass plot—there is so little green on our campus—to see a man with a small
hand powersaw, cleaning and stacking up the milk-white wood into neat piles.

A crowd of some 200 students and faculty stand around and hiss me as I
break through the circle to speak to him. "Man, am I glad you're here. They're
ready to crucify me." It turns out he's not employed by the university. He
works for a local contractor. I could never find out who was responsible: the
landscape artist who designed the new plot with poodle hedges, or his boss,
the landscape architect; the director of planning, or his boss the head of the
physical plant; the vice president for management and finance, the university
building committee, the executive vice president the committee reports to . . .

When I called them all together they numbered twenty, and they were
innocents all. All of us. Bureaucracies are beautiful mechanisms for the evasion
of responsibility and guilt.

Too far from the classroom, from the munitions plant, from the battlefield,
from the people, from love. That's pornography.

There are no easy answers—or options. The problem is immense and
invades all of our lives. Recently the Bureau of Census reported that only 1.5
percent of our employment rolls are made up of the "self-employed"; the rest
work, as you and I do (if we work), in large organizations. Less than 75 years
ago, that ratio was the opposite.

And it's far too simple (and unrealistic) to talk about "small is beautiful."
Smallness helps only if it prevents the episodic, disconnected experience that
characterizes so many of our leaders and administrators. And it does no good
to pretend closeness and a direct relationship with "the people," displaying the
candidate or governor wearing saffron robes, walking to work, eating vegeta-
rian dinners to a recording of Fritz Perls reading Zen Haiku. The "simple"
life—through a technotronic, quadraphonic TV tube. That's "soft porn" for the
intellectual, falsely lulling, and just as corrupt as the hard kind.

What's important, it seems to me, is the capacity to see things in wide
perspective, to receive impressions and gain experiences directly—not
vicariously—that point beyond the experiences and data themselves. Continuity and purpose.

To the pornographic leader, things and events of the world appear as
portable fragments. The long view is replaced by shortsightedness. Detail, but
no pattern. The fresh outlook yields to a stereotyped and biased one. Experi-

ences and impressions, what there are of them seen through the lucite gray of a limousine window, cannot be fully valued and enjoyed because their character is lost.

Our leaders must learn to embrace error and take risks, to explore in the presence of others. Almost like learning how to play the violin in public.

Unless they do (and we permit them to), they will continue to sound as if they are talking through a plate-glass window, distant, isolated, removed from the complex lives of living people on the other side.

2
The Seven Secrets of the Metroliner's Success
Walter Shapiro

Government has become synonymous with failure. The situation is so bleak that the new intellectual pastime is determining the last time in American history when everything actually worked—some choose World War II, and modernists hold out for the middle years of the Eisenhower Administration.

Admittedly, in the last decade, the notion that government can't do anything right has been backed by some pretty convincing evidence. Determined to avoid future debacles, we have tried assiduously to absorb the depressing lessons of the 1960's. But against the backdrop of current cynicism, it is difficult to suggest that we can learn from the government's successes—as well as its failures—without sounding like a character out of *Bambi*.

Part of the problem is simply a scarcity of programs that worked. The one which springs most quickly to mind is NASA's Apollo program, which put a man on the moon. Following the landing, newspaper editorials repeatedly asked, "If the government can send a man to the moon, why can't it repair those potholes on Main Street?" But this question was primarily rhetorical—no one looked seriously at the Apollo program for clues about how anything might be fixed. The space program's very extravagance prevented it from being taken as anything more than an expensive curiosity.

But there were elements in Apollo that just weren't that unique. There was, for example, another project with both modest goals and funding which followed many of the same patterns as the space program and worked. Amid a host of uncompleted programs, the 1960's managed to give birth to the Metroliner, the modern, electric-powered train which makes the 231-mile trip

From *The Washington Monthly*, March, 1973, pp. 194-205. Reprinted with permission from *The Washington Monthly*. Copyright 1973 by The Washington Monthly Co., 1028 Connecticut Ave., N.W. Washington, D.C. 20036.
Walter Shapiro was an editor of *The Washington Monthly* at time of writing this article.

between New York and Washington in less than three hours. Vast sums were not spent on the project. The government's investment was not much more than a paltry $10 million, with the railroad contributing $55 million. Although the Metroliner obviously did not match the complexity of a moon launch, the task of building an entirely new train from scratch did present some unique problems.

At a time when passenger service had deteriorated to a level reminiscent of third-class coaches on the old Trans-Siberian railroad, a partnership between the government and Penn Central to improve service was not designed to inspire confidence.

Picture the situation. Here was the government trying to create one of the world's most technologically advanced trains in conjunction with a railroad that was being systematically looted by its officers in the unseen prelude to the biggest bankruptcy in American business history. Here was a contractor, the Budd Company, which had remained in the railroad-car building business largely out of habit, working on only a handful of new projects since World War II. For more than a decade the New York City subway system was virtually Budd's only customer. With help from groups like this, creating the Metroliner was almost analogous to constructing a battleship from old chewing-gum wrappers.

Despite the problems, the Metroliner has been an unqualified success, starting with its first run in January, 1969. Luring businessmen and other travelers off the Eastern Airlines shuttle, the Metroliner's 14 round trips a day have brightened AMTRAK's balance sheet with profits of just under $10 million in 1972.

But there's more to the Metroliner story than just profits. At a time when clogged highways and overstacked airports have become environmentalist cliches, the Metroliner experiment has proven that when given adequate service, the public will still ride trains—our most ecologically sound method of transportation.

The glamour of NASA and its lavish budget gave the space program freedom from many bureaucratic roadblocks. But the Metroliner did not have it nearly as easy. The roots of the high-speed train are in the Northeast Corridor Project set up in the Commerce Department in 1963. In 1965, the Metroliner project itself was started in the new Office of High Speed Ground Transportation and survived a 1967 shift from Commerce to the newly created Department of Transportation (DOT) that would have sidetracked many larger programs. Unlike most government procurement contracts, authority for the actual construction of Metroliner rested with the railroad, which was putting up most of the money. This relationship was complicated by the 1968 merger that transformed the Pennsylvania Railroad into part of the soon-to-be-bankrupt Penn Central system.

Analyzing the complex history of the Metroliner project, seven simple steps seem to account for its success. They are not foolproof. But they do help give some idea how the good things happen.

Step One—A Clear Goal

A successful project can easily be distinguished from other bureaucratic efforts by the clarity of its goal. With the Metroliner the objective was to build a train which could make the trip between New York and Washington in less than three hours. With the Apollo program it was to put a man on the moon. While the wisdom of the goal is not necessarily important (witness the space program), its existence is indispensable. A clear objective provides a sense of mission where otherwise there would be bureaucratic lassitude. Who would dare take a three-hour lunch when we had to get to the moon before the Russians? On the other hand, who wouldn't leave the office early on Friday afternoon when all that was pending were projections of personnel needs for the General Services Administration?

The history of the Northeast Corridor Project indicates the kind of focus firm goals can provide. Set up on a temporary basis in 1963, it had only a vague mandate to examine rail passenger service between Boston and Washington. Open-ended goals like these are what make bureaucracy thrive. The absence of a clear-cut purpose also explains why Robert Nelson, the project's director, said, "At the time of the Kennedy assassination we were just floundering."

It took presidential intervention—a request for permanent legislation to improve rail service in the Northeast—to get the project moving (see step two). Since in 1964 passenger trains seemed almost as risky a proposition as dirigibles, the initial White House decision was to make this a low-budget effort. Such parsimony normally creates $30-million worth of inconclusive feasibility studies. In this case, however, it created the Metroliner because the Office of High Speed Ground Transportation was set up with a firm objective.

Bob Nelson had a hypothesis that transportation demand was particularly sensitive to time savings. Counting travel to and from the airport, a plane flight from New York to Washington took more than two hours. Although the Pennsylvania Railroad's best train did the trip in 3:35, the average trip was over four hours. All it took was for Nelson to ask, "How much would it cost to set up a demonstration project that would cut an hour off the running time to New York?" and get the answer, "Not much," and the Metroliner was born.

There is a minor catch. In seeking specific goals, you only get what you ask for. No matter what the objective, it will not be surpassed. Obviously, if you are going to the moon this is not a major problem. But the goal of a New York-to-Washington trip in less than three hours has resulted in trains with running times of exactly 2:59. A non-stop Metroliner which made the trip in 2:30 was quickly abandoned, for reasons ranging from poor scheduling to insufficient patronage to high maintenance costs. But the real explanation was an absence of motive; all the government's contract with the railroad mandated was a trip of less than three hours.

Step Two—Presidential Involvement

In almost every account of pre-revolutionary Russia there was an obligatory scene: an old woman watching Cossack troops loot her village, murmurs prayerfully, "If the tsar only knew."

"If the president only knew," might be inscribed on the walls of every federal office as a monument to all unsuccessful projects, both past and future. Although the bureaucracy can still thwart a project which has presidential support, it is virtually impossible for a program to succeed without strong White House backing—or the appearance of it.

Here again the space program provides a model. Not only did NASA have secure access to the White House before Apollo, but it was President Kennedy himself who publicly declared the national objective of landing a man on the moon. Apollo began under the supervision of Vice-President Johnson, and when he succeeded to the presidency, success was written in the sky.

. . . With the Metroliner, access to the president was through Rhode Island's patrician Senator Claiborne Pell. Pell played the role of a catalyst to perfection, convincing two different administrations of the need . . .

In retrospect, Pell's ideas about railroads seem quaintly naive on the one hand and fuzzily futuristic on the other. It's easy to wonder whether the senator would have been interested in railroads at all if service had been better on the sleeper he rode regularly from Providence to Washington. Passenger trains had few defenders during the early 1960's, and it must have taken a deep reluctance to fly and many long nights on sidings outside Trenton to turn Pell into Congress' leading advocate of improved rail service.

Senator Pell's pet notion was a multi-state transportation pact, modeled after the New York Port Authority, to run railroad service from Boston to Washington. At times, Pell just seemed to long for a return to the gentility which characterized the European railroads he remembered from his youth in a diplomatic family. But some of his ideas seemed to be lifted from Walt Disney's Tomorrowland as the senator conjured up visions of monorails, air-cushioned vehicles, and even rocket-propelled trains traveling the Northeast corridor.

But Pell's role did not require ideas, just access. After a few well-publicized speeches on the subject, Pell, whose ties with President Kennedy were both political and personal, approached the White House. The senator's intervention—and the aid of the Budget Bureau, which was trying to relinquish its role as the government's expert on a third-rate subject like passenger trains—led to the creation of the Northeast Corridor Project in 1963.

A year later, with a Texan as president, Pell feared the end of White House interest in Boston-to-Washington train service. Since linking the Northeast Corridor to a plan to upgrade rail service from Waco to El Paso was unlikely, Pell took a different tack, appealing to Johnson's political instincts in an election year. The Rhode Island Democrat presented the president with a terse memo on the program—stressing the total electoral vote represented by the states in the Northeast corridor.

Men's fates were often decided by a nod from the tsar. In this case, all it took was for Johnson to scrawl on the Pell memo, "Tell Commerce to get off its ass on this," and the Metroliner program was under way.

Even long after a president's attention has shifted elsewhere, a skillful project director (see step three) can nurture the illusion of continuing White House involvement. While risky when dealing with other branches of the government with their own access to the president, this strategy is virtually foolproof when dealing with those outside the government, who are in no position to call your bluff.

The Pennsylvania Railroad's interest in the Metroliner indicates the benefits of maintaining an aura of presidential support. Building the Metroliner required the PRR to invest $55 million in a project where the lion's share of the credit would go to the federal government. The Pennsy in fact had recently turned down an in-house proposal for a new New York-to-Washington train because investment capital was tight and most of the railroad's top management believed their own public rhetoric about passenger service being inherently unprofitable.

Enter an unlikely hero. "If Stuart Saunders hadn't been on the scene," said Jim Diffenderfer, the PRR official who proposed a new train, "the Metroliner project wouldn't have gotten started." Saunders, the railroad's president and later one of the unquestioned villains of the Penn Central bankruptcy, was never known for his compassion for passengers. But with the Penn Central merger in the offing, the reasons for his sudden interest in the Metroliner were not difficult to detect.

If $400,000 gifts to the Republican Party are how corporations like ITT get mergers approved in the Nixon Administration, providing capital for projects like high-speed trains was how things got done in the Johnson years. "I have no doubt," said Bob Nelson, "that Saunders' softness in negotiating the Metroliner contract with the government can be directly related to his feeling that this was one of the things he had to do to get the Penn Central merger approved." Saunders and the railroad weren't sure how much influence Nelson had on the government's decision to approve the Penn Central merger, but they couldn't take chances. The result was what one railroad official called "the worst contract ever negotiated in the 120-year history of the Pennsylvania Railroad."

Step Three—The Man

Despite all the civics-book rhetoric about government being made of laws not men, nothing could be farther from the truth in the quest for a successful project. What is needed is the kind of project director who is called "a tough son of a bitch" but gets the job done. The archetype for this breed was Jim Webb, who ran the Apollo program. Webb's roots were in the oil business of Oklahoma Senator Robert Kerr, but he wasn't a politician. Webb's aim wasn't making friends or keeping bureaucrats happy, it was landing a man on the moon. Webb, like the ideal director, was there from the beginning. No one could tell him, "We used to do it this way"; no one could challenge his authority by claiming a superior knowledge of the project. For Apollo began with Webb.

Although his background is far different from the wheeler-dealer world of Oklahoma oil, Bob Nelson shared a number of traits with Jim Webb. Like Webb, Nelson was there at the beginning. A professor of transportation economics at the University of Washington when he was recruited to head the Northeast Corridor Project in 1963, Nelson recalls that he "wasn't very much interested in passenger transportation at that time." Gordon Murray of the Budget Bureau played a key role in selecting Nelson, whom he knew from professional conferences. It also didn't hurt that Nelson taught in the home state of Warren Magnuson, chairman of the Senate Commerce Committee. Little in Nelson's background prepared him for the cutthroat world of bureaucratic infighting, but he had learned the game by 1965 when he became director of the new Office of High Speed Ground Transportation.

Understanding Nelson starts with his own simple admission, "I'm no train buff." Tall and white-haired, more interested in freight rates than railroad memorabilia, Nelson is not the sort to talk about the romance of the train whistle in the night. There is a severity about him, a kind of intellectual Calvinism, which meshes with the frugality of the Metroliner project in an era of cost overruns and inflated promises. Recalling his anger at the failure of the railroad and its contractors to honor their contract for the production of the train, Nelson said, "I'm old fashioned. I believe that commitments once made should be honored. Obviously, that wasn't the way they did things in the railroad business."

Few in the railroad business have fond memories of Bob Nelson. Even today the mere mention of his name in Penn Central offices creates involuntary shudders. When asked about Nelson or the Metroliner, officials of the Budd Company, the project's prime contractor, will only say, "It's a good train and we will not comment on past difficulties."

Jim Diffenderfer, who played a key role in promoting the Metroliner at the Pennsylvania Railroad, chuckles as he recalls how Nelson's name was "poison around here." Now with Penn Central, Diffenderfer said, "I used to be castigated for defending him. The problem with Bob Nelson was that he hated incompetence. He hated guys who didn't know what they were talking about. He'd see right through them and call their bluff."

The railroad's feelings about Nelson are easily understood. Nelson was interested in only one thing—the construction of the Metroliner. In early 1966, for example, he talked to a "federal official" about getting the White House to postpone announcing approval of the Penn Central merger until after Metroliner contract negotiations were finished.

Nelson was equally firm when the PRR's President Saunders announced that the railroad wanted Budd to postpone delivery of Metroliner cars until after the merger because of complicated railroad stock transfers. "Hell, no" replied Nelson. "It's not the federal government's business what the Pennsylvania Railroad's cash balance is at the time of the merger."

Because the government's contract was only with the railroad and not with the Budd Company, it took Nelson several months to discover that Saunders had ordered the contractor to delay Metroliner production anyway. Nelson said that when he discovered this, "I literally raised hell. For the next three weeks I was sitting on Budd's doorstep. I forced them to put on another production line."

A clear picture of Bob Nelson was provided by a colleague from the Department of Transportation. "He was abrasive, difficult, and terribly obstinate. At times we felt he was either a bloody ass or a genius. Neither are characteristics of an average bureaucrat."

But then, how many trains have average bureaucrats built lately?

Step Four–Project Autonomy

"I had far more decision-making power than anyone over at the Pennsylvania Railroad except for Stuart Saunders," Nelson recalled.

It's a rare government official who has anything resembling the authority of a corporation president, but this kind of autonomy is needed to overcome bureaucratic inertia. The Metroliner project director achieved it, even after being forced to mesh with two government departments—Commerce and Transportation.

If the Metroliner had been an ordinary project, the scenario Nelson and his small office would have faced in the Commerce Department might have gone something like this:

To negotiate a contract they would have had to call in Department lawyers; to hire an assistant they would have had to go through the Commerce personnel office; to order desks or typewriters they would have had to contact the Department's purchasing office. Each one of these divisions had priorities far different from those of Nelson and his office. If the Metroliner had not been a priority project, the contract with the PRR might have been shaped more by a Commerce lawyer than by Nelson himself. A simple purchase order might have taken months to be executed.

It should be clear by now that any office following its own goals, operating on its own timetable (see step five), can't afford to yield authority to external bureaucratic forces. Nelson managed to avoid most pitfalls of bureaucratic life by obtaining special status for the Metroliner through the support of two successive Secretaries of Commerce. Bob Nelson had freedom of action from the outset, but most administrators aren't so lucky.

In the beginning, the key to Nelson's autonomy was White House support for the Metroliner. Luther Hodges, Kennedy's Secretary of Commerce, had grave and well-justified fears about not being reappointed after the 1964 elections and was understandably sensitive to White House whim. Hodges set the pattern by making every effort to give Nelson free rein. His successor, John

Connors, was far more interested in national economic policy than he was in running the Commerce Department, and his preoccupation with White House intrigues permitted Alan Boyd, Undersecretary of Commerce for Transportation, to exercise broad authority. The number of transportation officials within Commerce was few enough so that Nelson's Office of High Speed Ground Transportation acted as an extension of Undersecretary Boyd's personal staff. Boyd, hoping to eventually be named to the new post of Secretary of Transportation, was also sensitive to White House sponsorship of the Metroliner project and gave Nelson virtually a free hand during the critical period in 1966 when the contract with the PRR was under negotiation.

The creation of a new cabinet department is to bureaucrats what the Oklahoma land rush was to homesteaders. A new department means a new hierarchy—with favored projects often directly linked to the secretary's office, where they flourish in the glare of high-level attention. When the Department of Transportation was set up in early 1967, Nelson had hoped to continue his close relationship with Alan Boyd, the new Transportation Secretary. Instead, Nelson's office became a division of the Federal Railroad Administration, almost the equivalent of exile to bureaucratic Siberia.

But in this case, banishment had its compensations. A. Scheffer Lang, the federal railroad administrator, had worked with Nelson in the Commerce Department and was sympathetic to the project. Although isolation might have been fatal if Nelson had had no preexisting relationship with Boyd or powerful friends outside DOT, the new arrangement worked. For one thing, being away from the Secretary's office freed Nelson from the distracting political battles which accompany the creation of any new cabinet department. "Perhaps my most important contribution to the Metroliner," said Lang, "was to keep the bureaucrats and the power-grabbers away from Nelson so he could get his work done in peace."

But outside intervention was needed in late 1967 to prevent Nelson's office from being subdivided as part of a DOT reorganization effort. No longer could Nelson count on help from a White House far too preoccupied with the Vietnam war to notice minor domestic projects. This time, a call from Senator Warren Magnuson (see step seven) to Alan Boyd was all that was needed to keep Nelson's domain intact.

Step Five—A Timetable

Without firm deadlines, the government operates with a languor that three-toed sloths might envy. The space program adjusted for this by having not one, but two deadlines:

1. to get a man to the moon before the Russians; and

2. when it appeared that the Russians were in no hurry to get there, a lunar landing by the end of the 1960's.

Once the bill authorizing the Metroliner passed Congress in 1965, Bob Nelson was in the newspapers (see step six) predicting the trains would be running by October, 1967. Unlike most deadlines, Nelson's public timetable wasn't designed to stimulate the federal bureaucracy, it was meant to motivate the equally intractable railroad and its contractors.

Aware that the railroad's enthusiasm for the project would quickly wane following approval of their cherished merger, Nelson saw the October, 1967, date as a bargaining chip rather than a realistic projection. Since the Metroliner's technical complexity was well beyond the contractors' initial production capacity, the train could never have been ready by the 1967 deadline, even with everyone's full cooperation.

But without the 1967 deadline, 1968 would not have brought a series of public inquiries about why the Metroliner was delayed. Without the 1968 furor, the train would never have been ready in early 1969.

Step Six—Project Visibility

From the outset, the Metroliner was a unique program—it attracted public attention. Newspaper involvement in the project began with Claiborne Pell's scheme for a multi-state transportation pact. Lunching in 1962 with Arthur Krock, then *The New York Times'* Washington bureau chief and an old family friend, Pell mentioned his plan as something which might be suitable for *The New York Times Magazine.* Instead, Krock transformed Pell's views into a front-page story and the impact of this article emboldened Pell to take his proposal to President Kennedy.

The public's interest in the Metroliner was not hard to understand. Obviously, a project which could cut an hour off travel time from New York to Washington has more widespread appeal than a reorganization of the field offices of the Manpower Administration. Nelson could effectively stage-manage his public deadlines only because the press took them seriously. In 1967 alone, *The New York Times* ran more than a dozen stories on the Metroliner and its production delays, and the Washington and Philadelphia papers also followed it closely.

Step Seven—Friends on the Hill

Claiborne Pell and Warren Magnuson were not the only senators keeping track of the Metroliner. By 1968 Nelson had developed a rapport with a wide variety of legislators; many were impressed with the clarity of his presentations during budget hearings.

When program delays began to snowball, Nelson decided the time was right for that classic scene—the angry congressional hearing. Nelson had nothing to lose by a public airing of the controversy, since even if the hearing backfired, no additional congressional funding was required to complete the project.

If this was the strategy behind the Senate Appropriations subcommittee hearings on the Metroliner in early June, 1968, then Republican Senator Gordon Allott of Colorado played the leading role. The interest of the GOP conservative in a railroad project more than 2,000 miles east of his constituents stemmed from a closeworking relationship that Nelson had developed with Paul Weyrich, one of Allott's aides.

The senator also had a political motivation for sponsoring the hearings—he seized upon the Metroliner as an example of the Great Society's inability to even make the trains run on time. But Nelson nonetheless credits Allott's hearings with bringing the "Metroliner into operation a year to a year and a half in advance of what it normally would." The hearings were unusual. Although subcommittee Chairman John Stennis opened the hearings, Allott presided over virtually the entire session (one of the rare occasions since the Democrats captured the Senate in 1955 that a Republican has run a televised hearing).

Even more striking was the tenor of the hearings. Allott, like a Capitol Hill Perry Mason, lined up Nelson and representatives of the Penn Central and the three contractors at the witness table and questioned them collectively. If one man claimed he didn't know the reason for a certain delay, Allott turned to the next and demanded an answer. As a public pillory, it was highly effective. The hearings, like the newspaper stories which preceded them, put pressure on the contractors where it hurt—right in the middle of their public image. It became a question of the lesser of two evils, and finishing the Metroliner was infinitely preferable to continued adverse publicity.

The seven steps are not classified information, but a look at the average federal employee explains why they are so rarely applied. Too many government workers resemble characters out of a Beckett play, sitting at their desks and waiting to be told what to do. Since many recognize the fundamental uselessness of their work, they are hounded by the continuing fear that someday someone will catch on and their jobs will be abolished. Completing anything, therefore, is a threatening experience because each finished task may bring retirement or dismissal one step closer. Sisyphus, eternally pushing the same boulder up the same hill, had the perfect government job. It was endless.

From this it's easy to understand the typical bureaucrat's aversion to goals and deadlines. Goals imply that a project can be completed and timetables—most ominously of all—tell when it will be finished. Visibility is only a step away from evaluation; and anyway, even the most innocent publicity may somehow spark an investigation. A dynamic administrator running the whole show is worse—he may even upset the status quo, being so new to government that he won't take sloth and inefficiency for granted.

Admittedly, project autonomy and friends in the White House and on Capitol Hill have their appeal, but for the wrong reasons. For most government workers, autonomy doesn't mean freedom to get the job done, it means the freedom to be left alone. Friends in high places are just another form of job security—"just let them try to abolish my job, and I'll have half the Congress on their backs in no time."

But not all bureaucrats fit these stereotypes. There are a few eccentrics who really want to get the job done. Finding enough of these governmental mavericks to keep a project going is an administrator's hardest task. And for that there are unfortunately no easy formulas.

3
How Outsiders
Overhauled a Public Agency

Arthur H. Spiegel III

O ne day in January 1972 this want ad addressed to "results-oriented MBAs and engineers" appeared in the financial pages of *The New York Times:* "We've been charged with turning around a three-billion-dollar government agency and have two years to do it." The ad was placed by the city's Human Resources Administration (HRA), and the mission was reform of the welfare system. The agency eventually hired some 600 managers, industrial engineers, and specialists—80% of them from business—at competitive salaries. The leader of the group, HRA's executive deputy administrator, is the author of this article. By the time the John Lindsay regime gave way to a new administration two years later, the team had overhauled the entire welfare operation. The author chronicles how it was accomplished—how, for instance, new controls and better screening trimmed the welfare case load and improved the way it was handled. And, to cite another example, he relates how the team learned the art of dealing with the possible in working with the civil service. Their experiences offer an object lesson in public administration, a fertile territory for enterprising executives.

Note

Mayor Lindsay created Mr. Spiegel's position at HRA for him in 1971 in order to facilitate the reform effort. As an executive of the New York City Housing and Development Administration, Mr. Spiegel had just devised a cost-effective rent program for the city's rent-controlled apartments when he joined HRA. He was 32 years old and four years out of the Harvard Business School. Since leaving city government a year ago, he has formed American Practice Management, Inc., which develops medical buildings that feature central managerial and professional services.

Ambitious men and women aspiring to the managerial ranks or already there have long disdained government service as unworthy of their training. With no competitive market to spur innovation and no apparent prospect for personal growth, government has been designated the realm of the second-raters.

This laissez-faire of the private sector has fostered an anomaly in our economy. Government operations now account for 22% of our gross national product. Federal, state, and local governments employ one sixth of our work force. Government is *the* growth sector today. Yet it has been galloping along virtually devoid of capable management, deprived of modern technology, and burdened with operating conditions that would challenge even the most blasé management reformer.

New York City's welfare operation is perhaps the epitome of this situation. In 1971 the Human Resources Administration was a 27,000-man agency that distributed welfare checks to 1.2 million people twice a month and claimed 31% of the city's municipal outlay. The agency's growth was out of control: its case load had doubled in the past five years and was still growing by 10,000 people a month. The case load explosion was accompanied by a myriad of complex new laws to administer—Medicaid; day care and other expansions in social services; welfare work programs, such as the federal work-incentive program for welfare mothers; and nationally mandated reorganization to separate "income maintenance" (welfare checks) from "social services" (rehabilitation).

The operation was in chaos. It was still functioning with the same basic— and largely manual—systems written at its inception 35 years previously. Handwritten forms, made out in triplicate by a high-turnover staff, passed through no fewer than 27 steps in procedures that changed almost monthly. Some 165,000 transactions were backlogged. Payment errors cropped up in 36% of the case load. Checks went out regularly to the wrong clients— $150 million worth in the course of a year. Recipients lined up before dawn to get inside the welfare centers by the 5 p.m. closing time, and violent attacks on the staff by angered clients became frequent.

The situation called for a drastic response. The response taken by Mayor John Lindsay was a decision to place the operation in the hands of professional management. He and Administrator Jule Sugarman brought me in to recruit a management team that would have two and a half years of strong mayoral support for whatever resources were needed to get welfare under control. It was an irresistible challenge. Although the welfare system needed total overhaul, its breakdown could not even be diagnosed because there was no clear documentation on how it worked. It took nearly a year of systems analysis just to complete the specification of objectives.

Nevertheless, by the end of the Lindsay administration in December 1973, we had wrested the operation into the shape of a modern, high-volume processing system. We had implemented a top-to-bottom overhaul that included an introduction of integrated, system-wide automation, a complete revamping of welfare center operations, and a general tightening of management controls. The team effort had reduced the agency's error rate by 50%, increased staff productivity some 16%, trimmed the case load by 109,000 people, and generated a $200 million savings in welfare payments. . . . Whereas the numbers increased at a rate of some 11,000 persons per month from July through December 1971, they declined at a rate of more than 7,000 a month from September 1972 through 1973 with a seasonal upturn in August.

When the next city administration took office, the overhaul was about 90% complete. Some of its components will inevitably deteriorate because of government's constantly changing top management. But most represent permanent system changes, sufficiently implanted in HRA to ensure their perpetuation. And the scale of the team's achievements suggests that the application of standard business practices and results-oriented people can produce high-magnitude gains in government.

I do not believe our situation was unique. New York's management problems, though larger in scale, are similar to those of other cities. Public operating agencies, so long neglected by management, are now opening up as a fertile site for managerial action. It is in such agencies that the rubber of government expansion meets the road and that our government's real productivity improvements can be made. For this reason, I believe that my bout with New York City welfare may provide some useful guidelines for other managers integrated in the public sector.

'An almost foreign culture'

Unlike commerce, government's raison d'être does not include a built-in need for productivity. An agency's status is a function of how much it spends, not of how much it earns. Success is a function of favorable press and ever bigger budget allocations. So the fundamental marketing maxim is to satisfy all of the people all of the time—and that means responding to all the exigencies of legislators, regulators, resource controllers, taxpayers, vote-controlling constituencies, and direct users of service.

Consequently, little is constant in the public sector. Laws, public pressure, personnel, entire organization charts change with mercurial speed and move operational priorities around as if they were portable heaters. The politics of a situation are really a struggle for top priority: that's where the money goes.

In such an atmosphere, efficiency is largely irrelevant, and so government agencies are not performance oriented. The executive who is so oriented must create, from scratch, a set of specific objectives and then educate his staff as to their purpose and their relationship to the agency's viability.

However, the government management structure is designed to diffuse control in order to prevent accumulation of political power. Any top manager knows that his position is temporary. His agency's only career managers are the civil servants, whose positions do not include the top posts. These are reserved for appointees such as himself, and it is understood throughout the system that appointees change with each administration. Furthermore, no agency executive ever fully controls his own operation. In New York City any significant shift in policy and every operational resource need, down to technical help, must win approval from three or four government bodies. Good relationships are vital because there are always two different procedures—the long one on the books and the shortcut.

Thus any recruit from the private sector faces an almost foreign culture. Government's different structure induces motivations, definitions of personal achievement, and modes of doing business that differ from those he is accustomed to. It is an environment that calls for tremendous versatility.

A fast start is a must

A government manager's success is largely determined during his first three months in office. He can complete only a finite number of improvements before the next election, and he will need resources for all of them. These are always most readily approved while he is still publicly at center stage—new, untested, and untarnished by attacks on his shortcomings. His ability to garner more resources later will depend heavily on his activities and the posture he establishes at this time in the public eye.

The first three months are overwhelming. Piecemeal operational problems, conflicting constituency demands, and distracting political issues are channeled daily to an agency administrator's office. He is expected to consider each one a crisis, as government managers always have. Thus it is crucial to establish early his approach to management—well-defined targets, clear priorities, and focused resources. But which ones? If he has been brought in for his management ability, it is probably because the operation is in utter disrepair and even its best line management cannot identify the causes. So he finds it difficult even to gain a perspective on the problems, much less establish policies for the organization.

In 1971 the New York City welfare agency had two fundamental problems: its budget was supporting too many ineligible recipients, and its operation was very inefficient. That was all we knew. The raging public debate over ineligibility "pinpointed" the problem as ranging from 3.5% to 37% of the case load, but no one could determine why ineligible applicants were accepted. Was the problem up front, where clients were accepted? Was it caused by poor monitoring of ongoing cases or failures in the case closing procedures? Was it employee error, recipient fraud, or the law itself? Or was failure spread throughout the operating system, entangled in labyrinthine office layouts, crisscrossed procedures, ill-trained staff, and ambiguous management controls?

The new manager must decide which problems to tackle before he understands where they are. I wrote my two-and-a-half-year agenda on the back of an envelope. It was a list of every obvious part of a welfare operation, each starting with analysis. In setting priorities, I used two criteria—the public, which put direct eligibility controls before operational reform, and, within that framework, the simplest problem first. This approach enabled us to produce early results while we were still defining our long-term program.

The abuses that outrage the public, though generated by deep-seated systemic dysfunctions, are usually specific enough to be mastered quickly. They lend themselves to quick-action projects that are also consistent with government's way of working. These projects are hole pluggers; they yield dramatic—and therefore political—results, denting staff and public scepticism and enhancing the new manager's credibility for long-term funding. At the same time, they offer the new management group clear-cut pathways into the operating system.

First on our agenda were three quick-action projects that could be completed with an embryonic management force. They focused on the agency's most acute public issues—addicts and fraud—where early results would gain high visibility. All three attacked easily identifiable, limited-scale problems; yet each took us into a different key aspect of the welfare operation. Furthermore, they injected the neophytes into the system. Charged to produce hands-on results rather than elegant studies, the new staff quickly lost its public-sector virginity and gained a solid grasp of the operation in the fastest way possible— through working closely with line personnel. Briefly, these were the projects:

Welfare-check fraud, in which a client illegally obtains duplicate assistance checks, actually involved only 0.02% of the welfare population. Locating that volume required much digging into the convoluted payment system.

Drug addicts, though they made up only 2.5% of the case load, were its fastest-growing and most troublesome segment. Transient, violent, and fraud-prone, they abused the procedures in ways that exposed every weakness in the client-processing system. We instituted several small but significant changes that reduced the problem. (More on that program later.)

Issuance of a photograhic ID card to every welfare client—a new antifraud requirement—gave us a complete course in client scheduling. As a special off-line undertaking, it also provided a high-visibility showcase for our managerial tools. Such opportunities are not rare in government, given the frequency with which mandates change.

Short-termers & old-timers

In government, how does one go about developing a skilled management force in a hurry? We started with a firm funding commitment from the mayor as a prerequisite for attracting talent. New York City, like most governments, will not pay head hunters, so we involved the mayor and budget personnel in a massive recruiting campaign that broadcast our objectives through personal contacts, brochures, and extensive advertising. The city's hiring practices are hopelessly ineffective; approvals and paper work for civil service job titles take from two to six months, and neither the existing titles nor job remuneration correlates with their counterparts in industry. To shortcut these practices and provide competitive compensation, we created new job titles wherever it was possible and instituted a salary-advance fund.

It was not difficult to attract good professionals to the project; our efforts generated some 10,000 résumés. Of the 322 persons we initially hired (this number was eventually doubled), 80% came directly from industry. Their average age was 31; average experience, seven years. Some were drawn by social commitment, but the majority saw a unique opportunity for developing entrepreneurial responsibility. In career terms, the experience gained would carry a value of $8,000 to $15,000 increases when they returned to business. At the top, the tremendous challenge of radical technological overhaul attracted top private-sector management from such organizations as Allied Chemical, Loews Corporation, Mobil Oil, and the American Stock Exchange.

In assigning new staff, we used a project-management focus. It allowed us to start functioning immediately, to hire managers and subordinates simultaneously, and to evalute individual staff members quickly.

Penetrating the line

Early in the overhaul effort our best industrial engineer devised a simple procedure to remove some of the pressure on welfare center interviewers. The union struck in protest. The employees did not understand the procedure because of the bald manner in which it was presented, and they resented its origin in the top management staff. A civil service supervisor rewrote the directive, burying the change in gobbledygook that referenced a score of old procedures. It was implemented immediately.

This anecdote reveals an immutable facet of government: the civil servants control the line, and they are immersed in an ethos that is incomprehensible to outsiders. In our not atypical welfare operation, the civil service is much like a fraternity. Supervisors and subordinates belong to the same unions. Promotion is by written exam, exams must be taken in a certain order, and there is no lateral entry. Dismissal is rare; some top-level civil servants have been in the department since the Depression.

The operation they sustain is incredibly complex. Its governing regulations, which come from nine different agencies and fill a four-foot shelf, are intricate, contradictory, and perpetually changing. Central office management spends at least one fourth of its time implementing the latest regulatory tinkering: a slight adjustment in the federal budgeting formula that requires a review of the entire case load, a state eligibility rule necessitating six new forms, or a national separation of social services from income maintenance that changes the nature of 20,000 jobs and contradicts both civil service and union rules. Meanwhile, in the antiquated, undermanned welfare centers, confused and frustrated workers face a jam of angry clients.

Civil service management is pragmatic. It tacks the new procedures onto the old and maintains the same basic work patterns. What looks like a garbled mess to the incoming executive is, in fact, a rational approach to the environment. The civil servants are a force for continuity in an operation that is never constant. In contrast, their politically appointed top managment is usually operations-ignorant and invariably committed to change. The skeptical attitude toward any new manager's objectives—"Commissioners come and go, but civil servants stay forever"—reflects a long history of overhead incompetence.

I experienced several pleasant surprises in dealing with the civil service. First, their support was available. It hinged on four factors—proof of our competence, the mayor's backing of our effort, our respect for their standard bureaucratic procedure, and insight into the mutuality of our objectives. Their support was not difficult to obtain. We brought a 30-year civil service executive out of retirement to be a consultant for the huge clerical staff he had recently headed. We had civil servants interview our recruits for the top line vacancy; then we chose a young man with 10 years' government experience and clear sympathy for the civil service. Our first major line action dealt with worker safety, the unions' greatest concern. We added 600 men to the welfare center security force and built protective partitions and reception areas in the 18 centers most disrupted by violence. These activities, plus the early results of our first projects, proved that we could produce.

Second, their support was invaluable. Many of our key start-up activities were initiated by a civil servant whose recommendations ranged from strategic action steps to specific personnel changes. She helped us immensely, while bowing out of the running for the top line job. The agency's fiscal director, though he had never instituted sound accounting systems, possessed an immense knowledge of budgeting and reimbursement. He contributed it to the effort and supported our proposal for project-by-project fiscal reform. In our behalf, the personnel chief made use of his extensive interagency connections. He also allowed us to move a tough private-sector administrator in under him.

Finally, we found a richness of management talent buried under the civil service promotion system. By working around the regulations, we were able to put these people into the strategic positions that called for professionals.

Platform for reform

Project management may be the government reformer's most valuable tool; it cuts a large job into workable pieces and combines analysis with action. However, the traditional concept—gathering a team of in-house technicians for a closely defined task—required adaptation for our use. This situation called for the input of people with varied backgrounds in managerial techniques but no grounding in standard agency procedures, no internal loyalties, and no conditioning to civil service defeatism.

So we staffed our project-management operation with outsiders and made it the central reform organization. Its "project" was to restructure the entire agency. Its personnel, at first acting as internal consultants and organized on a project-analysis basis, were later given responsibility for installing the new systems they had designed. As the overhaul progressed, we spun off staff employees as line managers or as members of line support groups and retained only a nucleus for long-term analytic work.

The management group's life cycle explains, in part, why HRA did not simply hire a consultant. We wanted a committed staff of specialists who would stay with the system, dirty their hands operationally, and remain accountable for results. We wanted to integrate them with line personnel in order to build a lasting body of government technology. The New York City operation, including our agency's own computer center, was riddled with consultant-designed systems created out of superficial analyses and canned private-sector procedures. The city lacked the internal expertise to evaluate the applicability of such systems to government's different kind of machinery.

Consequently, we brought civil servants into the reform effort as soon as each piece of analysis was complete. During systems design, we added 590 persons to the management group to work in small teams with analysts and industrial engineers. We adapted project plans to a traditional civil service conformation. At the same time, the civil servants felt the effects of the differences in our approach; they were not used to quantitative objectives, explicit timetables, or procedures that held them accountable for results.

The implementation was assigned to line management. We put our industrial engineers under welfare center managers and created new civil service positions for the systems analysts responsible for eligibility controls.

Establishing accountability

The public manager who hopes to accomplish something often has to invent targets. Usually his predecessors have been ignorant of tangible performance measures; people simply "did their best." During systems development, we set up timetables as targets, with the completed project plan as the bottom line. When each new system was turned on, we switched to performance measures.

The absence of standard performance criteria indicates a surplus of measures for results. Before an administrator can increase productivity, he has to define productivity. How should he measure—by error rates or units of work, by dollar costs or dollar losses, by pieces of paper or minutes of time, by transactions, cases, or people? All are interrelated, and which are used matters little. What does matter is having a clear focus on *any* specified results.

Performance objectives are tools, applicable only in settings that demand accountability and that reward performance. Public organizations are structured for neither. A results-oriented administrator has to be particularly pragmatic in developing management controls.

We manufactured an atmosphere of accountability through a shotgun approach. At the top we streamlined the structure by reducing six lines of command to one. At the bottom we instituted a time-keeping crackdown that cut the agency's 30% lateness rate by two thirds and reduced absenteeism by 29%. In the middle we introduced the concept of management reporting. The system, which began with project plans in the management shop, was gradually expanded into a series of agency-wide performance reports. We made them meaningful by employing the civil service's most effective management tool—peer opinion. The reports, containing a set of productivity measurements to rank the 45 welfare centers, received wide distribution. A special, top-level civil service unit subjected the lowest-ranking centers to intensive audits.

We also found the means to reward performance, although they were severely limited. Through the efforts of civil service top management, we created staff jobs for 19 inept center directors and provided for their replacement with "provisional" appointees recommended by their superiors.

Our most inclusive accountability tool, however, was the press. The press is government's information system, the only reporting system that touches everyone with the measures that count—what the mayor praises, what the public demands, what the union thinks, and what the next election is likely to change. We used the press to create a positive attitude toward accountability. With an announcement that our minimum accomplishment would be a case load reduction of 100,000 people, we made ourselves publicly accountable. We frightened agency bureaucrats by releasing the full results of our analyses. We publicly issued agency-wide performance objectives and published regular progress reports that clearly reflected on line management.

This strategy made us look like fools on the numerous occasions when we fell behind schedule and failed to meet objectives. But it succeded in building our credibility, both inside the agency and out, and put personal egos on the line against results. Moreover, it brought the agency out of its defensive posture, created a "can-do" atmosphere among staff, and made accountability a real issue.

New hardware, new software

The principles employed to overhaul an operationally bankrupt organization are probably little different in government from what they are in business. Top management works from the outside in, patching up the skin of the operation, then taking increasingly bigger chunks into its core. We began with the series of eligibility controls to stop the estimated $150 million flowing annually to unqualified recipients. Then we moved into operational reform by overhauling basic procedures in the welfare centers. Paralleling this action, we developed a $5 million computer system to bring into the modern age an operation that was processed mainly on paper.

The major difference between a government and a private overhaul is in degree. The lack of controls in government can allow serious deterioration to develop unchecked. As a result, when new blood comes in, the imminence of chaos gives stopgap measures priority over long-term reforms. There is no leeway; everything is at an explosion point. In one instance, when we missed a computer-room air conditioning installation deadline by one day, the lag in check printing brought a storm of 30,000 people into the centers. Such incidents are critical in an antiquated welfare center where every month 8,000 walk-in clients are already producing some 52,000 manually processed transactions and the clerks (often poorly trained) are trying to shuffle 320 different forms through a welfare payment pipeline two weeks long.

Given these conditions, we used an incremental approach to every aspect of operational reform. The eligibility controls, each a major operation in itself, were developed as separate programs and held off line until ready for installation. Procedural changes were put in center by center and step by step. The automation plan embodied an eight-subsystem design that permitted independent development and installation of each part.

We also brought in centralization as a major control tool in order to put most key eligibility-related processes under single management, eliminate error-producing paper work in the centers, and simplify automation. A fully computerized central case-closing operation reduced the center clerk's work to a single notification form. Special client centers were established for a computer-assisted, off-line program to recertify the entire case load on a regular basis through a document-supported personal interview with every client.

To centralize welfare work with addicts and other possible employables, we established four welfare centers solely for them. To control eligibility at the entry point, we trained special application groups in each center.

For the sweeping operational changes in the 45 welfare centers, we bowed to line management. Implementing plans differently from the way we would have, the line inched in changes that gave them more work but permitted the staff time to adjust. In converting each center to a central file, for example, we intended to eliminate the agency's senseless paper duplication through a terminal digit system. Line management chose to sift through the 8 million files twice, first to consolidate them alphabetically, then to refile them by terminal digit.

Operation drug addict

An illustration of our methodology is provided in microcosm by our simplest project—dealing with drug addicts. Classification of drug addicts under Aid to the Disabled in 1970 had exempted them from work requirements. During 1971 the addict case load doubled, becoming a $70 million category with 15% higher average grants per case than the next highest disabled group. Furthermore, while representing only 2.5% of the city's case load, they accounted for 12.5% of its processing volume, and the processing cost per addict's welfare check was ten times higher than average. What was worse, the swelling numbers of drug users, supporting their habit through welfare and required to pick up their checks in person, were terrorizing the welfare centers and surrounding neighborhoods.

The analysis needed to correct this situation covered processing, regulations, procedures in other cities, and medical consideraions. Out of it came a multi-phased program that began in late 1971 with a central registry to identify and track down addicts. By the following April we had computerized the registry and added a set of hard eligibility documentation requirements for the use of center workers. HRA then reinterpreted the regulations to mandate proof of addiction by medical exam and compulsory attendance in either treatment or work programs.

The program produced results. The new regulations took nearly half the addicts off the rolls, and the central registry reduced drug users' fraud attempts from a high of 206 per month to fewer than 15. The documented monitoring system eliminated the need for personal check pickup at the centers. At the same time the project allowed us to experiment, using a relatively small population and a number of approaches we would later extend system-wide.

The extent to which the drug program and the other approaches worked is an indication of both the amenability of the agency's personnel and the breadth of its problems. The application system reduced by half the number of new cases accepted. Centralized case closing has reduced the closing lag from six weeks to the two mandated by law, at an annual saving in grants of $25 million. At the time of this writing, the recertification program was closing 10% of the cases contacted and finding payment errors in an additional 33%

At the operational level, well over half of the 45 welfare centers were functioning under newly engineered systems that eliminate traffic jams and provide civilized service. Features of the system include client appointment scheduling, central files and file controls, separate phone and mail units, and specialized worker groups for quick-service problems, applications, and complex case changes. . . .

Our most surprising success, however, was the speedy implementation of the automation program, in an area where city job descriptions were limited to $17,000 first-generation computer technicians—and where new development had to wait for conversion of HRA's existing computer hodgepodge into a working third-generation system. By late 1974, the new system was fully operational, with its massive data base keyed to video terminal data entry and inquiry from the centers. We thought we had aimed too high, since the network includes both a medicaid system similar to California's and a subsystem geared entirely to management information. But both are now operating. The increased efficiency and control benefits are expected to save the taxpayers more than $100 million a year.

Reconstruction help wanted

It should be evident from our results that change is possible in big government. Beyond that, the experience leads me to believe that what can be done in—and by—a government agency is limited by the legal and political framework in which it functions.

One reason is that much of government's productivity problem may really be a problem of law. Most legislators have little time and financing to research the policies they set. The operating agencies, viewing themselves merely as implemental servants of the legal system, fail to investigate the realities of their public market and the effectiveness of their programs. As a result, laws are passed and new system layers mandated to solve problems that are defined by public perception rather than by substantive analysis.

We were fortunate to obtain the support to set up a 30-man policy research staff, supported by a RAND contract. While part of the group performed a multi-faceted anylysis of the city's welfare population, the remainder focused on two strategic legislative issues—the state's costly and inequitable system of supplying welfare rent money and the welfare work laws. We lost our fight to standardize rents, but succeeded in replacing the demeaning mandate that forced welfare clients to "work off" their grants, without pay, in a city agency.

This law exemplified the misdirection common in public programs. The state employment agency was able to find jobs for only 8% of the employable recipients at an administrative cost of $6 million. HRA's substitution transferred the welfare monies to the city agencies, to become real wages for real jobs.

It also put recipients into a system where long-term advancement was possible. So far, some 15,000 people have been enrolled in paid employment.

However important such gains may be, the most pressing work to be done today is reconstructing the systems that propel government operation. The outdated frameworks now in use are clearly counter-productive. Once installed, new hardware inevitably produces improvements; put a caseworker's files into a centralized terminal digit system, and he has no choice but to use it.

Improvements depending on management control are considerably less effective than technical improvements. The existence of a telephone service does not guarantee that employees will answer the phones. Performance measures will not work when the supervisors themselves take hour-long coffee breaks.

It may be impossible to build industry-level performance into public operations. The government system simply cannot be completely controlled; the lines of authority are too ambiguous, the top management changes too frequent, the bureaucracy too strong, and the public's attention span too short. The productivity mandate of our agency—the public pressure behind our success—virtually evaporated as soon as we began showing results. The operational tautness began disintegrating the day that John Lindsay announced his decision to leave office.

The cleanest solution to the government productivity issue is the direct involvement of the private sector. Government should contract its operations functions to industry, where incentives for performance are built in and the control structure is clear. First, however, public agencies must learn to measure results. Without the ability to monitor a contractor's performance, they will be unwilling (and politically unable) to relinquish operational control.

It is in this area that I believe management professionals can take up the gauntlet, both as vigilant outsiders and as effective participants. Government is extremely sensitive to public pressure; private power groups can drive public officials toward productivity if the pressure is steady enough. To instill private-sector techniques down the line, however, the direct participation of private-sector management is necessary. Since public agencies seem incapable of self-reform, the challenge and the opportunity for outsiders are there.

4
Watergate As A
Case Study in Management

Max Ways

Seldom if ever has a U.S. Administration fallen so far so fast as Nixon's did in a single year. Last November [1972] worldwide opinion applauded its diplomacy toward Moscow and Peking and its withdrawal of the U.S. from the Vietnam war. At home the more raucous and violent expressions of dissent had abated. The economy was on a steep upgrade. The voters were ready to give Nixon one of the most resounding victories in the U.S. electoral record. Now, Nixon's Administration has lost diplomatic momentum, and its initiatives in domestic affairs have become fitful and feeble. Many key men of the 1972 Nixon ascendancy have departed, some in disgrace and some in disgust. So low has the Nixon political estate sunk that Spiro Agnew's resignation may be viewed by the White House either as one more affliction of a Job-like President or as a respite that distracts attention from pressures nearer home.

The errant thread that, when pulled, unraveled Nixon's skein of triumph was, of course, Watergate, the weird sequence beginning in the summer of 1971 before the break-in at the psychiatrist's office and running on and on through the slow disintegration of the cover-up in 1973. Watergate will not become, as some of those hurt by it have suggested, a mere footnote to history. For generations ahead, political scientists, lawyers, and moralists will be sorting out this jumble of facts, quasi-facts, confessions, lies, and accusations. Since it involves organized activity, Watergate can also be approached as a study in management.

The prime measure of management is effectiveness—often expressed as a relation of benefit to cost. Although neither benefits nor costs need be monetary, effectiveness is a frankly pragmatic test, separated from larger considerations of legality and morality. Speaking managerially, one gang of assassins may be judged "better" than a rival gang. One monastery may be judged "better" than another although both pursue high ends with equal ardor. A well-run gang of assassins may even be "better"—managerially—than a sloppy monastery.

That kind of statement does not imply that management in real life has nothing to do with morality. Like any other specialized approach, a managerial analysis is incapable of expressing the whole truth about a messy mass of phenomena from which the material under study has been selected. A look at Watergate as management, then, is not meant to evade or supersede judgments made from political or legal or moral viewpoints. On the contrary, a management analysis may throw some peripheral light on larger issues, and vice versa.

Fortune, November, 1973, pp. 108-11; 196-201. Copyright Time Inc., 1973. Reprinted with permission.
Max Ways is a staff writer for *Fortune.*

An executive's nightmare

Managerially, Watergate is an obvious disaster area. Its participants—whoever they may be assumed to be—incurred "costs" so much larger than "benefits" that it would be hard to think of an organized peacetime operation with an effectiveness rating farther on the wrong side of zero. Bad luck will not begin to explain the Watergate calamity. No matter which of many possible assumptions is adopted about how much Nixon knew at what "points in time," Watergate from its start to the present reeks of mismanagement.

Especially conspicuous are defects in the lifeblood of organizations: accurate communication. . . . The well-known management malady called constipated feedback seems to have been especially severe in the White House during the period of the cover-up when the President, on his own version of events, was isolated from both the activities of his aides and from rising public concern.

No doubt the universal managerial problem of communication is particularly difficult in the White House, where awe of presidential power can foster both overkill in efforts to serve and undue reticence in reporting unpleasant information. Such tendencies must be countered by presidential vigilance. After all, the essence of a President's job is to stay in touch with the people. The main function of his staff is to help him do that. When the staff became more of a barrier than a conduit, failure in a central responsibility occurred.

An overcapitalized enterprise

But this is only one of a hundred managerial flaws that can be indentified in the Watergate record. Organizational objectives were ill selected and ill defined. Choice of people, that key management function, was poor, not so much in terms of their over-all quality but rather in the casting for the particular roles they played; somewhere a personnel manual must exist that warns against slotting the likes of Liddy, Hunt, and Dean in the operational spots they came to occupy. Coordination was weak. Cooperators, who needed to communicate, didn't. The enterprise was so overcapitalized that money was recklessly sloshed around in a way that facilitated detection. The burglaries were overmanned; nobody can argue with the judgment of the former New York cop, Anthony Ulasewicz, that professionals "would not have walked in with an army." Indeed, analysis of Watergate can be discouraged or misled by the very richness of its pathology. So many people at so many levels in and around the White House made so many different kinds of mistakes that the observer is first tempted to say that this was the stupidest lot of managers ever assembled.

That lazy hypothesis is demolished by the plain fact that neither Richard Nixon nor the men around him are stupid—managerially or otherwise. Nixon is believed by some shrewd observers of government to be the most management-minded of recent Presidents. Those who viewed the parade of witnesses before the Ervin committee knew they were listening to intelligent men. Management analysis of Watergate, then, must turn upon the question of why officials, whose ability ranged from average to very high, made so many mistakes.

Much of the answer must lie in the ambience of the group, the cognitive and emotional patterns that permeated and shaped its organizational style. Such a collective atmosphere is not necessarily the exact sum of the attitudes, ideas, suppositions, desires, and values of the individuals who make up the group. Every organization has its own character, its own way of acting and reacting, and this quality powerfully colors what its members feel, think, say, and do within the organization. We will dig around in some Watergate material, starting at the bottom with the burglaries themselves, in an attempt to find the poisoned spring from which so much error flowed.

Hindsight makes it perfectly clear that nobody in or around the White House should have dabbled in burglary. But one of the attributes of management is supposed to be foresight. The quality of the decision to embark upon burglary must be appraised on the basis of what the deciders knew—or could have known—at the time of decision. The question may be cast in a strictly managerial form, leaving aside consideration of legality and morality: should an organization, not usually in the burglary business, diversify its activities in that direction?

The basic economy of burglary

Superficially, the prospect may seem inviting, just as people who pay restaurant checks are often seduced into believing that the restauranteur has an automatic and infallible surplus of benefits over costs. (A little research would show that more than half of new restaurants fail within a year.) White House staffers (no career burglars among them) were, like most of us, victims or potential victims of burglary. From that viewpoint, the burglar's profit seems easy and assured. Again, a little research into the burglary industry would have disclosed a repellent picture.

Though the number of burglaries in the U.S. is high and rising (2,345,000 in 1972), the curve of growth has been flattening out—and no wonder. Total cost to the victims was an impressive $722 million (or $308 per job). But burglars, because of the severe markdown traditional in thieves' markets, do not gain nearly as much as their victims lose. The actual take is probably closer to $200 per job, and this often has to be split among two or more perpetrators.

In the vast majority of burglaries, operating costs are so low as to be negligible. But risks, which are costs *in posse*, are formidable. While an individual netting $150 per job would have to commit fifty burglaries a year to achieve a modest income of $7,500 (tax-free, to be sure), the basic risk statistics of the industry indicate that one burglary in every five ends up with an arrest. Among adults arrested, half of those charged with burglary are convicted. Consequent unemployment and other costs reinforce the conclusion that burglary is not an activity that commends itself to mature and prudent people. No doubt that explains why half of all those arrested for burglary are under eighteen years old; the other half includes a high proportion of drug addicts, school dropouts, and persons otherwise disadvantaged and/or disturbed.

Target selection: poor

As every manager knows, attractive "special situations" sometimes appear in even those industries that are statistically most bleak. In the case of the Watergate sequence of burglaries, we have to ask whether the specific rewards that could reasonably be expected were so great or the specific risks so low as to overbalance the general probability that shows burglary to be a game for losers.

The sad truth is that the Watergate burglaries were "special situations" only in a negative sense: their prospective rewards were lower and their operating costs and contingent costs (risks) were both very much higher than in the model U.S. burglary. The highest expectable benefit that could have been gained from the break-in at the office of Daniel Ellsberg's psychiatrist would have been a file containing otherwise unobtainable personal information about him, information that might have been used (although it isn't clear how) to discredit him or to stop leaks. None of the White House deciders paused to note: (1) that the Pentagon papers case turned on legal and political issues to which Ellsberg's personality and motives were largely irrelevant; (2) that knowledge of Ellsberg's emotional make-up would not have contributed to solving the general problem of Washington leaks, which derive from many different kinds of people, few of whom bear a psychological resemblance to Ellsberg; (3) that since Ellsberg is not a notably secretive man, lots of personal information about him, for what it was worth, could have been gathered, free of risk, around Harvard Yard, around the Pentagon, and around the Rand Corp. From the burglary at the psychiatrist's office that promised such meager rewards, the burglars got, in fact, precisely nothing.

Nevertheless, the same team with some unhelpful additions was retooled to break into the Democratic National Committee. Once again, target selection was deplorable. Here the main mission was to bug the phone of Lawrence O'Brien, a man of probity and circumspection, two qualities often found together—although some barefoot moralizers insist virtue has no need of prudence. Public officials and politicians have been wary of telephones ever since 1876 when Alexander Graham Bell, demonstrating his gadget in Philadelphia, unwittingly startled the visiting Emperor of Brazil. An O'Brien friend says: "If you had a verbatim transcript of every telephone conversation Larry has engaged in since he was nineteen years old, you wouldn't have enough to embarrass him." In short, the break-in at the Watergate office building had an expectable reward very close to zero.

The prevalence of ogres

These footless ventures would remain forever incomprehensible unless we turned to the beliefs and emotional patterns of the participants. Their attitudes were shaped in part by the general ambience that enveloped the White House and the Committee to Re-elect the President, and that ambience included a lot of fear, suspicion, and hostility. Although the word "paranoia," used by many people, is too strong, it is correct to say that a high level of self-pity influenced the style of the Nixon White House.

The seeds of this attitude were sown long before Watergate. Self-pity was evident, though excusable, in many of Nixon's periods of adversity, and it had not melted away in the warm sun of ambition fulfilled. The public utterances of President Nixon, and those he encouraged Vice President Agnew to make in the early years of their first terms, often contained a strong theme of complaint against the unfairness of adversaries. The internal atmosphere of the White House was even more marked by this air of hostility and suspicion toward such outside bodies as Congress, the federal bureaucarcy, and the press. All Presidents have had adversaries, but no other White House institutionalized its hostility by keeping, as Nixon's did, an "enemies list."

The U.S. organizes its political life, as well as its business life, through competition. Not only do we have competing parties, but government has many separate elements that are simultaneously in cooperation and competition with one another. Among the people themselves we don't expect—and don't want— a placid homogeneity of outlook and aims. In our kind of pluralist politics, a degree of combativeness, an awareness of adversaries, is inevitable and constructive. But there's a line, blurred but real, beyond which a normal self-assertion in the face of opposition can move over into either arrogance or self-pity.

Many business managers have seen in their own sphere examples of the damage that can be done when this blurred line is crossed. It is desirable, for instance, that a sales force be on its toes, alert to spot and to counter moves by its opposition. A given sales force can become too proud of its competitive ability and be made vulnerable by overconfidence. Or it can become demoralized by the pressure of competition. A sensitive executive would worry if his salesmen were constantly telling him and one another about the perfidy of their competitors, dwelling on their dirty tricks, exaggerating their unfairness. In that ambience his own salesmen would have a built-in excuse for poor performance, or they might goad themselves into foolish and imprudent acts.

The nearest business equivalent of the Watergate folly was the great electrical price-fixing conspiracy uncovered in 1962. The question that then ran through the business world was: how could experienced executives in well-run companies do anything so stupid? Much of the answer lay in the ambience of the conspirators. They felt overpressured—by their bosses, by rising costs, by government regulations they considered unfair. One executive in the industry, trying to explain his colleagues' gross misjudgment, told a *FORTUNE* reporter at the time that the conspirators did what they did because they were "distressed men."

The distress, of course, was not visible in their objective condition of opulence and success. The distress was in their minds. So, too, powerful men in the White House came to think of themselves as inhabitants of a beleaguered and distressed city, surrounded by enemies whose strength and malice they exaggerated. An intense will to win, coupled with the belief that the situation is desperate, can release a lot of energizing adrenalin. If it goes too far, such a state of mind can also trigger reckless misjudgments. Whom the gods would destroy they first make unduly sorry for themselves.

A surplus of sincerity

Nixon's White House, of course, was not the first to overstress the power and menace of its adversaries. Franklin Roosevelt had depicted himself as standing, along with the weak, against the "economic royalists" who, he implied, were really in charge of the country. This tactic was so brilliantly successful that all subsequent Presidents have flirted with it. But in Roosevelt's underdog posture there was always a saving measure of insincerity. He never really believed his histrionic pretense that the dragons he opposed were all that monstrous. Nor did the men around him, cheerfully manipulating the reins of power, lose themselves in the dramatic myth he had created. Nixon's aides, unfortunately, seem to have let the role of victim capture their hearts and minds.

In a culture that prizes justice, fears power, and roots for underdogs, the temptation to cast oneself as a victim is ever present. The average American, when looking privately at his own situation, resists this temptation rather effectively; he knows—most of the time—that he is not doing too badly. But in any public discourse or in any capacity where he represents others, the contemporary American tends toward donning the victim's robe.

Listening to the speeches of businessmen, with their frequent emphasis on the abuse of government and labor-union power, an observer may worry lest their self-pity blind them to the ever expanding scope of action that beckons to business. Spokesmen for blacks or women can express real grievances in terms so extravagant that their followers will not perceive actual opportunities; the result can be stagnation or angry, self-destructive action. This unhappy pattern even extends to sports. One September night this year in Baltimore the managers of both baseball teams were thrown out of the same game for protesting too raucously against the injustice of the umpires. Passionate complaint is the almost unvarying tone of those man-in-the-street interviews cherished by producers of TV news programs. If Americans ever became, in fact, as sorry for themselves as they sound in public discourse, the country as a whole might begin to act as foolishly as the "distressed" men who blindly stumbled into Watergate.

Nixon early recognized the danger in protest run wild. It was he who laudably set out to "bring us together" and admonished us to "lower our voices." One of the deepest ironies of Watergate is the public demoralization that has occurred because the Nixon White House got carried away by its own agonized indignation toward the "unfairness" of its adversaries. The public in

1973 would never have had occasion to "wallow in Watergate" (as the President expressed it) had not the White House, years before, wallowed in self-pity.

Aristotle would understand

Watergate is often referred to as a "tragedy," as indeed it is in the sense that it blasted lives and caused suffering. But Watergate imitates in many other ways the structure of classic tragedy as Aristotle described it. The action of the plot, he said, proceeds from a "flaw" (*hamartia*). This may be either a defect of knowledge (e.g., Oedipus didn't know that his wife, Jocasta, was his mother) or an emotional imbalance (e.g., Medea, filled with woe-is-me, overreacted to Jason's infidelity by killing their children). Sometimes the tragic flaw is a mingling of cognitive and emotional imperfections.

From the flaw emerges *hubris*, which has long been translated as pride or arrogance. But recent scholarship pushes toward a different understanding of *hubris*. Walter Kaufmann in *Tragedy and Philosophy* argues persuasively that *hubris* refers to the quality of the action that proceeds from the flaw; it is not the internal flaw itself. Greek writers used the word *hubris* in referring to rivers that overflow their banks. They applied *hubris* to armies that run riot, indulging in wanton behavior, or to anything—human, animal, vegetable, or inanimate—that rankly transgresses the usual order of its nature.

In the Watergate case, the flaw obviously was not pride, which scorns to slink about by night in other people's offices. If we think of self-pity as the tragic flaw in Watergate, then all the wild imprudence of the consequent actions, the *hubris*, becomes less baffling. The literary analogy may illuminate details of a problem in management analysis.

Act I, Scene I occurs in the summer of 1971, in the ruler's room of state. He is giving urgent orders to members of his staff. The precise content of his instruction is not known to us, but its tone and general import are clear. His government is bedeviled by leaks of information to a press deemed hostile. He invokes his highest responsibility, that in respect to the national security, as he tells them he wants his government sealed against leaks.

So far, there is nothing irrational about the ruler's attitude or the gist of his instruction. Leaks are no trivial matter. They can impair national security—and some have done so. More often they are devices employed by a government official to support a policy he favors, to hurt a rival, or advance his own career. Such leaks sow distrust among officials, inhibit frank discussion, and demoralize government. Now, publication of the Pentagon Papers, a veritable Niagara of a leak, requires drastic and immediate remedy.

At first the plumbers' unit interprets its responsibility in a normal and harmless way. Its members start to carry out a staff assignment to needle the chiefs of line departments and the regular investigatory agencies into greater vigilance against leaks. But progress, if any, is too slow. At this point the tragic flaw in the spiritual ambience of the White House group begins to manifest itself.

In and around the plumbers' unit, deviation from organizational normality takes two forms. The atmosphere of a besieged city overmotivates the staffers involved. They wish so intensely to succeed in their assigned task that restraints of ordinary prudence drop away. The second manifestation of the flaw is more specifically managerial: they transform a staff function into a line operation. They decide that they themselves will gather the evidence that will retard leaks.

Their master, the President, deploys under his hand the largest, most expensive, and most professional array of investigatory agencies this side of the Soviet border. Yet these agencies are bypassed when the plumbers' unit decides to go into clandestine operations—which is no woods for babes. Neither Egil Krogh nor David Young, who headed the plumbers, had relevant experience in this line of work. Their immediate superior, John Ehrlichman, had no investigatory experience. Liddy, who had worked for the FBI, and Hunt, who had worked for the CIA, did have relevant experience. But many instances are known where individuals can render valuable service within a large professionalized organization and yet be helpless or harmful when working without professional supervision and organized support. In the plumbers' unit, Liddy and Hunt plainly lacked the competence, restraint, and judgment to be found (one hopes) in the organizations that had previously girdled their exuberance.

A former aide to a different President believes that all White House staffs, becoming impatient with the regular line agencies of government, are from time to time tempted to get into operations themselves. They hardly ever do so, however, partly because of what he called "the danger of involving the President." He was talking about possible interventions far less dangerous to the presidential reputation than burglary. Why, then, was the Nixon White House so incautiously willing to bypass the regular agencies and place its honor in the hands of people who knew so little about what they were doing?

Should bureaucrats obey?

The decision was almost certainly influenced by an attitude of distrust toward the whole federal bureaucracy. This was one of the areas where members of the Nixon circle felt most sorry for themselves. One expert on government structure remembers a long meeting of Nixon staff men at San Clemente devoted to the question of how to make the bureaucracy more obedient.

A familiar management problem is involved here, as anybody knows who has taken over the top spot in a corporation, or a division, or even a small office. He is likely to have found there men and women who took their own responsibilities seriously and who are entrenched by their specialized competence. A wise executive does not try to command the servile obedience of such people. His responsibility for coordinating their efforts and changing the over-all direction of the organization can only be achieved through the patient arts of leadership. He has to talk, to listen, to persuade and be persuaded.

But from the first the Nixon inner circle seems to have misunderstood the nature of the difficulty. It saw bureaucratic resistance as arising from political philosophy. No doubt, most civil servants are Democrats and maybe even "liberals." But this is not as important a truth as the Nixon people thought it. Presidents Kennedy and Johnson also had trouble with the bureaucracy. A Nixon official who has been most effective in his leadership of civil servants is Secretary of the Treasury George Shultz, whose own political philosophy happens to be most remote from the presumed liberalism of the bureaucrats. Shultz talks and listens to his experts. Shultz does not withdraw into injured and persecuted silence because they won't obey him. In short, Shultz follows a pattern widespread among managers of corporations who anticipate resistance from their experts. They do not perceive it as disloyalty or hostility. They know that dealing with such resistance is just what they are hired to do.

When the big scene was bungled

But the Nixon Administration, with some distinguished exceptions, had never been notable for strong, independent personalities, secure enough to listen to the experts below and speak candidly to the chief above. The White House staff, the citadel of the beleaguered city, seems to have been chosen more for its zeal to protect the boss than for ability to serve him with information and argument. This criterion owed part of its origin to the tragic flaw, and it resulted in disaster at a crucial decision time.

Classic tragedy moves toward a point of "recognition," the scene where the flaw in all its horror is revealed to the audience and the dramatis personae. In the Watergate sequence, that point was reached in the summer of 1972 after the arrests, after the disclosure that large sums of money had been "laundered" in Mexico. Clearly, these were no ordinary burglars. They had backing at high levels.

If at that point the President or his former Attorney General had publicly recognized that a serious error had occurred, Watergate would never have grown to anything approaching its ultimate proportions. Such a public recognition would have been painful, but it almost certainly would not have cost Nixon either the election or the respect of several millions of Americans who lost confidence in him this year.

Nixon and the men around him bungled the recognition scene. Or to put the same thought in business terms, they failed to face the hard decision to cut their losses. Exactly what went on in the White House in the year following June, 1972, is still far from clear. But on any assumption about those months, there was serious managerial trouble in two big areas: personnel and communications.

In the most unlikely case, that Nixon knew exactly what was going on at every step, he was picking the wrong people to do the wrong things. On the much more likely assumption that Nixon didn't know much about the cover-up efforts, then those who were involved in it badly needed some coordinator—and they needed one with more authority, prudence, experience, and fiber than John Dean.

As a group, the White House staff contained too few men of the caliber and courage to make Nixon face the situation that the public, Nixon's audience, had long since recognized. On one version of events, it was not until April 15, 1973, that anybody told Nixon just how bad the situation was and what immediate steps he had to take. That messenger was Henry Petersen, not a member of Nixon's staff but one of the despised careerists, who had never spoken to the President until he stood before him in tennis shoes and old clothes on a Sunday afternoon and finally got the bad news across.

Nixon understands organizational information systems better, perhaps, than any previous President. But he showed in the Watergate sequence no sign that he grasped the most important fact about such systems: they are all far short of perfect. A prudent executive keeps testing his organization's ability to tell him what he needs to know about its own activities. A classic management story on this point goes back to 1924 and its hero is Alfred P. Sloan. In the spring of that year General Motors plants were turning out cars much faster than salesmen were getting rid of them. The established channels of information failed to bring this bad news to corporate headquarters. Corporate calamity was averted only because Sloan visited dealers in St. Louis, Kansas City, and Los Angeles, and himself counted the cars that had piled up in their lots. Nixon, on his version of what happened during the cover-up, never got down to personal investigation of widely published reports of what was being done in his name.

The press is unfair

It is quite possible that Nixon simply did not believe what the media were reporting concerning the cover-up because he had grown so accustomed to considering himself the victim of a press hostile to him.

The press is unfair to Nixon in a sense more fundamental than he knows. It has been unfair to all recent Presidents. It is unfair to businessmen, labor leaders, and everybody else responsible for carrying out action in a world whose complexity makes for dull writing. The inadequacy of the press in explaining to the public the actual working of government processes may be one of the most serious defects in contemporary democracy. Compared to this problem, the additional fact that many influential journalists don't much like Richard Nixon pales toward insignificance.

The Nixon White House diminishes its chances of constructive coverage by its attitude of pained withdrawal from the media. The exceptions demonstrate this general point. Henry Kissinger, who talks frequently and (relatively) frankly with reporters, manages to get through the media to the public. Nixon himself, on the rare occasions when he endures face-to-face contact with the media, handles press conferences with verve. His San Clemente press conference of August 22 was one of the few effective White House moves in the long Watergate sequence.

Nixon's relations with Congress also have that hurt and withdrawn look. Before he came to office, Congress was already becoming restless under what many of it members considered the undue power of the executive branch.

Nixon was bound to have trouble with Congress, no matter what its political coloration might have been. But Nixon seems to have taken congressional opposition as a personal affront. In its day-to-day contact with individual Congressmen, the Nixon White House has been less active, less persuasively communicative than previous Administrations, including Eisenhower's. In public Nixon has, as a President must, often summarized what was wrong about the record of Congress and what was right about his own record. But in his relations with Congress he has not, as they say in Seville, worked close to the bull.

Why we remember Hannibal

Deplorable tendencies in Congress, in the bureaucracy, and in the media are easier to denounce than to overcome. A President, nevertheless, will be appraised by how much headway he makes against such objective difficulties. Hannibal is remembered for actually crossing the Alps, not for whatever Carthaginian maledictions that he, frustrated in Gaul, might have hurled at the "unfair" gradients confronting him.

The flaw that mars Nixon's style in domestic affairs becomes the more glaring when it is limned against his foreign-policy successes. In dealing with Red China and the Soviet Union he has brilliantly demonstrated that he can rise above self-pity. He has studied these offshore adversaries so long and so intently that he can handle the problems they represent much more coolly, objectively, and effectively than he handles the onshore problems represented by Daniel Ellsberg or Larry O'Brien or the federal bureaucracy or the *Washington Post*. Nixon isn't thrown off stride by Peking's or Moscow's "dirty tricks." It never seems to occur to him that Brezhnev or Mao is "unfair." He manages his relations with them like a manager, not with the mien of a wounded deer.

Excessive self-pity is, of course, an emotional and moral flaw. It is often found entwined with an inaccurate cognitive picture of reality. Individuals or groups marked by such a flaw may be handicapped in practical affairs, even in those activities that are put in such specialized pigeonholes as politics or economics or management.

Machiavelli taught the world that politics, for instance, has rules of success that are independent of moral strictures. But he never taught that men who act in politics are to be considered unbound by moral law. Twenty years ago Professor Charles Singleton in a memorable lecture called "The Perspective of Art" pointed to a passage in Machiavelli's *Discourses* as a corrective to the popular view of what the Florentine believed. Machiavelli, in one of those typical passages about what a ruler must do to grasp and hold power, gives an example of some morally horrible but politically effective policies carried out by Philip of Macedon. Then Machiavelli says: "Doubtless these means are cruel and destructive of all civilized life, and neither Christian nor human, and should be avoided by everyone."

Now that politics is clearly recognized as an independent art, any practitioner faces a double hurdle. What he does must be good as politics, but must not be bad as morals. The point is even clearer in the relation of morals to economics. When Alfred Sloan, in the example given above, learned that unsold cars were piling up, he shut down the production lines. As a compassionate man, he regretted the consequent unemployment and suffering. But in the economic circumstances his decision was not immoral. On the contrary, once he knew the facts any other decision would have been economically, managerially, and morally irresponsible.

Allen Dulles, when he was head of the CIA, once told a group of journalists that anyone entering upon his job must leave all moral considerations outside the door. This dangerous proposition is an example of the vulgar misreading of the Machiavellian view. The head of the CIA works in circumstances that ordinary citizens do not encounter. Circumstances change cases, and the head of the CIA may morally do things which an ordinary citizen would have no compelling occasion and no moral right to do. But the head of the CIA must nevertheless weigh the morality of any such act by whatever standards are appropriate to the circumstances.

John Ehrlichman in his testimony indicated that he could think of circumstances involving, say, the threat of nuclear attack, in which a President could justifiably order a burglary. But does this mean that a President, by invoking the name of national security, can order *any* burglary? A weighing of circumstances becomes critical in government morality, as indeed it is in private morality. It is not only managerially shocking but morally shocking that so serious an offense as the Beverly Hills break-in was undertaken in circumstances that did not come within miles of requiring it.

Melancholy example

The moral standards of political life are, indeed, often more strict than those of private life. "Dirty tricks" that may be merely tasteless in undergraduate elections are seriously offensive when plotted by people on a White House staff. All that useless Dick-Tuckery revealed by the Ervin committee is one of the most appalling aspects of the Watergate disclosures. Another, and more melancholy, example is brought to mind by Spiro Agnew's resignation. Many people may not regard an ordinary citizen's failure to report taxable income as one of the graver moral offenses. But when a Vice President of the United States is exposed as having done that, we are all—quite logically—horrified.

In the Watergate sequence, self-pity blinded the participants to dangers that were political, managerial, legal, and moral. As their retribution unfolds, the rest of us may from time to time ask whether our own legitimate resentment against our share of the injustices that all men experience might not be making us so sorry for ourselves that we mismanage our practical affairs.

| PERSONALITY PROFILE |

5
When
Government Works
Anthony Lewis

Washington—One of the prickliest questions awaiting decision in Washington is whether to let Concorde land in this country. Britain and France have invested enormous sums and prestige in their supersonic airliner and urgently want an O.K. for commercial service. But the environmental safety objections—noise, threat to the atmosphere, marginal fuel reserves—are all so formidable.

The man who will decide is William T. Coleman Jr., the Secretary of Transportation. That kind of responsibility is often fudged in Washington, or subject to secret distortions. The British papers have already suggested that Secretary of State Kissinger or President Ford will really decide about Concorde. But Bill Coleman makes clear that he thinks it is his duty, that he has been left free to carry it out and that he will.

He is going about it a little like a judge. He has identified nine key issues on Concorde. He is trying to get answers on them from his own safety people, noise experts and the like. He has a letter from Henry Kissinger laying out the foreign policy considerations. In the next few weeks he will make the decision, and then do something really unusual for a Cabinet officer.

"I'm going to write an opinion," Coleman said in a conversation the other day. "I think there is a duty to articulate one's reasons on something this important." He added, smiling, "Then I'll get the hell out of town."

It will not be the first time he has explained a decision in that open way. When he resisted powerful bureaucratic and political forces and said no to a proposed super highway through the Virginia suburbs, I-66, he gave his reasons in an opinion.

Nor is it the first time he has faced up to controversy with apparent equanimity. Talking with Mr. Coleman, one gets the impression not that he enjoys battles but that he thinks the only point in his kind of job is to call them as he sees them.

Recently he annoyed a lot of people, including some friends and natural allies, by coming out against Federal aid to give the Northeast rail corridor 150-mile-an-hour trains. Mr. Coleman did it because he found that the cost had been grossly underestimated. A 1971 department study came up with the figure of $370 million. But when Mr. Coleman pressed for hard estimates, the total approached $5 billion. He suggested spending $1.2 billion to upgrade the service now, leaving open the possibility of high-speed trains later.

Another controversial decision was to impose user charges on the inland waterways. The Government has spent $8 billion on the waterways over the years, and Mr. Coleman reasoned that the barge companies—some of them large, or owned by conglomerates—should not get that capital free. Moreover, they pay no gasoline tax, and they compete with the railroads.

"We have a lot of changes to make in the transportation field," Mr. Coleman said, "and you have to make choices. You mostly disappoint people—you don't please them."

Part of his policy is to encourage mass transit. His most difficult political problem may lie in his proposals for change in the highway trust fund. It was set up in 1956, to run for twenty years. Mr. Coleman wants to revive the allocation formula so a portion of the tax money goes to complete the interstate highway network, the rest to states and localities for either roads or mass transit. But there is stiff resistance in Congress to any change.

"I'm willing to take the same $7 billion a year," he said, "and give people options. I say, 'If you want to spend your share all on highways, be my guest. But if you want to have transit, that is your choice.' I don't understand why people should be against that.

"President Eisenhower was right to choose a twenty-year trust fund for highways when he did. But gasoline was 17 cents a gallon then, and the supply seemed unlimited; we were not educated on environmental costs. Why can't we change our policy to reflect realities?"

Watergate showed, among other things, how power in Washington had drained to the White House, and been abused. One widely suggested safeguard against that corruption of power was to have in the Cabinet persons of independence, of substance, who could not be overborne in secret by an H. R. Haldeman.

Coleman is a post-Watergate example of a man of independence, accepting responsibility. There are others; one often mentioned is the Secretary of Labor, John Dunlop. The obvious element in common is that they do not need the job: John Dunlop can go back to being a professor happily any time, and Bill Coleman to being a prosperous lawyer. But that does not always assure independence. Some people who do not need office grow so fond of its trappings that they trim their judgment.

So there is some good news in Washington, along with the dreary. Credit is due to President Ford for confiding important issues to people of substance and letting them decide as their legal duty requires. Of course the fact that decisions are faced squarely and made openly does not guarantee that they will be right. But if they are not, someone will be accountable.

Topic Two

The Individual in Administration: Ethical Choices

Introduction

Ethics are the values that individuals use to guide them when making choices about their relationships with other people. "Historically ethics [have] been primarily concerned with determining what things are good or bad and what acts are right and wrong. ... [They deal] with problems of value and obligation."[1] In a more narrow sense of the word, ethics also means the rules or standards of conduct for members of a profession. Lawyers, teachers, doctors, accountants, and others have ethical codes which pertain only to their members and which establish certain standards of conduct among themselves and with the public. Our emphasis, however, is on the broader meaning of ethics.

An important distinction must be understood between an administrative act which is unethical and one which is illegal. Often the terms are used interchangeably when there should be a distinction. Public administrators who accept gifts from people whose interests they could further may be doing nothing illegal, but in the view of some people their conduct is clearly unethical. That is, the moral quality of the action by the administrators is being questioned rather than the legality of what is done. On the other hand, to label outright lawbreaking as unethical conduct is not only misleading but does a disservice to the public because it hides the seriousness of the act. Some of the professions mentioned above have censured their members for "unethical" practices which in fact were convictions for illegal activities. This may be done to protect the status of the profession, as unethical certainly carries less of a stigma than the term criminal activity.

In this Topic, we look at ethical choices among various kinds of action where no specific law exists to govern the situation or where the law is vague. The cases and examples cover a wide range of the most frequently encountered types of ethical problems, and they suggest a few answers and their consequences. We shall see some noble and some less than heroic responses to these ethical challenges. The important and difficult questions to be examined include: What ethical criteria should an administrator follow? What accounts for different ethical standards in various governmental jurisdictions? Is it ethical to break the law in the guise of protecting the public interest?

To begin the analysis, let us consider what might be the minimal ethical standards for public administrators regardless of the requirements of the law. One general guideline that has existed for some time can be stated: If what I am about to do in my job should later be seen on nationwide television, would I be able to explain and defend my action? If the answer is No, the guideline suggests that the administrator should not do it!

More specific criteria are offered by Glenn Stahl, a public administrator and a teacher. He believes that the fundamental principle of public administration must be to "serve the public in a manner that strengthens the integrity and processes of a democratic society."[2] To bring this about, three specific types of administrative behavior which are basic to ethical conduct must be practiced. These are "(1) that all the people must be served, equally and impartially; (2) that this must be achieved with full respect for and reliance on representative institutions; and (3) that internal administration in public agencies must be consistent with these modes of behavior."[3] While laws can be passed to try to make the above behavior mandatory, this will not work fully unless the individual administrators possess a desire and an understanding of the need for such attitudes. Without these individual values, laws and codes serve only to show the gap between performance and intent.

Many people in and out of government fail to see the connection between administrative competency and ethical practices along the lines suggested above. It is generally assumed that if administrators appear to be effective in their job, their particular administrative ethical values are of little concern. The theme of this Topic, however, presents an opposing view; namely, that a lack of high ethical practice by public administrators does indeed diminish their competency because they are not fulfilling all their administrative responsibilities to serve the public fully. "To serve the public fully" means more than just physically occupying a place in a public agency. Because of the special nature of governmental administration discussed in Topic One, public administrators have responsibilities other than their job functions. The public should expect its governmental administration to be conducted in a prescribed manner consistent with democratic procedures and by people who understand and respect those principles. Anything less in practice and attitude jeopardizes the entire political process.

Political Culture and Ethical Values

What is considered ethical administrative behavior in one part of the United States may not be acceptable practice somewhere else. Until recently, in some midwestern and eastern cities and states, there was the practice of public employees contributing part of their salary to the political party in power. Such "kick-backs" were considered part of the patronage system and the way politics was conducted. If there were prohibitory laws, they were not enforced vigorously except when it became politically expedient to do so. In other cities and states, especially in the West, such practices generally have been considered unethical and illegal, and the laws have been strictly enforced.

What accounts for these differences in ethical values which, in turn, influence the very practice of public administration? The general answer is political culture; that is, the attitudes, beliefs, and traditions people have about the political process. Where we find distinct political cultures, we find different values and political practices. The existence of particular political attitudes and traditions brings about or reinforces certain political institutional arrangements and procedures. Therefore, to understand why a particular administrative behavior is found in one geographic area and not in another, one needs to know about the basic political attitudes which have shaped various institutions and administrative practices.

There are many current political attitudes in the United States which are manifested in public administration and individual behavior. Jeffersonian and Jacksonian democracy are two longstanding examples. Jeffersonian democracy with its emphasis upon governmental decentralization and the importance of state and local governments is still a recurring issue in American politics. As a consequence, a fundamental question in public policy debates is which level of government should have administrative responsibility for a particular program.

In Jacksonian democracy the emphasis is on the "common-man" or citizen-politician in government. This means that no special professional or technical expertise is needed to run government; only good common sense is necessary. Jacksonian democracy also features patronage rather than a merit system to fill governmental positions.

Daniel Elazar has identified three other political cultures in the United States: Moralistic, Individualistic, and Traditionalistic.[4] A brief look at two of these will underscore the relationship among political culture, ethical values, and individual public administrators. Elazar's descriptions represent "pure" types but today one finds mixtures with a dominant strain of one political culture within a given geographical area.

Elazar's first political culture is called the "Moralistic" (referred to as the "M" culture). In this culture or political environment, the political system is perceived as a commonwealth. This is defined as "a state in which the whole people have an undivided interest—in which the citizens cooperate in an effort to create and maintain the best government in order to implement certain shared moral principles."[5] Politics in this culture is considered a virtuous activity, and it is related to the development of the good society and the establishment of the public good. A number of ethical values affecting individual behavior stem from these basic premises. For example, there is a moral obligation to serve in government. Individual goals are subordinated to the general good as defined by the community. Government itself is used to achieve community goals but not to further one's own personal ambitions or economic well-being.

In "M" culture areas ethical behavior is well defined and there is a high expectation that public employees will adhere to those standards. What might be merely unethical but not illegal elsewhere is subject to severe legal penalties where "M" culture values exist. In the issue of conflict of interest (which is discussed in detail later in this Introduction) there are usually clear restrictions and limits prohibiting such practices. In short, corruption, or even its appearance, is not tolerated. Finally, "M" culture cities and states are more likely to use a merit personnel system than a patronage system. Although this is based on the assumption that the public deserves the services of the most qualified in terms of skills instead of those whose principal loyalty is to a person or party, merit should not be seen as guaranteeing ethical practice or the highest service in the public interest.

Among the states that typify many of the "M" characteristics are Minnesota, Wisconsin, Utah, California, Oregon, and Washington. At their very best, "M" culture areas come close to the democratic ideal. Yet there is a potential adverse consequence of this culture. When a community defines "the public good," there may be little room for dissent or opposing views. Questions of right and wrong in absolute terms are found in "M" culture regions. Values become fixed and a narrowness and lack of toleration can easily replace the search for the public interest, thereby diminishing the "M" culture's positive influences on individuals and administration.

Elazar's second political culture is called the "Individualistic" or "I" culture. It contrasts sharply in premise and practice with the "M." In the "I" culture the political order is viewed as "a marketplace in which the primary public relationships are products for bargaining among individuals and groups acting out of self-interest."[6] Politics is not differentiated from other human activities. People enter politics as they would business: because they like it; they are proficient; they can make money; and they can fulfill other personal objectives.

From these assumptions a number of ethical and administrative practices follow. There is no moral obligation to serve in government. In fact, amateurs are discouraged, for it is believed that government is best run by the professional politician, although not necessarily by the professional administrator. The machinery of government is for the use of the people controlling it. Patronage, handing out governmental contracts to friends, and other similar practices are not subject to ethical judgments. Toleration of corruption is fairly loose, and what laws have been written on the subject generally are ignored.

In those cities and states where the "I" culture is predominant, such as Chicago, Maryland, New Jersey, and Indiana, there have been some famous scandals. At its worst, the "I" culture is undemocratic and corrupt. There has been one redeeming feature, however, which provides some balance to the picture. Historically, "I" culture areas have been more likely to provide the means for minority groups to enter the political process. Because political organizations have needed votes, and immigrants represented potential voters, efforts have been made to bring these people into the political system. Even though it was done for selfish reasons—that is to gain or retain political power—the "I" culture machines actually broadened the base of the political process.

These descriptions of some of the dominant political cultures in the United States suggest that specific ethical and administrative values do not occur by happenstance. Their origins and influences can be traced and analyzed. Equally important, however, but not included in this book, are the individual values derived from personal experiences, family, educational, and religious training. All these contribute to the kinds of responses individuals make to ethical questions.

Examples of Ethical Choices

We now turn to some of the specific types of ethical questions that public administrators encounter. Keep in mind that these situations are not governed by precise laws, and therefore are not simple matters of legal versus illegal. Individual judgments are required to determine what is right and wrong action.

1. Conflict of interest. One of the most common situations involving ethical choices is known as a conflict of interest. This condition exists when people in public office stand to gain personally from their public action. The conflict arises if in the course of conducting the public's business, administrators can directly affect their personal fortunes. For example, when an administrator sits on a public commission which regulates a particular business, and that commissioner has a direct financial or other personal interest in such a business, then a conflict may occur.

Various shades of opinion have developed on the propriety of conflicts of interest. The classic statement and defense of public officials using their offices to further their own interests are found in Selection 6. William Riordan, the author of this commentary, has recorded the views of George Washington Plunkitt, a Tammany Hall leader in the late 1800's. Plunkitt defines the difference between "honest graft" and "dishonest graft," saying that the former is perfectly acceptable. Using one's public office, according to Plunkitt, is just plain common sense and certainly should not be confused with outright dishonesty.

Today, almost a century later, many public officials echo Plunkitt when they defend what apparently are conflicts of interest (the modern-day term for "honest graft") as normal and acceptable practice. People in the Individualistic political culture look upon government as a means to promote their own interests, and believe every opportunity should be taken to use government for this purpose. Another group voices a slightly different view; namely, there is nothing unethical when the interests of a public administrator have been furthered so long as the public has also benefited. Only if the public official alone gains from the act would the action be considered an unethical practice. According to this same group, the public is served better by people who are knowledgeable because of their close personal connection or financial involvement in the issues of government.

Opponents of conflicts of interest argue that the appearance or even the hint of personal gain by a public administrator from a public act is unethical. They reason that the suspicion by the public of any wrongdoing by governmental employees can contribute as much toward undermining public confidence in government as actual lawbreaking. Potential or real conflicts of interest impair the fiduciary responsibilities of public administrators, and so every effort must be made to avoid these kinds of situations.

A wide variety of activity can constitute conflicts of interest. Public employees may be offered free tickets to all sorts of events; they may be sent on "fact-finding" trips paid by private groups; they can be invited to speak at conventions in exotic places (all expenses paid, of course); and they and their families can be given personal gifts. The possibilities are endless, and so are the attempts to circumvent laws which prevent outright gifts.

A basic question is, Does a public administrator become obligated to the person or group giving the favor? Virtually every public administrator will answer No, but there is less unanimity on whether gifts should be accepted in the first place. Some public employees are highly insulted when it is suggested they can be "bought" with such favors. Others say they cannot be swayed by any gift, but add that it is better to avoid the suggestion of improper influence.

Many laws attempt to control conflicts of interest, but most of them are either vague or not enforced. Existing federal regulations, for example, prohibit public employees from soliciting or accepting favors from persons having business dealings with their agency. The exceptions dilute the intent: "nominal" business meals and gifts based on "personal friendships" but not on business relationships may be accepted. Former federal governmental employees are prevented also for one year from representing private clients before their former agencies on any matter in which they were once involved. About half the federal agencies, however, have failed to set up any type of compliance mechanism to enforce that rule, according to the Senate Government Operations Committee.

Selection 7, "The Curious Case of the Indicted Meat Inspectors," illustrates many problems associated with conflicts of interest. The meat inspectors were caught in the middle of several conflicting forces and, in order to reconcile these, they were required to use their individual discretion daily. Federal law prohibited inspectors from receiving anything of value from the meat packers. At the same time, the administrators of the inspection program did not discourage their inspectors from taking "small" gifts so long as this did not affect their job. The administrators themselves often received gifts from the processors, sometimes out of friendship, other times for a more selfish reason.

The case depicts a working environment in which the professional, organizational, and ethical norms were vague, contradictory, and hypocritical. It could be argued that the administrators were as guilty as the inspectors for permitting such conditions to exist. They were asking the inspectors to implement a program which was unworkable given the inadequate resources available to the inspectors and the traditions which had developed over the years. The administrators in this situation had an ethical obligation to their own employees and to the public, and they failed both.

Another type of conflict of interest is known as the "revolving door" arrangement. This is a common practice at the national and state levels of government and the subject of much debate. It is called a "revolving door" because people come into public service as top-level administrators from industries over which they have power of regulation or influence in their new government job. Then, after a time in government, most of these individuals return to the same industry. It is this situation which creates the potential or actual conflict of interest. The critics of this practice believe that it is asking too much of people to be tough regulators of the companies and friends who are expected to offer them higher paying positions in two or three years.

The defenders of the system counter by saying that people of integrity understand the different functions they have in government, and that business executives can assume different responsibilities and loyalties for a period of time. Further, it is stated, government benefits by having administrators who are intimately familiar with the practices it is trying to regulate. Finally, they add that a rotation of personnel helps both government and business because people acquire new skills and perspectives with which to solve mutual problems.

"The Great Grain Robbery"

Some of the implications of the "revolving door" arrangement are dramatically illustrated in the following case.[7] The sale of wheat by the United States to the Soviet Union in 1972 was one of the most controversial events involving a possible conflict of interest because of a shuffling of top administraors back and forth between government and private industry.

These are the basic facts of the case. In 1972 the Soviet Union was in desperate need of wheat. Its shortage was potentially disastrous, but only a few top U.S. Department of Agriculture officials knew in the spring of that year the exact dimensions of the Soviet problem. A report had been prepared outlining the situation, but it was withheld from the American public. Sometime between May and July the six major American grain exporters learned of the Soviet needs. The last group to discover that the Soviets would have to buy large quantities of wheat, and therefore drive up the domestic and world prices, was the American wheat farmer. On July 8, 1972, President Nixon announced that the United States would sell wheat to the Soviet Union, but the amounts were minimized by both sides. Actually, by that date, substantial sale contracts had already been made between the Soviets and the American grain exporters who were very much aware of the scale of the Soviet purchases. Because information on the Soviet situation had been withheld from the American farmer by the Department of Agriculture until after mid-August, the grain exporters were able to buy wheat at much lower prices than if the farmers had known of the actual demand.

In addition to learning of the Soviet need for wheat before the American public and farmers did, the grain export companies also acquired a second piece of vital information before it was made public. The Department of Agriculture announced on August 25 that it was retroactively increasing the export subsidy for any wheat sales made through August 24. In other words, it was to the benefit of grain exporters to complete as many sale contracts as possible by August 24 because after that date the subsidy would be reduced. Even though the increase was announced retroactively (presumably to prevent last minute sales), Charles Pence of the Department of Agriculture on August 24 telephoned the six grain export companies to inform them of this special subsidy that would be phased out by the end of the day. It has been estimated that this special information to the companies reaped for them several million dollars in additional profits. All told, the Soviets bought one-fourth of the total American wheat crop at considerable cost to the American farmer and consumer.

Throughout this period which began in early May and ended in September, there was an evident "revolving door" situation. A listing of some of the principal people indicates the extent of the business to government to business relationship.[8] (1) Clarence Palmby—Assistant Secretary of Agriculture until June 1972 quit to become a vice-president of Continental Grain Co. (the major exporter in the Soviet deal). Palmby had been with Secretary of Agriculture Earl Butz in Moscow in the spring for the initial talks about Soviet purchases of wheat. (2) Carroll Brunthaver—an executive from Cook Industries (grain exporter) replaced Palmby as an Assistant Secretary of Agriculture. (3) George Shenkin—a Washington lobbyist for Bunge (grain exporter) left that position in January 1972 to become an assistant to Clifford Pulvermacher, the manager of the Department of Agriculture's Export Marketing Services. (4) Clifford Pulvermacher—manager of the Department of Agriculture's Export Marketing Services until June 1972 quit to become a Washington lobbyist for Bunge. (He traded places with Shenkin.) (5) William Pearce—a vice-president of Cargill (grain exporter)—left that job in December 1971 to become a White House special representative for trade negotiations.

The question all this poses is, Did these close relationships lead to inside information and favored treatment of the grain exporting companies?

2. *Loyalty to the agency and superiors.* Ethical choices arise for employees when they are forced to decide how much allegiance they owe their agency or their organizational leaders when they believe them to be wrong. Two hypothetical instances can illustrate these points. Your agency has adopted a policy with which you adamantly disagree on some ethical or public interest grounds. You may actually be required to take an action which offends

your sense of right. You have been with the agency for some time; the job market is tight and the opportunities for transfer are limited. At what point and under what conditions do you resign?

In another example, you suspect your immediate supervisor is doing something illegal. You are not positive, but the preliminary facts point in that direction. What do you do? Do you approach him or her? Do you notify others? Do you ignore what you think you are seeing? In this problem, you personally like the individual. He or she just promoted you, and so you have some respect for his or her judgment. Yet, you know you are supposed to be working for the public interest and not a particular employee. What do you do?[9]

A recent example of individuals demonstrating more loyalty to a person than to the public interest is found in the events surrounding the background investigation of Bert Lance for his nomination as Director of the national Office of Management and Budget (OMB). In congressional committee hearings nine months after Lance was confirmed by the Senate as OMB Director, testimony revealed that several government officials who earlier investigated Lance had withheld derogatory information or made decisions helpful to Lance in the hope that they would be retained in their jobs by the new Carter administration.

Jimmy Carter nominated Lance to the OMB on December 3, 1976. In December 1975, the U.S. Comptroller of the Currency had issued an "enforcement agreement" placing restrictions on Lance and a Georgia bank of which he was an officer. On November 22, 1976, Lance visited Donald Tarleton, the regional administrator of the Comptroller's office in Atlanta, and they discussed the agreement and the fact that Lance was going to be nominated as the head of OMB. After that meeting, Tarlton rescinded the "enforcement agreement," although he testified Lance never asked for that action. When Robert Bloom, the Acting Comptroller of the Currency for the United States, and Tarlton's boss, heard about this agreement being rescinded he was angry at first. Later, however, he took personal steps to protect Lance's reputation by not fully disclosing unfavorable facts to the Senate during its confirmation hearing. Bloom admitted to Lance that he wanted to be appointed Comptroller by Carter, and so Bloom withheld information about Lance's questionable financial status.[10]

A third governmental official figured prominently in the Lance investigation. The U.S. Attorney in Atlanta, John Stokes, closed the investigation by the Justice Department into Lance's financial practices on December 2, 1976, the day before Lance was nominated. The Justice Department inquiry had begun in December 1975, and while there was no ongoing investigation, the case had never been closed. On December 2, 1976, Lance's attorney called his long-time friend John Stokes to ask about the status of the investigation and to inquire whether there was any reason not to close it. Stokes closed the case officially the same day. He later denied that his decision was prompted by the fact that he needed only a few more months in office to be eligible for retirement. Stokes stated it was only coincidental that he closed the case one day before Carter nominated Lance for OMB Director.

As a closing note, neither Bloom nor Stokes was retained by the Carter adminstration despite their intentional or unintentional attempts to help Carter's close friend, Bert Lance.

3. *Secrecy in government.* Another ethical choice for administrators concerns when and whether the public should be made aware of sensitive information. A distinction exists between keeping government information secret for reasons of national security and deliberately withholding it because the facts are embarrassing to an agency or a person.

Except in the relatively few instances when national security is really at stake—think what examples truly qualify—the withholding of information or actual lying to the public is not much more than an expression of elitism and anti-democratic values by public administrators. The justification for their act is "the public won't understand" or "the people cannot really grasp all the complexities that we, the administrators, understand." An equally plausible interpretation is that the public would understand fully what any agency or administrator has done, and would be horrified by the display of incompetence or arrogance. An agency or an administrator should not be afraid to reveal the truth, even if the news is the worst kind. If the democratic process is to work, there must be an acceptance of two assumptions—the public should be properly informed and the public can make right decisions most of the time. Anything less verges on the undemocratic. (Selection 25 in Topic Five, "Vietnam Cover-Up: Playing War With Numbers," provides insight into this issue of withholding adverse information from the public.)

Often governmental secrecy is challenged on the basis of "the public's right to know." That proposition actually creates a false argument, as the public already has the right to know its own business. The question to be considered is "the government's right to withhold information." By focusing on that question, the people place the responsibility and burden where they belong—on the government to justify keeping information secret from the public.

4. *"Whistleblowing."* The most publicized cases involving public servants faced with ethical choices have focused on "whistleblowers." The term applies to individuals working in an agency who publicly criticize that agency's administrative practices by disclosing pertinent information to the public. If the employees are not merely disgruntled individuals who have been demoted or fired for legitimate reasons, real "whistleblowers" can be truly dedicated, public-spirited citizens in the finest traditions of public service.

Congress has created a "Catch-22" situation for "whistleblowers." The federal Code of Ethics passed by Congress states it is a federal employee's duty to "expose corruption wherever discovered." The same Code also says that government workers must not evade agency regulations which forbid their disclosing data from official files. Therefore, if an administrator gives information to the the press or even Congress, that person can be fired, although the original charges may later be proven accurate. In effect, the code requires "whistleblowers" to bring agency problems to the attention of people who may be the cause of the maladministration.

This is well illustrated in Selection 8, " 'Going Public' " and the Federal Code of Ethics." It is the story of two employees who were fired for trying to expose corruption in the General Services Administration. One of the employees, Robert Sullivan, used the Code of Ethics in his defense but met with disappointing results.

Selection 9, "The Price of Blowing the Whistle," presents several more cases of individuals who criticized their agencies publicly and then suffered severe consequences. It is evident that "whistleblowers" require great courage and patience. Selection 9 also indicates they could use some legal help. Several legal questions need to be answered if public employees are to continue to point out irregularities or illegalities to the public. What rights do public employees have to release internal memoranda pertaining to mismanagement? Should there be a First Amendment protection of free speech for publicly disclosing official misconduct? If "whistleblowers" are subject to law suits, who should pay their legal costs? If they win their case, can they collect costs and damages from the government? Until these issues are decided by the courts and legislatures more favorably for true "whistleblowers," public employees will continue to be reluctant to come forward with charges and proof of administrative incompetency and dishonesty.

Selections 8 and 9 show how employees can be intimidated, but despite all the personal costs and difficulties required to fulfill administrative responsibility in the fullest sense, we still have public administrators who do not shirk their duty. The personality profile of Stanley Sporkin (Selection 10) describes such a person. His real loyalty is to his sense of right and not to particular individuals who happen to occupy positions of power.

Notes

1. Carl Wellman, *The Language of Ethics* (Cambridge, Mass.: Harvard Univ. Press, 1961), p. 328.

2. O. Glenn Stahl, *Public Personnel Administration,* 7th ed. (New York: Harper & Row, 1976), p. 271.

3. *Ibid.*

4. Daniel Elazar, *American Federalism: A View From The States* (New York: Thomas Crowell, 1972), Chapter 4, on which much of this discussion has been based.

5. *Ibid.*, p. 90

6. *Ibid.*

7. Most materials for this case are drawn from "Wheat Harvest," *The New Republic*, September 30, 1972 (Vol. 167, No. 12), pp. 7-8; and "The Great Grain Robbery," *The Nation*, October 16, 1972, (Vol. 215, No. 11), pp. 324-325.

8. "Wheat Harvest," *op. cit.*, p. 8.

9. For a number of answers to these kinds of questions, see Edward Weisband, *Resignation in Protest* (New York: Penguin Books, 1975).

10. "Matters Relating to T. Bertram Lance," Hearings Before the Committee on Governmental Affairs, U.S. Senate, Part 4, September 1977, p. 456.

6

Honest Graft and Dishonest Graft

William Riordan

Everybody is talkin' these days about Tammany men growin' rich on graft, but nobody thinks of drawin' the distinction between honest graft and dishonest graft. There's all the difference in the world between the two. Yes, many of our men have grown rich in politics. I have myself. I've made a big fortune out of the game, and I'm gettin' richer every day, but I've not gone in for dishonest graft—blackmailin' gamblers, saloonkeepers, disorderly people, etc.—and neither has any of the men who have made big fortunes in politics.

There's an honest graft, and I'm an example of how it works. I might sum up the whole thing by sayin': "I seen my opportunities and I took 'em."

Just let me explain by examples. My party's in power in the city, and it's goin' to undertake a lot of public improvements. Well, I'm tipped off, say, that they're going to lay out a new park at a certain place.

I see my opportunity and I take it. I go to that place and I buy up all the land I can in the neighborhood. Then the board of this or that makes its plan public, and there is a rush to get my land, which nobody cared particular for before.

Ain't it perfectly honest to charge a good price and make a profit on my investment and foresight? Of course, it is. Well, that's honest graft.

Or supposin' it's a new bridge they're goin' to build. I get tipped off and I buy as much property as I can that has to be taken for approaches. I sell at my own price later on and drop some more money in the bank.

Wouldn't you? It's just like lookin' ahead in Wall Street or in the coffee or cotton market. It's honest graft, and I'm lookin' for it every day in the year. I will tell you frankly that I've got a good lot of it, too.

I'll tell you of one case. They were goin' to fix up a big park, no matter where. I got on to it, and went lookin' for land in that neighborhood.

I could get nothin' at a bargain but a big piece of swamp, but I took it fast enough and held on to it. What turned out was just what I counted on. They

---

From *Plunkitt of Tammany Hall* by William L. Riordan. Published by E. P. Dutton and reprinted with their permission.

William L. Riordan was a reporter for the *New York Evening Post*.

couldn't make the park complete without Plunkitt's swamp, and they had to pay a good price for it. Anything dishonest in that?

Up in the watershed I made some money, too. I bought up several bits of land there some years ago and made a pretty good guess that they would be bought up for water purposes later by the city.

Somehow, I always guessed about right, and shouldn't I enjoy the profit of my foresight? It was rather amusin' when the condemnation commissioners came along and found piece after piece of land in the name of George Plunkitt of the Fifteenth Assembly District, New York City. They wondered how I knew just what to buy. The answer is—I seen my opportunity and I took it. ...

7

The Curious Case of the Indicted Meat Inspectors

Peter Schuck

THE INSPECTORS "Alone in the lion's den"

At seven o'clock on the morning of October 8, 1971, Edward Wywiorski arrived for work at a meat-processing plant in Boston. He entered the plant, waving casually to employees inside the gate, and headed for the U.S. Government office at the rear of the building. As he walked slowly past the long, silent lines of processing machinery being hosed down for another day's work, Wywiorski's thoughts oscillated between his first morning as a U.S. Department of Agriculture meat inspector back in 1929, and the jubilee day, now less than two years off, when he would reach sixty-five and retire. He smiled to himself as he walked, trying to imagine how many carcasses he must have inspected in those forty-two years. The old man, unaccustomed to such flights of fancy, broke off the effort as he approached the office door. Glancing at the other inspectors already inside, he knew immediately that something was up.

For most federal meat inspectors, as for Edmund Wywiorski, theirs is a career, a life's work. More than perhaps any other federal career job, however, meat inspection is a grueling, exacting enterprise. Of all blue-collar work in our society, only that of the policeman on the beat begins to compare with meat inspection for the rigor of the intellectual, physical, social, and psychological demands on the job.

The meat inspector works under extremely unpleasant, if not nauseating,

From *Harper's Magazine*, September, 1972, pp. 81-88. Copyright 1972 by Peter Schuck and reprinted by permission of the author.
Peter Schuck is currently Deputy Assistant Secretary for Planning and Evaluation, U.S. Department of Health, Education and Welfare.

conditions. Most meat-processing plants are old, hot, noisy, and noisome. The constant sight and smell of rent flesh, blood, entrails, and offal are sensuous assaults to which the inspector may grow accustomed, but never immune. Twelve-hour work days are common. The inspector must often cover many "houses" in a circuit, traveling from plant to plant at some distance and at odd hours.

What the meat inspector must endure is nothing compared to what he must know. Many inspectors now start at a GS-5 level, earning less than $7,400 per year, yet they cannot perform a day's work without routinely applying vast knowledge of food chemistry, bacteriology, animal pathology, sampling techniques, food-processing machinery and technology, plant construction, and industrial hygiene. The regulations, guidelines, and directives the inspector must follow and enforce are so numerous, intricate, and technical that they seem like the bureaucratic equivalent of Mission Control at Cape Kennedy. There are detailed regulations specifying the nature and condition of the salt solutions that may be used on wetting cloths applied to dressed carcasses. There are extensive instructions pertaining to packaging, labeling, and transportation of inspected products. Section 310.10 of the Manual of Meat Inspection Procedures sets forth in fifteen single-spaced pages the requirements for the "routine" (other than final inspection) postmortem inspection of every carcass. A typical excerpt follows:

Examination of the liver should include opening the large bile duct. This should be done very carefully as cutting through the duct into the liver tissue will interfere with the detection of the small lancet liver fluke. The incision should extend at least an inch through the bile duct dorsally and in the other direction as far as possible. The beef liver should be palpated on the entire parietal surface and within the area of the renal impression. Palpation should be accomplished by exerting sufficient pressure with the hands and fingers to be able to detect deep abscesses or cysts within the liver. . . .

The complex regulations and instructions nevertheless leave the inspector with an irreducible residue of discretion within which he is empowered to impose grave sanctions against the processor, including closing down the plant. In part, this discretion derives from the inability of law to reconcile fully the imperatives of uniformity and diversity. The point at which a "remote product contamination," i.e., a dirty rail, becomes a "direct product contamination," i.e., a very dirty rail, is obviously a matter of degree, and the regulations concede as much. Yet the latter may justify the inspector's closing down production until the condition is remedied, while the former ordinarily will not.

But the inspector's discretion goes well beyond this. It is a commonplace in the industry, denied only by official USDA spokesmen, that if all meat-inspection regulations were enforced to the letter, no meat processor in

America would be open for business. This fact, probably common to all regulated industries, says as much about an agency's tendency to overregulate as about an industry's unwillingness to comply with the law, yet the net result is the same: the inspector is not expected to enforce strictly every rule, *but rather to decide which rules are worth enforcing at all.* In this process, USDA offers no official guidance, for it feels obliged, like all public agencies, to maintain the myth that all rules are rigidly enforced. Unofficially, the inspector is admonished by his USDA superiors to "use common sense," to do his job in a "reasonable way."

Ironically this amalgam of discretion—conferred by law, custom, and necessity—represents to the inspector not power but impotence. For he is obliged to exercise this discretion in a fluid, political context in which he is a pawn of those interests—the processor, its employees, and USDA—with the greatest stake in that exercise. The inspector is the focus, but not the locus, of responsibility.

Most meat processors (or packers) operate on a narrow margin of profitability. In a fiercely competitive industry the incentives to cut costs are practically irresistible. Watered hams, fatty sausages, chicken ingredients instead of beef—these are but a few of the stratagems of the resourceful, cost-conscious packer. A 1 per cent increase in the weight of poultry from added water, for example, has been estimated to cost consumers $32 million per year; government studies show excessive watering to be a routine practice. Violations of sanitation and construction standards are also profitable to the packer. There is every reason to delay compliance as long as possible and only one reason to comply at all—the threat that the inspector will stop production until the offending condition is remedied.

To forestall this threat, the packer relies upon a mixed strategy with the inspector, offering the carrot and wielding the stick. The carrots available to the packer are many, and perhaps the most significant is overtime. Since an inspector may earn thousands of dollars annually in overtime to supplement his meager USDA salary, availability of this perquisite is of crucial importance. The packer decides each day how long the plant will operate and bears the cost of all inspectors required beyond the normal eight hours. Inspectors insist that the subtle offer and withholding of overtime is a mainstay of the system of rewards and punishments by which they are encouraged to be "reasonable."

Another carrot is the gift or favor. Many items are necessary to the inspector's work—boots for the wet floors, freezer coats, pens, office supplies—yet USDA refuses to supply some of them, and scrimps on others. Some packer gifts seem animated by simple goodwill, the oil that lubricates the interactions of people working closely together in the plant day in and day out. A bag of doughnuts for the night shift, a Thanksgiving turkey, a bottle of Scotch at Christmas—these are routinely given to plant employees, and the inspectors are often included. Other gratuities grow naturally out of specific work situations. According to one inspector, "when you have to work overtime, the packer may send out for beer and sandwiches. If you insist on paying, they tell you to go out and get it yourself. It is to the packer's interest to have you eat on the job, so the line can keep running."

To the inspector, a gift of meat is even less suspect. The packer who throws away literally hundreds of pounds of edible product daily for one reason or another—and deducts it as a business expense—does not seem particularly insidious when he asks the inspector, "Need anything for Sunday dinner, Doc?" An inspector observing policemen, firemen, politicians, representatives of veterans groups, hospitals, and other charitable organizations, as well as the packer employees with whom he works, leaving the plant laden with free meat, is hard put to rationalize why he alone should refuse the proferred gift.

The practice is called "cumshaw"—accepting small amounts of product for one's own use at home. Inspectors argue that the pressure to conform to the practice begins from the first day on the job, and comes almost as much from other inspectors as from packers. "We are weaned on the tradition. The old-timers always say, 'It isn't a good inspector who pays for his Sunday dinner.' They tell you that everybody else does it and has always done it, that it has nothing to do with doing your duty, and that if you don't take it, someone else will. I figure the job is hard enough without having the other inspectors suspicious of you." There are unwritten ground rules, moral strictures transmitted from inspector to inspector, and these too are impressed on the new recruit: "Don't accept more meat than your family can use"; "Don't solicit the meat from the packer"; and by far the most important "Don't let cumshaw influence your judgment or the way you do your job."

To the inspector this distinction between accepting a gratuity and accepting a bribe is clear and morally based. The general federal bribery statutes recognize this distinction and reinforce this morality by making it a crime for a public official to receive anything of value "in return for . . . being influenced in his performance of any official act. . . .," or "for or because of any official act performed or to be performed by him."

The inspector readily acknowledges that what appears to be a gift may become a bribe—if it is large enough, takes certain forms, or is given under certain circumstances—but to him, the critical factor is always whether the gratuity induces him not to enforce the regulations in the normal manner. "Sure I'll accept bundles of meat to take home for my family," says one, echoing the sentiments of many. "But that doesn't affect my decisions in the plant one iota, and the packer knows that. The fact of the matter is that if you get on a high horse and *refuse* to take a bundle, it makes it much more difficult to get the job done. Everyone becomes edgy and suspicious. Enforcing the regulations requires reasonableness, cooperation, and flexibility, as USDA is always telling us. If the packer, his employees, or the other inspectors think I look down on them, they are not going to cooperate with me. How can it be morally wrong to do something that hurts nobody and helps me get the job done?"

In addition to the normal urge to self-justification, then, much in the meat inspector's daily life—the pressures of his work routine, temptations by the packer, the job socialization process, the traditions of the industry, the conventional morality of his fellow inspectors, the general bribery statute, and the imperatives of "getting the job done"—tells him that he may accept small gratuities from the packer with a clear conscience. Section 622 of the Wholesome Meat Act, however, tells him something very different. Where the packers are concerned this section conforms to the traditional ethic—a packer commits a felony in giving something of value to an inspector *only if* it is given "with intent to influence said inspector . . . in the discharge of any duty. . . ." A convicted packer does not forfeit the right to engage in the meat business. The inspector, on the other hand, commits a felony if he receives *anything* of value "given with any purpose or intent whatsoever." And a convicted inspector, in addition to bearing normal criminal penalties, "shall . . . be summarily discharged from office."

The rationale for this double standard is obscure. Federal employees must be held to a high standard of conduct, to be sure, but should it be any higher than that applicable to a packer extensively regulated and certified to do interstate business by USDA? Should one party to an illegal transaction be regarded as guiltless while another is branded a felon? On October 8, 1971, these questions suddenly lost their academic quality.

The Department of Agriculture
A case of nonsupport

Ed Wywiorski, seeing the other inspectors huddled over a newspaper, quickly entered the office and looked at the banner headline in the *Boston Globe*: 40 MEAT INSPECTORS INDICTED IN HUB. A stunned silence lay over the inspectors, each gripped by a private terror. Minutes later, the office phone began its relentless ringing as wives, children, and friends called to ask if it could really be true. Wywiorski cannot recall what he did for the rest of the day or how he made his way back to his West Roxbury home, but his wife recalls that he arrived "in a trance" clutching a notice from USDA suspending him from duty until further notice, effective immediately. "Ed has literally been in a state of shock ever since that day," his wife confides, "and I don't think he will ever get over it."

Later that day, Herbert Travers, then the United States Attorney for Massachusetts and the man who had obtained the grand jury indictments, held a televised press conference in Boston to announce the indictment and suspension of the inspectors, the largest group of federal employees ever indicted at one time, and to assure the public that no impure food had resulted from the inspectors' crimes. The indictments received extensive publicity in the national media, featuring the remark of a USDA spokesman that "We're expecting the worst scandal since meat inspection became mandatory in 1907." Shortly after the indictments became public, the governor appointed Travers to a Superior Court judgeship.

Several days after he was suspended, Wywiorski and thirty-nine other inspectors, almost two-thirds of the inspectors in the Boston circuit, were arraigned in federal court in Boston under indictments charging some of them with having accepted "things of value," some of them with having accepted bribes, and some of them with having done both. In addition, some were charged with having conspired with certain individuals to defraud the U.S. Government of the full value of their services. Many inspectors were not served with their indictments by the Government until they were arraigned. Judge Charles Wyzanski chastised the prosecutors for finding time to be on TV but not to serve the indictments. The inspectors pleaded not guilty. None had any prior criminal record.

On October 22, the inspectors were summoned to the USDA office in Boston. Each was handed a written advance notice of a proposal to suspend him from duty without pay "until the outcome of the proceedings resulting from the indictment is known." The notice gave them forty-eight hours to respond. USDA refused to give them more time to obtain counsel and prepare their responses, although the forty-eight hours covered a holiday weekend, and Civil Service regulations entitle the employee to "all the time he actually needs to prepare and submit his answer." Five inspectors obtained a federal court order extending their time to respond until November 5. Despite oral assurances by USDA officials that *all* of the inspectors could have the additional time, USDA suspended the other thirty-five inspectors on November 1. This was done by identical form letters, although the inspectors were charged with vastly different crimes, ranging from receiving "a handful of screws" to accepting a bribe of thousands of dollars. Even before the suspensions, USDA had already begun filling the suspended inspectors' positions with permanent replacements.

The inspectors then appealed their suspensions to the Civil Service Commission and USDA, contending that to suspend them before they had even been tried, much less convicted, was illegal, and that USDA had not complied with the procedural requirements for suspension. Twenty-six of the cases are still pending before the Commission. In six other cases, the Commission's Appeals Examiner ordered immediate reinstatement pending trial.

USDA has appealed five of these reinstatement decisions to the Commission's Board of Appeals and Review and refuses to reinstate the inspectors pending the outcome. USDA failed to appeal the case of inspector Frank Cavaleri, yet it refused to reinstate him for seven weeks, and then immediately served him with another notice of suspension. Seven inspectors appealed their suspensions within USDA and won, but USDA rejected the decision of its own hearing examiner as "unacceptable" and appealed to the Commission, refusing reinstatement in the meanwhile.

One union official, surveying the fruits of these hard-won administrative "victories," lamented, "USDA decided from the very beginning to throw these men to the wolves, and it is not going to let due process of law stand in its way." As a result, the inspectors have received no salary since October, and most have been unable to find any work while under indictment. Lack of income, coupled with high legal expenses, has driven all into debt and many to the point of utter financial ruin.

To an old-timer like Ed Wywiorski, who has spent two-thirds of his sixty-three years in USDA, the indifference of the Department to his plight has been profoundly dispiriting. After so many years, he had come to think of the Department possessively and metaphorically: it was "his" Department, it had nurtured him to manhood, it had trained him in a respected career, and it would provide for him in his old age. Now, it seemed, it had suddenly turned on him, almost rushing to condemn him before he had a chance to defend himself.

Many of the younger inspectors, however, see in the situation a confirmation of USDA's true allegiances. To them, the Department is simply a bureaucracy, cold and morally neutral, but possessed of an unerring instinct for political survival. One inspector puts it this way: "Look, we are probably the only regulatory officials who are required to go out among the regulated to do our job. We don't just visit them periodically, we just about marry them. Day after day, night after night, we are in the lion's den alone with the lion. How are we supposed to get along? USDA doesn't tell us. How are we supposed to resist the barrage of threats and temptations the packers constantly direct at us? USDA doesn't tell us. USDA *does* tell us to use our ingenuity to do our job, to use our common sense—but that's not very helpful when you're in the lion's den."

Every inspector has dozens of anecdotes about the failure of USDA supervisors to back him up in disputes with plant management. This pattern of nonsupport is clearly woven in the public records of USDA and outside investigative bodies. The conflict arises from the fact that the inspector, in the words of one old-timer, is "a shock absorber between USDA and the packer. If you tag too many violations, your supervisor will frequently say you are being too antagonistic and rigid. Then when you let some minor violations go, such as allowing 4 per cent milk powder in a sausage instead of 3.5 per cent, and the supervisor catches them, he blames it on you, not the packer."

Santa Mancina, the top USDA official in the Boston area, readily concedes that most inspector complaints about packer pressures are legitimate. "The packers up here are resistant as hell. I met with their trade association in an effort to communicate. They continually tried to pressure us. Hell, they threatened to go to Washington and cut our appropriations if we didn't play it their way. The packers, of course, complain about the inspectors, but I tend to believe the inspectors most of the time."

USDA files, only recently made public after a Freedom of Information Act suit, are filled with instances of vicious physical and verbal attacks on inspectors by packers or their employees. These assaults, criminal under the Wholesome Meat Act, elicit from USDA little more than gentle reproach and an exhortation to the packer to read the Act. The Act authorizes USDA to withdraw inspection permanently from serious or persistent violators, yet USDA has never invoked that authority. Reports by the General Accounting Office, the investigatory arm of Congress, repeatedly document the low morale of the inspection corps, attributing this in large part to USDA's failure to back up its inspectors.

USDA takes a rigidly legalistic position against the gratuity system while at the same time appearing to ignore—and even contribute to—the vortex of pressures and incentives that nourish this system. Once every year, USDA supervisors meet with inspectors to go over the regulations prohibiting acceptance of things of value from packers. According to many inspectors and supervisors, this is a very tongue-in-cheek affair. "The best analogy I can think of," says one, "is in the Army when they read you the Articles of War or instructions on how to respond to brainwashing. It is all very make-believe, and no one, least of all the supervisors, takes it seriously. If you press them about how to apply these lofty principles in the real world of the plant, they say, 'Oh, it's okay to take a cup of coffee or an occasional meal from the packer.' If you ask how they reconcile that with the regulations, they tell you, 'Use your common sense.' We leave that meeting thinking small gifts are okay so long as they don't affect the way we do our jobs."

USDA enforces these regulations against inspectors with a passion rarely found in its dealings with unregenerate packers. Consider the case of inspector Harry Topol, thirteen years an inspector and a recipient of the USDA Certificate of Merit in 1968 "for sustained superior performance in carrying out assigned responsibilities." One Saturday morning in July 1969, Topol, on duty at a new assignment in Boston, received a telephone call from his brother-in-law, Salvatore Cina, who said he needed about ten pounds of frankfurters, salami, and bologna for a barbecue that afternoon. Cina asked Topol to put in the order for him, and said he would pick the meat up at the plant before closing. The plant closed before Cina arrived, so Topol filled out a purchase slip and took the meat from the order clerk, arranging to pay Monday since no cashier was on duty. On Topol's way out, a USDA supervisor saw the package, stopped him, and ordered him to return the meat. Topol complied and proceeded to forget about the matter.

Three months later, Topol received a letter from USDA charging him with violation of the regulation and proposing that he be fired. Astonished, Topol requested a hearing and received one—before a circuit supervisor in the meat-inspection program. The supervisor recommended that Topol be fired on the ground that he had purchased meat from a plant that had no retail outlet, despite the uncontradicted testimony of at least four individuals that they routinely walked into the plant off the street and bought meat.

Topol appealed and finally obtained a hearing before an official not connected with the meat-inspection program, who found that the plant did sell to the public and that all charges should be dismissed. The resourceful Director of Personnel, however, while accepting these findings, managed to have the last word. Topol had obtained credit for the purchase until Monday, he ruled, "a personal accommodation which was out of the ordinary." He suspended Topol for four weeks without pay. Two weeks after his suspension, Topol suffered a heart attack. Shortly thereafter, his wife had a nervous breakdown that her physician attributed to the strain of the yearlong ordeal.

The Department of Justice
"It is more blessed to give than to receive"

In April 1972, Ed Wywiorski's trial began. He had been indicted on eight counts of receiving meat, "a thing of value," in 1967 and 1968. Six of the counts alleged the receipt of a quantity "unknown to the Grand Jury," the seventh stated a quantity of "eight pounds, more or less," and the eighth cited a quantity of "twenty-one pounds and two ounces, more or less." Before trial, the prosecution conceded that Wywiorski had been indicted on three counts he could not possibly have committed, having been on vacation or at different locations at the times alleged. Judge Andrew Caffrey permitted James Krasnoo, the young Assistant U.S. Attorney prosecuting the inspector cases, to drop these counts over the objection of Arnold Felton, Wywiorski's attorney, who argued that the jury should be able to see the kind of evidence on which the prosecution's case rested. A fourth count was dismissed on a technicality.

Krasnoo then offered Felton a deal. "Wywiorski's only a little fish in a big pond," Krasnoo told Felton. "If he pleads guilty before trial, I'll recommend two years probation to the judge." Felton relayed this offer to his client. Wywiorski decided to stand trial on charges of having received four bundles of meat from Jack Satter, Baldwin Vincent Scalesse, and John McNeil. Satter and Scalesse were and are executives of Colonial Provision Company, and McNeil had been a quality-control man with Colonial.

The only damaging witness against Wywiorski was McNeil. He testified that he had no independent memory of transactions with Wywiorski but that when he worked at Colonial he had given bundles of meat to inspectors on behalf of Colonial and had made notations on rack cards for each transaction, usually including the initials of the inspector, the date, and the amount of meat given. He had saved these cards, and he produced four bearing the notation "Ed Wy."

At the end of the first day of trial, Felton was confronted with an agonizing decision. Reviewing his thought processes, Felton says, "Wywiorski is an old, ineffectual, harmless guy, what people call a 'nebbish.' He would have made a terrible witness. Krasnoo would have made mincemeat of him. I decided he should plead guilty if we could get a favorable disposition." Felton called Krasnoo to ask if his offer to recommend probation on a guilty plea was still open. Krasnoo replied, "Tauro [the new U.S. Attorney] insists that we add on a $2,000 fine as a penalty for your having gone to trial." Wywiorski then called his wife from Felton's office. "I'm going to throw in the towel," he told her, "At least this way, I won't go to jail." Felton, Wywiorski, and Krasnoo then signed a form statement reciting that the determination as to a sentence recommendation "is *always* made after a verdict of Guilty or a Guilty plea has been entered, and *not before*. . . . Any statement relating to a recommendation by an Assistant U.S. Attorney made before a determination of guilt can only refer to his recommendation to be made to the U.S. Attorney, and does not refer to any recommendation to be made to the Court." The statement goes on to say that the final decision on sentence is that of the judge alone. The next day, Wywiorski entered a plea of guilty. Thus the trial ended before Felton could introduce evidence that on March 30, 1967, precisely the period during which McNeil said Wywiorski received meat, Wywiorski reported to his supervisor in writing that he had caught McNeil making entries of reports of laboratory results in official USDA folders without an inspector being present. The report concluded that McNeil left "in an annoyed and resentful manner."

On May 10, Wywiorski appeared before Judge Caffrey for sentencing. Caffrey told Wywiorski that before accepting his guilty plea and sentencing him, he wished to be satisfied that Wywiorski had in fact committed the crimes for which he was admitting guilt. Wywiorski stated that he had not. A surprised Caffrey reminded him that he could not accept a guilty plea unless he was actually guilty. Wywiorski again denied guilt. Caffrey suggested a short recess to resolve the confusion, during which Felton explained that Wywiorski could not plead guilty without admitting guilt and that if he did not plead guilty, the deal with Krasnoo would be off. When court resumed, Caffrey once again asked Wywiorski if he was guilty. Wywiorski muttered that he had given McNeil the keys to his car (where McNeil had said the meat was probably placed). Caffrey then asked Krasnoo for his sentence recommendation, and Krasnoo responded with the agreed-upon recommendation. Judge Caffrey proceeded to sentence Wywiorski to one year in prison and a $1,000 fine.

Mrs. Wywiorski recalls the scene. "When the judge pronounced his sentence on Ed, even Krasnoo seemed stunned. Ed was in a trance. He had never for one moment believed that he would go to jail. All he had talked about was retirement, an end to the pressures in the plant. When the U.S. Marshals dragged him away, he still did not seem to know what had hit him. He is a totally broken man. And all this over four bundles of meat."

Wywiorski is now serving his prison sentence.

As of June 1, eight Boston meat inspectors had reached trial and had either been convicted or pleaded guilty. All six who have been sentenced so far have received prison sentences, ranging up to three years. The "bigger fish"—other line inspectors, two subcircuit supervisors, and a circuit supervisor, some of whom are accused of accepting money as well as meat—are still to come.

Krasnoo scoffs at the suggestion that the sentences have been unduly harsh. In his view, the inspectors have not been dealt with harshly enough: "These were public officials invested with a high public trust." (To the inspectors, this view is bitterly ironic. "For years," says one, "we've been pieces of shit, lowly GS-5s and 7s, barely noticed, barely lower middle class. Now, all of a sudden, we are exalted public officials charged with weighty responsibilities and moral leadership.") The young prosecutor told one lawyer that the inspectors were damned lucky that he wasn't prosecuting their wives, who he felt must have had knowledge of their crimes.

Most of the forty inspectors, like Wywiorski, were indicted on the testimony of McNeil, and to a lesser extent Scalesse and Satter, before a federal grand jury first convened in early 1970. The prosecution's case at trial was and is based almost entirely upon the same evidence.

One of the intriguing questions that haunt these trials is why McNeil, who left Colonial in June 1967 to become a USDA inspector, and who is all too familiar with the gratuity system, decided to go before the grand jury and incriminate the inspectors. There is some evidence—based on McNeil's frequently expressed hostility toward Colonial, and on his threats to sue Colonial for compensation for injuries sustained by him and his wife while in Colonial's employ—that he thought his revelations would result in prosecutions not of the inspectors but of the "biggest fish" of all: Colonial Provision Company. Such an expectation would be a natural one, of course, for McNeil's testimony is at least as damaging to Colonial, a company with annual sales of over $50 million, as to a bunch of low-level inspectors, many of whom were charged with receiving small quantites of meat. And while the inspectors could be effectively disciplined administratively—by loss of pay, discharge, or otherwise—Colonial could be punished only by prosectuion and public obloquy.

If McNeil's intention was to damage Colonial, he has utterly failed to do so. The Department of Justice has actually contrived the meat-inspector prosecutions in such a way that Colonial has managed to emerge unscathed. That has not been easy to do, given the admissions of McNeil, Scalesse, and Satter that they routinely gave meat, money, and other things of value to numerous inspectors; that McNeil, at Colonial's behest, doctored samples, illegally gained access to the USDA retention cage, and chose dummy samples; that Scalesse lied to the grand jury in at least three sessions; that Satter lied to the grand jury and had tried to bring political pressure to bear from Washington against zealous inspectors. But the ingenuity of a political Department of Justice is not to be underestimated.

According to the Justice Department's own evidence, employees of Colonial and six other Boston area packers routinely and systematically gave meat, money, and other things of value to the forty inspectors on behalf of the packers. *Yet none of these packers or their employees has been, or probably ever will be, indicted for these transactions.* The reason is simple: after lying to the grand jury, Satter and Scalesse finally claimed the Fifth Amendment, refusing to answer further questions. The Department then granted them immunity from prosecution in order to induce them to testify against the inspectors.

When asked why the U.S. Attorney decided to grant immunity from prosecution to Colonial and six other packers and their employees, but not to the inspectors, prosecutor Krasnoo gave three reasons:

1) "I would never grant immunity to a witness who lied before the grand

jury." Yet Scalesse and Satter admittedly lied to the grand jury on several occasions prior to being granted immunity.

2) "The inspectors failed to cooperate by giving evidence to the grand jury." But the packer witnesses also failed to cooperate, until they were offered immunity, and there is every reason to believe that the inspectors would have cooperated had *they* been offered immunity. Well before the indictments were issued, at least one attorney representing a group of inspectors told Krasnoo his clients would "sing like canaries" in return for immunity. The offer was refused. To the inspectors, it was clear from their first appearance before the grand jury that they were the targets of the investigation.

3) "I know of no inspector who took the Fifth, so we couldn't offer them immunity." This is incorrect. A number of inspectors took the Fifth, as Krasnoo should certainly have known.

The real reasons that the Department of Justice pursued the minnows while protecting the whales probably lie elsewhere. As one former prosecutor put it: "From the Department's point of view, this was a smart prosecutive decision. By giving immunity to a relatively small number of influential packers who dealt with a relatively large number of inspectors, they could get a large number of convictions, a lot of publicity, and not step on any important toes. If they had prosecuted the packers, they would have had to prove 'intent to influence.' This way, the judge simply charges the jury that in order to convict, they need only find that the inspectors received anything of value. Since McNeil gets up with his cards and says they received, these are very easy cases to win."

The solicitude of the Department of Justice for Colonial, however, goes far beyond immunizing it from prosecution. For the Department has managed to draft indictments against the inspectors containing well over 2,000 counts, most of which involve gratuities given by key Colonial personnel, without ever mentioning Colonial by name. The same is true of the six other immunized packing companies. The indictments recite that things of value were given, and conspiracies entered into with the defendants, by certain named individuals—Satter, Scalesse, and McNeil in most cases—but they are not identified as employees or agents of Colonial. For all the public knows or *could* know from the indictments, Colonial and other immunized packers have been pure as the driven snow. Since the mass media have confined their attention entirely to the indictments and the sentences, there has been virtually no coverage of the trials, at which the involvement of Colonial and other packers is brought out.

The Department, to be sure, has secured indictments against three small packers, none of them involved with the forty inspectors. Only one case has been tried, and the outcome is most intriguing and bizarre. As the result of an FBI plant and the use of marked money, inspector Robert Gaff had apparently been caught redhanded immediately after receiving money from a packer, Waters & Litchfield Co. On October 29, 1971, Gaff pleaded guilty to four counts of receiving things of value from two packers. He was sentenced to serve a six-month sentence (half of that meted out to Wywiorski for accepting four bundles of meat). After Gaff completed his term and left prison, Waters & Litchfield was brought to trial in April. The Department of Justice, in a most extraordinary and inexplicable maneuver, *waived a jury,* knowing full well that a jury, particularly with the price of meat on their minds, would be far more likely to convict than a judge would be. Then Gaff took the stand as the prosecution's main witness, and his testimony—testimony that had supported his plea of guilty and the grand jury indictment of Waters & Litchfield—was so garbled that the judge directed a verdict of not guilty. So the Department's record remains clean as a hound's tooth: no packers convicted.

Other aspects of the meat-inspector cases also raise the question of whether the lady holding the Scales of Justice in front of the Department's headquarters is actually peeking from under her blindfold. On the day the indictments were returned against the inspectors, Herbert Travers, the then U.S. Attorney, took the extraordinary step in a case of this sort of applying for the issuance of bench warrants for the immediate arrest of the inspectors. This procedure was highly unusual because no inspector had a prior criminal record (this is a condition of being a USDA inspector), and they were obviously unlikely to flee. Travers had arranged for federal agents to sweep through the meat districts and make a dramatic and well-publicized mass arrest and incarceration of the inspectors. The judge, seeing no justification for arrests, refused to issue the warrants.

When the indictments were announced in October to an attentive press, many of the counts against the inspectors were so trivial as to lend comic relief to an otherwise relentlessly depressing affair. One inspector indicted for receiving "a thing of value to wit, a handful of screws," quipped, "I wouldn't mind if I had a big hand, but how many screws can I get in this?" Another inspector was indicted for receiving "a spiritual bouquet," a third for receiving a light bulb. Other "things of value" forming the basis for individual counts were half a can of shoe polish, "the picking up of one photograph," and a car wash. One inspector was charged with accepting a ride home for his daughter from a packer employee.

Many of the counts were not simply trivial, they were demonstrably mistaken. Frank Cavaleri, for example, was indicted on six counts, four of which occurred at times when he was not even working for the Government. Most inspectors had at least some counts of this order of accuracy. After all of the publicity and hoopla had been generated, of course, these counts were dropped by the U.S. Attorney's office, often over the objections of defense counsel who wished the jury to learn how casual the Department had been in securing indictments. The proliferation of counts had another purpose too. As one ex-prosecutor explained, "They threw indictments around like confetti to inundate the inspectors. Then Krasnoo could offer to drop most of the counts in exchange for a plea of guilty. Krasnoo was giving up nothing that was worth anything, of course, but to the inspectors, the offer must have seemed generous."

The Department of Justice has employed other questionable tactics. The indictments contain a large number of counts for accepting bribes—in which there is necessarily an allegation of intent to influence the inspector's official actions—as well as counts of simply receiving things of value, which include no such allegation. *Yet there has been no evidence that inspectors were bribed, and much evidence that they were not.* First, packer employees have admitted at the trials that the inspectors did their jobs and did not relax their application of the regulations. Second, Travers and Krasnoo have both stated publicly that the public has not been exposed to deficient meat products as a result of the indicted transactions. Third, Krasnoo has dropped all bribery counts before trial; he concedes that he has proved only the receipt of things of value by inspectors. Nevertheless, despite requests by defense attorneys not to do so, Krasnoo has used the term "bribery" in summations to the jury on a number of occasions.

The Department, in conjunction with the courts, also consistently penalizes those inspectors who invoke their right to go to trial. This practice is not unique to these cases, of course, but the result is not less unjust for being common. Inspector Hugh McDonald was indicted on 183 counts of receiving money, meat, and liquor; 163 counts were dropped before trial. Then Krasnoo induced him to plead guilty to nine counts of receiving meat and liquor, dropping the others. Krasnoo made no sentence recommendation to the judge. McDonald received one year in prison and a $1,000 suspended fine. Inspector Richard H. Murphy was indicted on 157 counts of receiving money and meat, 147 of which were dropped before trial. Krasnoo offered to make no sentence recommendation if Murphy pleaded guilty. Murphy insisted on going to trial and was convicted on ten counts of receiving money. Krasnoo then recommended a sentence of four years in prison, with a $4,000 suspended fine. Murphy received three years in prison and a $1,000 fine.

It is inconceivable that Murphy would have received so severe a sentence if he, like McDonald several weeks before, had pleaded guilty instead of invoking his right to put the Government to its proof in a trial. As Krasnoo well knows, Murphy's example has not been lost on the thirty-three inspectors still awaiting trial. "I have a strong case," says one, "but look at the risk I run by going to trial before jurors angry about the high cost of meat. I will have to plead guilty to avoid paying 'the Murphy premium.'"

With the Department of Justice at the bargaining table, negotiation for guilty pleas can be a nasty business. In the case of one married inspector, the prosecution threatened to show that he had had sexual relations with a female employee of the packer. The Internal Revenue Service, presumably with the connivance of the Department of Justice, has conducted tax audits on a number of inspectors in an effort to show that they were living beyond their means, evidence that would assist the prosecution's case. The IRS, after securing records and cooperation from the attorney for several inspectors, has refused either to return the records or to issue a ruling, thus enhancing the bargaining power of the Justice Department in negotiating with the inspectors for guilty pleas.

The Boston meat-inspector cases raise disturbing questions. A steady stream of inspectors are now entering prison, their careers and reputations irretrievably lost, their families plunged into unspeakable despair. Yet within a mile of the federal courthouse, Colonial Provision Company flourishes, processing millions of pounds of meat daily; Jack Satter drives his Cadillac to his new job as president of Colonial, and Vinnie Scalesse has been promoted to head of a Colonial subsidiary. These admitted perjurers and the other packers who admittedly gave things of value to the inspectors continue to do business as before. John McNeil continues as a USDA inspector, sometimes training new inspectors in their duties, despite having admitted doctoring and switching USDA samples as a Colonial employee and having been a key link in a chain of illegality. The public continues to subsidize this system in several ways—in higher meat prices, reflecting the costs of gratuities, and in higher taxes, reflecting the packers' practice of deducting these gratuities as part of their operational "shrinkage." It is likely, in addition, that the public is getting an inferior product for its money. "How much rigorous inspection do you think is going on today at Colonial or these other houses?" one inspector asks. "These packers bought insurance against strict inspection. How do you think the inspector is going to behave knowing that he can be prosecuted simply on the word of the packer he is supposed to regulate and that the packer will not be touched?"

A society truly concerned about crime must concern itself with those social systems—like the meat plant—in which crime seems to make sense to otherwise moral men. "Cumshaw" is such a system, and it flourishes. While some of its practitioners have been punished, the most powerful have not. For the latter, at least, the system has paid handsome dividends.

8

'Going Public' and the Federal Code of Ethics: The Cases of Tucker and Sullivan

In January of 1975, Robert F. Sullivan was one of a team of GSA [General Services Administration] criminal investigators assigned to interview Robert J. Tucker, a GSA electrical engineer. Their questioning focused on Tucker's removal of GSA files dealing with construction contracts awarded in

From a report "The Whistleblowers" by the Committee on Governmental Affairs, U.S. Senate, February 1978, pp. 274-280.

the New England region. Tucker was convinced that the GSA had been improperly awarding contracts to favored Boston area firms. He had confidentially contacted the FBI about his suspicions and had provided them with supporting documentation. The FBI proceeded to conduct an investigation and came to the conclusion that there was no evidence of wrongdoing on the part of the GSA.

Through an unusual series of contacts among the FBI, the U.S. Attorney's Office in Boston, and the Regional GSA Administrator, Tucker's identity was made known to GSA officials. Soon after, Tucker was fired for removing government files and refusing to answer questions from GSA investigators, including Robert Sullivan.

Robert Tucker was informed of his removal in April 1975, a few months after the completion of the FBI investigation into his charges. According to the notice of proposed removal he was fired for refusing to cooperate with GSA investigators looking into his release of documents, failure to comply with an authorized instruction to meet with the GSA investigators at a later date and, misconduct in removing official GSA files without authorization. General Services Administration officials stated that Tucker's unauthorized disclosure of the material was tantamount to "... defaming the reputation of the GSA and your fellow employees."

Along with his contact with the FBI, Tucker had provided copies of documents covering construction projects he considerd questionable to the press in late 1975. According to GSA management in the letter of removal, the effect of the articles was to severely damage GSA's reputation. They caused doubt in the minds of the public concerning the integrity of the employees of the GSA and adversely affected the morale and efficiency of the Construction Management Division of the GSA in Boston.

Robert Sullivan's downfall began while he was preparing to interview Robert Tucker concerning his part in the FBI investigation of the GSA. As background for that meeting, Sullivan was given the final reports produced by the FBI. Sullivan soon realized that the FBI effort had been far from complete. The reports showed evidence of favoritism, collusion and other contracting irregularities, but the FBI had not gone far enough.

When the GSA internal audit was released after Tucker's firing, it supported his allegations of irregularities including potential collusion and fraud, within the Construction Management Division of the GSA. Specifically, the auditors found that over half of the $9 million in contracts reviewed had been falsely labeled as emergency situations, allowing the GSA to have favored contractors negotiate on the projects. This was in violation of agency regulations and Federal law.

The reaction of GSA management to the internal audit report was minimal. Even in the face of Tucker's recent firing for his allegations in this area, the Chief Criminal Investigator for GSA-Boston and the Director of the GSA Investigative Division-Washington, did not feel it necessary to read the report, although they knew of its existence. It was routinely received, processed and sent to Washington for analysis.

Inaction on the part of GSA officials on the findings of the report, coupled with their quick action against Tucker, troubled Sullivan. For six months after Tucker's removal, Sullivan debated what, if anything, he should do. He felt that discussing the reports with agency officials would be futile since they already knew of their existence. The U.S. Attorney's office had proven to be closely allied with GSA during the Tucker/FBI episode and contact with them appeared to be fruitless. Furthermore, Sullivan was concerned about the fact that the GSA audit had been withheld from the FEAA [Federal Employee Appeals Authority] during Tucker's hearings. In his opinion, the press was the only avenue left for attempting to root out the problems at GSA. After consulting his priest and studying the Code of Ethics for Government Service, Sullivan decided to contact the Boston *Globe*.

In December 1975, Sullivan hand-carried copies of three (3) GSA audit reports (one recently released and two from 1974) and the six (6) FBI reports to the *Globe*. *Globe* reporters xeroxed the documents and Sullivan returned them to the GSA files. On Sunday, January 18, 1976 the story appeared.

Sullivan was interviewed by GSA investigators about his part in the *Globe* article on January 23. When asked, he admitted to having provided the paper with copies of the reports.

In the course of defending his actions, Sullivan relied heavily upon the Code of Ethics and the demands of his conscience. When interviewed by a GSA investigator, Sullivan summed up the reasons for his actions in these words:

I feel that it is and was my duty to act to stop this kind of conduct within the government (improper, illegal and questionable conduct) and to act to prevent it from reoccurring. All of my actions to date have been taken with this goal in mind.

Sullivan's sincerity was also noted by the FEAA in their review of his case:

Mr. Sullivan has throughout the proceedings sought to justify his actions by claiming that his motives for what he did were the highest, in that he was responding to the dictates of his conscience and to the expressions contained in the Code of Ethics for Government Employees. In essence, it is Mr. Sullivan's position that requirements of conscience and the Code of Ethics transcended all other regulations, guidelines and agency standards of conduct.

Even the GSA admitted that Sullivan's actions were "altruistic and well-intentioned" in their letter of removal.

The agency was faced with an employee who admitted to providing the press with embarrassing information and offered only conscience and the Code of Ethics as his defense.

In the decision letter of November 12, 1976, Sullivan was removed on the basis of four instances of misconduct:

1. He failed to report evidence of irregularities to his superiors.
2. He used government documents for personal reasons and thereby violated the "need to know" standard.
3. He allowed others the use of officials' information obtained in the course of his GSA employment.
4. He disclosed information, contained in the agency's system of records, without the prior written consent of the individuals to whom the record pertained.

The GSA offered the following argument to explain why these four actions justified Sullivan's firing:

Your (Sullivan's) actions have not only compromised the Office of Investigations, but have unjustifiably contributed to the continuation of public doubt concerning the integrity of all GSA employees in Region I and, if condoned, would certainly lead to administrative chaos.

When it received Sullivan's case on appeal, the FEAA was faced with a classic confrontation. Sullivan maintained that his actions were justified by GSA inaction and the demands of public service. The agency held that their rules and regulations were supreme, for without rules that are enforced and obeyed, the government cannot function.

In the course of the decision, the FEAA examiner who had ruled on the Tucker case, quickly settled any questions of procedure or fact and moved to the merits of both sides' actions. The GSA's charge that Sullivan had failed to inform his superiors of irregularities, was voided by the FEAA. This was done because Sullivan discovered no irregularities except those already in official reports. The three remaining charges relating to the improper use of official documents were sustained. The only item left to decide was whether there were any mitigating factors which would justify Sullivan's violation of agency regulations. In short, they were asking whether or not the Code of Ethics could be used as a defense.

FEAA's answer was no, and they summarized their view of Sullivan's case as complete disregard of agency regulations and an attempt to justify his actions on the grounds of conscience and the Code of Ethics. The decision continued:

While we do not in any way diminish the importance of the code. . ., we feel obligated to point out (1), that it is not law and (2), that the second paragraph includes a recognition by the Congress that employees should uphold laws and agency regulations and never be parties to their evasion. Our point is that there are laws that govern disclosure of information from agency records. For an employee to assume authority on his own initiative to make his own private decision as to what he will elect to remove from agency records and to turn over to an outside party when he is not the custodian of the records, and when the turnover is a personal, unofficial act, smacks of anarchy regardless of his motive.

In essence, they denied the use of the Code of Ethics as defense for violating agency regulations. At least in this case, their decision makes it clear that, in the eyes of the CSC, the demands of an agency for cohesion, order and public image far outweigh the need for federal employees to be able to follow the dictates of their conscience or the Code of Ethics.

The cases of Robert Sullivan and Robert Tucker are unique in their simplicity. In many instances of whistleblowing, the cause and effect relationship between the employee's action and the agency's response is difficult to establish. In these cases, however, the act of blowing the whistle is admitted by the agency as central to the actions taken against them. The experiences of Sullivan and Tucker provide a rare opportunity to look directly at a conflict between agency rules and regulations, and the demands of the "greater public good".

9

The Price of Blowing the Whistle

Helen Dudar

In the spring of 1974, Dr. Stanley Mazaleski, a Government scientist, began complaining about the sluggish pace at which his agency had set about designing safety standards for industrial workers exposed to carcinogenic chemicals. The following winter, Mazaleski's criticisms were leaked to the newspapers. Within a few months he was fired. And last May, after a two-year fight for reinstatement, he won a court decision ordering the Public Health Service to hold a new hearing. It was a modest victory, just enough to allow his attorney to try to open negotiations with the agency. After a while, the lawyer called with the report that he had been in touch with the agency's general counsel to no avail. "They said you're guilty," he told Mazaleski. "Guilty of what?" Mazaleski asked. "I don't know—they just said you're guilty."

Mazaleski's belief in his righteousness is whole and complete. He is driven by a fearsome persistence and by a myopic refusal to acknowledge that the system can possibly be as "unfair" as it has so far been to him. He is a

© 1977 by The New York Times Company. Reprinted by permission. From *The New York Times Magazine*, October 30, 1977.
Helen Dudar is a freelance writer.

"whistleblower"—a rather casual term for a risky business. Mazaleski belongs to a haunted little tribe of Federal employees who have transgressed against the bureaucracy—who, having seen something seriously wrong in a Government operation, made a noise about it.

The penalty for going public, for telling Congress or a reporter or even a superior a few steps up the chain of command can be harsh. Mazaleski lost his position at an agency hearing which he was not even invited to attend. A more sophisticated way of dealing with the overzealous bureaucrat is to have his job abolished. If the dissident is too well known to be dismissed, he can be "promoted" into another section of the agency where his expertise is useless. If he is obscure but likely to make a public fuss, he can be effectively immobilized by demotion to a lesser, lower-paying job where his expertise is also wasted. On the other hand, it may be decided that his behavior has been erratic. In that event, his superior may insist that he consult a psychiatrist in the expectation that he will be found to be unstable and thereby eligible for a disability discharge. Of course, he can refuse to submit to an examination. But then he may be fired for insubordination.

Theoretically, a bureaucrat who testifies before Congress is automatically protected from reprisal. Firing him is literally a crime. In practice, the system is "unenforceable," according to an aide for a powerful Senator. "What would you have the Senate do when a Pentagon employee testifies and is punished?" he asked. "Hold the Secretary of Defense in contempt?" A bureaucrat with a dismissal slip is entitled to a Civil Service hearing, but there the cards may be stacked, too.

The bureaucracy is a Goliath, and the machinery available to enforce its will is immense. Moreover, its will often extends far beyond its boundaries. A civil servant who has lost a post in a conflict that reached the press usually becomes unemployable. Advertised jobs in other Federal agencies prove to be illusory the day he applies; promising offerings in private enterprises that are dependent on the kindness of Government agencies vanish overnight. It takes merely a phone call to a former boss to learn that the applicant is considered just a trifle hard to get along with.

The Dean of Whistleblowers

Most people have neither the heart nor the means to begin a fight that may last for years. They quietly resign, they accept early retirement, they shut up. A. Ernest Fitzgerald, a Defense Department cost analyst who eight years ago went before a Congressional committee and testified that a Lockheed cargoplane was costing $2 billion more than the contracted price, is perhaps the best known of contemporary whistleblowers. He has been battling the Pentagon for eight years and is a one-man advisory committee to scores of Federal employees who consider doing what he did in the interests of exposing waste and corruption. People go to him for guidance all the time. "I never advise them," he says, "I just tell them the probable consequences of going public. Most of them never do." Those who stay the course seem, on casual encounter, to be quite nondescript, the sort of people Fitzgerald is fond of assigning to mainstream America. They wear lapel flags, he says, lift weights and belong to the National Rifle Association. They are special, he goes on, because they can't stand stealing. Experience has transformed some of them into cranks—rather exalted cranks who can be nagging, verbose, obsessed and sometimes difficult to be with and yet who are wholly admirable in their gritty stubbornness. What sets them apart and gives them distinction is a sublime innocence, a pure and compelling attachment to schoolroom lessons in morality. It is wrong to cheat. It is a sin to lie. There is no compromise with evil. Deceivers will be punished. Good will triumph.

Once in a while it does. But the process is so long and so lonely and so consuming and the psychic pain is so profound that nothing finally can obliterate the scars. Friends are lost and careers are blighted. In suburban precincts where every other homeowner can be a Federal employee, neighbors cruelly cease to be neighborly. How do you explain to a 5-year-old child why he's the only kid on his Oak Ridge block who wasn't invited to the Easter-egg hunt? On occasion, even reason is forfeited. "I cringe when they come to see me," says a Congressional staff man who has tried to help some victims. "They are walking wounds."

The quality of the damage is discoverable when the clan assembles in one place, an event that occurred early this year in Washington. For almost two years, the Institute for Policy Studies, a well-known haven for respectably leftish thinkers and doers, has been working on a program to develop legislative, legal and financial protection for the civil servant who steps out of line in the provable interests of the public good. Last June, I.P.S. organized a two-day conference of whistleblowers. Two hundred came. Some of them merely bore personal grudges against agency supervisors but many of them had, in Fitzgerald's felicitous phrase, "committed truth" and had suffered for it. According to several accounts, the sessions took place in an atmosphere of such raging anger and bitterness they could have been recorded as peaks and valleys on a seismograph. Moreover, the sense of futility projected by the conferees was almost gaudy in its intensity. Yet these people came and they stayed out of some freakishly inexhaustible hope that injustices could be remedied and that the system could be made to work.

What sustains that hope is unfathomable. The qualities they have in common hardly seem significant enough to illuminate any corner of their experiences. They all apparently tend to be careful with money, if not downright cheese-paring. Their politics seem mostly centrist and nonideological, and they are engagingly oblivious to the irony of receiving the support of a leftist organization on the order of I.P.S. While not necessarily formally religious, many of them count themselves believers. With some exceptions, they share a certain lack of imagination. It did not, at the outset, occur to most of them to anticipate the fury of official vengeance.

Some Consequences

The sign over Ernest Fitzgerald's door at the Pentagon reads "Deputy for Productivity Management." What, I ask—does a productivity manager do? Whatever he can, the best he can, enough to earn his $47,500 wage, he answers, but nothing like what he could do if he were allowed to exercise his skill and experience as a weapons cost analyst for the Air Force. Fitzgerald is, of course, a legend, the dean of Washington whistleblowers and folk hero to Federal employees who would like to emulate him. Shortly after he testified about how the military patronage system wastes great sums of money on its munitions and aerospace purchases, his job was abolished. And the Civil Service Commission—the court of last resort within the Government—ruled he was not a victim of reprisal.

What followed was nearly four years of legal battles, protracted by Government delays and by its appeals at every point. Finally, in 1973, a U.S. District Court ordered his reinstatement. By then, Fitzgerald, who had kept busy lecturing, writing a book and working for two Congressional committees, figured the fight could cost him $400,000 in legal fees. He sued to collect. In 1976, a Federal judge ruled that the Government must bear the cost of a "blatantly improper action" against Fitzgerald. Last May, the U.S. Court of Appeals agreed that the law requires that a wrongfully dismissed Federal employee be made "whole again" but does not permit the Government to pay his lawyers' bills. Fitzgerald, an industrial engineer who comes from Birmingham, Ala., is a remote but affable and jaunty-spirited man. However difficult these years have been, he has resisted any sense of martyrdom. He loved his work and was good at it. But he observes that the 1969 dismissal "effectively ended my career" as if he were commenting on the high price of dry cleaning. What he does now is "baby" stuff, the kind of assignments he worked on when he was just out of college. "That's sad," I commented. "That's bad," he corrected me.

Why stay? Where would he go? Subconsciously, he supposes he knew that his decision to testify could abort his career, "but I hadn't really prepared for it." When he was fired, Fitzgerald went job hunting and found he had speedily been marked "a bad guy." As time went on, the labeling became more imaginative. Eventually, he was to learn that the dossier the department had been building on him proposed that he was simultaneously a womanizer and a homosexual.

A registered Democrat, Fitzgerald describes his ideology as "tightwadded." He has a wife who he says has been unstintingly supportive and three children who he believes have not suffered unduly from his career problems.

But "The Case," a multi-million-dollar damage suit against Defense Department officials responsible for the loss of his job eight years ago, occupies a good deal of his time. Luckily for Fitzgerald, he finds life irrepressibly comic. Late last winter, he was invited to address a gathering of Defense rank-and-file employees. The Defense supergrader, with his G-17 rating, faced 100 members of the American Federation of Government Employees who would normally see him as management. They loved him, they cheered him and they gave him an award—a silver whistle. Fitzgerald was enormously pleased. But he noticed that it had been mounted on a plaque, and thereby rendered inoperable.

The Price for Questioning

Stanley Mazaleski's wife, Charlotte, tells him he can't win; his adversary is too powerful. Sometimes, Mazaleski thinks she may be right, but he can't give up. He really believes that "the truth will out." It has been more than two years since he was fired from his $17,800-a-year job with the Public Health Service, and his life is a shambles. A Ph.D. in preventive medicine, he could not find work in his field for 17 months. For a period, he worked nights as a security guard near his home in Monrovia, Md., and his teen-age daughter, eldest of his four children, took a job in a Hot Shoppe to help support the family. Last winter, money was so short that the family lived mostly on potatoes, which Mazaleski, a farm boy from Pennsylvania, had grown in the garden. The debts have piled up, and his creditors are pressing for payments he cannot make; the bank is threatening to foreclose the mortgage on his four-bedroom house; his marriage is desperately strained; friends have fallen away and relatives in Government service who are apparently nervous about their social connections exclude him from family gatherings.

In January, Mazaleski finally found work in Washington with the Environmental Protection Agency, but it is temporary and likely to end any day now. He writes letters incessantly to officials in and out of Government, beseeching help which never comes.

A large, genial, sad-eyed man, Mazaleski went to work for the National Institute of Occupational Safety and Health, a P.H.S. agency, four years ago. His job was to write reports on a variety of dangerous and possibly carcinogenic chemicals used in industry and to develop standards, required by new legislation, for protecting the health of workers exposed to these materials.

Before the year was out, Mazaleski was in trouble. He insisted, against considerable resistance by the medical authorities over him, that the chemical cadmium may cause prostate cancer. A year later, the professional literature proved him right. He said the industry should be required to keep medical records for 20 years on workers exposed to chloroform, a suspected cause of cancer and birth defects; over his protest, the N.I.O.S.H. management reduced the period to a worthless five years. He filed a grievance against a superior who had dealt rudely with him. He complained to superiors that evidence he needed for his work was being withheld. He wrote letters to Congressmen bemoaning delays in setting safety standards, delays that probably made life easier for industry but surely imperiled the health of millions of workers. His criticism found its way into The New York Times early in 1975.

In March 1975, he was fired for "marginal and substandard performance" and for "insubordination." Mazaleski's fate, said Albert R. Lauderbaugh, a senior P.H.S. official who tried to help settle the affair before it reached the firing stage, was "an almost classic example of management's reaction to an internal critic." Mazeleski's former boss, Dr. John May, insists, "His charges have no validity whatsoever. He was fired because he didn't do his job."

What is so bewildering to Mazaleski is that he had spent a lifetime doing the right thing. When the Korean War began, he was about to enter college and he gave up a scholarship to enlist in the Navy. After four years of service, he came home and worked hard on his father's farm, spending six years in evening studies to earn a college degree. He has always been a popular and successful student. He is 44, an exceedingly earnest man who believes in God, the Constitution and conservative government. Sitting in a cramped little office we had borrowed for the interview, I wondered aloud whether Mazaleski was the kind of householder who regularly hung out the American flag on patriotic holidays. Yes, yes, he did. And on Veterans Day, he related, he always took the family on a pilgrimage to Gettysburg National Park. Abruptly, Mazaleski's eyes filled with tears and for several minutes he could not talk.

Dr. Morris and the FDA

In the spring of 1976, after President Ford said he wanted every man, woman and child in the country vaccinated against swine flu, the only scientific voice raised against the program belonged to Dr. J. Anthony Morris, a virologist. Even in intimate conversation, the voice is lecture-hall loud; the speech is fluent and precise, the tone self-confident, the inflections an echo of his boyhood in Maryland. Tony Morris, a Ph.D., is a vaccine specialist and he is especially knowledgeable about flu vaccine. He has worked productively and successfully for the Government for most of his life and he has been in trouble with the bureaucracy before for protesting rather insistently that there is no such thing as an effective flu shot—a judgment that could only bring unhappiness to the businesses that make flu vaccines and the doctors who inject them by the millions each year. Taking on the bureaucracy is, at best, risky; tangling with an entire administration is an act of breathtaking nerve. In his zeal to alert the public last year, Morris had seminars on the N.I.H. campus in Bethesda, Md., sent letters to newspapers and Federal health officials and talked to reporters. His message was that no evidence whatsoever existed that swine flu embodied the virulence of the 1918 pandemic and that, in any event, the vaccine on hand was totally worthless. Most serious of all, it was certainly dangerous. Morris could not predict that it would paralyze and kill anybody, but he did know and warn that it could cause a hypersensitivity in some people that would trigger a whole range of grave illnesses.

That is precisely what happened the following December. By then, Morris, at 58, had been fired from his $32,000 research job at the Bureau of Biologics by Food and Drug Administrator Alexander Schmidt. Schmidt found him guilty of "insubordination and inefficiency." Moreover, his behavior toward his colleagues and superiors "directly challenged the integrity of scientific progress." The Civil Service Commission has upheld the insubordination charge even while acknowledging that Morris's science was sound, and the case is now on its way into the courts.

In 35 years of Government service, Morris had prudently put away money for his retirement, savings that were to have financed travels with his wife. It's almost all gone. He is inflexibly cheerful about all this. Morris says he would rather have his problems than carry on his conscience the burdens of people killed or crippled as a result of a staggering sweep of official stupidity.

An extremely reticent man, Morris does not like to talk about his experience in personal terms. But he was willing, finally, to share one lasting lesson of his life. "In 1940, I went to work for one of the truly great men of science, Joe Smadel." After training under Smadel, Morris moved on to other jobs, until Smadel called him back. Smadel had become associate director of the National Institutes of Health.

But Smadel had changed. He had been a dedicated and important advocate of polio vaccine since its release. But a research worker at N.I.H. discovered that the monkey kidney tissue in which polio vaccine had been propagated contained a virus called SV-40 which caused tumors in hamsters. There was no way of knowing whether medical science had conquered polio at the risk of provoking a new affliction. "Joe Smadel couldn't believe it. It was a frightening thing. It's still frightening. That information was held up for two years before it was made public, and I saw Joe Smadel fall apart under the pressure of keeping it quiet. He had gotten himself into a tremendous intellectual box. I said then that never, if I had anything to do about it, would I be caught in an intellectual box like Joe found himself in."

Promotion into Oblivion

"I get a kick out of outfoxing the bastards. Where else could I be such a son of a bitch and be on the right side?" If there is an ideal position from which to pursue whistleblowing as a steady avocation, Dr. John Nestor occupies it. For 16 years, he has been bedeviling the Food and Drug Administration, which employs him. Since he is a bachelor, there is no family to worry about. He has a crusty self-assurance reminiscent of all the authoritative older-doctor roles Lionel Barrymore used to play. Rude, abrasive, difficult, obstreperous, rigid, inflexible—Nestor has been called all that and more. He will obligingly recite the complaints, observing that none of these flaws is as grievous as the official mendacity he sees all the time.

Nestor, now nearing 65, went to work for F.D.A. in 1961 as a reviewer of drugs for heart and kidney ailments. Nestor was not at F.D.A. long before he concluded that the agency was and had always been the captive of the industry it is supposed to regulate and so he has testified in numerous appearances at Congressional hearings.

In 1972, Nestor was "promoted" into the F.D.A. Office of Compliance— which oversees industry compliance with agency rules—an activity for which he had neither the appetite nor the experience. He has been kicking and fussing ever since. Three years ago, he and a dozen other F.D.A employees appeared at a hearing before an inquiry conducted by Senator Edward Kennedy and offered testimony charging the agency with corrupt practices in drug approval and with the harassment of dissident employees. The complaints have been investigated, most recently by a special panel which delivered a 766-page report last April. It concluded that the charges were accurate. It also said that officials had lied. The report said Nestor was owed a formal apology, payment of his legal costs and a new position where his talents would be used. He is still waiting.

Nestor is an assiduous leaker. What he knows and what other agency employees feed him (Ernest Fitzgerald calls them "closet patriots") finds its way steadily into the files of Congressional investigators, consumer advocates and media folk. "Let me tell you," he commented over a beer, "the Freedom of Information Act hasn't opened up the Government. The duplicating machine has. I have kept very busy."

Ripskis and HUD

Al Louis Ripskis, a slender, mild-mannered bachelor of 40, now has the routine job of program analyst at the Department of Housing and Urban Development. "Papershuffling," he calls it contemptuously. The job has no psychic rewards, a dreary state of affairs for a man who went to Federal housing 16 years ago with more idealism than was good for him. But Impact fills the need.

Impact is a "leaksheet," a neatly mimeographed, $5-a-year report of almost everything that can go wrong at one public agency. Ripskis writes it with the help of anonymous regional correspondents, and on publication morning, before he signs in for work, he is to be found brashly hawking it on the sidewalk in front of H.U.D. Its subscribers include H.U.D. employees, some high agency officials he hopes to alert to the latest criticism, muckraking reporters in and out of Washington, the Office of Management and Budget and the Library of Congress. The H.U.D. Secretary gets one free. Ripskis says he is out of pocket about $3,000 a year on production costs.

In five years of publication, he has chronicled mismanagement, incompetence, waste and stupidity at his agency, assembling in print the kind of details that rarely get beyond the gossip hour around the water cooler. He flashily reported that a new housing project in Minneapolis lacked adequate elevators but had a brothel and that a high-ranking H.U.D. official seldom traveled anywhere without his mistress. In recent years, he has nagged at H.U.D. for its neglect of the lead-paint problems in housing. In the middle of President Ford's drive against inflation, Impact was reporting that H.U.D. Secretary Carla Hills had spent $82,000 for new air-conditioning for a conference room.

Born in Lithuania, Ripskis spent four years in a D.P. camp in Germany, and remembers it all: the dirt, the crowding, the lack of privacy. As a refugee in America, he lived in Chicago tenements. Out of school, Ripskis got a job with the Public Housing Administration in 1961, planning to stay no longer than two years. "It was to be my own domestic Peace Corps effort." But he began moving up the bureaucratic ladder and he was full of widely admired and widely ignored ideas for making public housing look more like homes than barracks. In 1965, after H.U.D. had become the umbrella agent for housing, Ripskis's innovative approaches carried him to Washington into a key task force called Social Concerns of H.U.D. The notion was that this time the Government was really going to build human concerns into public housing. Ripskis remembers that period as a wonderful time. The group, he says, wrote a wonderful report. And, in the end, it was interred wherever good Government reports go to die.

That and the fate of a H.U.D. co-worker laid the groundwork for Impact. The newsletter's predecessor was Quest, an in-house underground journal published by a friend who, as a result, was briefly exiled to Alaska. Setting out on his own soon after, Ripskis planned the way with canny caution. "I have managed to survive with a minimum of harassment, and it was not by accident. The critical choices came in the beginning. If they decide to fire you at the start, it's hard to reverse the bureaucracy once it gets rolling. But I started muckraking and kicking up a lot of publicity, and I became well known, so the department knew it would be bloody if they canned me."

Ripskis's modest success is instructive. The whistleblower must not only be strong and knowledgeable, but exceptionally careful. Most people who wind up in the fraternity begin almost accidentally, expecting gratitude and encountering, instead, a stone wall of either indifference or hostility.

Some people have mused that the hazards were so great it might be sensible for the public-spirited bureaucrat to stay on the job, stay anonymous and simply "leak for life." That choice, of course, is made daily by hundreds of middle-management employees who become regular and protected sources for reporters and Congressional investigators. It's one way to serve the public interest without pain and intense public drama. What would recent American history have been, for example, without those grand panjandrums of whistle-blowing, Daniel Ellsberg, who Xeroxed the Pentagon Papers, and Victor Marchetti, the first to tell us how the C.I.A. really works.

On the other hand, nothing about this activity guarantees it will fill a real need or gain wide public support. One of the celebrated whistleblowers of the early 1960's was Otto Otepka, the chief of security at the State Department, who earnestly believed that subversives held down Government jobs in his agency. He leaked confidential loyalty files to the Senate Internal Security subcommittee, which was still pursuing "Reds" in Government. Otepka was demoted, wiretapped and harassed in other illegal ways. In that case, it was not the advocates of free speech or open government who came to his support; Otepka found his modest constituency in the John Birch Society.

As it stands now, the civil servant who squawks is apt to be regarded at worst as a Judas, at best as a foolish aberration. One of the main priorities of the I.P.S. Project for Government Accountability is to institutionalize whistleblowing, to create a climate where it is easier and even commonplace for a public servant to deliver up to the public details of waste and deceit in his agency.

Carter's Views

"We don't want saints and heroes," says Ralph Stavins, an I.P.S. fellow who heads the project. "We want this made automatic and procedural."

The I.P.S. literature on the subject includes a flashy red-white-and-blue brochure with a cover exhorting Federal workers to "Point Out Illegality, Inefficiency and Waste." Its final words are from one of President Carter's campaign speeches. Ten days before the election, Carter declared, "I intend to seek strong legislation to protect our Federal employees from harassment and dismissal if they find out and report waste or dishonesty by their superiors or others. The Fitzgerald case, where a dedicated civil servant was fired from the Defense Department for reporting cost overruns, must never be repeated."

A number of people, including Fitzgerald, took heart from that notice, but not much has happened lately to suggest a safer future. Carter's Civil Service Commission chairman, Alan Campbell, went to the conference and brought greetings from the President and extremely cautious expressions of his own sympathies.

When I talked to him a few weeks later, Campbell said no legislation was ready and none likely to be until early next year. Moreover, while the Administration might eventually offer some protection to future whistleblowers, retroactivity for those who had suffered penalties was unlikely. But he felt it important to stress a new spirit in the commission demonstrated by a recent in-house inquiry. An investigation had just concluded that two officials in the General Services Administration in Philadelphia had been improperly demoted after protesting Nixonian abuses of the merit system. Exoneration had required a four-year fight. Campbell hopes the whole process can be accelerated.

Civil Service Commission

Campbell's views on the entire subject are clearly divided. On the one hand, he has the Sisyphean job of getting the bureaucracy functioning more efficiently; on the other hand, he seems to see the task as separate from and possibly complicated by the problems of an individual bureaucrat who protests inefficiencies that make it hard to work efficiently. He had just come back from a tour of regional offices where he found middle-level management personnel complaining they were stifled by restrictions against penalizing employees. "If anything," he said, "one can argue that the system is too cumbersome if what you are concerned with is getting on with the job. A whistleblower may be a perfectly straight and absolutely right person or he may be a troublemaker. One can't assume."

In Campbell's view, there are "inevitable limitations" on employees' rights to speak out. After all, a middle-management executive in private industry who peaches on his boss can expect immediate dismissal. As an example of the Government's right to curtail free speech where it interferes with policy, he cites the Carter recall of General Singlaub from Korea. Campbell says he sees no real difference between a U.S. Army general objecting to the removal of U.S. troops from Korea and a Pentagon cost analyst telling Congress about a gross waste of public funds. But there is a difference: A general in the United States, by tradition, is forbidden to make foreign-policy statements. A competent and honest bureaucrat is a permanent public servant who owes his allegiance to the Government and, beyond that, the taxpayer.

A New Agency?

Campbell is thinking of moving the Civil Service appeals procedure into a separate agency so that the commission is no longer in the position of both making the rules and judging whether they have been violated. Otherwise, he is not entirely sure that any new law can be composed that would provide better protection than now exists. Congress does not entirely agree. At the most recent count, at least six legislators were considering new approaches to the problem. One is an I.P.S. model bill called "Openness in Government," which not only would pay legal costs to the wronged civil servant but would also punish his punisher.

A controversial proposal in the bill would set up an Office of Administrative Oversight, an ombudsman agency that would advise whistleblowers and investigate complaints of unfair, punitive treatment. Of course, that would mean yet another bureaucracy. And there is no telling how long it would be before some civil servant from the Office of Administrative Oversight blew the whistle on the ombudsman for whistleblowers.

10
Stanley Sporkin, Honest Man, Puts Carter on the Spot

Mary McGrory

Washington—Stanley Sporkin is the chief of the enforcement section of the Securities and Exchange Commission, and some people think he overdoes it.

The State Department calls him a bull in a China shop, crashing around in foreign policy. Some people in the Commerce Department think he's a one-man recession, wrecking foreign trade. Certain scalded corporation heads regard him as a "young (J. Edgar) Hoover."

To others, however, he is simply the most honest and effective man in

From the *Los Angeles Times*, November 27, 1977. Copyright 1977 by the Washington Star Syndicate. Reprinted by permission.
Mary McGrory is a syndicated columnist in Washington.

government. And his operation attracts the kind of young lawyers who three years ago were beating down the doors to work for Watergate Special Prosecutor Archibald Cox.

"Stanley is the only game in town," said a former Watergate tiger.

The 45-year-old watchdog of business bites big shots without a second thought. Just this week it was learned that he had recommended that Bert Lance be barred, at least temporarily, from the banking business.

The charge of "double standard," which has been floating around in the wake of the Helms case, has never been leveled at his office, which is, incidentally, so unpretentious it doesn't even have a coffee pot.

"It's like law-school exams here," he says cheerfully. "Our files have numbers, not names. But we never permit any games to be played. We never wiretapped anybody. We do everything as it is supposed to be done."

Sporkin has been sniffing out corruption in boardrooms for 16 years. He succeeded his idol, Irving Pollack, as chief enforcer when Pollack went on to the commission. The law is in his blood. His father was a prosecutor and a judge in his native Philadelphia.

Right now, he's in the grip of his biggest case. He was instrumental in dumping into Jimmy Carter's lap one of the stickiest issues imaginable for an administration that is trying desperately to win over the business community. Atty. Gen. Griffin Bell and President Carter, as a result of Sporkin's crusading instincts, must decide on the possible prosecution of some 400 corporations who made what they prefer to term "sensitive payments"—Sporkin starkly labels them bribes—to foreign governments.

NBC broke the story a couple of weeks ago, and instantly familiar noises came from State and Commerce. Trials, which would disclose the bribed along with the bribers, could damage our foreign relations. They would be bad for business.

Sporkin doesn't mind. To him it's a simple matter of right and wrong—and this is what drives his critics, who have included such luminaries as Henry Kissinger and Elliot Richardson, crazy.

"Look," says Sporkin, "the competitive system is the greatest system in the world and it works only with public confidence. If it goes unchecked, it will destroy itself. Some of our corporations were making foreign policy—look at ITT in Chile—and they weren't elected to do that.

"And I don't think you should take our best and brightest people and train them to be dishonest. They learn ethics at the Harvard Business School and then somebody says to them, 'You've got to take a black bag and run two sets of books.' "

There is no law that says big, or even little, corporations can't pay foreign politicians to get orders, although Sen. William Proxmire (D-Wis.) is currently engaged in trying to pass one that will make the corrupt—and common—practice illegal.

But SEC regulations require that businesses make an accounting to stockholders and submit accurate reports to the SEC. And that is why in some 400 boardrooms there is anxiety over just how far the attorney general, who is no crusader, is willing to go in prosecuting executives who falsified financial reports or income-tax returns to conceal their disbursements to foreign officials.

The trouble for them all began in September, 1974, in the dying days of the Senate Watergate hearings, when Sporkin was watching his friend Sam Dash question executives of Gulf and Northrop about illegal campaign payments from slush funds that were laundered in other countries.

Sporkin's mind began to work in its usual way. "How do they book transactions like this?" he wondered. "Was it extortion?"

The SEC commissioners okayed an investigation. Sporkin was amazed by what he found: millions of dollars, unrecorded, being used to grease important palms around the world. He invited corporations to make "voluntary disclosure." Sen. Frank Church (D-Ida.) opened public hearings, which shook up governments in Italy, Holland and Japan.

Four hundred corporations that were warned that they would not be immune to prosecution, came in and confessed. Their records were sent over to the Justice Department to be screened for criminal content. A task force of 17 attorneys, aided by two SEC lawyers, went to work full time.

Nobody knows how many of the cases will end up in court.

It's all up to the President and the attorney general. They thought they were suffering their worst moments with the Helms and FBI cases. Now Stanley Sporkin has handed them the moral equivalent of a nightmare—and just when they were convincing big business that it *could* do business with the Carter Administration.

Topic Three

The Individual and the Organization

Introduction

In the first two Topics, we observed the effects that several major external factors have on individuals and public organizations in the administrative process. These included the governmental framework of American politics, the special role of public administration in society, and the various dominant cultural values that influence administrative behavior.

The subject of Topic Three is more specific. It concerns the relationship between the individual and the organization where that person works. This Introduction and the selections examine some of the influences which shape that relationship. Organizational theory, as this area is often called, may at first sound abstract. In fact, however, many current research findings have an immediate and practical application for those charged with the responsibility of running organizations. While disagreement is present among administrators and others about "the best way" to deal with certain organization-worker problems, most agree that the key to successful administration is the ability of an administrator to find solutions. As a consequence, innovative ways are being tried in Western Europe and the United States to organize individuals into effective work groups.

A Fundamental Organizational Problem

A mutual relationship exists between the individual employee and the organization. It is mutual since each of them needs the other even though the degree of dependence may vary because of unique conditions. Saul Gellerman has analyzed this symbiotic relationship in detail in *The Management of Human Resources*. He points out that "while organizations are totally dependent on individual effort, they are compelled to risk suppressing it or diverting it into unproductive channels."[1] That is, they must at some point direct human effort toward the organizational goal, or the organization will cease to function as it was intended. Later, Gellerman writes: "The organization exists, thrives, and survives by harnessing the talents of individuals. Its internal problem is to do so without hobbling those talents or turning them against itself."[2] Without individuals, organizations would not exist. Conversely, most people could not work or receive many kinds of rewards without organizations. Thus, the mutual dependency is established. The terms of the relationship are generally understood—organizations can expect, even extract, certain talents, skills, and labor from their members. Employees in turn can expect to derive from their organization economic, psychological, and social benefits.

The managerial problem facing administrators is how to strike a balance between what the organization wants and is willing to give, and what the workers are willing to give and accept from the organization. The implicit assumption in this relationship is that people in organizations possess imagination, energy, and abilities. The question for administrators is, Will these resources be directed into serving the general goals of the agency or will the employees use their time and effort to subvert and even destroy the organization and its administrators?

Ways of Structuring Organizations

One of the most fundamental decisions a top administrator has to make is how the organization should be structured. There are basically two organizational models that can be followed, although each has many variations. The first is often called the "machine" model; the other, the "humanistic." What difference does it really make to administrators and employees which type is used? It makes a great deal of difference according to the literature in organizational theory which generally assumes that the way people are organized influences their effectiveness and productivity on the job.

A dilemma for managers is that each organizational model has diametrically opposed premises about human nature and what motivates people. While ideally some middle-ground type of organization would be desirable, in practice there is usually a bias in favor of one model or the other.

The "machine" model is based on the assumption that the average worker needs considerable close supervision. The organization is conceived of as a machine. It is composed of many different parts (people and functions), all interrelated and vital to the smooth functioning of the organization. Because a breakdown in one part will adversely affect all others, the organization relies heavily upon a narrow span of control, a hierarchy of authority, and a downward communication flow. Tasks in the organization are simplified as much as possible so the employee has a minimum of responsibility but is able to master what is assigned.

The "humanistic" model views human nature in a completely opposite manner. Administrators in the "humanistic" model put much greater stress upon motivating workers than upon coercing them. Opportunities for allowing individuals to express their abilities become more important than formal organizational charts and lines of authority. For example, individuals or groups of employees are encouraged to set their own work schedules and ways to achieve their goals. Sweden and West Germany have taken the lead in redesigning tedious jobs into more imaginative methods of production. In the United States some public agencies have gone into flexible work schedules and more team project approaches that are intended to downplay the traditional superior-subordinate relationship which at times can stifle creativity. "Humantistic" type organizations, therefore, are much less hierarchical in form and in some cases scarcely resemble traditional ways of organizing people.

In 1960 Douglas McGregor introduced the terms "Theory X" and "Theory Y" to describe sets of beliefs held by administrators about workers.[3] These two designations correspond to the "machine" and "humanistic" model premises. For example, a "Theory X" manager thinks that the average worker dislikes working and will try to avoid responsibility wherever possible. Most workers, it is said, want to be supervised closely. Management, therefore, feels justified in establishing tight, rigid authority within an organization and in using threats or other forms of coercion to extract work from individuals.

A "Theory Y" administrator believes that employees are willing and able to assume responsibility in an organization without much supervision. Too much authority is counterproductive because employees will be diverted from accomplishing what they should be doing by their efforts to evade managerial control.

This background material should show that organizational forms are not accidental. Organizations take on certain characteristics largely due to the basic attitudes that administrators have about their employees. There are other factors, of course, that shape organizational structures. For example, a military or para-military organization would be expected to be more hierarchical than a research laboratory because of the need for tighter authority relationships. Yet, even within those two opposite organizations, the views of human nature held by administrators can immensely influence the administrative practices and relationships.

Why Organizations Come Into Existence

The character of organizations is also determined by the reason for which the agency was created. There are seven distinct ways organizations can come into being, and each will influence the organization's structure, political relationships, and social importance. Here are the seven ways.

1. Function. An organization is created to carry out a specific task. A need arises, and people are brought together to perform a function. This is probably the most common reason for establishing organizations.

2. Clientele. Some agencies are established to service specific groups in society. Labor, veterans, and Indians are three illustrations. A trend in American politics has been to gain "group protection" within the administrative bureaucracy by having a separate department or even Cabinet-level agency formed. Much legislation now is drafted by administrators rather than by legislators. As a consequence, lobbying is no longer directed only at the legislative branch. Instead, administrators and their staffs become prime targets for interest group and clientele activities.

3. *Place.* Often the basis for establishing an agency or its field office is to serve a particular geographic location. For both political and administrative reasons a trend has developed toward decentralizing the federal bureaucracy, which has meant the creation of more field offices. At the federal, state, or local level an accurate gauge of a legislator's power may be the number or size of field offices in that representative's district.

4. *Person.* Organizations are sometimes formed around an individual or his or her ideas. Religious groups provide several notable examples. Political candidates and officeholders develop personal organizations. Ralph Nader has been the dominant personality in the consumer movement, so much in fact that the specific organizations and study projects which he has created remain relatively obscure compared to his name alone. The administrative problem for personal organizations is whether or not they can or should continue to exist when the person is no longer able to lead the organization. In some public agencies, administrators have in effect created their own "personal" organization by shaping the agencies to fit their personalities. One of the most famous examples was the Federal Bureau of Investigation under J. Edgar Hoover. Recent revelations have disclosed the extent to which that public agency became a private organization. To have a personal imprint upon a public agency is not necessarily undesirable. In fact, it may be exactly what is needed to make the organization effective. What must be remembered, however, is that the purpose is to serve the public and not the head administrator.

5. *Policy Promotion.* Some organizations come into being because people want to see particular policies adopted. Three examples from recent decades are civil rights, the anti-Vietnam war, and environmental protection. In two of these—civil rights and environment—governmental agencies were eventually created but only after the nongovernmental organizations gained sufficient influence to bring them into existence. Sometimes it is difficult to determine if an organization has developed around a policy or a personality as in the cases of civil rights and Dr. Martin Luther King Jr. or Ralph Nader and the consumer protection movement. The organization and its leader become as one, and it is almost impossible to think of them separately.

6. *Organizational Spin-offs.* Some organizations are split from existing agencies to become completely independent. While they are "new" in one sense, they are different from other just-created agencies because they bring with them existing structure, staff, resources, and clientele support. Such an organization's beginning, therefore, differs from an agency started entirely without previous existence. In the federal government, the major example is the U.S. Air Force which was originally part of the Army until it became a totally separate military service. There has been a marked decline at the federal

level in organizational spin-offs. The trend instead has been toward organizational mergers or consolidations.

7. *Consolidation of Existing Agencies Into A Single New One.* In recent years at all levels of government so-called "super agencies" have been created. These are consolidations of existing agencies or programs into a single new organization. The intent is "to streamline," "make efficient," and "coordinate under one roof" the dozens of programs and policies which already are in operation but which for various reasons are deemed to be not effective.

The administrative question is whether the results will be better by having one agency responsible for all related programs (at the expense of not having any one closely supervised), or if smaller agencies do a more effective job (even if they are unaware of the policies of other agencies). In the policy area of energy, the President and the Congress decided in favor of establishing a single agency, which will make it possible in the immediate years ahead to examine this question directly.

Selection 11 discusses this most recent example at the federal level of an organization created by consolidation. The Department of Energy (DOE) came into being on October 1, 1977, as a Cabinet-level department. It consists of the personnel and programs of two agencies which became parts of DOE and ceased to exist as separate organizations: the Federal Energy Administration (FEA) and the Energy Research and Development Administration (ERDA). DOE also collected energy-related programs from the Departments of the Interior, Navy, and Commerce and the Interstate Commerce Commission.

Richard Corrigan in Selection 11 shows the peculiar problems faced by DOE because of the way it was started. Under the most favorable circumstances, it would be a challenging administrative task to establish such a major organization but, in addition, the administrators of DOE have had to spend their time seeking support for President Carter's energy program. To complicate their responsibilities further, DOE administrators have been frustrated by the Department of Defense (DOD) which has been able to delay vacating the Forrestal Building. In June 1977, President Carter designated that building as the headquarters for DOE and "ordered" 5,000 DOD employees to be moved elsewhere. By April 1978 only a few top DOE officials had been able to move in, and the latest estimate is that it will be another two years before all of the DOE employees will be located in the same place.

In Washington the struggle between the DOD employees and the DOE administrators has become almost as important as the energy policy itself. The Defense employees have formed special committees to prevent their being moved, while James Schlesinger, the Energy Secretary, has told Congress that the solution of the nation's energy problem was being imperiled because his Department could not occupy the Forrestal Building.[4]

What this seemingly ludicrous situation illustrates is the importance of personal factors in managing people and policies. Very few books mention that top administrators will drop other matters and will spend several months trying to move in or prevent being moved out of an office building. Yet in the case of DOE that problem has been raised to the point of a "policy issue" and given high-level attention.

The fact, therefore, that there can be seven reasons why organizations come into being indicates a variety of employee attitudes and perceptions about their organizations that may be manifested. Administrators must try to manage and direct their agencies even as employees are entering and leaving, policies are being formulated, or the organization itself is undergoing a transformation. Some overall sense of direction is needed, and that is where organizational goals may be of use to administrators.

Organizational Goals

If the members of an organization do not have a clear idea of their agency's goals or overall objectives, a number of problems can result. A lack of clear goals can affect an agency's efforts to maintain its autonomy, obtain budget requests, implement policies, and evaluate its performance. In a general sense, an organizational goal will be related to one of the seven reasons why the organization came into existence. Over time, however, that may not be specific enough to give its administrators a definite sense of direction.

Just how important a well-defined, unifying goal is to an organization is the subject of Jennifer Oldfield's case study (Selection 12). The Permanent Commission on the Status of Women (PCSW) of Connecticut was set up in 1973, and from the beginning it had been unable to reach agreement on its goals. Oldfield shows the vital importance that individual perceptions play in achieving consensus, and the obstacles that arise as members of the same organization define agency purposes and issues differently. When this occurs, the effectiveness of the organization is dramatically undermined.

Well-publicized goals for public organizations aid greatly in preserving the identity and autonomy of that agency. If the legislators and clientele have a clear notion of the purpose of the organization, this awareness can generate support which will provide a defense against territorial encroachments by other organizations. Of course, administrators run some risk if they make their organizations too visible, especially if they fail to achieve what has been publicly announced. On the other hand, agencies without public identity and constituency support will find they may be the first to be cut in the budgetary process. (This point is well illustrated in Selection 31 in Topic Six on the National Bureau of Standards.)

To what extent is it proper for a public agency to use public money for public relations campaigns? Should an organization be permitted to lobby legislators and the public in order to gain backing for its policies? There are many indirect and subtle forms of lobbying which can be just as effective as having a paid representative appear before a group. Advocates contend that the dissemination of information about the activities and objectives of a public agency is proper and necessary. What bothers some of the opponents of public relations is the possibility of "image-making" overshadowing straight news releases. Where one ends and the other begins is a fine line. The issue of public relations is connected, however, to the administrative responsibility of goal setting and communicating to the public. How and in what manner these are done are both ethical and technical questions.

Reorganization

Reorganization is a technique used frequently by administrators in their attempts to deal with many kinds of organizational problems. In its most superficial form, reorganization is nothing more than changing titles or shifting people around on organizational charts. Little really is altered except on paper. In its most serious application, however, reorganization is essential to the effectiveness of an agency if basic changes in an organization's basic goals, technologies, personnel, or status have occurred. Which kinds of reorganization happen most often? While there is no hard evidence either way, the suspicion by many observers is that most reorganizations tend to be surface modifications and, after awhile, the same problem returns which prompted the change in the first place.

Why then do so many administrators get involved with reorganizations? A new administrator coming into an agency may feel the need to make a "fresh" start or to have a dramatic beginning. A long-time administrator in an agency may reason that a reorganization is visible indication that activity is going on. There will be a lot of movement and it looks like the manager is "on top" of the organization doing what administrators are paid to do.

A recent example of a reorganization illustrates how people attach as much importance to appearance as they do to substance. In April 1978 the U.S. Information Agency (USIA) became the International Communication Agency (ICA). As is customary, a formal ceremony to swear in the new director took place, and the Vice President of the United States was in attendance. The old USIA—it was known as the United States Information Service (USIS) overseas—had as its purpose "Telling America's story to the world." Under the congressional reorganization legislation, the ICA was to engage in "conversation" with the world rather than in one-way dissemination of information. It was this change in agency purpose that caused the name change and subsequent reorganization. Yet even before the paint on the new name plates of the agency had dried, the Senate Foreign Relations Committee approved new legislation to change the ICA's name to the "Agency for Information and Cultural Exchange" (AICA). The Senators' complaint was that ICA's name was ambiguous in meaning. While few people could argue against having the USIA, USIS or ICA engage in more two-way communication, many might seriously ask whether that policy shift was sufficiently substantial to warrant the name, personnel, and organizational changes that took place.

What conditions might demand substantive reorganization?[5] First, there might be a major change in an agency's purpose or function. If an organization completes, eliminates, or adds a large program, such a development could necessitate appropriate organizational changes. For example, when the Apollo

Program of NASA was completed, people and resources had to be transferred or eliminated. Similarly, it can be expected that those agencies mentioned in Selection 11 which lost their programs to the Department of Energy will reorganize to fill the gaps.

Second, technological changes inside or outside an agency could trigger a reorganization. The introduction of a new information retrieval system, for instance, might require the formation of a whole new division. A technological breakthrough on the outside—inexpensive solar energy for homes—might require additional responsibilities for an agency and subsequent changes in its organization.

Third, different kinds of personnel might be required in an agency, thus necessitating a major reorganization. If either of the first two conditions described above occurred (either a policy or technological change), then there likely would be a corresponding adjustment in the requirements for personnel in terms of their numbers, training, education, or experience. A sudden influx or exodus of people would cause administrators to reshape their organization to conform to these new personnel conditions.

Finally, a reorganization might result if the political or social importance of an agency were altered. A change in elected leadership or the political climate can drastically affect relationships and standings of organizations. Chief executives like to establish close communication with their favorite agencies and administrators, but when those elected officials are no longer in office, reorganizations may occur because the personal importance of the agency has been diminished. In the early 1960s, several poverty and urban-related agencies such as the Office of Economic Opportunity had great prestige. Then, almost as quickly, the political situation changed (Vietnam became the issue) and these agencies lost their political power base and became invisible.

What are the obstacles to effective reorganization? A short answer is that a lack of attention by top administrators to the human considerations when reorganizations are being planned or carried out create fear, insecurity, and distrust. By nature, most people are reluctant to change from a condition with which they are familiar or relatively comfortable. Since a true reorganization will bring about fundamental changes in the way people work or in their relationships to other people, the administrative challenge is to consider the human side of the organizational change and not only the technical or theoretical aspects.

Kathy Sawyer's "Federal Staffs Are Fearful of Shake-Up Plans" (Selection 13) presents the reactions of several people going through or anticipating a reorganization. The process is made worse by the fact that so many top administrators, apparently including the President of the United States, are unclear as to exactly what will be reorganized and when. This uncertainty, coupled with poor communication with the affected employees, depresses morale. Even if, as the President has stated, few employees will lose their jobs (an inconsistent objective with the original intent of the reorganizations), severe organizational problems have developed because of the manner in which the workers have been treated.

Selection 13 also suggests that employees are defenseless against their employers. This, however, is not always the whole story. The last two selections (16 and 17) in this Topic indicate that there is more that workers can do than simply be frustrated and disgruntled. In effect, a kind of organizational guerilla warfare may erupt. (In the Introduction to Topic Six a story is related about the National Park Service which is pertinent to this point as well.)

Ronald Ostrow (Selection 14) gives a view of the conflict between U.S. Attorney-General Griffin Bell and his own employees. According to Bell, he has identified seven "principles" that Justice Department people have used to try to control him. Significantly, Bell believes that governmental employees acting by themselves would not engage in these practices. He attributes this antagonistic behavior to the fact that "they collectively are in some sort of bureaucracy where you don't have private sector discipline." It should be recalled that this view was discussed in Topic One in both Bennis (Selection 1) and Spiegel (Selection 3).

The personality profile of Lilith Reynolds (Selection 15) is of an individual who has completed one more reorganization. She has been given virtually no responsibility (we do not know why), and so she has had to fill her time with her own interests. At the beginning of this Topic Introduction, the point was made that individuals will use their time, energy, and talent in some manner. The administrator's job is to direct these toward the organization without stifling the individual. In Lilith Reynold's case, this was not done. As a result, both the organization and the individual suffered. Because we have only a part of one side of the story, it would be unfair to pass judgment. What can be questioned, however, is a personnel system that would permit such a situation to continue for very long. That issue will be covered in the next Topic (Four).

Notes

1. Saul Gellerman, *The Management of Human Resources* (Hinsdale, Ill.: The Dryden Press, 1976), p. 1.
2. *Ibid.*, p. 13.
3. Douglas McGregor, *The Human Side of Enterprise*, (New York: McGraw Hill, 1960).
4. For more background on the "politics of moving," see Karen House, "Energy Agency Finds Bureaucracy Doesn't Move Energetically," *Wall Street Journal*, January 17, 1978.
5. For further development of some of these conditions, see Anthony Downs *Inside Bureaucracy* (Boston: Little, Brown and Co., 1967), Chapter 16.

11
The Department of Energy's
Continuing, Confusing Shake-Down

Richard Corrigan

Jack H. Ray was steaming.

It was bad enough that the Energy Department had just messed up two multi-billion-dollar natural gas deals that his company was trying to close.

But what really riled him was the way the department had gone about it—in one case, as Ray described it, by letting a deadline slide by on a contract for Algerian gas without issuing a long-awaited decision or even giving a word of explanation for the delay; in the other, by stomping on negotiations for Mexican gas before Ray's company had time to file its applications or muster its arguments.

Ray, the president of Tennessee Gas Transmission Corp., a division of Tenneco Inc., said he would rather do business with the old Federal Power Commission (FPC) than with this new superagency. "If it had just been the FPC," he said, "I think we would have done all right on both cases. At least I don't think the FPC would have gone down to Mexico and intervened."

Ray's arguments might be taken as self-serving, and the nation may be better off because these two projects have not yet gotten clearance on his terms.

But when Ray slams the Energy Department, he is not alone. After four months in operation, Secretary James R. Schlesinger's fledgling department is drawing complaints from all sides.

"At the policy-making level, we see the same sort of lack of interest in solar [energy] that we saw at ERDA [the Energy Research and Development Administration]," said Sheldon H. Butt, president of the Solar Energy Industries Association and a marketing executive with Olin Corp. "There's just no visible evidence that Dr. Schlesinger and his policy-making crew ever give a moment's thought to it."

"I think that there's utter chaos and a potential for real disaster over there," said James F. Flug, director of Energy Action, a public interest lobby. "There are people with nothing to do, people who don't have bosses, bosses who don't make decisions because they don't know if they're coming or going."

"The view that I think permeates the organization is that their role is far greater than it can possibly be," said Glenn R. Schleede, vice president for policy planning at the National Coal Association. "The important energy deci-

From the *National Journal*, February 4, 1978, pp. 184-187. Copyright 1978 by National Journal. Reprinted with permission.
Richard Corrigan is a staff correspondent for the *National Journal*.

sions are made throughout the economy by millions of people and organizations, and there's no possibility that DOE can understand all that and come up with solutions to all the problems."

On policy questions, the Administration has been roundly criticized for not putting more emphasis on domestic energy production in its legislative package. And the new department's first budget, for fiscal 1979, did not reveal any major initiatives in this direction—either through more federal research and development spending or through further incentives to energy companies. *(For a report on the energy budget, see NJ, 1/28/78, p. 139.)* But officials now say that a new emphasis on energy production is influencing their planning.

On the subject of nuclear energy, meanwhile, the department is decidedly in favor of the accelerated use of atomic-powered electricity. While President Carter said during his campaign that nuclear energy should be employed only as a "last resort," it has since become clear that the Administration is relying on a steady expansion in the number of conventional light-water power reactors.

The department's commitment to this energy source has not been enough to please the nuclear industry, which has been traumatized by the Administration's frosty attitude toward breeder reactor technology and exports of nuclear equipment. Nor has it pleased the substantial anti-nuclear lobby, which was hoping the Administration would turn away from the nuclear option.

Thus, complaints about the department cover a multitude of topics: policies and the lack of them, the people in charge and the slots still vacant, priorities that are upside-down or the same as ever or not yet on the list.

It is not so surprising that the department is coming under attack. The department (including some semi-autonomous offices that are under its umbrella) was given immense powers by the reorganization legislation that Congress approved last year.

What threatens the department's image most, however, seems to be the widely held view that it has not yet gotten its act together.

"I think the situation is probably worse right now than if nothing had happened," said William T. McCormick, vice president for policy analysis at the American Gas Association. Department insiders, he said, "will privately admit that it is a zoo."

Further evidence of the department's failure to get organized is the fact that its constituent parts are still scattered around Washington, as department officials have been stymied in their attempt to take over the Forrestal Building on Independence Avenue from the Defense Department. How can this department grapple with what it sees as a worldwide energy crisis, the argument goes, if it cannot even move itself into new headquarters?

Taking Command

Schlesinger, in an interview, said the department has made rapid progress but added that "hard work on organization is critical."

"In one sense I'm not satisfied because I'm always demanding more," said the ex-boss of the Atomic Energy Commission, Central Intelligence Agency and Defense Department. "Quite obviously these [constituent] agencies are now responsive to guidance from the top," he said, while adding that "some elements of the agencies have not recognized that there is a larger department."

Schlesinger, operating out of a cozy office in the White House through lieutenants stationed next door in the Old Executive Office Building, has tried to impose a command system on the reshuffled energy bureaucracy.

Within the Office of the Secretary, for example, there is an Executive Secretariat, which contains the document control center, the document analysis and coordination center and the Action Coordination and Tracking System (ACTS) management center.

With these and other tools, the department's high command tries to keep watch and gain control over the people and programs it collected from ERDA, the Federal Energy Administration (FEA), the FPC, the Interior Department and elsewhere.

On Tuesday mornings, Schlesinger usually presides over a meeting of the Energy Policy Council, whose members include a raft of assistant secretaries and other top aides.

Other high-level staff sessions are held regularly by deputy secretary John F. O'Leary and undersecretary Dale D. Myers.

When the high command gets together, officials say, Schlesinger's Energy Department really seems to come alive. "Jim is not someone who just likes to check a box," said one assistant. "He likes to go eyeball-to-eyeball on something and talk it through."

"I think it's working quite well at the top." John M. Deutch, director of the department's energy research office, said. But down at the operating level, he added, "It takes an awful lot of time to get things done."

"The problem is," said a department employee, "we don't know what the top level is doing." And another employee, when asked how the reorganization was working out, said glumly, "It's going to take time. That's all I'll say about it."

Getting Organized

For all the advance planning that went into the launching of the Energy Department, its rocky start is understandable.

This is the first Cabinet-level department to be formed since the birth of the Transportation Department in the mid-1960s. Assembling 19,000 employees and some $10 billion worth of programs under a new organization chart is no small task.

This also is a green Administration that, in its first year in office, attempted to establish a new department while trying to get Congress to approve a hastily drawn national energy program. Schlesinger and his associates have worried more about the progress of the legislation than the department.

The department was envisioned as much more than a new command center that would oversee existing activities. On paper at least, entire agencies have been atomized and their employees reassigned.

While ERDA was set up mostly on fuel-by-fuel divisions, for example, the Energy Department has clustered fuels by evolutionary stages. Thus, instead of all coal-related programs falling under the responsibility of one boss, coal programs now are found under various bosses, whose responsibilities range from basic research to commercial applications.

Congress also insisted on a major change in the Administration's reorganization proposal. As the bill emerged from Congress, much authority over oil and natural gas pricing regulations was vested in an independent unit of the department, the Federal Energy Regulatory Commission (FERC). Schlesinger had wanted direct control over pricing policies rather than having to share jurisdiction with a commission that need not obey his directives.

As matters now stand, the department's Economic Regulatory Administration handles some oil and gas regulatory functions while FERC handles others. Jurisdictional questions are still being sorted out.

Adding to the department's troubles in its first months have been key vacancies.

Some nominees have not yet cleared the Senate, and two of them have run into opposition: Robert D. Thorne, acting assistant secretary for energy technology, and Lynn R. Coleman, selected for the post of general counsel.

Many other officials are holding jobs on an acting basis until they—or others—are assigned permanent titles. The White House has not yet found a nominee for the post of assistant secretary for environment, and Schlesinger has not yet named 10 regional representatives for the department.

Awaiting Decisions

Jack Ray's gas import ventures seem to be among the early victims of the new department's organizational throes. What happened to these projects illustrates the difficulties of dealing with a new institution whose policies still are in flux.

In the Algerian gas case, Tenneco had been seeking permission from the FPC to import liquefied natural gas (LNG) at a rate of one billion cubic feet a day for 20 years. The project's total capital cost was estimated at up to $5 billion.

Ray said his company had spent some $400,000 just in filing fees with the FPC and had been promised a decision by the end of 1977, the expiration date of the sales contract with the Algerians.

Under the reorganization legislation, which took effect last Oct. 1, responsibility for gas import applications was shifted to the Economic Regulatory Administration. And that office, despite anxious phone calls and telegrams from the company, has not yet issued a decision, leaving the whole project in limbo.

A spokesman for David J. Bardin, the administrator of the Economic

Regulatory Administration, said "Bardin does not feel he can decide responsibly on cases involving billions of dollars without a thorough review."

On the Mexican gas application, Tenneco has been among a half-dozen firms seeking to bring in about two billion cubic feet of gas a day through an overland pipeline. . . .

Negotiations for this gas were halted after Schlesinger said the Administration would not accept the sales terms, which would have priced the gas at about $2.60 per thousand cubic feet and linked future prices to world oil prices.

Schlesinger said Mexico should be allowed "reasonably generous" prices, which he suggested would amount to about $2.16, the price that Canada now collects for its gas exports to this nation.

It also appears that Schlesinger does not want to permit a large infusion of liquefied natural gas or fix a price formula for Mexican gas until Congress has resolved the issue of how much money American gas should fetch.

Policy Directions

The delays in the decision-making process that Jack Ray and others have encountered can be blamed in part on the organizational confusion that seems to exist at the department.

But policy decisions also play a role in how the new department is operating. The outlines of at least three such decisions have become clear as the new department gets organized. They are to reduce paperwork, enforce prior pricing regulations and push production of energy in the near term.

This is how the department's Energy Information Administration (EIA) says it intends to cut down on paperwork: "In order to accomplish this initial consolidation, the EIA must conduct detailed functional and user requirements analyses, systems analyses, programmatic and respondent impact studies and cost/benefit analyses, as well as program, document, and implement all cancellations, modifications, and consolidations.

The EIA is the new central data bank inside the department. It is supposed to become everybody's best source of information about the world of energy.

One of the office's first missions is to cut back the number of reporting forms that the government has been collecting from the energy industry. Its approach shows that it takes paperwork to fight paperwork.

Last August, a "special activation task force" decided, based on a contractor's study, that at least 250 different energy reporting systems were in effect and that at least 30 could be eliminated quickly and not be greatly missed.

After extensive reviews and comments, this task force report made its way to Schlesinger and then to Lincoln E. Moses, an academic statistician who has been brought in to run the EIA.

In a recent memorandum to department officials (from which the earlier quote was taken), Moses said he intended to carry out the task force recommendation by the end of this fiscal year.

He is establishing an energy information systems review group, which will review proposals to cut out or consolidate the reams of material that EIA now handles, he said.

This may seem an unnecessarily elaborate way to cut out red tape, but EIA has inherited a series of congressional directives and regulatory decrees to collect specific kinds of data. Each collection process has become a part of the routine for reporters and reportees, and presumably much of the information proves useful to people in and out of government.

As further evidence of the department's commitment to reducing paperwork, Schlesinger has appointed a regulatory reform task force, to be chaired by O'Leary. It will look for ways to lighten the regulatory burdens on producers. The department says it wants to see producers drilling for oil or gas, not wasting time on unnecessary forms.

The effort to reduce the paperwork burden may draw praise from outsiders. The drive to enforce pricing regulations may draw bitter opposition.

As administrator of the old Federal Energy Administration, O'Leary set in motion last year a major overhaul of regulatory activities. Now, as the No. 2 man in the new department, he is overseeing an expansion of regulatory activity within the new Economic Regulatory Administration (ERA).

In accordance with the recommendations of the Sporkin task force report (named after Stanley Sporkin, director of the Securities and Exchange Commission's Bureau of Enforcement), the department has established a special counsel's office within ERA. Its task is to review the activities of the nation's major oil companies during the period of the Arab oil embargo of 1973-74 and in succeeding years to investigate possible overcharges. The Sporkin report said the overcharges might run into the billions of dollars.

The problem is, as O'Leary calls it, "transubstantiation." It is the process of transforming "old" oil into "new" oil and charging higher prices for it, something that isn't supposed to happen. "People are breaking the law," O'Leary said, and the department must "go in and see to it that the law was obeyed and is being obeyed."

Paul Bloom is the special counsel in charge of the investigation. "I have been instructed to take the resources I am given and get the job done in the quickest, most professional way that I can," he said.

Bloom's office, which was established in December, already has served subpoenas on more than a dozen major oil companies as part of an intensified effort to audit company records. And the office has issued "notices of probable violations" to Exxon Corp. and Texaco Inc., accusing them of violations of price regulations totaling more than $600 million—such as collecting higher "upper-tier" prices for "old" oil that was supposed to sell at a cheaper price.

Exxon and Texaco have denied the allegations, accusing the department of trying to make retroactive changes in its oil pricing rules, which the companies said they obeyed during the periods in question.

Bloom, a jovial man—he cheerfully showed a visitor how his air conditioning unit kept running on a bitterly cold day—may soon become one of the most controversial figures in government as his investigative team pursues its work.

Production

As far as production is concerned, the current buzz-word around the Energy Department is "near-term."

The push is on, said one of Schlesinger's associates, "to produce what we can produce now, or next year, or the year after."

Officials say they are trying to identify promising technologies that can be yanked out of the research and development stages and put into the marketplace—as quickly as possible.

Schlesinger made it clear that this effort is still in the talking stage. He said no decisions have yet been made, for example, on whether or how the department might try to subsidize the introduction of major new technologies such as big coal gasification or liquefaction plants.

But the emphasis, he said, is on finding technologies that offer the promise of a "reasonably near-term payoff" over the next decade, instead of looking "35 or 40 years out" to such exotic energy sources as fusion power.

O'Leary put it this way: "We're taking a look at the entire ERDA side of the business to see which of these technologies is ready to come off the shelf, and at what it takes to take it off the shelf."

"We can afford to waste money but we can't afford to waste time," an aide to O'Leary said.

Some steps could be taken right now, O'Leary said, such as the lifting of price controls for oil that is produced through enhanced recovery techniques.

However, the department clearly is waiting for Congress to approve the pending energy legislation before it moves, through legislative or administrative channels, to take such steps.

Evidently, department officials feel that such "sweeteners" should not be offered to oil and gas producers before the issues still pending on Capitol Hill have been resolved.

Officials talk of projects that soon may make the "evolutionary jump"—even if the research and development specialists do not want to let them go.

"I've got to look at the big payoffs," said Dale Myers, the department's No. 3 official, who oversees the research to commercialization divisions of the department. "And it looks like the big payoffs now are coal and nuclear." He later added solar energy to his list of promising sources.

Department officials still are trying to reach agreement within the Carter Administration on a nuclear power plant siting bill. The long-pending legislation is one of the initiatives that department officials cite as part of their near-term production policy. (*For a report on the legislation, see NJ, 11/19/77, p. 1821.*)

"Let me tell you what the overriding problem is," said Alvin I. Alm, assistant secretary of the department for policy and analysis. "There is a tremendous incentive to hold on to ongoing research projects. This department can develop the most marvelous technologies. But if they're not put into the commercial sector, the whole effort is in vain."

Just how the department will get these products into the commercial sector is a matter of some debate. O'Leary, who has favored all-out development of so-called synthetic fuels, now warns that even with federal subsidies, coal gasification plants might face so many financial and regulatory and environmental constraints that the government might build one "toy" and the industry will say, "So what?"

And Alm said, "If people knew what our policy was in terms of rolled-in price versus incremental price, it would give people an assurance of what incentive they will have" for projects such as gasification.

But the department does not yet have such a policy to proclaim, and in any case the pricing decisions might ultimately be made by FERC, and might run counter to Schlesinger's policy.

Some of the department's work involves reviews of what is called MOPPS, for Market Oriented Program Planning Study. This was a project launched within ERDA during the Ford Administration. Its purpose was to match emerging technologies with estimates of fuel-by-fuel demand in future years.

"The problem was that anything ERDA did really had to meet a market test in the real world," said Robert W. Fri, former acting administrator of ERDA who started the study. "You don't develop energy devices for government use, like the Pentagon develops a B-1."

The study was kept under wraps by the Carter Administration after it came to the startling conclusion that, at a higher price than the Administration was willing to allow, the natural gas shortage might be ended. "What MOPPS finally came out with," said Fri, now an investment adviser, "was that after you get the price up to $2.50 [per thousand cubic feet of gas], it gets questionable whether you need that much more gas."

The findings have not yet been accepted by high officials, but the information will be fed into high-level reviews of which technologies deserve a nudge. The studies, one department official said, remain optimistic about future natural gas reserves and pessimistic on possibilities for oil.

"In the next 10 years, there's absolutely no magic as to how to get more supply," said Eric R. Zausner, a former FEA official now a senior vice president at the firm of Booz Allen & Hamilton Inc. "You've got to make sure the utilities can in fact build all the coal and nuclear plants they have scheduled. And the other side is to make sure all those guys who drill for oil and gas have the incentive and the certainty to go out and poke holes in the ground.

"Trying to find some poor Ph.D. physicist and bending his arm and telling him to work [faster] on something that's 10 years away instead of five years away I don't think is going to do much," Zausner added.

The Ford and Carter Administrations held different views about how much incentive should be offered to producers of conventional and unconventional energy sources. The Ford Administration ultimately endorsed both the lifting of price controls and a $100 billion federal aid package.

The Carter Administration is not taking that route. But officials in the Energy Department hint that, once Congress approves the energy package, they will put a major effort into new energy production plans.

"We're going to go down that road," a senior official said, dismissing any notion that the Energy Department favors a no-growth approach. "It just doesn't look that way."

12
A Case Study on the Impact of Public Policy Affecting Women
Jennifer Dorn Oldfield

Lost in government's preoccupation with organization is perhaps the most fundamental problem in its dealings with women's rights: Does the "status of women" provide a unified goal around which one can organize a government program? Or is the concept just another form of sexism, assuming the presence of a coherent group that, in fact, does not exist?

Connecticut's Permanent Commission on the Status of Women underscores the significance of this issue. While its legislative mandate assumes a unified goal for women, its actual operation casts serious doubt on such unity. The following case study explores the implications of this diversity as they affect the policy development of a legislative commission for women.

From its inception, the commission has been unable to come to agreement on its mission. This basic disagreement has manifested itself in three areas critical to the fulfillment of its mandate: (1) in the commission's composition, (2) in its operating style, and (3) in the issues it chooses to confront.

The study also points up a second issue: Can the advocacy role be performed by a government agency?

Creation and Climate

Connecticut's Permanent Commission on the Status of Women (PCSW) was established in 1973. It was an idea whose time had come.[1] In fact, its time had nearly come and passed. Almost 12 years had elapsed since John F. Kennedy created the national Commission on the Status of Women, and by 1972, 48 states had functioning groups of their own.

Reprinted from *Public Administration Review*, July/August 1976. © 1976 by The American Society for Public Administration, 1225 Connecticut Avenue, N.W., Washington, D.C. All rights reserved.

Jennifer Oldfield is on the staff of U.S. Senator Mark Hatfield.

Many members of the Connecticut General Assembly believed the function of such a commission superfluous, but may have felt a subtle pressure to keep up with their colleague states and establish a government body to deal with the concerns of women.[2]

The pressure of a powerful coalition of women's groups was not nearly so subtle. Legislators could not underestimate the influence of a lobby which had, during the previous year, skillfully rallied the votes for passage of the State Equal Rights Amendment, and now urged the creation of an advocate group for women.

While the legislative support was at least passive, the governor had to be coaxed into not opposing the bill. In spite of this half-hearted acceptance of a commission for women, the PCSW was given a broad charter to combat sex discrimination.

The commission was directed to:
• Review the general statutes with regard to sex discrimination and recommend legislative revisions to the General Assembly.
• Inform the community—including business, education, state and local governments—of sex discrimination practices and enlist its support to change such practices.
• Serve as a liaison between government and private interest groups concerned with services for women.
• Promote consideration of qualified women for all levels of government positions.
• Oversee coordination, and assess programs and practices in all state agencies as they affect women.

The PCSW was to be directed by a body of 17 commissioners, five of whom were appointed by the governor, four by the speaker of the house, and four by the president pro-tempore of the senate. Its membership also included the co-chairman of the joint standing committee on human rights and opportunities, and the ranking minority representative and senator of this committee.

The commission was authorized to hire an executive director and staff (although its initial budget was just $30,000), and to perform a variety of quasi-judicial functions. These included the right to hold fact-finding hearings, with the mandate to subpoena witnesses and records, to receive and refer complaints of sex discrimination to the State Commission on Human Rights and Opportunities; to recommend policies to state agencies to promulgate such regulations, and, finally, to request and receive from all state agencies "such information and assistance as the commission may require."

Problems of Definition

In the last few years, women's liberation has become a household word.[3] But in every household, it generates a different word. To some, perhaps the minority, women's liberation is an unnecessary and negative concept. To others, it is an issue of equal rights only, rights which are to be achieved quietly, through legislation. To still others, it is an issue of women's liberation in the full sense, requiring a transformation of roles in society, by more activist "radical" methods.

Connecticut's Commission on the Status of Women was a microcosm of this diversity.[4]

Yet the assumption in the legislative mandate was a common agreement on goals. That agreement, whether in concept or technique, was rare in the PCSW.[5] When agreement did occur, it was with the most non-controversial issues. Indeed, that magic spiritual bond which has been said to unite all women in a crusade for justice,[6] was mere fantasy. Each of the commissioners had a personal philosophy and a private agenda for the commission, and pulling together as a team was difficult.

Said a former staff member:

The commission could never seem to come to a consensus about its mission. As a result, its projects tended to ricochet from one enthusiastic idea to another.

The group was constantly shifting its emphasis or response to a situation. Often, issues would be brought before the commissioners for reconsideration, after a decision had been made. This resulted in confusion and a great deal of inactivity.

From month to month, the commission would change its policy or decisions … As a group, it would make a decision, and then individually, members would come in and whack away at it, giving other directions to the executive director. And then they would criticize her for whatever she had done.

Commission Composition

Philosophical and practical disagreements on the issues were reinforced by the type of appointments made to the commission.

Some have suggested that the governor, who opposed the establishment of the PCSW, deliberately appointed persons who would not be as effective as others, in order to reduce the commission's ability to perform.[7]

Said one former PCSW staff member:

Many well-known feminists in the state had looked forward to serving on the commission, and then the appointments seemed to be political favors, to women who had no experience, and frankly, no interest in feminist things.

The significance of such political appointments to the commission lies with the priority given the women's issue by some of these members.

According to one commissioner:

Originally, there were three people who had been working in the feminist fields on the commission. The rest were political appointments. ... Those people have problems because they have allegiances to their respective parties, which come first. ... All commissioners who are beholden to the Democratic party or to the Republican party will unite against a feminist who is not beholden to either party. ... I think the Democrats and the Republicans are feminists as long as it is okay with the party. And it is okay with the party as long as it doesn't make too many waves.

Party allegiance provided just one more methodological difference among an already diverse body. Those without party allegiance and not accustomed to using the political ropes believed in a different approach to problem solving. In the view of the same commissioner:

The political appointees were generally more conservative. They moved slowly, doing what the appropriations committee told them, trying to get along by personal interview ... "Joe, or whomever, on the appropriations committee is a friend of mine, and I'll call him up and ask him what we should do about our budget". ... That kind of thing is really difficult for a feminist to handle.

The party-feminist conflict provided another cross division of commissioners. It was not only Democrat versus Republican, but also old hands versus idealists.[8]

According to one commissioner, the "old political hands" were dealing in old ways:

The activists are the effective new politicians. After all, we (the activists) got the commission established. The old political hands had nothing to do with it. ... It is my view that the activists would never have been so shoved around by the legislature if they had run this commission, and the PCSW role would be entirely different today.

Compounding the problems of party allegiance and political-feminist backgrounds, was the fact that several of the appointees were relatively unaware of the problems of women. Before the PCSW could even begin to discuss its mission, it had to help educate and raise the consciousness of its own members. This resulted in a slowdown on the commission's action front.

The diversity of group affiliation within the commission was also bound to produce a wide range of views. Organizations as dissimilar in membership, purpose, and technique as the National Organization for Women, the League of Women Voters, the Women's Political Caucus, and the Business and Professional Women's Club, were represented on the commission.

And, like many other commissions, the Connecticut body was composed of a group of strong and dominant personalities, most of whom had been "kingpins" in their own organizations. While cooperative action under these circumstances is difficult, it was magnified in the PCSW by the multiplicity of goals and strategies which emerged from those group loyalties.

Operating Style

The disagreement on objectives and approach was reflected in the PCSW's operating style. "Delegation" was not in the commission's vocabulary. A group can only delegate responsibilities with confidence if all are agreed as to what should be done. Since indeed they were not, the strategy was high participation by all commissioners.

Said one:

We take on a lot of the work ourselves. We want to become involved in the work of the agency. We've fought for the idea that individual commissioners' talents and ideas should be used where it is appropriate, and that has happened purely because of the force of the personalities of the various commissioners.

However, that "force of personalities" often overstepped its function of policy making and became involved in the minutiae of day-to-day operations. Duplication of effort with the staff often resulted in confusion and embarrassment. At one point, the executive director found that she was five minutes behind a commissioner in making technical arrangements for the publication of an ERA brochure—an obvious function of the staff.

A commitment to high participation was one of the organizing principles of the commission. Early in its existence, the commissioners voted against the formation of an executive committee, because they wanted all to participate in decisions.[9] And although they did elect a chairperson, she served as a mere figurehead, as many commissioners would often speak and act on behalf of the group.

Ironically, while the commissioners accepted this "leaderless" group concept as appropriate to their own operation, they could not accept the same style of management for the staff.

The former executive director was a "team" person, one who did not believe in hierarchy, operating in perhaps the most hierarchical of structures—a government agency. She espoused what she called the "feminist way," where the five-member staff was not on different levels, but worked together.

However, some commissioners believed strongly in the need for a hierarchical staff structure:

The "feminist process," in which there is an attempt to achieve some level of equality among members of the organization, has become confused with getting a job done. That requires a tough executive director, who is capable of establishing stations, of giving orders.

This conflict in style led to a complete changeover in the five-member staff in just two years.[10]

In some respects, the former executive director may have been "an idea whose time had not yet come." She was a strong director acting firmly on what she saw as direction from the commission, in a time when the commission's directions were often contradictory. As she noted, "the telephone was always ringing with controversial directions from individual commissioners," telling her how to move from point A to point B, or suggesting that she not move in that direction at all, despite a recent vote by the commission.

The leaderless style of operation could not be supported by a mandate so broad, or a group so diverse.

Issue Avoidance

The disagreement on PCSW objectives also caused it to concentrate basically on procedural issues and non-controversial matters. The body was indeed a firm subscriber to Seidman's Law: Controversial decisions which can be deferred, are deferred.[11]

In its first year of operation, the commission took very few policy stands, concentrating instead on the so-called "safe" issues.[12] Its stance has moved only moderately from that point in its second year. Certainly, the commission has not tapped the extensive power given in its mandate, and has rather focused on its research and education functions.

The sensibility of such an approach is dubious to the "Activists" on the commission. One commissioner said cynically:

The commission wants to study whether or not discrimination exists when everyone knows it exists.

But another staunchly defends that approach:

If we wanted to play it a certain way as a commission we could come up with all kinds of information in the area of discrimination against women . . . and publish it right away and create an absolute hailstorm. But that's not a good way of handling it, particularly when a lot of men don't understand that women are discriminated against at all. . . . It is better to do an education program first and save these kinds of rockets for some other time when you feel the legislature is thoroughly informed and thoroughly educated.

The "political realists" believed that if they took on controversial topics too soon they might jeopardize the commission and its development.[13] The opposing faction felt that the commission was there to serve the women of the state and it should deal with all areas—including difficult issues like abortion. Staff members, as well as some commissioners, regretted that the commission seemed reluctant to take stands on this, as well as other issues such as the problems of welfare women, and the sex discrimination case of waitress Judith Quist, who was fired because she refused to shave her legs.

Government Agency as Advocate

When the commission did unite in project and approach, it soon discovered its own limitations. Serving at once as an advocate, and as a state agency, became a difficult balancing act.

There was always the overriding . . . problem that we had as a state agency, in terms of the political realities: We had to make sure we didn't step on people's toes. When working in a political situation, we obviously have to consider the point of view of the administration on an issue, and the point of view of the various people on committees who are going to say "yes" or "no" to our budget, and the things we want to do.

For example, the PCSW has had a stormy history with the Committee on Legislative Management, the powerful group charged with reviewing all commission expenditures over $250. It has often said "no" to the things the commission has wanted to do. In one instance, the committee refused to allow the PCSW to spend $1,000 on pamphlets supporting the passage of the Equal Rights Amendment, in spite of two state attorney generals' rulings that it was within the commission's mandate to do so. The legislative group would approve the expenditure only if the publication was revised into simply an informative, rather than an endorsement piece.

Its status as a legislative commission has cast severe limitations on its impact on other state agencies, as well.

Of course, if a state agency is not fulfilling its responsibility in the area of equal rights, said one commissioner, "We must make a stink about it. But what kind of a stink can a state agency make about another state agency?"

The commission has instead chosen a more delicate approach to the problem, relying on the cooperation/education technique with the establishment of formal interagency committees.

Sensitive to its structure as a tax-supported agency, the PCSW takes a hard line on its nonalignment strategy with other women's groups. This, too, is a subject for conflict within the commission:

What the commission could have been was a focal point in the state for all those groups—NOW, the Women's Political Caucus, the League of Women Voters, etc.—but what it tried to do was get away from these groups. They did not want to be like them, and they would become nervous. . . . That's crazy. They have all those women out there who are dying to help, but they (the commissioners) didn't want to be contaminated, or be confused with these groups which they thought were too radical, or too vocal.

As an agency dealing with a broad constituency and a controversial, sensitive issue, the commission's interest groups were many and diverse. To represent and serve as an advocate for *all* women in the state was an incredible mandate—a mandate impossible to carry out to the satisfaction of even a small number of organized women's groups. Methodologies, ideologies, and opinions of the PCSW were all over the map, from "too conservative" or "too radical" to "we don't need an advocate for women" or "we need a more active group to be our ombudsperson."

However, it has been the active women's groups who have been the most critical of the PCSW's mild approach to the problems of women in the state. While the commission has been sensitive to this, its organizational maintenance (perhaps the only basis for agreement among commissioners) has received top priority. The PCSW's survival is dependent on legislative good will. And many commissioners feel the only way to maintain that passive support is with a "tiptoe" approach to the problem of sex discrimination.

A Concluding Note

Does the "status of women" provide a unified goal around which one can organize a government program? In the case of the Connecticut Commission, the answer is clearly no. Indeed, the existence of a commission assumes the presence of a coherent group that does not exist.

However, given the present scope of the problem of sex discrimination, and the pressure to formulate such public advocate agencies, government may not have the luxury of choice. Certainly, Connecticut government was not accustomed to having an advocate within its own ranks, and many within the commission, as well, found themselves uncomfortably bound in a public agency.

The basic challenge for government, then, is to recognize this diversity and its ramifications for a public agency, and to attempt to organize within and around it. Connecticut's commission was unable to do that, for its diversity was emphasized and magnified by other forces.

Changes in the structure, the scope of the mandate, and the composition of such a body may serve to accommodate such diversity. These are surely issues which government must examine. In the end, however, it is the women themselves who must develop an acceptable operating style and approach, within the confines of a public agency, if they are to help unite this broad-based group in a modified "crusade for justice."

Notes

1. Harold Seidman, "Decisional Strategies in Public Administration," lecture (University of Connecticut, October 1975).

2. Personal interview with PCSW commissioner (October 1975).

3. J. Freeman, "The Women's Liberation Movement: Its Origins, Structures, Impact and Ideas" in J. Freeman (ed.), *Women: A Feminist Perspective* (New York: Mayfield Publishing Co., 1975), p. 451.

4. Personal interview with PCSW commissioner.

5. Even the publicaion of a pro-Equal Rights Amendment brochure for Connecticut voters was disputed by some commissioners. And even the vote in support of the

Supreme Court decision allowing abortion, an issue that many consider to be a basic female right, was split eight to four.

6. Freeman, *op. cit.*

7. Personal interview with PCSW staff member (October 1975).

8. Personal interview with PCSW commissioner (October 1975).

9. *Ibid.*

10. According to the commission's former executive director, this situation was not unique to other commissions on the status of women, which have also had a high turnover rate in staff.

11. Seidman, *op. cit.*

12. The commission was reluctant to tackle controversial issues. Said the former executive director: "One of the first things the commissioners were interested in was child care. Some of the less sophisticated members felt somehow this would be a safe issue. ..." One commissioner admitted that the PCSW had saved perhaps the most explosive issue for last, family law: "I think the reason the commission has delayed on the family law is because this is the real crunch. ... Women's existence in the home and the marriage is going to be the hardest thing of all to change, and we all know that. It's going to cause a revolution for these middle-aged men."

13. Personal interview with PCSW's former executive director (October 1975).

13
Federal Staffs Are Fearful
of Shake-Up Plans
Kathy Sawyer

"**S**o much is being done to us that it's hard to tell who is doing what to who and for which reason," sighed a midlevel bureaucrat in the Department of Health, Education and Welfare, where thousands of employees are facing demotions, transfers, layoffs and other terrors.

Just about everybody has declared open season on their kind, government workers point out, and they are braced for a rain of possible adversities from the Carter administration: various types and sizes of reorganization, government programs of "job reclassification" (which often means demotions) and a spate of proposals to alter pay scales and take away a measure of their job security.

Many of the reorganizations and other actions still are on the drawing board and their ultimate dimensions are unknown. Officials insist that, for at least some workers, current fears may turn out to be more painful than anything that actually happens to them at government hands.

From the *Washington Post*, January 30, 1978. Copyright 1978 *The Washington Post*. Reprinted with permission.
Kathy Sawyer is a *Washington Post* staff writer.

"I don't know where I stand anymore," said Gela Portee, 52, a GS-13 budget analyst at the Commerce Department. She is one of six employes in her eight-person office who have been told they might be demoted.

"You don't spend 21 years giving the best of your service and then not get upset over a thing like that. This kills federal employes off," Portee said. "It's like a slap in the face. You can't ever feel the same about your job again."

"We keep saying around here that things can't get any worse—but things keep getting worse," said Al Ripskis, a GS-13 program analyst at the Department of Housing and Urban Development. He vents his frustrations by publishing a feisty newsletter called Impact, which lambastes the bureaucracy every couple of months.

Ripskis' most recent target is the new HUD reorganization gearing up to replace the reorganization that had commenced under the preceding administration. He notes that this is the 20th reorganization there since 1960.

"The gloom is so thick you can almost see it, and people are walking around like zombies," Ripskis said.

Such talk is easy to hear these days at most federal agencies, although people generally do not want to be quoted by name on such a topic.

Despite President Carter's attempts to exorcise them, frustration, fear and rumor continue to prowl the corridors of his bureaucracy, driving the morale of the work force to what some oldtimers are calling an all-time low.

The antigovernment crosstides, which threaten federal workers' self-esteem and job security, have swept in from several sources—from the public, in polls; from the press, in headlines about overpaid and underworked or incompetent government workers who "can't be fired," and from Jimmy Carter, a reform-minded president whose administration has vowed to nail to the wall this floundering jelly of a bureaucracy.

Some of the antigovernment feeling comes from the federal workers themselves, they note pointedly, because they are the ones who deal daily with the same infamous problems that have prompted the moves toward reform in the bureaucracy. "It's a snake trying to bite its own other end," a frustrated State Department employe said.

Another factor is that the government operates on its own employes the same way it operates generally—very slowly. "They're giving us too much time to think about things before they happen," the bureaucrat added.

Some employes say, also, that the malaise reflects the disappointment their coworkers feel about the new Democratic administration, which promised a spirit of humanism and reform.

"It's the same old thing," said a GS-13 in the Commerce Department. "The man in charge saying we will do things in a humane way, and the people who are really in control saying, 'we're going to go ahead and do it our way.'"

Some union leaders feel that federal managers here and there are using reorganization as "an opportunity to shove it to the people they didn't get along with," as Greg Kenefick, a spokesman for the America Federation of Government Employees, put it.

Two philosophies operate during a personnel upheaval, according to a GS-15 social planner at HEW. "You can either put your energy into showing what a good job you can do, or you try to show how much you're being hurt. I think you do better with the former, but I see a lot of movement around here in the latter direction," he said.

The planner and others at HEW complained about continuing leadership vacuums and unfilled vacancies down the line, some in programs charged with dispensing millions of dollars in federal checks. The results, they said, include infighting about jurisdictions and "some people who try to move on their own, and others afraid to step out into that policy hiatus, so they aren't doing anything much."

A GS-14 working in a health care program said: "Everybody around here is an 'acting' something. Our supervisor, his supervisor and HIS supervisor are all in an 'acting' capacity. I call it the 'vanishing authority concept.' I can't pin anybody down to sign anything."

At the same time, he said, "there's plenty of 'fat' around here. You could go through the place and wipe out a third of the people and still have effective programs. The question is, which ones go?"

Many government workers emphasize that they favor improving the system, getting rid of incompetents and making programs more effective so their own work is more valuable and appreciated.

"The majority of dedicated, competent employes feel they are being vilified because of a handful of incompetents," said Rep. Gladys Spellman (D-Md.). Her Washington-area constituency includes a high percentage of federal employes, and she also heads a subcommittee that will handle the president's civil service reform legislation proposals.

"Federal employes are not happy about being bogged down in a machine which by its very nature stifles innovation," Spellman said, reacting to charges by some administration aides that she plans to obstruct reform legislation.

"But, while we don't expect federal employes to be 'more equal' than other workers," she added, "we also want them not to be the whipping boys of disenchantment with government in general."

Traditionally, civil servants have "felt happier" with the big-government oriented Democrats in power, noted a long-time government worker now retired and working in the private sector. "Today the whole business of conservatism and liberalism is changing its meaning. It's hard for any national figure, politically, to stand up for the government worker today.

"I think federal employes have probably seen their best days," this worker said.

Carter's plans include not only a major reorganization of unknown dimensions, to streamline government agencies, but also proposals to change radically the way the government manages its work force. The proposals range from facilitating hiring, firing and promoting employes to revising pay scales.

In addition, the normal turbulences that keep the bureaucratic alphabet soup stirring have been intensified by an accumulation of leftover problems, including some neglected during Watergate.

Thousands of employes already have been demoted in the last year because of the government's job reclassification program, an evaluation process that often determines that an employe is overpaid for the work he is doing and results in the worker's being "bustered" (downgraded). Thousands of others still face the prospect in connection with various shakeups—office closings, layoffs and reorganizations and government error in job classification.

When a 49-year-old Commerce Department worker killed himself by jumping from the top of the seven-story Commerce building last October, some friends and coworkers attributed the suicide in part to depression about his demotion. "It wasn't just the demotion. It was the cold and callous way it was done," a fellow employe said.

In repeated attempts to defuse bureaucratic hostility to his reorganization plans, Carter has promised federal workers that none will be hurt by his shakeups. Some agencies clearly were not abiding by that policy, administration officials said, so the president last month underscored his intention by approving a plan to prevent federal agencies from firing workers or demoting them as a result of his reorganization.

Carter also said he would support legislation to restore grade and pay levels for at least two years to those demoted for reasons beyond their control during 1977. He urged federal managers generally to be as humane as possible.

Still, some managers and their employes remain confused. Edward Preston, an official with the Office of Management and Budget, explained that this is partly because the president's commitment does not extend to so-called internal reorganizations, closing of military bases and other managerial actions that are not part of Carter's own reorganization.

Preston also said there are problems sometimes in defining exactly which shakeups are those of Carter and which are those of someone else.

Among reorganizations clearly bearing the Carter label, according to administration officials, are consolidation of scattered energy programs into a single Department of Energy, consolidation of a State Department bureau and the United States Information Agency into an International Communication Agency and the proposal for an independent agency for Education, wresting the "E" out of the massive HEW apparatus.

The recently announced layoff of 800 agents of the Central Intelligence Agency, which was followed by plummeting morale and rebellious mutterings in intelligence community ranks, obviously did not fall under the president's policy of protection.

Of the various internal or otherwise non-Carter actions, the most massive so far is the reorganization at HEW that eventually could affect as many as 10,000 employes in ways ranging from a change in their door plaques to being fired, officials said.

In addition, for reasons other than the reorganization, the officials expect an estimated 2,500 positions to be demoted to a lower pay level. Most of those positions are at the Social Security Administration.

"Nobody ever mentions the 33 million (Social Security) checks these people send out every month," said Harold Roof, president of the American Federation of Government Employees union local at SSA headquarters in Baltimore. "These employes are not going to give you the same dedication they gave you before. You've got the backbone of the (federal) work force totally frustrated."

But HEW, among the agencies, is "following the same pledge" that the president made for his own reorganizations and will not "throw anybody out," according to Thomas McFee, assistant secretary for personnel administration at HEW.

McFee said the agency is developing special placement programs and hopes to arrange an early retirement program to free some slots. These steps, combined with policies affecting downgrading, should mean that the downgrading might involve "only the jobs, not the people in them." McFee said in any case, "it should be at least four years before the downgradings affect people in their pocketbooks."

14
Bell Figuring Out How to Outfox the Bureaucrats

Ronald J. Ostrow

Washington— Atty. Gen. Griffin B. Bell thinks he finally has figured out how to outmaneuver the wily Justice Department bureaucrats he is supposed to control.

But the issue is still in doubt.

For example, one of Bell's first targets for criticism was the Law Enforcement Assistance Administration, the multimillion-dollar grant-giving agency. Bell ordered the LEAA to do away with its advisory boards, some of whose members were receiving LEAA funds.

It was a clear conflict-of-interest situation, as the new attorney general saw it.

"The next thing I knew they cut out two grants I was interested in," Bell recalls, "a clear application of the retaliation principle."

The problems Bell has encountered are not peculiar to the 53,000-employe Justice Department or to the Carter Administration. Administrations come and go, but bureaucracy endures—and prevails, cabinet heads often find.

From the *Los Angeles Times*, November 7, 1977, Part I, p. 1. Copyright, 1977, *Los Angeles Times*. Reprinted by permission.
Ronald J. Ostrow is a *Times* staff writer.

In an interview last week, Bell detailed seven basic techniques or "principles" he believes the bureaucrats use in their efforts to control him. Besides retaliation, the principles are "flooding, burying, leaking, crying politics, avoiding decisionmaking and expanding."

Soon after taking office, Bell said, he found himself flooded with lengthy papers, particularly from the Justice Department's antitrust division and the department's office of management and finance.

"They were telling me what they were doing." Bell recalls. "I don't know really what their motive was, but they were keeping me off balance. I was getting more information than I needed, and it was taking all my time.

"I assume it was a method of control—or keeping me from controlling," Bell said. "I was just getting so many papers that I couldn't think about how to get the place under control."

Bell's solution was to tell his staff that he could not understand material when it ran more than three pages.

"The burying principle," Bell says, is the technique of submerging a controversial proposal deep within a long report in hopes the high official responsible for making the decision will approve it without realizing the significance of what he had done.

There are limits to how far the bureaucracy dares to go, of course.

"A bureaucrat won't risk being fired," Bell said. "He won't do anything too drastic, but he'll do something he probably ought not to do and something that is against your policy."

"Of course, he would just as soon not hear about your policy. That's one reason I make so many speeches. I announce policies in speeches because I have not been able to get my own people's minds open."

Of all the techniques, however, Bell is most offended by leaking.

"It's really terrible on a person who has just come in," he said. "You're embarrassed and confused by constant leaks concerning matters which have not come to your attention. This puts you in the position of playing catch-up all the time, rather than being in charge."

The "most vicious" use of the leak, Bell believes, is when the aim is to control conduct.

A published report that Bell planned to authorize the indictment of several FBI officials is one example.

"Some thought I might not authorize the indictments, and a story was thus promptly leaked that I would," Bell said. "This was designed to put me in the position of appearing to change my mind rather than to make up my mind."

Instead, no indictments have been authorized and Bell ordered an investigation into the source of the leak.

The published story "quoted out of a report that I had locked up in the safe," Bell said. He treated the material so gingerly that he took the report across Pennsylvania from the Justice Department to his hideaway office in the FBI to study it all day.

The investigation led to yet another discovery—"There's rarely one copy of anything in government.

"I learned there were at least five other copies of the report. Folks will just make copies because it makes everybody feel important to have a copy—a status symbol," Bell said.

The "cry politics" principle often goes into operation "if some member of Congress happens to inquire about a matter." Bell said. "It is easy for those immediately in charge of the matter to contend there has been an effort to politicize and thus wrest control from the attorney general or other person in charge.

"Ninety-nine percent of such inquiries are proper in a representative form of government such as ours and quite harmless," Bell said.

He said he viewed the "cry politics" technique as "a Watergate aftermath."

"The average lawyer around here doesn't know that much about me," Bell said. "They may be testing me to see if I am a person who will stand up for the right principles."

Avoiding decision-making can be accomplished either by sending a matter up the ladder of authority with the expectation that it will be returned for further study or sending it down for study at a lower level. "In either event, decision-making can be avoided.," Bell said.

The "expansion" principle is at work when a government agency tries to develop its own litigating capacity rather than rely on the Justice Department to perform its traditional function.

As Bell seees it, "the result will be Balkanization. The legal voice of the government will be split into many parts."

Despite the variety of techniques for manipulating him that Bell has encountered, he voices confidence that he can overcome them.

Sounding much like a hunter toting a bag of quail over his shoulder, Bell says: "I think I've caught on to these simple techniques. They're no problem for me. If the bureaucracy is going to overcome me, they're going to have to get up something more sophisticated."

Bell says he believes that, acting individually, government workers probably "would cut out this foolishness and get to work. It's the fact that they collectively are in some sort of a bureaucarcy where you don't have private sector discipline" that causes the problem, he believes.

15
Lilith
Reynolds

Studs Terkel

It's hard for me to describe what I'm doing right now. It may sound like gobbledygook. It's hard to understand all the initials. It's like alphabet soup. We just went through a reorganization, which is typical of government. Reorganization comes at a rapid rate these days. My job has changed not only in name but in status.

She has worked for the federal government for nine years. "I work for the OEO. I was assistant to the regional director. I was what's called the regional council liasion person. There's something called the Inter-Agency Regional Council, which is made up of five agencies: OEO, HEW, Welfare, Labor, Transportation, and Housing. This group meets once a month.

"Agencies don't really want to coordinate their efforts. They want to operate their programs their way and the hell with the others. OEO has been unique in that we're funded directly to communities without going through other government structures.[1]

"The regional councils are really directed from Washington. They're told what to do by the Office of Management and Budget. They are just a little political thing. One of the big pushes was to make better contact with six governors of the region and the mayors—from appointments secretary to planning staffs to budget departments. Getting the money you need for the programs you want, getting it down to the people. We spent most of our time doing that."

It's amazing how little information there really is around. How systematically it's kept from getting around. Some of the Spanish-speaking community groups got fairly good at harassing the regional director. They wanted answers to questions. How many Spanish-speaking people are employed in our office? That wasn't hard—two. How many are employed by agencies to which we were giving grants? How many people are being served by the programs we're funding? These were legitimate questions. The way we went about getting the answers was ridiculous. We just couldn't come up with the statistics. We made an educated guess. It's hard to change the rules. People take the course of least resistance.

There's a theory I have. An employee's advancement depends on what his

From *Working: People Talk About What They Do All Day and How They Feel About What They Do,* by Studs Terkel. Copyright © 1972, 1974, by Studs Terkel. Reprinted by permission of Pantheon Books, a division of Random House, Inc.
Studs Terkel is an author of several books on the American scene.

supervisor thinks of him, not on what the people working for him think. The regional director's job depends on his friendship in Washington. So the best thing for him to do is not challenge the system, not make waves. His future depends on being nice to the people who are making the decisions to make the cuts that are hurting his employees. So he's silent. But the people down here, the field representatives, who know what's going on, make waves. So the director tries to get rid of the most troublesome.

At our office there's less and less talk about poor people. It's mainly about how we should do things. I don't know if this was always so. It's just more obvious now. Local politicians have more and more say in the programs. In Chicago, Mayor Daley runs it. In other cities, it depends on the power structure. We talk more of local institutions these days, not of poor people.

I have been very active in the union.[2] We've frequently confronted management with problems we insisted they solve. We tried to get them to upgrade the secretaries. They're being underpaid for the jobs they're doing. Management fought us. We've tried to have a say in policy making. We've urged them to fund poor groups directly. Management fought us.

For instance, the union has backed the Midwest Poor People's Coalition. We tried to get funds directly to the Chicago Indian Village and a poor group in Indiana. Almost always, the agency has balked. We've attacked management because they're just not carrying out the Economic Opportunity Act.

The employees should help make policy, since they're closest to what's going on. It's probably the same as in auto plants. A lot of times workers can make better decisions about production than managers. The managers aren't down there often enough to know what's going on.

Your education prepares you to go into a job and accept what you're told as being correct. I worked several years for the Social Security Administration. It has a fantastic number of rules and regulations. For a long time I believed they were correct and it was my job to carry out these rules. After I got to OEO it became more and more obvious to me that a lot of these rules were wrong, that rules were not sacrosanct. I think this is happening to workers all over. They're challenging the rules. That's what we're in the process of doing.

Through the union people have been bringing up ideas and management is forced more and more to listen. They hadn't taken us very seriously up to now. But we just got a national contract which calls for union-management committees. I think our union has challenged management a lot more than most government unions. That's largely because of the kind of people OEO has attracted. They believe in being advocates of the poor. They believe in organizing people to challenge the system. It's a natural carryover to organize a union which also challenges the system.

I'm among the top fifteen people in the decision making process in the office. As the union became more aggressive—it was on the issue of the Indians, the director tried to fire our president—I got into a big hassle. We developed thirty-three charges against the director and made a mass mailing to all community agencies, to all the grantees, to all the senators and congressmen in the region. After that, I was no longer assistant to the regional director. (Laughs.)

That's another typical thing in government. When management wants to get rid of you, they don't fire you. What they do is take your work away. That's what happened to me. He didn't even tell me what my new job would be. They sent somebody down to go through my personnel file. "My God, what can we do with her?" They had a problem because I'm a high-grade employee. I'm grade 14. The regional director's a 17. One of the deputy directors told me, "You're going to be economic development specialist." (Laugh.)

I'm very discouraged about my job right now. I have nothing to do. For the last four or five weeks I haven't been doing any official work, because they really don't expect anything. They just want me to be quiet. What they've said is it's a sixty-day detail. I'm to come up with some kind of paper on economic development. It won't be very hard because there's little that can be done. At the end of sixty days I'll present the paper. But because of the reorganization that's come up I'll probably never be asked about the paper.

It's extremely frustrating. But, ironically, I've felt more productive in the last few weeks doing what I've wanted to do than I have in the last year doing what I was officially supposed to be doing. Officially I'm loafing. I've been working on organizing women and on union activities. It's been great.

If they would let me loose a little more, I could really do something. We've got plenty of statistics to show incredible sex discrimination. Black women have the lowest average grade. White women have the next lowest. Then black men. Then white men. I'm sure these are the statistics for our whole society. We believe that in organizing women we can make changes in all directions. We've already started to do that.

There's no reason why we can't carry this to the community action agencies. Many of them deal with welfare mothers, with all kinds of households headed by women. If women knew more about their rights, they'd have an easier time. If we could get into the whole issue of law suits, we'd get real changes. My office is trying to stop us.

When you do something you're really turned on about, you'll do it off-hours too. I put more of myself into it, acting like I'm a capable person. When you're doing something you're turned off on, you don't use what talents you have. There are a lot of people in our office who are doing very, very little, simply because their jobs are so meaningless.

Some of these jobs will appear meaningful on paper. The idea of the antipoverty program is exciting. But people are stifled by bureaucratic decisions and non-decisions. When you're in the field and get into sticky situations with politicians, you can't count on your office to support you. You'll be punished—like having your job taken away from you. (Laughs.)

Since I've been doing what I want to do, my day goes much faster. When I was assistant to the regional director, an awful lot of my time was taken up with endless meetings. I spent easily twenty or more hours a week in meetings. Very, very nonproductive. Though now I'm doing what I want to do, I know it's not gonna last.

I have to hide the stuff I'm doing. If anybody walks into the office, you have to quick shove the stuff out of the way. It's fairly well known now that I'm not doing any official work, because this huge controversy has been going on between the union and the director. People are either on one side or the other. Most people who come in to see me are on the union side. I'm not hiding the fact that I'm not doing any official work.

I hide the stuff because I feel a little guilty. This is probably my Protestant upbringing. I've been work oriented all my life. I can't go on drawing a paycheck doing what I want to do—that's my conditioning. My dad worked in a factory. I was taught work is something you *have* to do. You do that to get money. It's not your life, but you must do it. Now I believe—I'm getting around to it (laughs)—you should get paid for doing what you want to do. I know its happening to me. But I still have this conditioning: it's too good to be true.

I've had discussions with friends of mine to the right and to the left of me. The people to the left say you shouldn't take any part in a corrupt system. To give them your time and take money from them is a no-no. People to the right say you have no right to take the taxpayers' money for doing nothing. You're not doing official work, therefore you shouldn't be paid for it.

I feel much less guilty about this than I would have a year ago. I have less and less confidence that management people should be telling me what to do. They know less than I do. I trust my own judgment more. I believe that what I'm doing is important.

What would be my recommendation? I read Bellamy's *Looking Back-ward*, which is about a utopian society. Getting paid for breathing is what it amounts to. I believe we'd be a lot better off if people got paid for what they want to do. You would certainly get a bigger contribution from the individual. I think it would make for exciting change. It'd be great.

The reasons people get paid now are wrong. I think the reward system should be different. I think we should have a basic security—a decent place to live, decent food, decent clothing, and all that. So people in a work situation wouldn't be so frightened. People are intimidated and the system works to emphasize that. They get what they want out of people by threatening them economically. It makes people apple polishers and ass kissers. I used to hear people say, "Work needs to be redefined." I thought they were crazy. Now I know they're not.

Notes

1."The Nixon administration has accelerated the movement toward patient, prudent evaluation, particularly in the Office of Economic Opportunity. . . . Prominent among the victims was the OEO, flagship of old ways, but also home of the new."(Jack Rosenthal, *New York Times,* February 4, 1973).

2. American Federation of Government Employees.

Topic Four

The Individual in the Public Personnel Process

Introduction

For many years public personnel administration was considered by most administrators to be little more than a minor staff function. Most of the work in personnel was routine and clerical in nature, often far removed from the key policy decisions of the organization. In short, people did not go into personnel work by choice. Instead, it was an area to be avoided because there were so few interesting programs or assignments.

That description no longer applies to personnel administration. Since the mid-1960s people working in personnel have been involved with some of the most exciting, challenging, and controversial issues in public administration. Some of these are employee training, affirmative action, employee productivity, reorganization, and labor relations including unionism and the right to strike. As a result, personnel administrators are considered to be an integral part of top management, and they find themselves being consulted on decisions much earlier instead of merely responding to policies already adopted.

There are two general reasons why personnel administrators have attained more status. First has been the increasing recognition, if not full acceptance, of some of the "humanistic" theories discussed in Topic Three. As more organizational leaders see that a variety of influences motivate people and that these are connected with policy administration and effectiveness, personnel administrators skilled in employee development are being used more widely. The job of people in personnel is no longer considered completed once a position has been filled. Responsibilities now last throughout the entire association of the employee with the agency.

The second reason why personnel administrators have acquired increased responsibilities is because of the rising number and rapid changes in the laws pertaining to individual employee rights. Affirmative action and labor relations in particular have become overriding issues in virtually all organizations. The consequences of improperly administering these laws can be so detrimental to an agency that it can no longer afford to leave these programs in the hands of untrained people isolated in a corner of the building. Administrators are being watched constantly by interest groups and enforcement agencies, and the slightest apparent irregularity in the administration of a law is likely to precipitate immediate litigation.

Public personnel administrators have a broad scope of activities. These include the recruitment, allocation, development, retention, and retirement of people. The selections in this Topic offer glimpses of a few of the particular adminstrative and individual problems in some of these areas. For example, Selection 16, "A Boss Takes His Job Personally," tells us of an employer in the private sector who typifies thousands of sincere, concerned and frustrated bosses across the country. These administrators are caught in the vortex of several forces. Employers want to be flexible and lenient with their employees, yet they have other obligations as well. They must ultimately be responsible to a profit and loss statement, stockholders, civil service regulations or state and federal laws. These employers are expected to take into account the personal factors of their employees when making work assignments or personnel decisions, yet by law, employers are forbidden to ask certain personal questions of prospective applicants even though they might aid the administrator at a later date. We see the need, therefore, for administrators to resolve two laudable yet contradictory goals: humanistic treatment of personnel and complete objectivity in hiring and promoting.

The Merit System

Public organizations use two methods to fill their job positions: patronage and merit. It should be remembered that just as not all "merit" appointments are truly meritorious, so all "patronage" administrators are not incompetent or corrupt. Patronage is the power to distribute governmental positions based on various criteria which may include such unrelated job skills as personal and political affiliations. Often equated with the "spoils system," patronage at its worst brings into governmental service people who have no ability or training but simply know someone in the right place. At its very best, however, patronage can provide workers who are extremely competent and who also are loyal and responsive to the elected leaders making the appointments. If such public employees know that their jobs depend upon satisfying an official who must in turn be re-elected, that relationship can create a responsive and accountable bureaucracy.

A true merit system is one in which all extraneous factors not related to performing the specific job are excluded in the selection process. It is accurate to say that there have been very few, if any, pure merit systems devised because of several technical and human considerations. (Some of these problems pertaining to qualifications and testing are discussed later.) In the so-called merit system used by the federal government and other jurisdictions, we find glaring exceptions to the idea that only relevant criteria are considered in selecting applicants. Some examples are accepting applications only from people already working in an agency, adding veterans' preference points to examination scores, giving oral instead of objective tests, and using the "rule of three" in which the actual top-rated candidate does not have to be chosen. All of these nullify the notion that "merit" alone determines who gets a job. While there may be justifiable social and administrative reasons for these practices, calling a personnel system "merit" does not necessarily make it so.

The merit system at the federal level was established as a reaction to some of the worst kinds of patronage ever practiced. Under merit, employees were to be judged by their job performance and not be subject to arbitrary and capricious behavior of employers. What began as a necessary reform of a deplorable situation, eventually developed as many problems as the old "spoils system." Consequently, many people including administrators and those from the public have raised some serious questions about perpetuating merit systems in their present form.

The criticisms of merit systems focus upon the following four points. (1) Merit is difficult to define, and even when it can be measured, it is not and should not be the only criterion used in personnel decisions. (2) Merit systems overprotect the incompetent employee while at the same time underreward the outstanding worker. (3) Merit is not an important factor in yearly salary reviews because nearly all governmental agencies use a "step increase" method whereby each employee is raised a step with an automatic commensurate increase in pay. (4) Merit encourages unresponsiveness and unaccountability in employees because they feel confident that severe disciplinary action against them is unlikely or will not be successful.

Reform Proposals

What can be done to preserve the desirable and necessary protections for public employees while eliminating those regulations which hinder or destroy the existence of an accountable governmental bureaucracy? President Carter has made several specific proposals for overhauling the federal civil service. In the past, presidents received little popular support for such policies, but recent public opinion polls reveal general support for the direction the President has outlined. The current "taxpayer revolts" at the state and local levels aimed at the size and cost of government suggest that the usual mundane subject of civil service reform may at last have some political campaign appeal.

The gist of Carter's proposals is that governmental reorganization cannot be effective until there are also major changes in the rules governing the way workers are hired, promoted, and fired. Unless the manner in which individuals work is modified, reorganization is merely window-dressing and no substantive changes in the way government conducts its business will occur. At the core of the Carter reform proposals is the idea that poorly performing employees will be demoted or fired without a long drawn out process while outstanding performances by employees can be rewarded quickly to encourage initiative. (To emphasize the magnitude of the problem, it should be noted that in 1977 only 226 federal employees out of a civilian work force of nearly 3 million actually lost their jobs because of poor performance.) A major contributing cause to this lack of job discipline is the fact that it can take up to three years and require a disproportionate amount of an administrator's time to obtain the dismissal of an employee.

President Carter proposed that there be an end to automatic pay raises for managers and supervisors, substituting true merit pay increases if earned. Managers would be given greater authority to dismiss personnel, and although there would be appeals, this procedure would take less time than it does now. A new category of top-level supervisors would be eligible for pay bonuses for outstanding performance. Military service veterans would receive bonus points and job preference consideration for only ten years after military duty. Finally, the President called for replacing the current Civil Service Commission with two separate agencies—a merit system protection board responsible for protecting the rights of employees, including "whistleblowers;" and an agency for personnel management carrying on the functions presently handled by the Civil Service Commission.

As might be expected, most of the reform suggestions are under attack by employee unions, veterans groups, and some members of Congress. What kind of bill will emerge from Congress, if indeed one actually does, is uncertain at this time. The need for fundamental changes, however, is essential as the next two selections clearly show.

Selection 17 by Karen House presents some dramatic examples of how meritless the merit system can be in Washington, D.C. She pictures administrators frustrated in their attempts to work with or around employees who are incompetent. Managers must devise imaginative ways to circumvent civil service rules—"turkey farms," for example—because they know the impracticality of trying to fire anyone.

Barbara Rasmussen (Selection 18) writes from the perspective of a supervisor in the office of the Mayor of Los Angeles who had to deal with local civil service regulations. In addition to outlining some general problems created by these rules, she concentrates on two practices not confined to Los Angeles: prevailing-wage clauses and automatic step-increases in salary. Her comments on these problems and on the advantage that city workers have in so-called "open" examinations for jobs underscore how some "merit" systems are nothing more than sophisticated mechanisms to protect employees already in an organization.

Before a reaction sets in and there is a demand for the abolition of all merit systems and civil service rules, the public should be cautioned. It is essential to be able to fire an incompetent worker within a reasonable period of time, but only according to a predetermined method. Procedural rights should not be so cumbersome that they discourage the administrator from taking appropriate action. At the same time, if public service is to attract and retain the highest quality individuals, there must be protections for employees so that they can discharge their duties in the manner necessary to carry out the essence of governmental administration discussed in Topic One. If the reforms go too far and make dismissal too arbitrary and unpredictable, people in government may avoid the really difficult administrative problems and decisions and the public will be no better served than they are now. Selection 19, "The Oppenheimer Case," is an excellent example of what happens when procedural regulations do not exist or are disregarded.

Administrative Procedures and the Case of Robert Oppenheimer

The case or "trial" of Robert Oppenheimer is probably the most famous administrative hearing in American public administration. Magazine articles, books, and a play have been written about the events from different perspectives. Several issues pertinent to public and personnel administration were raised in the hearing, and Selection 19 draws attention to two related issues—the nature of an administrative hearing and the scope of administrative discretion.

An administrative hearing and a regular courtroom trial differ. In a hearing, which is what Oppenheimer had, the proceedings are more informal than in a court of law. If conducted fairly, a hearing may enable the hearing officers to reach a conclusion more quickly and inexpensively than in a court trial because formal rules of evidence and cross-examination are not required. There can be advantages, therefore, to both sides in having a hearing instead of going to court. Yet, the biggest distinction between the two can also be the most important disadvantage. It is the lack of formal safeguards for the person being investigated in a hearing. In Selection 19, for instance, the attorney for Oppenheimer was denied access to certain records and was prevented from physically representing his client at one point.

A second issue throughout the Oppenheimer hearing was that of administrative discretion. The Atomic Energy Commission was both prosecutor and judge. Several examples cited by Harold Green show how the laws were abused to obtain the final verdict that the chairman and the commission wanted. Overall, the Oppenheimer case demonstrates that while there are times when an agency needs to make investigations of its employees, the workers must be protected from irresponsible administrative action. How to do both effectively is a continuing concern of administrative law and personnel administrators.

Recruitment and Selection Procedures

Attracting, selecting, and hiring the most qualified people are essential to the effectiveness of an organization. There are five steps in the recruitment-selection process.[1] (1) An organization must determine what characteristics—skills, experiences, and education—its new members must have. (2) The organization must be able to identify these desired characteristics in the people who apply for the job. (3) The organization has to direct its recruitment toward those individuals most likely to possess the needed characteristics. (4) The agency has to persuade the most attractive applicants to come to work for the organization. (5) The agency needs to keep the best qualified people in its organization.

Each of these five steps has its own set of problems, but the first two will be given special attention here. Step one, determining what characteristics an applicant for a position should have, is fundamental in the recruitment process. If an agency does not have a clear idea of what its employees should or will be doing, then personnel officials will not know what kinds of applicants to seek. Beyond this, however, there is a further problem. Once the organization decides what the job responsibilities are, there still must be agreement on what characteristics in people are needed to do that job.

Selection 20, "The New Face Of The Peace Corps," illustrates that disagreements may occur among administrators about what types of people should be recruited for jobs. The generalist versus specialist question is an old one in public administration and is basic in the Chris Kenrick selection. There must be a very close link between what an agency wants to do and the kind of personnel it has. If these two are not in agreement, problems will arise. The administrators of the Peace Corps are attempting to restructure and revive the agency as well as to provide a different kind of service to the host countries by deliberately recruiting people with general backgrounds rather than with professional skills. Sam Brown, the head of ACTION, believes that "people can matter more than mere skills" and that the generalist without any previous specific training can serve a useful purpose in the Peace Corps. Whether or not this orientation will be successful depends upon several factors. At the top, is the ability of the agency to define its goals precisely and then to identify the people best able to achieve those objectives.

This leads to the second step in the recruitment-selection process. Personnel administrators must be able to identify in applicants those characteristics and skills that have been judged the most important. If the characteristics are general and vague, identification will be more difficult. Selection 20 also illustrates this. Sam Brown talks of Peace Corps workers who are "adaptable," "perservering," and willing to address themselves to "basic human needs." Determining which applicants have these traits can be much more difficult than finding which individuals can perform specific tasks in agriculture, plumbing, or teaching.

Testing

A continuing problem for personnel administrators is devising techniques with which to identify the desired characteristics in prospective employees. Written, oral, and performance tests are used to measure certain qualities and skills, but even when they are employed very carefully most tests are imperfect measuring instruments. For several years the courts have recognized the intentional or unintentional limitations of tests. As a result, there are now many legal requirements pertaining to the content and the manner of administration

of examinations for job applicants. For example, two of the minimum requirements are that the questions on the test be "job-related" and that the entire test
must be "valid." Validity means that the test measures what it intends to
measure: the possession of certain characteristics or abilities to perform a job.
A perfectly valid examination, therefore, will rate applicants in the same order
they will be ranked after they have been on the job. The top scorer on the test
should be the highest performer on the job. While the courts have not
required perfect validity, they have demanded that a correlation exist between
the test and either the functions of the job or the training for the job. (In
Selection 22, by Anthony Balzer, there is a discussion of testing including what
is necessary for validation and the problems in achieving it.)

Selection 21, "A Success on the Job, She Flunked the Test," provides a
poignant personality profile of an individual trapped by the selection and
testing process. It summarizes many issues and problems that were covered in
the two sections of the Topic immediately preceding this one on testing. The
story is of an employee who had been performing well on her job, and then
because of a position reclassification was required to take an examination for
her own position. She flunked the test and was fired. While we have limited
information on this situation, one can speculate about the validity of the
examination. Did the test measure a person's ability to perform on the job or
did it evaluate an individual's talent to pass the examination? The same question should be asked about the college degree requirement in this instance.
Was it essential for job performance—a difficult point to defend in view of the
fact that a noncollege person was already doing well in the position—or was it
a means to reduce the number of applicants?

We cannot judge the motives of the test administrators in this case, but it
is true that examinations in the hands of untrained or biased administrators
have screened segments of society from organizations. Because of the potential
for misuse and intentional discrimination, testing is now a major issue in
personnel administration.

Affirmative Action

Affirmative action is the government's term for the policy of encouraging
or requiring employers to hire underutilized groups in society. The primary
intent is to open to women and minorities employment opportunities that
have been closed because of overt or subtle discriminatory practices. While
most people would not argue against the objective of affirmative action, what
has been the point of contention administratively and legally has been the
manner in which to implement its policy goals.

Affirmative action has many different meanings. For some groups it is a
long-range goal of "equal opportunity" but with no specific timetable or
numbers of women and minorities who need to be employed to reflect that
objective. For others, affirmative action is a form of "representative bureaucracy" which means an organization's membership must reflect mathematically
the group composition of the community it serves. As an example, if a certain

percentage of the community is composed of black females, then the agency must have the same composition in its work force.

Despite all the current attention to the policy of equal opportunity in hiring and promoting, the concept is not new. Franklin Roosevelt issued the first executive order against employment bias in 1941. In a broader sense, the attempt to expand employment opportunities to particular groups goes back as far as Andrew Jackson. As the first President from a state other than Massachusetts or Virginia, Jackson wanted to provide jobs in the national government for "westerners" and the "common" people. He did this through the patronage system and, although there were several abuses, one result was the beginning of a broader geographical and social representation in governmental employment.

At present, affirmative action programs often clash with other policies which reasonably could be considered to be in the public interest. It becomes necessary, therefore, for administrators, the courts, and the public to reconcile these and to find an acceptable middle ground. Organizational and personal dilemmas are created as individuals try to work through and resolve apparently contradictory policies. Selection 22 by Anthony Balzer is written from the perspective of a police officer personally involved in and affected by an affirmative action program, and it touches upon several problems.

Much of the discussion on affirmative action stems from the conflict between two fundamental philosophies about the relationship of individuals to society. These contrasting views of human nature and society can be translated into specific attitudes about the purpose and composition of organizations and the role affirmative action programs should carry out. One approach is called "the merit view" and the other, "the quota and equity" philosophy. A discussion of merit versus quota and equity may put the general concept of affirmative action as well as some of the specific discussion in Selection 22 into perspective. It should be suggested first, however, that some of the discussion on *both* sides of affirmative action is pure rhetoric and hypocrisy couched in these philosophical terms. Behind lofty arguments, defenders and opponents are really basing their views on fear and insecurity, political power-building and discrimination. These are not legitimate defenses and criticisms of affirmative action. There are reasonable arguments that can be offered on both sides of the issue, and this is what the following discussion tries to summarize.

The fundamental assumption behind the merit philosophy is that the individual is "the basic unit of society; therefore the group affiliations of an individual are irrelevant to an individual's ranking in the meritocracy."[2] Merit is measured in terms of individual talent and should be the only determining factor for receiving society's rewards, including jobs. Those who are most talented will and should receive a greater share of benefits than those who are less talented. There must be an equality of opportunity to use individual talents, but there will be no guarantees that each person will be successful. Under these principles, advocates of the merit view believe everyone, the talented and less talented, gains. Society as a whole benefits when the most meritorious make their full contribution. This is most likely to occur only if the rewards distributed are uneven and go most generously to those most capable. Therefore, any forms of special preferences, "reverse discrimination," or quotas no matter how "justified" they may appear to be, in the long run will adversely affect everyone in society including those they were designed to help.

The quota and equity philosophies start with a different basic assumption. Social groups, and not individuals, constitute the essential units of society. As a result, individual talents are a product of group influences as much as of any other factor. For this reason, a society should distribute its rewards, such as jobs, among groups and in proportion to each group's number in the total population. Without the group affiliation, individuals would lack certain norms, values and identification which enable each person to compete in society.

The equity argument is related to this group theory of society. Equity as used in the affirmative action context means remedying today the past wrongs which had been perpetrated against certain groups. Equity considerations are a means of compensating for past discrimination or unequal treatment, services or facilities. This view contends that all members of the same group were treated in the same manner in the past and that they must be given the same additional help today. One way to expiate past wrongs is to give preferential treatment in hiring or promoting.

It is at this point that the quota-equity views collide with the merit philosophy. Probably no other single employment policy has caused as much discussion and controversy during the past twenty-five years as affirmative action. Because there are telling arguments on all sides of the question, no simple solution is politically or socially acceptable. The Allan Bakke case against the University of California Regents and the U.C. medical school (1978) did provide some answers, although many questions remain. Affirmative action programs in education are constitutional but not if they use rigid racial quotas. The Court ruled that race may be taken into account as one of several considerations in a flexible admissions policy, but that race cannot be the single overriding criterion.

A week after the Bakke decision, the U.S. Supreme Court supported affirmative action programs again, this time in the area of hiring and promoting policies in private industry. The court let stand a "model" affirmative action program adopted by the American Telephone & Telegraph Co. which alloted two-thirds of new jobs and promotions to women and members of minority groups. No opinions were given in this Court action, so specific guidelines to employers and employees are not available. Other cases in the lower courts which are challenging affirmative action programs are headed toward the Supreme Court. Once they are decided by the Court, it is expected that they will define more precisely the meaning of affirmative action.

Notes

1. For additional discussion about some of these steps see Anthony Downs, *Inside Bureaucracy* (Boston: Little, Brown and Company, 1967), pp. 229-233.
2. Thomas R. Conrad, "The Debate About Qutoa Systems: An Analysis," *American Journal of Political Science*, February 1976 (Vol. 20, No. 1), pp. 135-149. Much of the discussion on merit and quota philosophies is drawn from this article.

16

A Boss Takes His Job Personally— and His Persons Expect It

Ellen Goodman

I know a man who is a boss. Not a Big Boss, and not a very bossy boss. But he does have a title on his door and an Oriental rug on his floor, and he takes his job very personally—which is the problem.

You see, when this boss was in business school he assumed that management was a question of profits and losses. Now he finds himself spending a great deal of time worrying about the cost-accounting of personnel problems. Personal personnel problems.

Moreover, he says, it's going around. He keeps reading articles about "corporate irresponsibility" toward private lives. He hears how often business plays the heavy in family crises. But from where he's sitting, in a corner office looking down on the rest of the city, he sees something else.

He sees employees who want to be treated strictly professionally one moment, and then personally the next moment. He sees the conflicts faced by his employees, but also the conflicts of being a boss. He is often in a no-win situation.

The boss had three stories to tell me.

The first was about his secretary. Last January, when he interviewed her he was warned by the personnel office to keep the questions strictly professional. On pain of a lawsuit, he could not quiz her on her marital status or child care. So he stuck to the facts, just the facts—stenography and typing and other work experience. Then last month, when one of her children was home sick, he was expected to understand why she had to be home. He saw the situation this way: One month he wasn't allowed to ask if she had children, the next month he was supposed to care that they were sick.

Then there was the junior executive whom he wanted to promote. The man was clearly ambitious and good. The boss had judged him on the basis of

---

Ellen Goodman writes a syndicated column in Boston.

his work, he'd groomed him and watched him. Then he'd handed him a big promotion to the Southwest. But the junior executive asked to be excused. He didn't want to make this trip, because he just couldn't move his family at this time. But, the boss said, the man had never described himself as immovable on account of teen-age children. Now the boss was asked to make allowances.

The third story was actually somewhat ironic, because it happened in the personnel department itself. The assitant director of personnel was a man who administered the most careful, scientific, professional testing service that the boss had ever seen. It screened people in and out of the company, up and down the hierarchy, on the basis of multiple-choice answers. But now this man had just obtained custody of two small chidren. He had come in to ask for flexible hours. Under the circumstances, he wanted to know whether he could make some special arrangements that would help his personal life.

This particular boss isn't a Simon Legree. Nor is he the sort of man who treats people like interchangeable plastic parts. So he adjusted to his secretary. He adjusted to his junior executive. He adjusted to the assistant director of personnel. He did it because, well, a happy employe is probably a productive employe, and all that.

He did it because a person's private life is a factor in his professional life, and all that. He did it because he believed that business should be more flexible. To a point.

But he feels a certain frustration. People want him to treat them professionally when it's to their advantage, and personally when it's to their advantage. While he understands the family-business conflict, he also understands the conflict that comes with the title on the door and the Oriental rug on the floor.

Every day this boss has to decide at what point the best personal interests of his employes conflict with the best business interests of his company. Where is it writ, he asks, that business increasingly has to deal with personal personnel issues? How do you balance the needs of the company and the needs of the workers?

Sometimes this man is afraid that he's running a family agency instead of a corporate division. Other times he's afraid he's being a heel.

The boss doesn't expect any sympathy. He doesn't want his name in the paper. People don't sympathize with bosses, anyway, he says, because it's hard to sympathize with someone who has the power to hire and fire you. He understands that.

But the fact is that he's responsible for 150 lives and one corporate balance sheet. And he takes both of these jobs very personally.

17

Civil Service Rule Book May Bury Carter's Bid To Achieve Efficiency

Karen Elliott House

Washington—As things go in the bureaucracy, the confrontation was particularly grim.

A top Carter appointee at the Department of Housing and Urban Development discovered that a $25,000-a-year economist was actually doing no work and called him in for a dressing-down. The economist blandly admitted doing nothing except writing personal free-lance articles, but warned his new boss that civil service regulations make it almost impossible to fire him.

"I'll spend whatever time it takes," the HUD official recalls saying. "You'll see," the economist confidently replied, "I'll wait you out just like I did all the others."

Whether he does or not, the dialogue is a vivid illustration of why government experts believe President Carter's promise to reorganize the bureaucracy faces deep trouble.

Reorganization, the President has said, will mean a wholesale shifting of the 2.8 million federal workers to eliminate duplication and to make the best use of their talents. Yet tangled civil service regulations almost prevent reassignment of employes according to talent. Indeed, so complex are the regulations that a manager seeking to reduce his staff often must use a computer to sort out who is entitled to stay and who must go.

Massive Regulations

As the regulations have ballooned to fill 21 volumes some five feet thick, government managers have found it increasingly difficult to fire employes. At the same time, promotions and merit pay raises have become almost automatic. The result is a bureaucracy nearly devoid of incentives and largely beyond anyone's control—even the determined Jimmy Carter.

"The civil service system makes managing government very difficult," says Jule Sugarman, vice chairman of the Civil Service Commission, which writes the regulations and oversees their administration by other government departments and agencies. "We must simplify the system."

But this won't be easy. Underlying the regulations are 400 laws enacted by Congress and an unknown number of executive orders, possibly 600. Any major changes in the system aren't likely to breeze through Congress, where federal workers' unions are influential.

To complicate reorganization further, President Carter has promised to do the job without firing or demoting anyone, a promise that leaves government managers aghast. "If reorganization means reducing duplication and inefficiency, someone has to get hurt," says Raymond Jacobsen, executive director of the Civil Service Commission.

"Asking the Impossible"

Adds one Commerce Department official: "The President is asking the impossible. He wants efficiency, but he's tied our hands by saying no one can be demoted."

Considering these shackles, the only way to reorganize, experienced government managers say, is to go around the system—a practice already common. For instance, almost every department has a "turkey farm," a special division created to pool many of the department's incompetent workers where they can do minimum damage.

"You have to know how to legally circumvent the system to get anything done," says Albert Dimcoff, Deputy Executive Director at the Consumer Product Safety Commission, who has worked in five other government agencies. "People like myself have built careers on knowing how" to do this, he says.

White House officials concede reorganization is going to be much tougher than President Carter imagined when he campaigned against the "horrible, disorganized and wasteful bureaucracy in Washington."

Privately, these officials say Mr. Carter may be able to do little more in his current four-year term than reshuffle organizational boxes. "We can move the boxes," says a member of the Carter reorganization team, "but getting rid of the incompetent or unwilling workers will be very difficult without major reforms in the system, and those could take years to push through Congress."

Ironical History

Ironically, the civil service system was created 94 years ago to bring merit to federal hiring. Previously, each new President swept out federal workers and replaced them with his own cronies. But over the years, regulations grew until workers not only are protected from the spoils system but from almost any managerial direction.

Today, life is pleasant in the bureaucracy, the average annual salary is $15,343, and most employes are due to get a 7.05% pay raise in October. Of the one million people eligible last year for merit raises, only 600 didn't receive them. Almost no one is fired; less than 1% of federal workers lost their jobs last year. In fact, firing isn't even in the government vocabulary: The term, is "removal action."

To this bureaucracy, reorganization is nothing new. Managers constantly are reshuffling people, often in an effort to work around unsatisfactory employes they can't fire. What's new is President Carter's promise that his reorganization will result in more efficient and responsive government. That would mean, officials say, weeding out bad employes and rewarding good ones. But the civil service system now thwarts such efforts.

In recent weeks, the White House and the Civil Service Commission have begun ways to overhaul the system. One of the few proposals made so far is aimed at getting around the President's promise of no demotions. The administration has asked Congress for authority to downgrade jobs during a reorganization yet guarantee employes their present salaries for the duration of government service.

Overpaying some federal workers is a "small price to pay for more flexibility to reorganize," says Alan Campbell, the Carter-appointed chairman of the Civil Service Commission.

Even if Congress goes along with this plan, hulking obstacles to efficient reorganization will remain.

Many government administrators, anxious to preserve their power, prestige and pay, will resist any remodeling that threatens to shrink their empires. Civil service seniority rules and special preferences for veterans also will interfere with change for the better. If a reorganization results in fewer jobs, the most senior employes get those jobs, and veterans have priority over nonveterans. Talent counts little: An outstanding rating from a supervisor is worth only four years' experience in counting seniority.

So, if an agency head wants to reorganize one of his bureaus to reduce the number of workers from 300 to 250, an employe who loses his job may displace someone less senior in another job of the same rank. That employe in turn may "bump" another more junior employe and so on until possibly everyone in the bureau is changing jobs—a giant game of musical chairs. In the process, the bureau may lose some of its best workers and end up with others in important jobs for which they aren't suited. A recently completed reorganization of the Environmental Protection Agency's Research and Development Office took two years to carry out, and all 300 employes wound up changing jobs, some of them several times.

Endless Appeals

Beyond the headaches of seniority is the agony of appeals of government personnel decisions. Almost any decision by a manager may be challenged in a lengthy process that begins in his agency and may proceed through two Civil Service Commission units and wind up in federal court. Among other things, a worker may appeal his supervisor's decision to fire him, to rate his performance unsatisfactory or to deny him a merit pay increase. Because these appeals take months or even years, most managers simply work around incompetent employes, rate everyone satisfactory and hand out the pay increases.

The case of Albert G. Tase Jr. indicates how nightmarish the appeals delays can be. Mr. Tase was fired in December 1974 for allegedly mishandling his job as a personnel officer for a U.S. Navy office in Norfolk, Va. Nearly three years later, his case still isn't resolved.

With a lawyer's help, Mr. Tase charged numerous violations of civil service regulations surrounded his dismissal. Among other things, he said he wasn't given time to make an adequate answer to his supervisor's charges, which were supported by a 2,000-page record. The hearing before the commission's Federal Employe Appeals Authority dragged on for 29 days, creating more than 4,000 pages of transcript. In April 1976, the FEAA ruled he shouldn't have been fired. The Navy asked the commission's nine-member appeals board to review the decision. After another year of delay, the board decided in June to remand the case to the FEAA for reconsideration on several issues. Now Mr. Tase is asking the three civil service commissioners to review the appeals board decision.

"To fire an employe you've got to be willing to spend most of your time for several months documenting and defending your decision," says Don Wortman, Deputy Commissioner of the Social Security Administration. "If it's a woman or black, you have to be extra-careful because of the suspicion you're a white chauvinist honky. And there's always a risk of procedural error."

For example, former Federal Energy Administrator Frank Zarb last year demoted his chief press spokesman, Robert Nipp, for among other things, allegedly fabricating a document given to a congressional subcommittee. Recently, the commission's appeals authority upheld Mr. Zarb's findings but reversed his decision on a procedural technicality: Notice of the effective date of Mr. Nipps's demotion arrived 12 hours too late to comply with civil service rules. The energy agency is appealing the decision.

Because civil service regulations make personnel management so difficult, many managers resort to subterfuge to get rid of incompetent employes. Trading them to other agencies is a favorite technique. For instance, the general counsel of one major department has prevailed upon two former assistants now in other agencies each to take on for one year a lawyer who he believes is incompetent but who would be difficult to fire.

Using Useless Jobs

Kicking unsatisfactory employes upstairs is another device for getting them out of the way. If a bureaucrat in a key position can't handle his job, his boss may promote him to "special assistant," where he may have little if any responsibility. Or he may be given a year off for training. "It's far better for the taxpayer if I abuse the system by sending a nonperformer to school for a year than allow him to foul up an important job," says a top official at the Department of Health, Educaton and Welfare.

The Carter administration almost certainly will have to resort to such subterfuges to reorganize the bureaucracy for more effective performance. It may find the task eased slightly by Chairman Campbell's promise that his agency will review reorganization plans with an eye toward helping an administrator carry them out rather than telling him why the regulations make them impossible.

"But," Mr. Campbell says, "there are inhibiting rules, and neither we nor the President can change them."

Problems With Attrition

President Carter also hopes the natural attrition in the federal work force—due to deaths, retirement and other departures—will further ease reorganization problems. But the number of employes leaving the government each year amounts to only about 10% of the total. "Attrition can't be the universal solvent," Mr. Jacobsen says, "because it occurs unevenly at various levels of government."

Even if Mr. Carter does achieve some success in reshaping the machinery of government, he may well find that no magical gains in efficiency result.

"There is so much that reorganization doesn't accomplish," says John Cole, director of the Civil Service Commission's Bureau of Personnel Management. "It creates new boxes on organizational charts and new stationery, but the history of reorganization is simply reshuffling."

18
Civil Service:
a Shocking Inside View

Barbara Rasmussen

The Los Angeles civil-service system is a mixed bag. Our City Council knows it, the public knows it, but no one knows quite what to do about it.

In all fairness, the system does provide a stable work force for the city that functions with minimal political patronage and cronyism. Nevertheless, serious shortcomings in the system breed inefficiency and stifle excellence.

Take the city charter's prevailing-wage clause, one of the most controversial issues at City Hall. The clause requires the city to pay its employes wages at least equal to those of their counterparts in the private sector. Moreover, it results in annual across-the-board pay increases.

Councilman Ernani Bernardi wants to dump this provision, but has failed in recent weeks to obtain enough valid signatures to place a repeal initiative on the June primary ballot.

Many citizens, including members of labor unions, vehemently oppose efforts to scuttle the prevailing-wage concept. Yet I wonder whether many voters really understand how it fits into the overall civil-service salary structure. Until 1974, when I began a three-year stint with the city, I myself had no idea how quickly city workers' paychecks grew.

I was unaware, for example, that the yearly increase required by the prevailing-wage clause is not the only automatic raise that employes receive.

From the *Los Angeles Times*, March 28, 1978. Copyright 1978 by Barbara Rasmussen. Reprinted with permission.
Barbara Rasmussen is a public relations consultant in Pacific Palisades, California.

"Step" increases are also awarded after a worker is hired or promoted. Such increases accrue solely on the basis of length of service, without regard to merit.

Say that an accountant were to join the city's labor force or receive a promotion this April 1. Exactly three months later, at the beginning of fiscal year 1978-79, he would automatically receive the prevailing-wage boost. For the past five years, such a raise has averaged 5.6% of a typical employe's salary.

Then, after completion of his six-month probationary period on Oct. 1, the accountant would receive an automatic step increase that, if recent experience is a measure, would amount to approximately 5.6% of his salary. The next prevailing-wage increase would arrive like clockwork in July, 1979, and the second annual step increase in October. Totaled up, automatic salary increases would boost the accountant's starting salary by roughly 25% in just a year and a half.

But the raises would not necessarily stop there. Since most civil-service job classifications have five steps, the accountant would, by staying at the same job for just three more years, make 55% more than his starting salary by October, 1982.

What is particularly shocking about this is that the accountant would not have to do anything more to earn these increases than to show up for work 10 months of each year.

That's right—*10 months*. Municipal workers receive 10.5 holidays each year, not counting general election days. In addition, every new employe is entitled to two week's vacation after a year of service. (Employes with seniority get longer vacations.) Add to that 12 days' sick leave for most employes, as well as another, rather unusual benefit: one additional week of sick leave at 75% pay, and still one more at half pay.

As a supervisor in a city office, I began feeling rather sick myself in late December on signing a multitude of attendance slips that authorized pay for my subordinates' last few hours of 50% sick leave for the year.

But discouraging as it was to watch lackluster employes collect one automatic raise after another, it was even more frustrating to know that I could not recommend pay hikes for workers under my supervision who showed exceptional dedication and diligence. The only way a civil-service employe can increase his base salary is by taking an exam to qualify for a higher-paying position.

But even that procedure is not as straight-forward as it sounds, for the exams are fraught with problems. To begin with, certain employes automatically score "bonus" points on the tests for reasons having nothing to do with merit.

This inequity drew wide public criticism during the process of selecting Los Angeles' new police chief. Though Santa Monica's chief of police, George P. Tielsch, received the highest score for his answers to oral and written questions, he was disqualified as a finalist because of bonus points granted to other candidates as rewards for their years of city service. Daryl Gates, who was named chief of police on Friday, was among those who received this bonus.

Police officers with seniority are not the only beneficiaries of bonus points. Earlier this month the City Council debated the fairness of automatically granting 10 points to veterans who seek jobs with the city. By a narrow margin, the council voted to instruct the city attorney to draft a charter amendment significantly altering this arrangement—a measure that will appear on the November ballot.

Unfortunately, however, more is wrong with civil-service tests than the scoring system. Often questions have little bearing on the job at stake. What point is there, for instance, in demanding that an employe be able to take shorthand at 90 words a minute if he is trying out for a supervisor's job? Or why demand that he quote verbatim from the city charter when a reference copy is available in each office?

I can offer no foolproof formula for screening out inept supervisorial prospects. Indeed, most of the myriad difficulties of the present system have me stymied, along with everyone else. I firmly believe, however, that the repeal of the prevailing-wage clause is an important first step on the road to making hard work pay.

Repeal would not mean that city workers would no longer be fairly compensated. To begin with, they could receive an annual increase keyed to the cost of living. More important, salary step increases should be awarded according to the amount and quality of work performed. Thus, once the prevailing-wage clause was repealed, the Civil Service Commission should revise its testing procedures to allow department supervisors to participate in establishing criteria for jobs in their respective areas.

Until reforms like these are instituted, taxpayers (many of whom are also city workers) will fail to receive full value for their tax dollar. Worse yet, some civil servants will continue to be neither *civil* to, nor *servants* of, the public that pays their salaries.

19
The Oppenheimer case: A study in the abuse of law

Harold P. Green

Almost a quarter of a century after the event, the case of J. Robert Oppenheimer continues to attract the attention of both scholars and the general public. To many observers the Oppenheimer case represented the high point of the McCarthy sickness, or a kind of American Dreyfus case, in which the victim was "framed" to punish him for his beliefs. In any event, we now know as a result of recent disclosures that there were many abuses of human rights in the name of America's internal security. And it is useful to re-examine the Oppenheimer case in light of this new background. The basic facts can be briefly stated.

Oppenheimer—American-born, educated at Harvard, Cambridge, Gottigen, and Leyden—was a charismatic teacher who built a great school of theoretical physics at Berkeley. He also had wide-ranging political interests. In the latter 1930s and early 1940s some of the people with whom he had close family and social ties were communists or communist sympathizers. To make matters worse for him, as it turned out later, some of the people with whom he associated in those days were believed by security officers to be high officials of the Communist Party or Soviet espionage agents. (It should be stressed here, and kept in mind, that virtually all of the information concerning Oppenheimer's political associations had always been known to government security officials.)

Oppenheimer began full-time work on the atomic bomb project in May of 1942, and from November 1942 until November 1945 he served as director of the Los Alamos Scientific Laboratory. Widely hailed as the "father of the atomic bomb," he became chairman of the prestigious General Advisory Committee to the Atomic Energy Commission (a position he held until June 30, 1952) and director of the Institute for Advanced Study at Princeton. During the period 1946 to 1953 he served on numerous other government advisory committees and was generally recognized as one of the most influential consultants to government agencies concerned with atomic energy, scientific, defense, and international matters.

In January 1953, following the start of the Cold War, the collapse of Chiang Kai-shek's China, the invasion of South Korea and an election campaign based on charges that previous Administrations had been "soft on com-

From the *Bulletin of the Atomic Scientists* 33 (Sept. 1977) pp. 12-16, 56-61. Reprinted by permission of the Bulletin of the Atomic Scientists. Copyright (c) 1977 by the Educational Foundation for Nuclear Science.
Harold Green was formerly with the Office of the General Counsel, U.S. Atomic Energy Commission. He is now professor of law at George Washington University.

munism," the Eisenhower administration came to power. It set about developing a new security program designed to generate statistics on the large number of dangerous subversives allegedly brought into the government during the preceding 20 years of Democratic administrations.

On November 7, 1953, the day after Attorney General Herbert Brownell alleged in a Chicago speech that President Truman had promoted a known Soviet spy (Harry Dexter White) to high office, William Borden, who had recently resigned as executive director of the Joint Congressional Committee on Atomic Energy, dispatched a letter to FBI Director J. Edgar Hoover. Borden stated that in his view, "based upon years of study of the available classified evidence that, more probably than not, J. Robert Oppenheimer is an agent of the Soviet Union." Borden's letter reached the desk of President Eisenhower.

On December 3, 1953, although stating that he was not prejudging the case, Eisenhower directed that a "blank wall be placed between Dr. Oppenheimer and secret data," and that established procedures be followed. The AEC implemented this directive on December 23 by serving on Oppenheimer a letter advising him of the security charge against him, of the suspension of his security clearance, and of his right to a hearing on the charges. The charges against Oppenheimer included allegations that he had obstructed President Truman's decision, taken about four years earlier, to proceed with development of a hydrogen bomb.

The security hearing was held from April 12 through May 6, 1954, before a three-member board chaired by Gordon Gray, then president of the University of North Carolina. Gray had previously served in a variety of important government positions including Secretary of the Army. The other members were Thomas A. Morgan, an industrialist who two years before had retired as chairman of the board of the Sperry Corporation; and Ward V. Evans, a professor of chemistry at Loyola University in Chicago.

Following a lengthy hearing at which numerous eminent scientists, businessmen, and former and present prominent government officials testified, the Gray Board voted two-to-one (Evans dissenting) against restoration of Oppenheimer's clearance. Although the majority reached the "clear conclusion" that he was a "loyal citizen" who had "a high degree of discretion, reflecting an unusual ability to keep to himself vital secrets," they based their decision on findings that Oppenheimer's conduct reflected "a serious disregard for the requirements of the security system," that he had "a susceptibility to influence," that his conduct in the hydrogen bomb program was "disturbing," and that he was "less than candid" in his testimony.

Kenneth D. Nichols, the AEC's General Manager, recommended to the Commission that the Gray Board's findings and recommendation of May 27, 1954, be accepted, and the Commission on June 28, 1954, issued its four-to-one decision (Henry D. Smyth dissented) against restoration of Oppenheimer's clearance.

The Oppenheimer case generated great public controversy at the time, and over the years has been the subject of numerous books and articles. Most commentators have interpreted the case as a vendetta on the part of Lewis L. Strauss, then chairman of the AEC, or of military officials (generally the Air Force) against Oppenheimer on the basis of personality and/or policy clashes. The most recent assessment, by Jack Holl, one of the official historians of the atomic energy program was presented at the American Historical Association's general meeting in December 1975. This assessment is likely to be given considerable credence because of the professional status and integrity of the official historians and because the account is based on total, uninhibited access to AEC files.

In a nutshell, the Holl account disputes the view that the case originated in a Strauss vendetta against Oppenheimer. Rather, Borden's triggering letter to J. Edgar Hoover is seen by Holl as an attempt by Borden to vindicate his own record in security that had become tarnished because of John Wheeler's loss of a highly classified document in a sleeping car while en route by overnight train to a meeting with Borden at the Joint Committee on Atomic Energy early in 1953.

Wheeler, a Princeton physicist who was a consultant to the AEC on the thermonuclear program, was also employed by the Joint Committee to assist in preparation of a chronology of the hydrogen bomb program that Borden was pushing to complete in order to warn the incoming Eisenhower administration about the dangers of complacency. The lost document was related to this effort.

President Eisenhower, appalled that Borden had commissioned the condensation of so many thermonuclear secrets in this single document, demanded that the Joint Committee's staff be reorganized so that such a thing could not happen again. Borden's departure was a direct consequence of this demand.

In Holl's view, President Eisenhower overreacted with his "blank wall" directive to "demonstrate forceful leadership to a troubled inner circle," and the AEC made an "uncertain response to the President's directive" and was unable to negotiate a compromise with Oppenheimer. Neither the FBI nor the AEC was really concerned about Oppenheimer's loyalty, according to Holl. Thus, the case was a kind of blunder that no one wanted to initiate, that everyone wanted to terminate, and that no one knew how to stop gracefully.

Holl's version, like all of the others advanced to date, misses the mark by a wide margin. All of the various explanations of the Oppenheimer case to date have attempted to explain what happened in largely unitary terms. The true explanation, as I know it from my personal involvement, is much more complex and multi-faceted.

My role in the Oppenheimer case is well described in Philip Stern's book, *The Oppenheimer Case: Security on Trial*. I was responsible for drafting General Manager K. D. Nichol's letter to Oppenheimer notifying him of the security charges against him and advising him of the procedures that would be followed. I was, therefore, fully familiar with the security files pertaining to Oppenheimer. Thereafter, for a brief period of time, I participated in further aspects of the case.

My participation ended in early February 1954, when, for reasons of personal conscience, I asked to be relieved of any further responsibilities in the case. These same reasons of conscience led me, immediately upon reading the Gray Board decision, to notify the General Counsel that I would shortly resign. I submitted my resignation, effective six weeks later, immediately upon reading the Commission's final decision.

My knowledge about the Oppenheimer case comes not only from my direct involvement in it, but also as a consequence of my role for three years as counsel to the AEC's Division of Security and my close personal relationships then and since then with high AEC security officials.

Although I have wanted to tell what I know, a combination of factors has deterred me from doing so: a reluctance to embarrass some who have been good friends and some who were, in a sense, my clients, when I was an AEC lawyer; and my concern about pitting my story, largely unsupportable by documentary evidence available to me, against the inevitable stonewalling fury of J. Edgar Hoover.

I did undertake to tell the story when I entered into a collaboration with Philip Stern several years ago, but for various reasons the Stern book includes only a small portion of the relevant information.

Now, however, Watergate and its aftermath have freed me of my inhibitions, and I regard it as important that my personal knowledge and recollection become part of the record. As I do not wish to repeat much of what has already been written and is generally known by interested persons, I shall limit the discussion here to a number of events and forces that contributed to the Oppenheimer tragedy.

Security Concepts

To begin with, one must take account of the ideological struggle over the concept of security. In the early months of the AEC's existence, the battle was between those who urged the "Caesar's wife" concept and those who urged the "whole man" concept.

"Caesar's wife" approach. In this view, security clearance was "a privilege and not a right." There were so many competent people seeking work in the program that the AEC did not have to take a chance on anyone with blemishing derogatory information in his security files. Thus, if there was any significant derogatory information at all that might be true, clearance should not be granted; and there was no need to waste time and money in trying to find out whether or not the information was true.

"Whole man" approach. In this view, it was unfair to those enmeshed in the security net and to the atomic energy program itself to deny security clearance merely on the basis of derogatory information without giving the individual an opportunity to set the record straight and without considering

favorable information that might outweigh the blemishes, as well as the importance of the individual to the nuclear program.

It was this view that prevailed, and the AEC security criteria and procedures promulgated in the late 1940s to codify this approach were widely hailed as the most liberal and equitable in the government. One consequence of the acceptance of the "whole man" concept was that Oppenheimer and others with blemished backgrounds were granted Q-clearance over the strong misgivings of "Caesar's wife" advocates such as J. Edgar Hoover and Lewis Strauss.

Executive Order 10450

In November 1952, Dwight Eisenhower was elected to the presidency on a platform that promised the rooting out of communists, subversives and security risks in government and the defense industry which, it was said, had been tolerated by the Roosevelt and Truman administrations. And one of Eisenhower's first actions was promulgation in April 1953 of Executive Order 10450 establishing a government-wide security program.

This order was inartfully drafted by new officials who knew only myth and not fact about the security problem. It was susceptible to interpretation, and was in fact widely interpreted, as requiring agencies to use the "Caesar's wife" approach, and to rid government service of any person concerning whom there was any derogatory information that was determined to be true.

Promulgation of Executive Order 10450 required drastic adjustments in most federal agencies, since only a few had previously subjected employees to security screening. The AEC, however, had had a security program, mandated under the Atomic Energy Act of 1946, since its very inception. As a result of an exchange of correspondence and a conference between the AEC and the Department of Justice, Deputy Attorney General William P. Rogers wrote the AEC on June 8, 1953 that, since the AEC's preexisting security program "exceeds the minimum standards of Executive Order 10450," the Executive Order "requires no change" in the AEC's program.

It will be observed, nevertheless, that the AEC initiated the proceeding against Oppenheimer under *both its own security program and Executive Order 10450*. Although the procedures followed were essentially its own, the AEC measured the significance of the derogatory information on Oppenheimer at least as much under the Executive Order's criteria as the AEC's own criteria. Thus, once it was established that substantial derogatory information about Oppenheimer was true, it followed under the "Caesar's wife" interpretation of the Eisenhower Order that clearance was to be denied. Under the AEC's own standards, on the other hand, the derogatory information would have had to be balanced against favorable information.

When the Eisenhower administration took office, Lewis Strauss served on the White House staff as the President's special assistant for atomic energy. It was widely expected, moreover, that he would be appointed AEC chairman upon the expiration of Gordon Dean's term on June 30, 1953.

In private life, Strauss had been a Wall Street investment banker. A close associate of Herbert Hoover, his political sympathies lay with the conservative wing of the Republican Party. He had been an original member of the AEC when it was established in 1946, and was known as a security zealot of the "Caesar's wife" school. Strauss' return to the atomic energy scene not surprisingly sent shock waves through those parts of the AEC concerned with security.

As security cases crossed my desk, I could see obvious indications of a changing order in the fact that security issues, which always had been dealt with in a tough (but fair) manner, were now being scrutinized under unarticulated tougher standards with less concern for fairness. I found, for example, that a high official in the general manager's office was pressing to deny clearance because the individual in question was represented at the security hearing without fee by a house counsel of a "communist organization," that is, a staff attorney for the American Civil Liberties Union.

Operating through loyalists in the AEC's security apparatus, Strauss began compiling dossiers on the attitudes of key personnel toward security. I was, for example, asked to provide information as to the attitudes of my colleagues in the general counsel's office. More importantly, word coming from the White House was that Strauss would settle old scores and would, in particular, reopen long closed security cases about which he had concern when he had been a commissioner from 1947 to 1950.

When Strauss assumed the chairmanship of the Commission in July 1953, I began to see old security files, long closed, on the desks of the general counsel and other high commission officials. Without exception, these were files of security cases of important individuals that had been decided in favor of clearance, but with some misgivings or controversy, during Strauss' previous incumbency as a commissioner.

In addition, I soon learned from AEC security officials (some of whom were notorious gossips), who received their information from FBI sources, that Strauss had made a promise to J. Edgar Hoover to purge the Commission of several persons who were bones in Hoover's throat. One of these was Oppenheimer, who was anathema to Hoover because of his former left-wing affiliations and what Hoover regarded as moral and character deficiencies, particularly in that Oppenheimer had told contradictory stories at different times to security officers and FBI agents about whether or not his friend Haakon Chevalier had approached him in 1943 for information about the atomic bomb project on behalf of a Russian agent.

Another Hoover target, curiously, was a high official in the AEC security program whom Hoover had once fired from the FBI and, therefore, detested.

Purging Methods

Strauss proceeded with consummate artistry to effect the desired purges. It was not his style to fire people. Instead, he used his contacts in industry, foundations, and educational institutions to produce career opportunities that the objects of his purges could not turn down.

It was somewhat more difficult in the case of the security official who was to be eliminated. Strauss told this man that he was concerned that his loyalty to Strauss through the years would leave him exposed to Strauss' enemies when his term as chairman came to an end. Therefore, Strauss was actively seeking employment opportunities for his devoted friend.

A succession of attractive job opportunities were presented, but the security official rejected each one because he really wanted to keep his government position. He knew though that he was really being forced out. Finally, Strauss was forced to tell him that this was it: either he accepted the offered position or he would be dismissed. He accepted and departed with lavish tributes from Strauss for his loyalty and devotion.

This episode is by no means unique. It was the usual Strauss *modus operandi* for getting rid of people he did not want or like and, indeed, for persuading colleagues to do as he wished.

Strauss' greatest weakness in the earlier portion of his chairmanship, including the entire period of the Oppenheimer case, was his almost paranoid distrust of the regular AEC staff, particularly with respect to security questions, and his tendency to rely primarily on his personal staff and a few others. A major figure in the inner circle was Charles Bates, a special agent of the FBI who was the FBI's liaison with the atomic energy program.

Bates was an able but shadowy figure who spent a portion of every day at the AEC's premises moving from one security office to another and with uninhibited access to the offices of the commissioners and the general manager. He came to pass on information, complaints, advice, and words of wisdom from Hoover. His activities were behind the scenes and off the record. Most of the sensitive communications between the AEC and the FBI were made orally through Bates, so there is no written record for the official historians to tap.

If Strauss used the velvet glove in dealing with personnel, the same was not true of General Manager K. D. Nichols. On several occasions I was summoned to the general manager's office, handed security files, and told "see what you can do with this one." This meant that a decision had been made that the individual in question must be purged, and it was my task to draft a statement of security charges that could be used as persuasion.

This was fairly simple to do, since there were very few files that did not contain some data that could be used as the basis for a security action, such as slowness in paying bills, an episode of intoxication, or an informant's interpretation of the individual's behavior as odd. The scenario was to confront the individual with the charges informally in the hope that he would offer to resign rather than fight. The ploy was almost always successful. This was, of course, essentially what was tried with Oppenheimer, but it did not produce the desired result.

The victims of this technique included a high-ranking AEC official who had served in important management positions since the days of the Manhattan Project, and a lesser official who has since become a prominent political figure. No one could rationally regard these people as security risks, but the security charges were used as leverage to force them out.

Strauss had some difficulties in making good on his promise to Hoover to get rid of Oppenheimer. At the time he became chairman, there were three incumbent commissioners—Thomas E. Murray (a prominent Catholic layman and former idustrialist), Eugene M. Zuckert (a lawyer with 15 years' experience in a variety of government positions), and Henry D. Smyth (a Princeton physicist)—who had been appointed by President Truman, and were, in general, sympathetic with the past AEC security policies.

Shortly after his arrival as chairman, Strauss convened an extraordinary assembly of all AEC personnel to introduce the newly appointed fifth commissioner, Joseph Campbell (an accountant and former vice-president of Columbia University). And Strauss made it clear to those assembled that President Eisenhower had nominated Campbell at Strauss' request. No one had any doubt that Campbell would be a Strauss ally. Still, Strauss could be outvoted three to two.

As Agency Head

Up until Strauss' appointment, the chairman had been regarded as the "first among equals" and as the AEC's official spokesman, with no rights or powers greater than those of the other commissioners. But from the moment of his arrival on the scene, Strauss began maneuvering to establish himself as the "agency head" with power to make unilateral decisions on important and sensitive matters. In this maneuvering, he used as leverage his continuing position as a special assistant to the President, which gave him access to White House information pertaining to the atomic energy program—information, he said, he was duty bound to keep from his fellow commissioners in order to preserve the confidentiality of presidential discussions.

Within a few weeks, there commenced a barrage of memoranda from the chairman's office to the AEC general counsel, William Mitchell, seeking to nibble away at the established AEC structure and particularly at the procedures used in security cases.

Mitchell's Opinion Memo

The most dramatic was a memorandum from Strauss personally asking for confirmation of his opinion that since, under the Eisenhower Security Order, each "head of agency" had a duty to make security clearance determinations, he, as chairman, was the head of the agency and had personal authority and responsibility independent of the other commissioners to revoke and deny security clearance. It so happened that, beyond any doubt whatsoever, Strauss' opinion was dead wrong, and the general counsel so informed Strauss in a reply memorandum setting forth the legal bases for his conclusion.

On January 18, 1954, Strauss then wrote Attorney General Brownell

requesting his opinion on precisely the same question. The timing is significant, since this was the period (within a month after initiation of the proceeding against Oppenheimer) during which the commission was considering
procedures for handling that case. To my personal knowledge, the letter to
Brownell was written following discussions between Strauss and Hoover, via
Special Agent Bates.

Strauss and Hoover were concerned that, if the final Oppenheimer decision were to be made by the full commission, the three holdover commissioners would vote for continuation of Oppenheimer's clearance. Therefore, to
ensure Oppenheimer's ouster, it was necessary that the AEC General Counsel's
opinion be overruled so that Strauss personally and solely would decide the
matter. Bates informed Strauss that Hoover discussed the matter with Brownell. Hoover had received a commitment from Brownell that he would—if
Strauss sought his opinion—give Strauss the legal opinion he wanted that
would establish Strauss, contrary to Mitchell's opinion, as agency head with
sole responsibility and authority for making security clearance decisions.

Remarkably, Strauss did not inform Mitchell that he was going over his
head to the Attorney General. Nor did Strauss forward to the Attorney General
a copy of Mitchell's opinion memorandum on the question. I became aware of
the situation through my Security Division clients and informed Mitchell that
Strauss had requested the Attorney General's opinion. Mitchell was visibly
shaken, shrugged his shoulders and said, "Well, if that's what the chairman
wants to do, there's nothing I can do about it." In actuality, Brownell could not
and did not deliver.

In a reply to Strauss dated January 29, 1954, Deputy Attorney General
Rogers avoided coming to grips with the question, pointing out that the
chairman of a commission "is generally considered to be the head of that
agency unless the full . . . commission affirmatively votes to limit the power of
its Chairman." Even this unhelpful reply was tempered to avoid torpedoing the
Strauss objective, since Rogers could and should have told Strauss that the
statute on which the Executive Order was based contained language explicitly
inserted to make it clear that the chairman of the AEC had no authority to act
independently of the full Commission.*

Strauss never really understood the relationship of Executive Order
10450 to the AEC's security program. In 1954, the Eisenhower administration
was engaged in its infamous "numbers game" to generate statistics showing
that thousands of federal employees inherited from the previous administra-

---

*Executive Order 10450 was based on Public Law 81-733 enacted in 1950 which authorized
certain agency heads summarily to suspend employees as security risks. The agency heads given
this authority were all listed as individuals (for example, the Secretary of the Army, the Chairman
of the National Security Resources Board, etc.), except that in the case of the AEC the authority
was given to "the Atomic Energy Commission."

In an earlier version of the bill, the authority would have been given to the "Chairman of the
Atomic Energy Commission," but this was changed for the explicitly stated reason that the
chairman possessed no authority independent of the full commission.

tion were being discharged as security risks under the Executive Order. When, as part of this effort, the AEC had to respond to a Civil Service Commission questionnaire, Strauss repeatedly refused to sign the transmittal letter because the reply form showed that only one employee (Oppenheimer) had been suspended on security grounds since the Executive Order became effective. Strauss sent the papers back to the Director of Security with a note saying, "John, are we really this good?" And he demanded that the numbers be beefed up.

What Strauss failed to recognize was that, unlike other agencies, the AEC always had a security program at least as stringent as that prescribed under Executive Order 10450. Thus, since security risks had already been screened out, obviously there would be occasion to take security action against only a very few, if any, incumbent employees who had previously been investigated and cleared.

In this connection, Strauss' published memoirs contain an illuminating passage. In describing the White House meeting on December 3, 1953 at which Eisenhower issued his "blank wall" directive, Strauss reports that the President asked whether the AEC had conducted a hearing on the charges against Oppenheimer as required by the Executive Order.

Strauss replied "that there had been no hearing since the order was promulgated, but that the AEC was engaged in applying the directive to all employees," including consultants such as Oppenheimer. Strauss' statement was totally untrue since, in reliance on Deputy Attorney General Rogers' letter of June 8, 1953, the AEC regarded the Executive Order as totally inapplicable to its security program and had taken no action whatsoever to implement the order.

I do not know what prompted William Borden to write the letter to Hoover that initiated the case. It was, however, a culmination of a long concern about Oppenheimer's loyalty and trustworthiness. And it came as no surprise that someone pulled the trigger to fire the shot I had expected ever since I learned that Strauss had promised Hoover that he would purge Oppenheimer.

The fact that Oppenheimer was the subject of long-standing security interest is vividly disclosed in the dissenting opinion of Commissioner Henry Smyth telling us that "for much of the last 11 years [that is, since 1943] he has been under actual surveillance, his movements watched, his conversations noted, his mail and telephone calls checked." This surveillance, obviously would have been under the aegis of the FBI, at least from 1946 on.

That Oppenheimer was a target is also demonstrated by certain events, not previously disclosed, concerning the perjury prosecution of Joseph Weinberg (the so-called "Scientist X") in 1952.

Weinberg episode. A former student of Oppenheimer's at Berkeley, Weinberg was employed at the Radiation Laboratory and was believed by the FBI to have been a communist and to have been involved in Soviet espionage. He was indicted for perjuring himself in denying that he had attended a closed meeting of the Communist Party in Oppenheimer's Berkeley home in 1941.

In 1952, a week or so before the Weinberg trial was to begin, a security official of the AEC and I were called to attend a meeting in the Criminal Division of the Department of Justice. We were informed that Oppenheimer would be called as a witness in the Weinberg trial, that it was expected that he would perjure himself in denying that such a meeting had been held at his home, and that the Department of Justice would attempt to impeach his credibility and perhaps indict him for perjury. We were asked to inform the Commission in order that it could prepare for the public relations and political impact.

At the trial, it was clear that the prosecutor, Assistant United States Attorney William Hitz, was thinking more about Oppenheimer than Weinberg. At one time during the trial, in a context totally unrelated to Oppenheimer, he referred to Weinberg as "Dr. Oppenheimer." Precipitously, however, Hitz rested his case without getting into areas involving Oppenheimer.

Every lawyer in the courtroom recognized, when Hitz rested his case, that there had to be an acquittal, even without defense testimony, since the perjury case simply had not been made. It is my belief, based entirely on circumstantial considerations, that President Truman ordered the Attorney General to order Hitz to refrain from introducing the Oppenheimer-related evidence that would have been necessary to convict Weinberg.

Although Dr. Holl stated in his 1975 paper (citing Chairman Gordon Dean's diary) that from the outset AEC officials knew that there was no substance to the allegations implicating Oppenheimer, this is not accurate. Oppenheimer's defense (that is, the evidence placing him at a distant location on the day in question) was known to AEC officials, but they also knew of impressive evidence to the contrary.

In any event, the brush with political disaster in the Weinberg case led to Oppenheimer's departure from the General Advisory Committee and to the beginning of a gradual winding down in Oppenheimer's access to atomic energy secrets.

Role of FBI. In assessing the origins of the Oppenheimer case, it is relevant to consider some events that transpired after the case was initiated. The most important of these was the role of the FBI.

In my personal involvement with hundreds of AEC personnel security cases, I had never encountered one in which the FBI played an affirmatively cooperative role. In Hoover's view, the FBI's role ended when it delivered its investigative reports to the AEC, and requests for additional information were invariably met with, at best, grudging compliance. When, however, I was drafting the charges against Oppenheimer, I found myself the recipient of a telephone call from an FBI official urging that I call upon the Bureau for any assistance or further information I might need.

Once the charges were handed to Oppenheimer he was kept under particularly close FBI surveillance. Holl stated in his paper that Hoover, although "careful not to reveal the source of his information, ... kept the

Commission posted on Oppenheimer's search for legal counsel and other matters pertaining to the case."

In January 1954, I personally saw an FBI report that unmistakably was based upon electronic surveillance of the offices of attorneys whom the FBI correctly assumed Oppenheimer would consult immediately upon being informed of the charges against him. This FBI report undoubtedly crossed my desk by mistake. It was the kind of document that was to be destroyed after reading or kept in special files with sharply limited access to preclude its becoming a part of history, current or otherwise.

Moreover, a horde of FBI agents was at AEC attorney Roger Robb's disposal during the hearing itself to check out witnesses, run down new information, etc., just as if it were a criminal prosecution. As a matter of fact, throughout the hearing, Robb was the beneficiary of instant reports on the most intimate conversations among Oppenheimer and his counsel. Indeed, the AEC prosecutors and FBI aides joined in a victory dinner at the Chevy Chase Country Club when the Gray Board announced its decision. This FBI involvement would not have been possible in the absence of outright zeal by Hoover to "get" Oppenheimer.

Abnormal Procedures

I agree with Holl's opinion that the Oppenheimer case cannot properly be explained as a Strauss vendetta against Oppenheimer. Although Strauss promised Hoover that he would purge Oppenheimer, my own view is that Strauss wanted and intended to accomplish this more gently and with subtlety. The Strauss scenario was, however, interrupted by Eisenhower's "blank wall" directive. The commissioners, the general manager, and the general counsel—none of whom had any particular knowledge of or experience with the commission's security procedures—reached the conclusion, unguided by the security professionals, that the President's directive required the initiation of a formal security proceeding against Oppenheimer.

Once this decision was made, as Holl notes, both the commission and Oppenheimer were locked into the formal proceeding with no feasible way to compromise or make a graceful exit.

More importantly, however, once the decision was made, the situation evolved into a savage prosecution. Hoover was determined that this time Oppenheimer would not emerge with his credibility and reputation intact, and the Administration was determined to exact the pound of flesh demanded by Executive Order 10450. Moreover, the case was seen in political terms as another opportunity to demonstrate that the previous Democratic administrations were harboring dangerous subversives.

In the discussion period following Holl's presentation at the December 1975 meeting of the American Historical Association, he disclosed the following previously unreported bit of history. During the final days of the AEC's consideration of the case, Strauss informed President Eisenhower of his concern that Commissioners Smyth, Zuckert, and Murray would vote to restore Oppenheimer's clearance. According to Strauss' memorandum of this conversation, the President urged him to use all his efforts to bring these commissioners around. A few days after the commission's decision, Eisenhower wrote Strauss congratulating him on the result.

Never before had an AEC security proceeding been launched with the predetermined objective of establishing that the individual concerned was a security risk. Indeed, in the past it could fairly be said that the AEC security hearings were intended primarily as a vehicle for clearing the individuals involved. However, in this case there was a special prosecutor, Roger Robb, renowned for his ability as a cross-examiner. Of more significance, perhaps, the case was taken entirely out of the hands of the AEC's Division of Security. Only one member of the AEC's security staff was directly involved in the case — C. Arthur Rolander, deputy director of the Security Division, who had had virtually no prior experience in the personnel security program. Rolander was, however, completey detached from his regular duties to work with Robb.

The personnel security professionals, although they had some concern about Oppenheimer's background, were generally of the view that he was not a security risk. Moreover, schooled in the tradition that a security hearing was "an inquiry and not a trial," they would not be temperamentally suited to play a prosecutorial role.

Teller's testimony. One illustration of the role of Robb related to the testimony of Edward Teller. A number of the charges against Oppenheimer were taken from a statement given to the FBI by Teller. When he testified (under oath) before the Gray Board, Teller's testimony was tame, bearing little relationship to what he told the FBI off the record.

Inexplicably, Robb was willing to accept this watering down of his case. If he were interested in establishing the truth, however that might cut, as was his obligation under both the AEC's procedures and Executive Order 10450, he should have attempted to impeach Teller's credibility. Alternatively, if his objective was to make the case against Oppenheimer as effectively as possible, Robb should have pressed Teller to repeat under oath his earlier allegations.

More importantly, the Gray Board itself, which had before it Teller's statements to the FBI, was apparently not interested in ascertaining why Teller had so changed his opinions.

Gray Board. Another matter of interest was the selection of the Gray Board. When it became clear in mid-January that Oppenheimer would demand a hearing, William Mitchell, the general counsel, was assigned the task of recruiting a three-member Personnel Security Board.

When he sought my views, I urged that the board be selected from among those persons with substantial previous experience on AEC Personnel Security Boards. Each AEC office maintained a panel, consisting principally of prominent local residents, from which these board members were drawn on an ad hoc basis. Some of these boards had impressed me with their ability, fairness, and toughness, and I urged that a board be chosen from the Chicago Operations Office panel, which had handled several very difficult cases in a particularly impressive manner.

Mitchell told me the commission rejected this idea because it thought that the members of the board should, in order to gain public acceptance of the decision, be of stature comparable to Oppenheimer's.

Mitchell traveled around the country seeking recruits. The first member signed on was Gordon Gray. The second was industrialist Thomas Morgan. Neither of them had had any previous involvement in AEC security cases. It was decided that the third member should be a scientist who had previously served on an AEC board. AEC security officials were asked to delve into old files to identify candidates and to form an estimate from the record as to the "softness" or "toughness" of each. After intensive compilation and analysis of attitudes and voting records, Ward V. Evans was chosen as the third member of the panel.

Evans had previously served as a member of Chicago boards, and I recognized him as one who was particularly "tough." Ironically, he dissented from the Gray Board's recommendation that Oppenheimer's clearance be revoked.

There was no question, as the Board was being recruited, that the AEC was looking for three members who would have a predisposition to find against Oppenheimer. Although pains were taken to maintain a facade of seeking members with a fair and judicious attitude, the major consideration was whether the candidate would shrink from revoking Oppenheimer's clearance. My knowledge that a "hanging jury" was being chosen was one of the reasons that I asked to be relieved of any further role in the case.

To reinforce the board's assumed predisposition, the board was brought to Washington a week before the hearing commenced for indoctrination by Rolander and Robb. Not only were they given an outline of the derogatory information against Oppenheimer; but, more critically, they were given indoctrination into the letter, spirit, and meaning of the AEC and Executive Order 10450 security criteria and procedures. This was, in a sense, "the blind leading the blind," since neither Robb nor Rolander had any real comprehension of what was involved or of the traditions of the AEC personnel security program.

It was clear to me at the time that the board was being authoritatively, but incorrectly, told by Rolander and Robb that the AEC's security program was based on a kind of "Caesar's wife" principle.

In fact, the Gray Board opinion on its face shows that it did not understand the AEC procedures. For example, despite the clear mandate of the AEC's procedures that the Board act as "practical men of affairs ... guided by the same considerations that would guide them in making a sound decision in the administration of their own lives" on the basis of an "overall, commonsense judgment" taking into account all relevant information, favorable or unfavorable, the Gray Board asserted that it might have been able to find in favor of Oppenheimer "if we were allowed to exercise mature practical judgment."

Mythology of security. Perhaps the most striking aspect of the Oppenheimer case is the fact that, on the government's side, every action that was taken was by persons who were not actually involved in and knowledgeable about personnel security matters.

These included the President, the Attorney General, the five AEC commissioners (who only rarely were exposed to particular security cases), the AEC general counsel, Robb and Rolander, and two of the three members of the Gray Board. Even General Nichols, the AEC's general manager, had very little contact with security cases, since the general manager's authority in these cases had been delegated to a subordinate.

One consequence of this was that decisions in the case were made more on the basis of a mythology of security than on the basis of any genuine principle.

Transcript released. On June 15, 1954, the 992-page printed transcript of the entire Oppenheimer hearing was released to the press. This was two weeks prior to the commission's final decision in the case and violated the assurance given to each of the 40 witnesses that the proceedings were to be treated as confidential and that the AEC would not initiate any public release.

In his *Men and Decisions*, Strauss states that the commission printed and released the transcript because a member of the commission had lost "a portion of his transcript" on a train; in fact, it was a digest of portions of the transcript. According to Strauss, it was this event that led the commission to "make a general release in advance of a possible unofficial publication" of the lost document. Strauss also stated that consent of all witnesses to such publication was obtained.

The Strauss version is inaccurate. The fact is that publication of the transcript was first considered at a meeting of the commission on June 7, four days prior to loss of the document, although the decision to send the transcript to the public printer was not made until June 12. Actual release of the transcript was authorized at a commission meeting on June 14, a full day after the lost document had been found and returned to AEC.

On June 14 and 15, after the decision to release the transcript was made, Nichols, Mitchell and Rolander worked around the clock to contact all 40 witnesses, not for the purpose of obtaining their consent but only to inform them of the AEC's decision.

The fact of the matter is that an electronic bug had picked up a conversation among Oppenheimer's attorneys to the effect that publication of the transcript would have a devastating effect on Oppenheimer's image. This suggested to Strauss that the transcript *should* be published to bring Smyth, Zuckert and Murray into line. Zuckert's loss of the document was nothing more than a convenient excuse for Strauss to use to force publication.

Lieutenant General Leslie R. Groves had served in the United States Army from 1916 to 1948, and during World War II he directed the atomic bomb project. In his testimony before the Gray Board he stated, in response to a question by Roger Robb, that "The Army as a whole didn't deal with matters of security until after the atomic bomb burst on the world because it was the first time that the Army really knew there was such a thing."

True, the Army always had a security program. But Groves' point was that through the World War II era security judgments rested primarily upon the informal appraisal by superior personnel of their personal confidence in their subordinates. It was not until the mid to latter 1940s, when many Americans came to fear a communist threat to internal security, that a security program was created involving rigid requirements for investigation, appraisal of trustworthiness against written criteria, and determinations of eligibility for clearance in formal proceedings that had many trappings of the judicial process.

The Oppenheimer case arose within the first decade of this new demijurisprudence.

There were few individuals knowledgeable or expert in the field. There were no established traditions.

There were no publicly available precedents on which to rely for guidance. And there were no judicial expositions of relevant constitutional principle.

This demi-jurisprudence was administered by officials motivated by an amalgam of patriotism, xenophobia, rigid morality, fear of conspiracy, self righteousness, and a desire to survive in the bureaucratic jungle. In the absence of any established procedures for judicial review, compounded by the initial reluctance of the federal judiciary to become involved, the law of security was what these officials said it was. Countless thousands of good Americans, Oppenheimer among them, were hounded from their jobs by these officials for the sake of protecting the nation against a handful who might, in fact, be dangerous.

One is tempted in the post-Watergate climate to characterize the Oppenheimer case in terms of "abuse of power." In my view, it was more an "abuse of law"—the invention and application of a body of law that, in fact, had very little claim to existence except in the minds of its ministers.

I have little doubt that Hoover, Strauss, Robb, Gray, and others did, with respect to Oppenheimer, precisely what they sincerely believed the law (perhaps aided by a higher morality) required them to do. Eisenhower and Strauss, for example, were undoubtedly of the view from the very outset that the law required a hearing to give legal blessing to the final revocation of Oppenheimer's clearance which, they believed, was inexorably mandated by law.

Other factors, such as personal animus and Republican politics, although obviously present, were incidental rather than motivating factors.

The abuse of law that was the essence of the Oppenheimer case was rectified within the next decade as the courts stepped in to bring the demijurisprudence of security into consonance with the requirements of due process. The costs of the abuse, in human misery and disruption of government function, were incalculably enormous.

Viewed as abuse of law, the Oppenheimer case has much in common with the Watergate affair. Hopefully, we have learned more from the latter than we did from the former.

20
The New Face Of
The Peace Corps
Chris Kenrick

When Detroit Peace Corps recruiter Julia Meck makes the rounds of college campuses these days, she doesn't avoid the humanities majors as she used to.

In the recent past, Miss Meck said, there were very few slots available for generalists in a Peace Corps determined to recruit the technically skilled.

Today, although she still has nothing specific to offer the hundreds of eager humanities graduates she encounters each year, Miss Meck cautiously tells them there may be some jobs by next summer. The Peace Corps, she explains, has a new director who is trying once again to make room for the "B.A. generalist."

If the new group in charge in Washington gets its way, the Peace Corps of the Jimmy Carter era will become bigger, less professionally oriented, more visible to the American public, and more expansive in its image—in sharp contrast to the organization that in the past decade shrunk to nearly one-third its former size and came to stress "professionalization" over the once-prominent notion of the idealistic—if unskilled—volunteer.

The Peace Corps will continue aggressively to seek individuals skilled in agronomy, plumbing, or medicine who want to devote two years of their lives to serve as low-paid international development workers. But recruiters say such volunteers are increasingly difficult to find.

Available new recruits are more likely to be recent liberal arts graduates who are willing to be trained in prawn culture, grain storage, or nutrition, or for service as math or science teachers in Africa, animal husbandry technicians in Latin America, or reforestation workers in Sahel.

If Peace Corps officials in Washington have big plans for the B.A. generalist, the 62 developing countries that currently play host to some 6,000 Peace Corps volunteers seem to have other things in mind. As these countries make their own economic and technological progress, many of them have begun to request from the Peace Corps fewer generalists and more specially skilled volunteers.

From *The Christian Science Monitor*, November 14, 1977. Reprinted by permission from *The Christian Science Monitor.* © 1977 The Christian Science Publishing Society. All rights reserved. Chris Kenrick is a staff correspondent of *The Christian Science Monitor.*

Peace Corps placement director Woody Jewett admits a recent study indicated that trends in host country requests for volunteers "appear to be continuing toward the more difficult to find volunteer."

At a time when the developing world is crying out for technicians, why is the Peace Corps talking about expanding its ranks of generalists? Much of the answer lies with Sam Brown, the antiwar leader turned bureaucrat who heads Peace Corps' parent agency, ACTION, and who passionately believes that "people can matter more than mere skills."

An Iowa boy educated at a small California college and Harvard Divinity School, Samuel Winfred Brown Jr. first came to Washington in the late 1960s with a handful of students to try to end the Vietnam war. By late 1969, his genius for organizing had made him a symbol of the national youth movement. In the words of one columnist, he ruled it "like a ward boss."

About the same time, Mr. Brown was called in briefly as a consultant to the Peace Corps. In those days, he said, he regarded the corps as "the sheep's clothing on American adventurism abroad."

In 1970 Mr. Brown moved to Colorado, where he served as state treasurer before being called to Washington by Jimmy Carter last February.

Second in command at ACTION is Mary King, a member of Mr. Carter's inner circle during the campaign who regards her background of civil rights and liberal political activism as "just applied Christianity."

The new Peace Corps director, appointed in September, is Carolyn Payton, a Howard University psychologist with experience as an overseas Peace Corps administrator during the '60s.

Eagerness to revamp

Seasoned in liberal Democratic politics, the new team seems eager to revamp the image of the Peace Corps as a scaled-down technocrat corps decreed during the Nixon and Ford administrations.

Mr. Brown talks of expanding the corps to 10,000 volunteers by 1980.

He talks of a new, concerted effort to assign Peace Corps volunteers to address "basic human needs" at the village level rather than working in government ministries or catering to an urban elite of a developing country.

And he talks of once again trying to capitalize on the enthusiasm of the B.A. generalist volunteer who may be less skilled but is often considered more adaptable and persevering than the technically trained professional when confronted with a difficult assignment.

Sam Brown is convinced that the B.A. generalist can help revive the Peace Corps in both numbers and spirit. He envisions restructured training programs to allow the generalist recruit to come in without any particular knowledge and by the end of 12 weeks be thoroughly trained in a narrow but practical technique such as rice growing, immunization, or fish culture.

Mr. Brown admitted that when he came to Washington last winter he was "prejudiced and skeptical" about the type of volunteer who might have been drawn to the Peace Corps during the Nixon and Ford years.

Volunteers are older

"But I was 180 degrees wrong," he said. "It turned out that those people who volunteered during the years of public cynicism were a remarkable bunch—enthused, committed, and very caring—perhaps more so than their earlier counterparts."

Mr. Brown credits Nixon appointees with bringing more older volunteers into the Peace Corps—the average volunteer age has risen from 24.5 to 27.6 and some 5 percent of the current volunteers are over 50.

But he has few kind words for other policies of recent Republican administrators.

The Nixon-era trend of emphasizing skilled volunteers with advanced degrees, Mr. Brown said in a recent interview, "began to shut out many applicants with commitment and dedication who might not have had PhDs or MDs.

The development philosophy reflected in Republican management of the corps—stressing aid at the higher levels of a society with the hope that it would trickle down—"is precisely what the Peace Corps shouldn't stand for," he said.

The number of volunteers shrank from a high of 15,000 in 1966 to some 6,000 ten years later. The agency's budget, in constant 1972 dollars, dropped from $148.6 million in 1966 to $56.6 million in 1977.

In 1971, the Peace Corps was merged with existing U.S. domestic volunteer programs such as VISTA to form the umbrella agency ACTION.

No director for five years

Mr. Brown maintains that attempts by President Nixon to stifle the Peace Corps were deliberate and nearly successful. Advertising, he said, obscured the roles of Peace Corps, VISTA, and ACTION. Peace Corps employees were forbidden to answer the telephone "Peace Corps." The position of Peace Corps director technically was left vacant for five years, he said.

Mr. Brown says he would like to mold a new organization that is in better tune with the committed, humanitarian spirit of the volunteers, whom he considers "the saving grace of the Peace Corps." But he is careful to distinguish his vision of the agency from the sweeping utopianism of the early, Kennedy-era corps. He seems careful to avoid the word "idealistic."

"The Peace Corps is tougher in some ways now than it used to be," says Mr. Brown. "It has much more to do with what the host countries are like. Ten or 15 years ago they were likely to be just coming out of a colonial heritage, the governments were just getting on their feet, and the infrastructures were weak.

"But we've been through a lot since then and the countries are different now. They have a much firmer sense of their identities and agendas. Fifteen years ago we thought we knew more than we think we know now.

"We can no longer go in idealistically ... but we have to go in with professionalism, understanding the third world's real needs and not its needs as we perceive them."

Because the host countries recently have come to expect more—not fewer—skilled professional volunteers, the Peace Corps administration currently is negotiating with them to promote the "trained generalist" approach.

"A host country might say, 'We need ten physicians to set up an intensive care unit in our capital city,'" Miss King explained. "We talk with the minister of health about things like how many people an intensive care unit would really serve, how they would maintain the expensive machinery, and what they would do when it broke down.

"The minister is likely to end up saying that really his country's greatest health needs are among the poorest villagers where trained paramedics could help.

"It's in the village that the Peace Corps can have its greatest impact," Miss King says. "And that impact is potentially of the greatest consequence for the U.S. emerging in a world order based on humanitarianism rather than on power considerations."

Peace Corps director Carolyn Payton thinks generalists tend to make more "altruistic" volunteers and that such recruits can be placed in remote locations "where trained personnel or even host country nationals won't go."

In a 1976 survey, she says, the altruistic volunteer was found to get the best ratings in job satisfaction, effectiveness, social relationships, and morale.

The new trained generalist direction of the Peace Corps is not without its skeptics and critics, however.

Says recruiter Julia Meck: "As a former volunteer in West Africa, I have some philosophical problems with Sam Brown saying, 'This is what we're going to do' without knowing whether the host countries really want it."

"There's a certain amount of salesmanship [to the host countries] involved," admits New England recruiter Alan Wernicke.

Perhaps the harshest critic of the return to the Peace Corps generalist is Joseph Blatchford, now a Washington attorney, who headed the corps from 1969 to 1972 and instilled it with a more professional and skilled blue-collar image.

"It's American arrogance to expect these [host] countries to let us make their decisions on who we're going to send," Mr. Blatchford said. "The Peace Corps should be saying 'What do these countries need and how can we provide it?'

"I'm in favor of using people with social commitment, but if we're going to do this in great numbers we should first experiment with it in our own land. . . . We can't afford to let young people work out a period of their lives at the expense of these very poor countries."

Mr. Blatchford points to the Peace Corps attrition rate, which currently runs at 30 percent and in some programs reaches 50 percent.

"The fact is, Americans aren't particularly self-reliant, cutting the jungle on their own in a foreign land. There are a percentage of real pioneers and there should be room for them in the Peace Corps. But these people are rare."

Mr. Blatchford argues that the new Peace Corps administration is overly concerned with "the numbers game" and short on concern for quality.

Critics write book

His skepticism is aired by C. Payne Lucas, a former Peace Corps director in Africa, and Kevin Lowther, a mid-'60s volunteer, who have written a forthcoming book on the "unmet hope" of the Peace Corps.

In recent congressional testimony they charged that the Peace Corps, long "dominated by white middle-class volunteers ... has failed to accomplish much of any enduring consequences to its hosts."

The Peace Corps has largely failed to provide skilled help, they said, and only a small percentage of volunteers ever truly adapt to the cross-cultural aspects of their assignments. Mr. Lucas and Mr. Lowther prescribe more intensive training programs and a greater stress on cross-cultural readiness.

Although their new training programs are mostly still in the planning stages, Mr. Brown, Miss King, and Dr. Payton answer their critics with confidence.

They are convinced that their new breed of "highly trained but not necessarily highly certified" volunteers will be able to make an enormous difference in the poorest communities of the developing world. Equally stressed around Peace Corps headquarters these days is the need for volunteers to learn from their host countries.

In one recently begun program, volunteers are asked to make note of what they learn and what they improvise in the village to contribute to a growing storehouse of "appropriate technology" strategies being collected in Washington.

"We should be looking for a lot of small answers, not a few big ones," Sam Brown says.

PERSONALITY PROFILE

21
A Success on the Job, She Flunked the Test

William Raspberry

WASHINGTON—If our judicial system included a Court of Common Sense, Margaret Townsend would be an easy winner. As it is, only a lawyer could find any justice in what's happened to her.

Townsend, a black woman, went to work in the Nassau County (N.Y.) Medical Center blood bank back in 1965. Despite the fact that she possessed only a high-school diploma, she worked out very well indeed. A year and a half after she started, she was promoted, provisionally, to the position of senior laboratory technician.

Then, following a survey by a management consulting firm, Nassau County reclassified all its civil-service positions. Townsend was placed—again, provisionally,—in the new competitive position of medical technologist. She stayed there until 1973.

During that time, she was an exemplary employe, performing not only her technical duties but a variety of administrative ones as well. She became an assistant supervisor and, when the supervisor left, assumed the position of acting supervisor. Her responsibilities included teaching blood-banking techniques.

But the same reclassification that changed her job title also changed the entry requirements for her job. It was now necessary to have a bachelor of science degree and to pass an examination. Townsend had no degree, but under a "grandfather clause" in the new regulations she was permitted to take the exam for medical technologist I. She failed.

When that first examination produced an insufficient number of qualified applicants, it was given again. This time, however, the grandfather clause did not apply, and Townsend was not permitted to take it. The second exam did produce a sufficient list of eligibles, though, and Townsend was fired.

Three months later, she was rehired by the blood bank, this time as a lower-paid laboratory technician II, although her duties were precisely what they had been before.

She sued, making what apparently was the only claim available to her: that the requirement of a college degree, whose job-relatedness had not been demonstrated, amounted to racial discrimination. (Her lawers argued that because of the lower proportion of black college graduates in Nassau County and New York state, the requirement operated disproportionately against blacks.)

The U.S. Supreme Court, in an earlier case, had held that rules which have a discriminatory effect—whether the discrimination is intentional or not—are unlawful unless they are shown to be job-related.

The U.S. District Court of the Eastern District of New York bought Townsend's argument and ordered her restored, retroactive to the date of her dismissal. The decision was overturned by the 2nd Court of Appeals. Then, earlier this month, the U.S. Supreme Court refused to review the case.

The justices didn't give any reason for their refusal; they never do. Perhaps they bought the reasoning of the appelate court, which observed that "the adoption of a college-degree requirement cannot, merely because of the general racial composition of college graduates, be considered discriminatory."

Perhaps they were influenced by the fact that four blood-bank employes were caught in the trap that caught Townsend, and that the other three were white. In any case, if they found no evidence of discrimination, they were powerless, under the Constitution, to remedy what must have struck them as an obvious injustice.

If there were a Court of Common Sense, Townsend's lawyers would never have had to claim racial discrimination in the first place.

They would have pointed out that both the college-degree requirement and the written examination are nothing but convenient, if imperfect, devices for predicting who will be able to perform successfully on the job. As a general rule, they might have conceded, it may make sense to rely on such devices.

But in Townsend's case, they would have said, the best evidence of her ability to perform on the job was the fact that for 10 exemplary years she had performed successfully on the job.

22
Quotas and the San Francisco Police: A Sergeant's Dilemma
Anthony J. Balzer

The San Francisco Police Department (SFPD) has had more than its share of controversy and publicity recently between its involvement in the Zebra Case, the Patty Hearst-SLA Case, and the unprecedented police and fire strike of August 1975. But my concern in this article is with a somewhat less publicized controversy: the ongoing struggle to obtain court-ordered quotas of minority group members in SFPD hiring. Though perhaps less sensational than random street shootings and political kidnappings, quota hiring presents social and economic issues that directly affect most medium and large-sized employers today. Hence, I would like to share some of the SFPD's experiences with quota hiring, and present some of my own reactions to them.

The Setting and the Ruling

The SFPD's involvement with quota hiring began in April 1973 when Public Advocates, Inc. (a non-profit law firm funded by the Ford Foundation to litigate class action suits in the "public interest"), brought a civil rights suit in the U.S. District Court, Northern District of California, against the San Francisco Police Commission and the San Francisco Civil Service Commission.[1] The Court was asked to enjoin further use of the SFPD's entrance examination (consisting of multiple choice questions intended to measure the applicant's aptitude and intelligence) and the SFPD's promotional examinations for sergeant, lieutenant, and captain (consisting of multiple choice questions

Reprinted from *Public Administration Review*, May/June 1977. © 1977 by The American Society for Public Administration, 1225 Connecticut Avenue, N.W., Washington, D.C. All rights reserved. Anthony Balzer has been a member of the San Francisco Police Department since 1968.

intended to measure the applicant's ability to memorize a given body of materials felt relevant to the particular level in question). The Court was also asked to impose specific quotas of minority group members on all hiring at the entrance and promotional levels, and to monitor directly the construction and administration of any new examinations that might be proposed. The plaintiffs prevailed in both of their requests. On November 23, 1973, Judge Robert Peckham announced a preliminary decision prohibiting further use of the written tests for patrolman and sergeant. He also ordered specified quotas to be placed on all hiring at the patrolman and sergeant levels until a representative number of minority group members was attained. Because adequate data was not yet available, no quotas were ordered for the lieutenant or captain levels. And the Court retained direct supervision over the whole case.

On May 2, 1975, Judge Peckham modified his preliminary decision by abolishing the original quotas of ethnic minorities, and by ordering that an experimental quota of 60 women be hired as police officers at a ratio of 15 women per 60 member class of recruits. This modified decision was based on the new results produced by a newly developed entrance examination. And as this article is being written, the second group of 15 women officers is just completing recruit training and "hitting the streets."

The Parties and Their Interests

Just who are the parties behind this suit, and what are their reasons for bringing suit? Actually, neither of these questions is as simple as first impressions might suggest. Among the plaintiffs named in the suit are the Officers for Justice, the NAACP, the National Organization of Women, and others.[2] These plaintiffs, represented by Public Advocates, Inc. attorneys, seek to represent a class composed of:

... all those Blacks, Latins, and Asians ... and women who i) have failed either in entry-level or promotional examinations promulgated by the Civil Service Commission and the Police Commission for a position in the San Francisco Police Department and are fully qualified therefore, or ii) may become eligible to take such examinations to be given in the near future, or iii) have passed such examinations but have not yet been appointed to the position applied for, or v) have been eliminated from contention for the position of sworn officer by reasons of certain biased elements in the applicant screening procedures of the Civil Service Commission and the Police Commission or their delegates, or vi) will in the future be subjected to any of the discriminatory treatment alleged ... or vii) have in the past been dissuaded or discouraged from even attempting to join the department due to the discriminatory reputation of its selection standards, devices, and practices, or viii) have been discriminated against in assignments, choice of duty, or other incidents of employment, or ix) who as a result of the above detailed practices and their exclusionary effects are deprived of protection and safety in minority neighborhoods equal to that available in non-minority areas. (The numbering here is the Court's.)[3]

The plaintiffs' basic interest, therefore, was jobs. But how does this proposed class relate to the population of San Francisco as a whole? The Census
Bureau predicted that by 1975, 51 per cent of San Francisco's population
would be composed of ethnic minority group members.[4] The Census Bureau
definition of minorities does not include women (who are included in the
above litigation class) or the large group of homosexuals who reside in San
Francisco (whose inclusion in the above litigation class has been proposed).
But even without homosexuals, the minority groups now represented in the
above litigation class together constitute a clear numerical majority of San
Francisco's population today. Of course, the Court does not use the term
"minority group" in reference to the numerical strength of the groups in
question, but rather to the socioeconomic status of the groups members. And
in arbitrating disputes over what criteria define a minority group and who
should be considered members of those groups, the Court chose to rely on the
large, semi-autonomous Equal Employment Opportunities Commission
(EEOC), which operates through its own rule-making and adjudicative
machinery.

Meanwhile, as defendants in this case, the SFPD and the Civil Service
Commission found themselves in a dilemma when the Court issued its preliminary injunction and order (November 23, 1973). On one hand, they were
enjoined from using their old examination system to hire and promote; and
any new examinations developed to take their place would have to secure
Judge Peckham's approval, based on rigorous EEOC validation criteria. On the
other hand, the defendants were faced with a pressing need to hire new patrol
persons and to promote new sergeants. This lawsuit had caught the defendants
with their "empirical pants down." No comprehensive job analyses had been
completed within the SFPD; little conceptual work had been done to develop a
tangible model of what constitutes "good police work"; and no serious attempts had been made to validate existing civil service examinations by
modern empirical methods. This is not intended to disparage the SFPD or the
Civil Service Commission for not having done these things; their reasons are
both understandable and compelling.[5] But there should be no surprise that
these defendants were unable to demonstrate the validity of their written tests
within the eight months leading up to Judge Peckham's preliminary decision.
Only now is some of the necessary conceptual and empirical work being
completed.[6] And it seems likely that had this lawsuit *not* been filed, many of
the basic issues brought out in this case would still be festering beneath the
surface of conscious debate, building up to a considerably more violent form of
expression at some point in the future. When seen in this light, the Public
Advocates, Inc., suit is indeed in the public interest—we should face these
issues now.

From the outset, the parties comprising the defense in this case agreed to
endure necessary hardships and take necessary initiatives to preserve existing
screening standards. This agreement probably reflected some elements of
emotional conservatism, plain self-interest, and perhaps even racism. But these

elements are present to some degree in all of us. And many of the defendants could have benefited individually by merely "accepting" the Court's preliminary decision rather than actively questioning and opposing it. Even the San Francisco Police Officers' Association, a traditionally divided and bickering group, promptly unified and assessed each of its active members $50 to help defend this case. In short, a deliberate, unanimous commitment emerged to support at least *some* standards of merit in the screening of SFPD applications and promotions, even though the sought-after "merit" and "standards" would undoubtedly be tough to define, measure, and predict.

The Applicable Federal Law

The importance of developing adequate conceptual and empirical justification for whatever screening devices may be utilized is vividly brought home by a look at the emerging body of federal law related to job discrimination. Lt. Richard Treub, Officer in Charge of the SFPD Legal Office, has traced the development of this body of law from the passage of the Civil Rights Act of 1964 (particularly Title VII, which is addressed to discrimination by large private employers) through the signing by President Nixon in March 1973 of the "Affirmative Action Amendment," which extended this body of law to encompass job discrimination by federally funded public employers as well.[7] The logic of this law, as currently applied by federal courts, proceeds roughly as follows:[8] First, the aggrieved plaintiffs must demonstrate the "fact" of adverse discrimination in hiring or promotions based on their race, sex, or national origin. Such discrimination may be shown to operate either de jure (by law) or de facto (in fact). This then establishes a *prima facie* case for the plaintiffs, and a heavy burden of proof shifts onto the defendants to demonstrate the "validity" of their screening devices; that is, that their screening devices are reasonably related to the employment positions in question. If the defendants fail to meet their burden of proof, the court may then exercise wide equity powers to prevent further discrimination and to compensate the plaintiffs for past discrimination suffered. Typically, the courts have exercised their equity powers in the form of preliminary injunction and imposition of hiring quotas.

In the present case, the plaintiffs established their *prima facie* case of de facto discrimination by means of statistics. They showed, for example, that while only 9 per cent of the SFPD's 1920 sworn personnel were correctly classified as minorities, fully 43 per cent of San Francisco's population at large were minorities.[9] In like manner, the plaintiffs showed that whites passed the SFPD entrance examination from 1969 through 1972 with a frequency of more than five to one over minorities; and that whites passed the 1971 sergeant's examination with a frequency of over three to one over minorities. These statistics, in themselves, were held to establish a *prima facie* case for the plaintiffs.[10]

At this point, the burden of proof shifted to the defendants, who were not, as I have pointed out, adequately prepared to demonstrate, by approved empirical techniques, their tests' validity. The Court's adopted standard of proving validity was taken from EEOC guidelines listed at 29 CFR Sect. 1607(c):

Evidence of a test's validity should consist of empirical data demonstrating that the test is predictive of or significantly correlated with important elements of work behavior which comprise or are relevant to the job or jobs for which the candidates are being evaluated.[11]

As broken down by the Court, these EEOC guidelines permit validation by one of two processes. The first of these, predictive validation, requires substantial evidence that "... there is a correlation between a candidate's performance on the test and his actual performance on the job."[12] This, it should be noted, is essentially a form of post-validation. The second permissible procedure, content validation, demands "... a detailed analysis of the requirements of the job and the translation of that analysis into carefully formulated test questions."[13] The Court held that the present defendants did not adequately validate their entry-level examination or their promotion-level sergeant examination by *any* acceptable form of validation. But at this preliminary stage, the Court did not decide whether predictive validation (the higher standard of proof) alone would meet the defendant's burden of proof. Predictive validation is generally required in cases brought under Title VII of the Civil Rights Act of 1964; the present case is brought under the Equal Protection Clause of the 14th Amendment and the Civil Rights Act of 1871.[14]

A Defense Counterproposal

Realistically assessing their position at the time this suit was first filed, the defendants promptly embarked on a somewhat belated twofold counterproposal. First, a new entrance examination was developed based on a pair of detailed professional job analyses; one relating to the psychological aspects of police work, the other relating to the physical aspects of police work. Second, the San Francisco Police Officers' Association hired the California Selection Consulting Center, a state agency formally recognized by the Court, to post-validate scientifically the old promotional examinations.

At this point, a look at the two job analyses supporting the new entrance examination would be useful. The first study, relating to the psychological aspects of police work, was conducted by Dr. Richard Shavelson of Stanford University and Dr. Leonard Beckum of the SFPD Personnel Unit.[15] It employs a concept called "criterion sampling." This means that applicants are evaluated by how well they perform certain elements or tasks selected directly from what a patrol person actually does on the job. The examination derived from this concept employs not only samples of written reports and forms used daily by SFPD personnel, but also a creative application of audio-visual simulations of relevant patrol situations. Of course, there are practical limits to the degree of realism attainable in testing sampled criteria of actual patrol work: cost limits, time limits, danger limits, and others. Still, this new testing concept does provide some answer to the challenge of job-relevance.

The second study, relating to the physical aspects of patrol work, was conducted by Dr. Frank Verducci of San Francisco State University.[16] This study is very similar in basic methodology to the Shavelson-Beckum study. It seeks to identify actual physical tasks regularly performed on the job and to break these tasks down into specific movements and techniques. Here, again, the emphasis is on job-relevance.

Some Progress, But Much Still Left To Do . . .

The initial application of the new entrance examination produced a passage ratio considerably more favorable to all participating minorities, with the exception of women, most of whom could not meet certain strength criteria identified in the Verducci study. In response, the plaintiffs claimed that the disqualifying strength criteria were not essential to the performance of police work—at least as it *should* be performed today. They stressed the alleged superior ability of most women to empathize and to persuade in adverse situations, thus obviating the need for resorting to physical force. Now my own experiences in the SFPD cause me seriously to question the practicality of the plaintiff's contentions here—but my own experiences reflect a basically conventional view of police work. Who is to say that the community does not want a more "humane" and less "aggressive" interpretation of the police role in society? And who is to say that most women cannot in fact do the job as it is now usually interpreted? Both of these questions, it seems to me, are legitimate topics for further study.

The Shavelson-Beckum and Verducci studies are serious innovative steps in the right direction. But they possess one potential flaw in relation to the present suit: they are both essentially examples of content validation. And the Court may still decide that only predictive validation will suffice to meet the defendants' burden of proving their tests' validity. Such a decision by the Court would be unfortunate; it would effectively preclude the defendants from designing their own examinations to meet their own specific needs. Instead, they would be forced to obtain examinations already pre-validated by some outside agency. For predictive validation requires that a detailed comparison be made between an applicant's performance on the test and his subsequent performance on the job. And if you cannot administer a particular test because it is *prima facie* discriminatory, how can you measure the subsequent job performance of those who might pass that test? It is my hope that some empirical data will soon become available for predictive validation purposes from a careful monitoring of the relative job performance of the 60 women ordered hired by the Court under relaxed entrance criteria.

Some Side Effects, and My Personal Reaction

Meanwhile, as a practicing sergeant of police, I do not pretend to view the SFPD's present position without feeling certain basic concerns; some purely selfish, other mainly professional, and most of them shared with the rest of the SFPD. The SFPD is now at least 150 members below its normal operating strength. Each individual member's share of the total workload has proportionately increased. The personnel shortage is felt most severely at the district stations among the ranks of uniformed patrolmen working night shifts. These are perhaps the least congenial jobs in the SFPD, but they contribute, in my estimation, the most important and productive services the SFPD has to offer. The attainment of overall SFPD objectives is threatened, vacations, days off, and requested intradepartmental transfers must be postponed or cancelled. Patrolmen are often required to assume sergeants' responsibilities. Promotional opportunities are at a standstill. The generally popular traditional system of determining merit—open, competitive, objective civil service examinations—is now attacked by a powerful coalition of minority groups as discriminatory in both intent and effect, and as a totally unreliable predictor of desirable job-related qualities of competing candidates. And the long-established practices, values, and social integration of the SFPD itself are now threatened by the impending influx of over 150 new police persons who constitute an "unknown quantity" in terms of their attitudes, motivations, and abilities.

Therefore, for me and for many others both inside and outside the SFPD, more is at stake in this lawsuit than merely opening for disadvantaged minority group members a fair opportunity to secure desirable SFPD jobs and promotions. (Although I do not mean to deny that this last objective is valid and important). Implicit in this civil rights attack on the civil service merit system is a more fundamental challenge of exactly what "merit" means or should mean when applied to police work. For if the existing standards of selection and promotion are to be impugned and discarded, what is to take their place?

Are Quotas the Answer?

If we assume, for the sake of argument, that quota representation of all minority groups in the SFPD is a desirable public policy goal, we are immediately faced with an array of tough practical problems.[17] First, we must decide who is a minority group member and who is not. In this area, the EEOC's arbitration efforts produced some rather arbitrary results—an apparently unavoidable situation. It was decided, for example, that policemen claiming American Indian ancestry were not minority group members unless they could demonstrate at least 1/4 Indian blood *and* adoption of an essentially "American Indian lifestyle."[18] And myriad similar problems are immediately suggested: at what point does a person of Chinese ancestry become a minority group member: 1/8 Chinese blood? 1/16 Chinese blood with a Chinese accent? Does it make any difference if the prospective minority group member's parents earn over $30,000 per year?

Second, we must somehow reconcile some individuals' concurrent membership in more than one minority group with our hypothetical scheme for calculating representation. For example, how should we "count" a black woman with a Spanish surname? And once we have decided how to "count" her, do we then grant her *threefold* preference in our quota system? Whatever we do in these regards, we cannot avoid being somewhat arbitrary.

A third problem in establishing a quota system lies in deciding what geographical unit to adopt as our basis for calculating minority group distribution. Should it be a neighborhood?—a city?—the whole state? Serious arguments could be advanced in behalf of any of these units; and the outcome of our decision here would directly affect how we set up our quotas.

And a fourth problem lies in defining the minority groups themselves. Why should we restrict our definition of minority groups to include only those groups exhibiting certain racial, ethnic, and sex characteristics? Why not expand our definition in order to provide quotas for groups characterized by certain political and religious beliefs as well? This last question seems difficult to ignore if you accept the general principle of minority group representation from the beginning. In fact, all four of these problems just mentioned must be confronted if a rational system of quotas is to be developed.

But the next question then arises: what is expected to be gained by imposing minority group quotas on SFPD testing procedures? The plaintiffs claim that five general benefits would accrue—all of which were formally adopted into the Court's preliminary decision. First, quotas are expected to nullify unlawful discrimination in SFPD testing practices. Second, quotas are expected to compensate injured minority group members who have been victimized by past discrimination in SFPD testing. Third, the attainment through quotas of greater racial, ethnic, and sex balance throughout the SFPD would theoretically make the SFPD more "sensitive" and effective in dealing with unique, pressing minority group problems. Fourth, quotas are expected to provide valuable job and promotional opportunities for deserving minority group members. And fifth, quotas are expected to facilitate increased direct minority group participation in SFPD decision making, and thereby reduce destructive minority group frustration and hostility directed at the SFPD and at civil society in general. Hence, in the plaintiff's logic, greater social harmony would be attained throughout the whole city.

Now whether all of these five proposed benefits would in fact accrue is purely a matter of speculation; however, I have definite misgivings about each of them. First, I am bothered by the term "unlawful discrimination" when used to describe SFPD testing procedures. The Court has held that the de facto discrimination proved statistically by the plaintiffs resulted from neither deliberate legislative intent nor from conscious design in the administration of a neutral statute. In fact, before the "Affirmative Action Amendment" was passed in 1973, there was no general legal cognizance of de facto discrimination in municipal police testing. And the de facto discrimination established in the present case is "unlawful" only because the tests in question have not yet been adequately validated by demanding EEOC standards. Hence, what we really have here is a situation in which an established civil service testing system which unintentionally favors whites over minorities is suddenly made unlawful in 1973 by the passage of a federal law. Curiously, however, current post-validation efforts may soon prove the whole system to be lawful again. The standard of "legality" seems rather ambiguous here; and this ambiguity relates directly to a point I shall attempt to make later.

Second, I am bothered by the idea of using quotas to compensate minority group members for past discriminations suffered. Assuming that unfair discrimination can be established in the first place, it seems arbitrary to set up a whole ambiguous *class* as the intended beneficiary of compensatory efforts. The particular minority group members who actually suffered the discrimination may not be the ones who actually reap the benefits of preferential hiring and promotions.

Third, I have doubts about the practicality of using quotas to attain greater SFPD sensitivity toward minority group problems. While some increase in police-minority empathy probably would result, there are countervailing disadvantages that probably would arise also. For no matter how "fair" and "justified" court-ordered quotas may appear with respect to some mythical "objective" standard, they are bound to produce almost universal resentment throughout the SFPD. *Any* sudden change in the existing system of allocating jobs, assignments, and promotions would have this effect. For the existing civil service system must be seen as the product of over 40 years of debate, experience, and legitimizing. And the imposition of preferential quotas would be particularly resented due to their perceived arbitrary racial nature, and because of their origin in the courts which are themselves summarily distrusted by many policemen from the beginning. Hence, while some desirable sensitizing probably would occur, considerable *undesirable* sensitizing would also possibly occur.

Fourth, I have misgivings about using quotas as a means of securing desirable SFPD jobs and promotions for minority group members. Certainly, many deserving minority group members would benefit from increased opportunities for SFPD jobs and promotions. But for every deserving minority group member who is provided a job or promotion through preferential quotas, there is also a deserving non-minority person who is thereby deprived of a job or promotion. What we accomplish here is to substitute one form of discrimination for another. And what is the new basis for discrimination? The taxpaying community, it seems to me, is entitled to the services of the most qualified police candidates and supervisors, whatever "qualified" turns out to mean. But to focus primarily on a candidate's race, ethnic background, or sex—ascriptive criteria over which the candidate has no control—is to deemphasize that candidate's own relative abilities and his total worth as an individual. It shortchanges not only the community (in the potential reduction of individual excellence in its public servants) but the alleged beneficiary as well. For he is promptly labeled as unable to survive on his own merits; he is resented and distrusted by his co-workers; and he may in fact be unable to meet his new responsibilities. He is, in short, "alienated."

And fifth, I have misgivings about using preferential quotas as a means of facilitating increased minority group participation in SFPD decision making. My argument here is not effectiveness; quotas would undoubtedly increase minority representation throughout the SFPD's decision making structure. They would also probably co-opt some portions of the minority communities. And both of these objectives are certainly desirable. But I would argue that quotas are perhaps the least desirable means we have available for attaining these goals. For quotas, again, alienate the intended beneficiaries, produce potentially inferior police services, and incite divisive resentment within the SFPD. Much of what might be gained through increased minority group participation and co-optation may well be tragically lost through the negative side effects of the quotas themselves.

The Lawsuit in Broader Perspective

Digressing briefly, I would now like to suggest a broader social and historical perspective for viewing this lawsuit. Three interrelated factors appear to have particular relevance: our inability as a polity to define what we mean by "equality," our tide of rising expectations, and the emergence of a relatively new socio-political concept, "neoliberalism."

Two Conflicting Models of Equality

Parties on both sides of this civil rights suit sincerely claim to champion the cause of equality. Their respective positions on this issue implicitly reflect a broader on-going struggle for dominance in all of our social institutions between two ostensibly conflicting models of "equality:" "equality of opportunity" and "equality of results."[19] The "equality of opportunity" model emphasizes facilitating individual achievement and self-actualization. It admits that some socioeconomic inequalities will probably result when individuals possessing different natural physical abilities, mental abilities, and "luck" all take off from the same "starting line" in competitive pursuit of optimum wealth, power, and prestige. But these resulting inequalities are themselves valued as incentives for greater individual productivity and self-improvement. And while successful competitors do indeed obtain a larger share of society's rewards than the "losers," everyone gains in the end due to an absolute gain in the total rewards available for distribution. The role of government is viewed as guaranteeing that the competition proceeds fairly; that the "rules of the race" are observed equally by all.

On the other hand, the "equality of results" model emphasizes a uniform distribution of society's rewards without regard to individual qualities or achievements. It contends that no one individual is any "better" or "more deserving" than any other; that the present social competition proceeds unfairly (either by design or by circumstance); and that the competition itself is often corrupting to the "winners" and demoralizing to the "losers." And the end product of this unfair competition—an unequal distribution of wealth, power, and prestige— produces social resentment, conflict, and destructiveness. Consequently, the role of government—indeed the *duty* of government—is viewed as ensuring that each member of society, regardless of his social condition, is provided a share of society's rewards equal to that of every other member.

Of course, neither of these two models of "equality" adequately describes American society today. And although they appear antagonistic, they are more likely complementary than mutually exclusive. Still, there are unmistakable reflections of both models in the arguments of our present plaintiffs and defendants; and a final decision in this case to impose quotas would be an implicit application of the "equality of results" model. Such a decision, as an examination of our two models will readily show, has socioeconomic implications of which we should be aware..

Our Tide of Rising Expectations

A second factor with direct bearing on the present lawsuit is our tide of rising expectations. Irving Kristol describes this phenomenon as follows: "To see something on television is to feel entitled to it; to be promised something by a politician is to feel deprived of it."[20] And Kristol goes on to describe the way in which "felt deprivation" is often expressed:

... there is mounting irritability, impatience, distemper and mistrust. Each individual and every organized group (racial, economic, professional, etc.) seeing no justification for self-discipline—indeed holding the idea of self-discipline in a kind of contempt—calls for greater discipline to be exercised against the rest.[21]

Now it seems reasonable that all of the negative feelings described above would be experienced most intensely by minority group members, who are reminded daily through a variety of media of the gaping disparity between their own meager share of society's rewards and that of their more fortunate neighbors. This brings us back to the matter of SFPD jobs.

A logical first step toward securing a greater share of our society's rewards is to obtain a good job. And while some minority group members might feel a bit uneasy about entering police work, there is a great deal to recommend it today: good starting pay, good job security, challenge, excitement, and an opportunity to help directly alleviate many pressing social problems. The press, television, and the movies have helped make police work more attractive by creating a romantic new image for the police person—an image that includes minority group members: "Christy Love" (Theresa Graves), "Mr. Tibbs" (Sidney Poitier), and "Pepper Anderson" (Angie Dickenson), just to name a few. At the same time, there is a growing shortage of jobs throughout the economy as a whole. All of these factors have combined to convert many minority group members' efforts to improve their position in society into efforts to obtain SFPD jobs.

But minority group members are not the only ones who have been feeling unemployment and responding to the call of SFPD jobs. Increasing numbers of non-minority persons have been making this move too. And many of this latter group have enjoyed the advantage of varying levels of college education. Hence, competition in civil service examinations (which have traditionally emphasized verbal skills) has increased; and the minimum passing scores have been pushed upward; not from a deliberate intent to discriminate against minority groups, but from a need to discriminate, period. Every applicant cannot be given an SFPD job; there simply aren't enough to go around. And the established means for resolving the competition is the civil service testing system.

Increased competition for SFPD jobs and a higher cut-off score on civil service examinations have produced two general effects. First, the SFPD has been able to hire and to promote an increasing number of college-educated middle class candidates—a phenomenon encouraged and acclaimed by many as a step toward more professional police services.[22] Second, it has become increasingly difficult for many less educated minority group members to gain entry into the SFPD—a phenomenon which frustrates their rising expectations and adds to their already mounting irritability, distemper, and mistrust. Hence, a basic "trade-off" is suggested between higher "standards" for police work and greater minority group employment. I shall return to this issue later.

Meanwhile, where is much of this minority group hostility directed? Right at the "gatekeeper," the civil service testing system. In early 1972, San Francisco voters approved a municipal charter amendment which placed the Civil Service Commission in control over virtually all major paths of advancement in the SFPD. This promptly brought the Officers for Justice into the fight.[23] For it eliminated the practice of patronage appointments to the detective division—a practice that had produced many minority group promotions in the past. And what was substituted was a highly competitive system of written examinations which the OFJ felt would not benefit their interests. Hence, this present lawsuit was initiated.

Neoliberalism

A third social factor with direct bearing on our present lawsuit is the development of a socio-political concept termed "neoliberalism:"

It is liberal in that it is still based on the Lockean belief in society as a congeries of special interests all seeking their own private gain and in that it regards economic growth as the major source of human motivation. It differs from traditional liberalism, however, in that the competitors for power and profit are now no longer individuals but organized groups: industrialists, farmers, workers, professions, churches, educational and scientific communities, ethnic groups, and so on.[24]

Of course, the idea of organizing to attain political power is not new. But what does appear to be new is the degree to which we tend to define and express almost all of our political demands through the particular groups with which we identify. And these groups are increasingly defined along lines of sex, ethnic background, and occupation.[25] We tend to view ourselves less as individual consumers of society's rewards than as group consumers; less as "I, an American" than as "we, women Spanish American students." The reasons for this development probably lie deep in the dynamics of our crowded, interdependent, competitive, mobile society. But whatever its causes, it is real; and it has implications. It explains much of the logic behind class action suits and the demand for minority group quotas.

The End Result of Our Three Factors

But class action suits and a demand for minority group quotas reflect more than a neoliberal outlook; they also reflect a basic snag in our political system itself. Our inability to reach consensus over what "equality" should mean in our society—our popular ambivalence—has "paralyzed" our political branches of government. Indeed, how can the politicians "respond" if the voters do not know what they want? Nor have any of our current batch of politicians—for whatever reason—displayed sufficient leadership and "guts" to organize a consensus capable of breaking this deadlock. Consequently, basic equality issues usually cannot be resolved with respect to deliberately formulated legislative guidelines; such guidelines either don't exist or they aren't clear enough to be of much practical use. Hence, these basic equality issues are usually left alone until they reduce themselves into specific and immediate cases suitable for judicial resolution—if they are to be resolved by formal civil means at all.

On the other hand, many federal courts have recently combined on "equality of results" ideal with a "neoliberal" logic in accepting jurisdiction over class action suits at a point, in my opinion, far before they reach sufficient specificity and immediacy for appropriate judicial resolution. What the courts are doing here is dealing with broad classes of parties and general social issues. Their decisions in these cases then assume the effect of new law covering similar conflicts under similar situations. Now to act in this manner is to function as a legislative body—but without the traditional widespread public input, without the direct popular accountability, and without the broad expertise and perspective of the duly constituted legislative body.[26] Admittedly, courts are occasionally "forced" into this role by a default of the regular legislature; but it is still a practice that should be minimized. The product of such ad hoc legislation is a public policy characterized by inconsistency, unresponsiveness, and a lack of expertise.

Conclusion and a Proposal

Finally, where does all of this discussion leave us? The most immediate problem presented by this lawsuit is the need to reconcile two apparently conflicting goals: (1) the maintaining and even raising of standards of excellence in the performance of police services; and (2) the hiring and promoting of more minority group members in the SFPD. I accept both of these goals as valid. But I do not feel that preferential quotas are the best means available to us for attaining these two goals. Quotas are arbitrary, degrading, alienating, resented, and largely self-defeating. But is there an alternative to quotas? I believe there is. And some positive innovative steps have already been taken in this direction.

What I would propose consists of six steps. First, conduct a detailed job analysis, using approved empirical techniques, to identify personal attributes and abilities required for the performance of police work as it is now practiced in the SFPD. Two, devise a scheme for measuring those attributes and abilities in competing candidates, again using approved empirical techniques. Three, to the extent that interested minority group members cannot initially meet the minimum criteria for qualifying, conduct an SFPD-sponsored training program, free to both minorities and non-minorities alike, to help these parties overcome their initial deficiencies. Four, engage in a vigorous program of minority recruitment, tempering the "pitch" with a realistic assessment of what will eventually be required to succeed. Five, expand the Cadet Program (a kind of apprenticeship program) to provide interim part-time employment in the SFPD while candidates are developing qualifications required for full-time employment as police persons. And six, engage in a continuing process of post-validating all examinations for "predictive validity."

But even if all of these proposed steps are faithfully followed, there is one glowing flaw in the whole scheme: it sidesteps the normative issue. Everything is based on a description of how police work is now being practiced in the SFPD, ignoring the issue of how police work *ought* to be practiced therein. In the last analysis, all arguments about what it takes to become either a police officer or a sergeant fall flat without reference to some ideal model of what constitutes "good police work."

Hence, if the above selection scheme (or any other proposed selection scheme) is to attain popular legitimacy, it must be expanded to include some concept of ideal police work—a concept that is shared and generally accepted throughout the community to be served. But as this present lawsuit has made devastatingly clear, we do not, at present, have such a concept. What we have is an old civil service merit system that is "vulnerable," in Irving Kristol's words, "for no other reason than it exists—and because the citizenry no longer feels any particular responsibility for its existence, any instinctive obligation to sustain or even reform it."[27] But the fact that the civil service system is now challenged and vulnerable does not mean that we should fatalistically abandon it. That would be irresponsible, nihilistic, and ultimately self-defeating. What we should do is conduct a serious, responsible "salvage operation" in deliberate pursuit of defining "good police work." This approach will certainly not be the easy way; but the potential rewards fully justify the effort. For no less is at stake than better police services for all and a discovery of professional police "identity."

Notes

1. *Officers for Justice v. SF Civil Service Commission,* Civil No. C-73-1657 RFP, Memorandum and Order, 1973.

2. Additional plaintiffs are the Chinese for Affirmative Action and several other women's groups.

3. *OFJ v. SF Civil Service,* p. 2.

4. *Ibid.,* p. 25.

5. Three rationale immediately come to mind: the high cost of such studies in terms of money and time; the lack of warning prior to this suit, and the heavy workload of on-going operational matters.

6. I refer here to three studies in particular: the Shavelson-Beckum Study and the Verducci Study (both outlined later in this article), and Lt. Richard Treub, *An Analysis of Height v. Ability to Perform Police Functions* (SFPD Legal Office, 1973).

7. Treub, p. 2.

8. This is my interpretation of USC 1981, 1983, and 2000 (annotated) in *Lawyer's Edition of US Codes* (1974 Amended), along with the present decision.

9. *OFJ v. SF Civil Service,* p. 5.

10. *Ibid.,* pp. 5, 7.

11. *Ibid.,* p. 14.

12. *Ibid.,* p. 14.

13. *Ibid.,* p. 14.

14. *Ibid.,* pp. 1, 15.

15. Richard Shavelson and Leonard Peckum, *Criterion Sampling Approach to Selecting Patrolmen* (unpublished, copyrighted study conducted for the SFPD Personnel Unit and the SF Civil Service Commission, 1973).

16. Frank Verducci, (title unavailable), an unpublished study of physical requirements for patrol work conducted for the SF Civil Service Commission, 1974. My summary is based on Dr. Verducci's testimony in the present case.

17. This analysis is based on Daniel Bell, *The Coming of Post Industrial Society* (New York: Basic Books, 1973), pp. 418-419.

18. This was the case of Sgt. David Duggar, who is now assigned to Central Station, SFPD Patrol Division.

19. I have borrowed these two concepts from *Bell,* pp. 424-432; and I have modified them to illustrate the divergent arguments presented in this case.

20. Irving Kristol, *On the Democratic Idea in America* (New York: Harper and Row, 1973), p. 26.

21. Kristol, pp. 26-27.

22. Perhaps the most influential advocate of educated policemen was the Report of the Katzenbach Commission: *The Challenge of Crime in a Free Society* (Washington, D.C.: U.S. Government Printing Office, 1967), at pp. 107-113.

23. This was the hard-fought, narrowly passed Proposition "E," which was later incorporated into the Police Sections of the SF City Charter.

24. Victor Ferkiss, *The Future of Technological Civilization* (New York: George Braziller, 1974), p. 44.

25. This concept was taken from Bell, p. 377.

26. This description of "legislation," as contrasted with "adjudication," is taken from Oliver Wendell Holmes, quoted in Kenneth Culp Davis, *Administrative Law* (St. Paul: West, 1973), pp. 227-228.

27. Kristol, p. 24.

Topic Five

The Administrator as Decisionmaker and Policymaker

Introduction

So far we have seen administrators in a wide variety of circumstances in which they had to make decisions. In some cases the decisions made were the right ones: the subsequent events turned out well for all concerned. In other situations, the decisions were wrong, and other decisions were needed to correct the previous ones. We have even seen administrators decide not to make any decision, which of course is a decision itself.

People are making decisions all the time in the administrative process. A number of important questions surround this fact, and some of these will be considered in this Topic. What is a decision and how does it differ from a policy? What are the different ways decisions can be made and what are their implications for individual administrators? How does a person know if a right decision has been made?

Some basic definitions should be helpful. A decision is the passing of judgment or the reaching of a conclusion about a particular issue, whereas a policy is a plan or course of action designed to influence and to determine particular decisions. "A policy differs from a decision largely in scope or magnitude. [It] usually establishes a framework according to which individual, particular decisions can be made."[1] In either case, the making of decisions or policies is a process, rather than a single, separate unrelated act. How "rational" this process really is and should be are major considerations of this Introduction. The five selections focus on individuals involved in making decisions or policies. We shall examine the personal factors that are important and that give public administration a human quality and dimension.

Decisionmaking Models

There have been several efforts to describe the basic components of the decisionmaking or policymaking process. (For purposes of this discussion, decisions and policies will be treated as being the same except where specifically noted.) Models, or simplified versions of reality, have been created to explain how people make decisions in the administrative process. Graham Allison has described three approaches, and they will be described to provide background for the selections.[2] The question to be considered is, Do any of these models adequately portray and explain the decisionmaking process in the cases?

The first model is called the "rational policy" or "rational actor" decisionmaking process. Many writers and administrators believe that ideally this is the one to follow, although as we shall see, it is very difficult to do so. The assumption of the rational model is that a person (an "actor") should reach a decision by going through four steps, each logically following the other. The four steps are (1) to identify precisely the problem that needs a solution; (2) to identify all the possible solutions to the problem; (3) to compare and evaluate all the consequences of the alternatives identified in Step 2; and (4) to select the best solution based on the empirical evidence in Step 3.

An administrator faces problems in trying to implement these steps. First, the problems may not be easily defined. Political groups may perceive the issue differently and, therefore, there will be little agreement on what precisely is the problem. Second, administrators may not identify all the possible solutions to the problem, or more important, they may not identify the right ones. The rational model assumes that the best decision cannot be made unless the best solutions are considered. Third, methodological deficiencies exist in analyzing whatever alternatives have been presented to an administrator. Even if all possible solutions are known, significant limitations are present in measuring their consequences and implications, especially in trying to quantify results of social programs. Fourth, assuming the above three conditions could be met, the "best" or most "rational" answer to the problem might not be politically feasible. Empirically, an administrator could defend the selection of a particular decision, but if it ignored political reality—interest groups or personal preferences of elected officials—then that decision might have to undergo extensive modification to conform to political forces in the administrative process.

To point out all the drawbacks of the rational approach should not be construed to mean that logical and reasoned thinking have no place in administrative decisionmaking. Rather, it suggests that individual administrators must decide important questions within a less than ideal environment.

The second decisionmaking model tries to recognize the limits of the rational model. Allison called it the "organizational process" model. By this he meant that rational decisionmakers are constrained in their decisionmaking because organizations have vested interests in specific decisions and policies and, therefore, organizations act as impediments to the rational process. Another writer, Charles Lindblom, refers to this second approach to decision-making as "incrementalism" in his book, *The Policy Making Process* (1968). This stresses that administrators can consider only a limited number of variables at the same time and, as a result, decisions tend to build gradually (incrementally) upon each other. They are not abrupt changes drastically altering previous directions. Consequently, where the rational approach seeks the "best" solution, the incremental model accepts a "satisfactory" answer to problems.

How the incremental approach works in practice was described by a former British prime minister. He was quoted as saying: "I am not sure that there is really such a thing as 'power' or 'decision.' I would certainly find it very hard to give you an example of when I have ever experienced power or taken a decision. For one thing, there is just a build-up of big and small factors, and they may not be brought to your notice until the issue has already been decided; and when you eventually have to decide, it may be in response to the smallest of them all. That is not 'power' or 'decision.' "[3]

The third decisionmaking model Allison calls the "bureaucratic-politics" model. It emphasizes that decisions largely result from the interaction within and among large organizations, and that these are mostly incremental in scope. This third model de-emphasizes the importance of the individual and attributes decisions to inherent characteristics of large bureaucracies (some of which were discussed in Topic Three) and the dynamics of the political process itself. Decisions result not so much from what individuals do and think, but from the fact that certain patterns of behavior are created by the existence of processes in complex organizations.

In the next section, which starts in the next paragraph, we look at some specific administrators as they make decisions or are involved in a decision-making process. These examples illustrate how and why some public decisions and policies are made under certain conditions.

Individuals in the Decisionmaking Process

Selection 23, "General Hershey and His Proposed Induction of Draft Protestors," shows clearly the power and influence that some administrators are able to wield. Lewis Hershey, as national director of the Selective Service System, issued in 1967 a statement on his own that in effect became a major policy for the entire nation. The author of this case, Larry Wade, writes: "This was a policy decision arrived at by one man, a man not subject to elections; a policy that was never subjected to a vote of any type; a policy that was instigated before any public discussion was solicited; and a policy that was, as later shown, illegal in light of existing law." Even though Hershey received little public support for his policy announcement, he was not forced to revoke it. Most other public officials were cautious in their criticism of Hershey, although after a few months Congress took action to invalidate the Hershey statement.

Until this incident in 1967, Hershey had experienced unchallenged power over the Selective Service System. How did one person get into a position of being able to make policy single-handedly? A major reason why Hershey and other administrators are able to achieve so much power is because of the length of time they serve in the same position. Hershey had been the only director of the Selective Service since its inception in 1940. So, at the time of his policy statement, he had been in charge for twenty-seven years, and he had built up considerable strength and support in his own bureaucracy as well as in Congress and the executive branch. Congress and the President had turned over more responsibilities each year to Hershey and, as might be expected in such a loose relationship, he felt he was not very accountable to elected officials. It was not until Hershey's administrative actions ran counter to some basic principles—thus embarrassing President Johnson who was sensitive to the political consequences of Hershey's order—that Hershey was criticized publicly.

Hershey's power because of his length of time in office was not unique. J. Edgar Hoover certainly owed much of his power to the fact that he had been the only director of the FBI since its founding. For various reasons, elected officials are reluctant to remove long-standing administrators. As long as bureaucrats can make and implement policy without creating public controversies, politicians reason that administrators should be left alone. This frees the elected officials to spend their time on more visible and campaign-worthy issues than overseeing vast bureaucracies. Such an attitude, of course, diminishes the possibility of ensuring accountability of public administrators, and it can lead to some severe abuses of power.

A long-term administrator becomes a prominent and stable feature on the political landscape. Politicians know that in the administrator's particular policy area, constituency problems can be expedited. As more people seek the administrator's help, power flows to that individual in terms of budget increases and additional authority in policy matters, and the administrator builds and secures a power base. Power begets more power, and so the administrator is assured permanency.

If legislators and elected executives cannot be counted on to control an administrator, then one solution is to limit by law the length of time a person can occupy the same position. Congress did this after Hoover was out of the FBI by setting a ten-year limit for the director. Of course, no law was needed, as the director serves at the pleasure of the President. Given the purported kinds of information Hoover had in his files, however, no President was willing to remove Hoover. The arguments against limitations on the length of service in a top administrative post are similar to those against mandatory retirement for any worker. Yet, an agency head does not have to leave government service, but only be transferred to another organization after a period of time. This rotation practice might minimize administrators thinking in terms of "their" agency as well as provide some new approaches in administering an organization.

Who really makes policy? Art Buchwald's satirical answer is not farfetched when one considers the previous case on Hershey and the following one on the CIA. Selection 24, "The Seditious Plot Thickens," tells about Plotkin, typical of thousands of administrators who have immense discretion in the administration of public policies. Because of the way policies are drafted in the political process, they tend to be vague and ambiguous. Therefore, when it comes to implementation, wide latitude is permitted in interpretation. The specifics of the legislative program are often left to the bureaucracy—the Plotkins of this world. Not all public servants are as timid or unwilling to make decisions as Plotkin, but we did observe in Topic Three a disinclination by many civil servants to show initiative and to be held accountable.

Further evidence of insulated administrators making key decisions is found in "Vietnam Cover-Up: Playing War With Numbers" (Selection 25). It is an incredible story that cuts across several topic areas covered in this book. In addition to the problem of decisionmaking and policymaking, "Vietnam Cover-Up" calls attention to organizational behavior, administrative accountability, and ethical choices facing administrators. All of these issues and the decisionmaking process are interrelated. The case profiles the struggles, persistence, and frustration of one person—Sam Adams—who was trying to have a positive impact on the administrative system. What happened to him has consequences for us all.

In this selection, we see that major decisions were based on limited amounts of information. Certainly, the rational model was not employed in the decisions described by Adams. New information was intentionally ignored or old data falsified by CIA personnel charged with collecting intelligence and processing it for use by military and civilian strategists.

Why would people ignore new information that could be useful in decisionmaking? Several reasons are likely. The two discussed here show the personal dimension in decisionmaking. One reason for refusing to consider the statistics developed by Adams was that they were thought to be politically unacceptable to the public and to top elected leaders. Whether or not this was true about the public's reaction at the time, top CIA administrators wanted to report only what they believed their superiors—including the President— wanted to hear. We saw this identical phenomenon in Topic Two. There administrators were anxious to please the new Carter administration in hopes of being appointed to important governmental jobs, and so they overlooked or failed to disclose in their official investigation reports questionable banking procedures by Bert Lance.

Another reason for the CIA and others to ignore the reports submitted by Adams was that the information challenged the existing assumptions of current strategies and the eventual outcome of the war. Decisions were being made incrementally, and to suddenly accept Adams' figures would necessitate some fundamental changes in policy and possibly organizational structures. Further, if administrators admitted that they had been working with incomplete or false data, that could have set off a full-scale investigation, and more than policy might be changed. To many people, therefore, keeping the status quo was to their advantage, and Adams and his persistence represented a real threat.

The way so many individuals acted in this case study should remind readers of the first selection in this book, "The Pornography of Everyday Life." Warren Bennis commented on what unsocial behavior can develop in individuals who work for large organizations. They become indifferent to the consequences that result from what they and their organizations are doing. All kinds of excuses were offered by people in the CIA for not sending Adams' intelligence estimates to other governmental officials. Yet there were significant political, military, and moral implications and consequences if the most accurate information did not reach the highest levels of policymakers in the White House. (Of course, the White House had a responsibility to consider seriously contrary information as well). Few people in the CIA were willing or able to look beyond their own personal careers and to take the risks that Adams did.

Top-level administrators need to know what their organizations are doing and how well. Certainly some formal organizational mechanisms are necessary, but as we saw in the Adams case, there is no guarantee that these offices within an agency will be very effective. How to obtain a degree of rationality in administration while at the same time recognizing the influence of personal factors is a central concern of management. In the next section, "Management by Objectives," the focus is on one technique designed to solve this problem.

Management by Objectives

In 1954 Peter Drucker introduced the term "management by objectives" (MBO) in his book, *The Practice of Management*. MBO was intended to be a technique to assist administrators in being more effective managers. Since then, it has been adopted widely in the business sector. Government was slower in trying MBO, but in the past ten years many federal and state agencies have been employing its principles.

MBO is an important concept because it has several practical applications. Administrators can use it in the following functions: decisionmaking and policymaking, personnel motivation, policy evaluation, and budgeting. Its versatility is evident when one notes that many current standard textbooks on public administration do not place their discussion of MBO under the same topic headings. It can be found in several different sections of a textbook.

MBO is placed in this Topic Introduction since it can be perceived as a bridge between the discussion on decisionmaking and the next Topic which is on the use of budgets and the evaluation of programs.

MBO is a method to improve the performance of programs and the people administering them. This is done by setting general program goals and then decentralizing the means to achieve them. The specific decisions on how to reach those goals are left to the middle- and lower-level personnel. MBO also employs a constant monitoring of the program so that everyone involved is aware of the progress or problems as they occur. When a difficulty comes up, the sub-units affected are expected to handle their own situation and not look to top management for answers or authority to resolve the problem.

Selection 26, "MBO Goes to Work in the Public Sector," analyzes the application of this system in the U.S. Department of Health, Education and Welfare (HEW). As Rodney Brady explains the working of MBO in this case study, there are six different phases in the process: (1) legislative proposals, (2) budget decisions, (3) objectives and plans set, (4) tracking, (5) bimonthly evaluation, (6) long-range planning.

As used in HEW, MBO takes into account political considerations early through the legislative proposal phase. It also links the entire program to budget decisions throughout the six phases. This gives administrators greater control over the program, and it enables them to add or subtract resources at different points as conditions warrant, instead of having to wait until the end of the fiscal year to make corrections in the program. By that time, of course, so many difficulties may have occurred that the program is in jeopardy.

There are several advantages in using MBO.[4] In the process of selecting goals, it usually identifies conflicting objectives and makes those that are to be pursued more explicit. MBO also provides the opportunity for personnel at all levels of the agency to participate in decisions pertaining to the ways to achieve the goals. Because of this participation, personnel accept some individual responsibility for the results of the agency. This can increase both motivation and accountability. Finally, MBO has built-in control and evaluation procedures so that administrators and others can be made aware constantly of what the organization and its employees are doing.

MBO is not without problems. Brady describes a few of those encountered when MBO was implemented at HEW. Some of the limitations noted are reminiscent of the problems in using the rational model in decisionmaking. Another set of problems is getting people to accept changes in the way decisions were to be made at HEW. Brady points out the importance of preparing employees for new techniques such as MBO in organizations. It might be recalled that Topic Three discussed some of the problems in organizational change and the fact that people's efforts can be directed against innovation or toward supporting goals and changes. In short, an administrator must recognize the importance of several elements if MBO is to be successful in the public sector. Brady concludes the case study by outlining these considerations, especially the significance of the individual administrator and the characteristics of the public sector environment.

Rationality and the Human Element

Charts, diagrams, models, and techniques alone will not guarantee effective management of human resources. The final selection of this Topic puts some of this introductory material into perspective. "Management vs. Man" by August Heckscher (Selection 27) argues against too much rationality in the decisionmaking process. As the head of the New York City park system, Heckscher was faced with having to make his agency "productive" at the expense of other considerations. His commentary deals with public administrators trying to reconcile several conflicting values, such as efficiency and public service. These are not always in opposition, but to strike a balance requires great administrative skill. Heckscher's observations raise an important question: What criteria are going to be used to measure the success or failure of a program? The answer tells us more about the kinds of functions public administration should be performing in society.

Notes

1. Robert Presthus, *Public Administration* (New York: The Ronald Press, 1975), p. 14.
2. Graham Allison, "Conceptual Models and the Cuban Missile Crisis," *American Political Science Review,* September 1969 (Vol. 63 No. 3), pp. 689-718; also by the same author, *Essence of Decision* (Boston: Little, Brown and Company, 1971), pp. 71-72.
3. Henry Fairlie, "Johnson and the Intellectuals," *Commentary*, October 1965 (Vol. 40, No. 4), p. 52.
4. Bruce H. De Woolfson, Jr., "Public Sector MBO and PPB: Cross Fertilization in Management Systems," *Public Administration Review,* July/August 1975 (Vol. 35, No. 4), pp. 388-389.

23
General Hershey and His Proposed Induction of Draft Protestors
Larry Wade

The policy incident discussed below involves a statement sent on October 26, 1967, to the nation's 4,087 local draft boards. The statement was issued by General Lewis B. Hershey, national director of the Selective Service System. In the wake of student protests against the draft during 1967, Hershey suggested that local boards review the draft status of anyone who (1) interfered with military recruiting on campus, (2) invaded a selective service office, or (3) burned or mutilated a draft card. Hershey recommended that, if such persons were draft eligible (classified 1-A), they be inducted immediately. He further suggested that if the protestors held a draft deferment, such as a student's II-S, their deferment be revoked by the local board and the registrant inducted into military service as soon as possible. Hershey suggested that all of the above decisions be made by administrative action at the local board level. The net result of this particular bureaucratic policy decision was failure in the sense that the decision produced a response quite contrary to the effect

From *The Elements of Public Policy* by Larry Wade, pp. 113-122. Copyright 1972 by the Charles E. Merrill Publishing Co. Reprinted with permission.
Larry Wade is a professor at the University of California, Davis.

desired by General Hershey. Draft protest was not curbed, but was in fact spurred to greater heights in the face of Hershey's recommendation. It appears that the failure of the policy was due to the violation by Hershey of certain features of a widely-held democratic myth, together with other reasons discussed below.

Since policy can and does often reflect the personality of the individuals formulating it, it is relevant to this study to include the following observations concerning General Hershey.

Hershey was the first and, until late 1969, when he was asked to resign by President Nixon, only head of the twenty-nine-year-old Selective Service System. He was appointed by President Roosevelt in 1940 to head a draft system that had been established as an emergency measure prior to World War II. In 1969 Hershey was 76 years old and the nation's oldest military officer on active duty. Throughout his tenure as Selective Service Director, the general staunchly opposed any radical change in the system, and public policy with respect to conscription had remained, with relatively minor exceptions, unchanged since it was developed in 1940. *Time* magazine called Hershey a "nineteenth century man unread in constitutional law, but totally dedicated to what used to be called Americanism." The general's opinions about the draft and draftees had remained rather constant over the years. During the Korean War, he had said that he felt "six out of ten draft rejects were faking disability on their induction physicals." In an interview in 1960, Hershey made the following comments about draft protestors: "I'm afraid this talk of objecting to the draft is some more of our softness—our desire to do no work, to shirk our responsibility as citizens. We want everything as painless as possible, everything with comfort and ease." When asked in 1967 how he felt about the president's proposal to abolish local draft boards, Hershey replied, "such action would violate most everything we have gained in democracy."

Although references such as these provide no adequate basis for a full assessment of Hershey's personality or political philosophy, they do suggest that important relationships exist between personality and public policy. In Hershey's case it is not unreasonable to believe that his personal sense of patriotism had much to do with his formulation of a policy calling for the induction of protestors. The fact that an important official in the executive branch could recommend actions that could so easily be construed as a threat to constitutional rights of speech, assembly, and petition poses interesting questions concerning personality, bureaucracy, and policy formation.

The Selective Service Act deals with all aspects of the draft. The law establishes the rules for the registration, induction, and discharge of all draft-age men. The law also outlines what it is that constitutes violation of the draft act, as well as the penalties applicable to such violations.

The president has legal responsibility for administering the draft. He appoints the director of the Selective Service who reports directly to him. As with many routinely functioning bureaucracies, Hershey had administered the system with little or no presidential involvement, at least up until the time of the incident in question. He had already survived five presidents and was, at the time of his famous letter, serving under a sixth. He was, indeed, a well-entrenched bureaucrat with whom presidents, Congress, and the courts found it inconvenient, or unnecessary, to intervene in the conduct of his office.

Under the Selective Service Act, the president has the power to determine the guidelines for induction, as shown by the wording of the law, which reads, in part: "The selection of persons for training and service ... shall be made in an impartial manner under such rules as the President may prescribe. ..." So while Hershey was the appointed head of the Selective Service, he held no *legal* authority of his own to establish induction priorities. Such authority rests with the president, acting by executive order, or with Congress, acting through the statutory amendment process. But with few exceptions, presidents had for all practical purposes delegated the responsibility for developing induction guidelines to General Hershey. This is important to remember when assessing Hershey's October, 1967, letter: he had for many years been the effective promulgator of induction standards.

Another aspect of the law which should be made clear concerns the theoretical legal autonomy of local draft boards. This autonomy lies with the manner in which local boards implement presidential guidelines for induction. Ostensibly, the president establishes age limits, registration procedures, methods of classification, rules for deferments, and so forth. Local boards interpret these guidelines to fit their own peculiar community needs. National Selective Service headquarters is supposed to furnish local boards with the quotas to be filled, and local boards in turn are to furnish the individuals according to previously established presidential rules. There is to be no governmental pressure concerning whether or not particular individuals are inducted. The head of the Selective Service is expected to *monitor* local board activities to insure compliance with presidential directive, but he is not supposed to *dictate* to the boards.

In reality, however, Hershey exercised a good deal of control over local boards, stemming less from legal authority than from the ideological or normative bureaucratic leadership he was in a position to provide. This moral suasion served to reduce sharply the autonomy of local boards. Norman S. Poole, assistant secretary of Defense for Manpower under President Johnson, said in 1965 that Hershey "strongly influences" local boards. When asked if the boards were autonomous, Poole replied, "They are autonomous *under* General Hershey." Continued Poole, "It is important to note that word *under*."

The Act also outlines the legal punishments applicable to draft law violators. None of these penalties includes induction or reclassification as proposed by Hershey. And what must also be noted is that such activities as draft card burning were not in themselves violations of the law in 1967. It was not until 1968 that Congress amended the law to make draft card burning a specific crime under the statute. So while there was little explicit legal backing for Hershey's attempt to induct draft protestors, the realities of his past influence in administering the system may well have led him to attempt to make such induction a matter of operative public policy.

The Selective Service is an agency that deals with a well-defined segment of the population, i.e., males aged 18 to 35. Its decisions, however, impinge upon and invoke reaction from, a far greater segment of society, e.g., inductees' families, employers, peace groups, patriotic organizations. Consequently, the Selective Service System places demands upon, and seeks the support of, a substantial proportion of the entire population.

The initial public action taken by Hershey against draft protestors occurred in January, 1966. Several students in Ann Arbor, Michigan, were arrested for a sit-in at the local draft board. The young men were later found guilty of violating a civil ordinance and were fined. Subsequently, General Hershey suggested that their cases be reviewed by their local boards for possible action. This was done, and some of the students were reclassified as I-A. A similar episode occurred in New York in late 1966, when four pacifists burned their draft cards on the steps of a federal court building. Although at that time there existed no laws against such conduct, Hershey suggested that the pacifists be relieved of their deferments by their draft boards and inducted immediately. Similar events continued over the next year in many places.

Several members of Congress questioned the legality of Hershey's actions in the above cases. Emanuel Cellar (Dem.—N.Y.), chairman of the House Judiciary Committee, sent Hershey a letter asking him to clarify his position with respect to the induction of protestors. In his reply, Hershey reaffirmed his stance on the question. He said, in answer to Cellar, that, "It has always been my view that any young man who violates the Selective Service Act should be given an opportunity to enter the armed forces rather than being prosecuted for his violation of the law." As the volume of protests against the war and the draft had grown in 1967, Hershey had translated his established personal views into a form of official Selective Service policy. The factors that led him to issue the policy statement cannot be known with certainty; perhaps Hershey himself is the only person who knows exactly why he did it. In any case, Hershey issued a statement on October 26, 1967, calling for local boards to immediately reclassify and induct anyone who burned his draft card, interfered with campus recruitment, or staged a sit-in at a local board.

This was a policy decision arrived at by one man, a man not subject to election; a policy that was never subjected to a vote of any type; a policy that was instigated before any public discussion was solicited; and a policy that was, as later shown, illegal in light of existing law. It was also a policy that failed. Before considering possible reasons for its failure, let us consider some examples of public reaction to the statement.

The reaction to Hershey making official what he had previously kept personal was immediate, and, as far as can be documented, overwhelmingly negative.

Although Hershey claimed that he had cleared the matter with the White

House prior to issuing the directive, a White House statement in the wake of the controversy claimed otherwise. The statement, presumably issued with presidential approval, although never publicly attributed to President Johnson, said, "The draft should not be used as a means of punishing dissent." Regardless of whether prior White House approval had been sought or not, the White House thus moved quickly to dissociate itself from the statement. Representative John Moss (Dem.—Calif.) threatened to call Hershey before the House Armed Services Committee unless the order was rescinded. In keeping with his earlier objections to Hershey's tactics, Representative Cellar condemned the Selective Service Director for his "flagrant disregard for the law" and said the draft "should not be used by Hershey as an instrument to punish or compel adherence to any political belief." The Justice Department's first reaction to the Hershey decision was a statement saying that the order would be difficult to uphold on constitutional grounds. The *New York Times*, in a December editorial, called the proposal "controversial."

Hershey's stand in the face of this controversy was a reaffirmation of his position. In a December *Washington Post* interview, the director claimed that "deferments were a privilege, and if a person violated the rules, he lost his deferment." In the same interview Hershey stated that a "student's school record does not form the entire basis for such deferments, but that obeyance of United States law also enters into the picture." He further contended that, "Decisions on the legality of a student's activities can be determined by the administrative action of local boards." *U.S. News and World Report* quoted Hershey as saying, "It is obvious that any action violating the military Selective Service act or related processes cannot be in the national interest." In these statements Hershey seemed clearly to reject the need for judge, jury, and trial in determining innocence and guilt. Joseph A. Califano, then special aid to President Johnson, issued an opinion contrary to Hershey's when he said, "Draft boards do not have the legal right to judge individual conduct."

The culmination of administration opposition to Hershey came on December 9, at a joint news conference attended by Hershey and Attorney General Ramsey Clark. At this conference Hershey insisted that the Selective Service system had the right to induct protestors who, in the opinion of local boards, had violated the Selective Service Act. Attorney General Clark dissented, saying that the Justice Department had not laid down any specific rules for handling protestors. Reaction from the general public to Hershey's induction edict is difficult if not impossible to assess.

The year drew to a close with General Hershey and much of the government still at odds. Direct public controversy between the administration and Hershey ended at the close of 1967. Whatever in-governmental fighting continued beyond this point can only be a matter for speculation.

In order to explain Hershey's failure, it is necessary to first establish it. The record shows that the Justice Department, under presidential sanction, reaffirmed in early 1968 its stand that the draft could not be used as a means of punishing dissent. General Hershey, on the other hand, staunchly refused to countermand his order of October 26 and continued to insist that local boards had the right to induct protestors. But the administration's disapproval of such action was apparently enough to dissuade local boards from implementing Hershey's statement, since no further cases of protestors being inducted were reported. Congress did move to amend the draft law to include draft card burning as an illegal act, but the punishments for draft law offenders remained what they had been, that is, fines and imprisonment following due process, and not induction.

In August of 1969, the Supreme Court added the final defeat to the controversial directive when it overturned the induction of a New York pacifist on a 1967 draft card burning charge. Hershey's action was repudiated therefore by the administration, the Court, and most of the press. These were the obvious results of Hershey's policy directive.

There were many contributing factors to the failure of Hershey's effort at policy making and some, of course, played a larger role than others. Several suggestions on this subject are advanced below, some of which undoubtedly made a significant contribution to failure, and some which possibly had no effect on the outcomes at all. The reader may want to add to, or criticize, these speculative explanations in terms of whether or not they contribute to an understanding of this, and perhaps other, unilateral, bureaucratically-based failures at policy making.

The first, and seemingly most obvious, cause of failure consisted in the fact that Hershey's induction directive was technically illegal in light of existing law. Induction and reclassification were not outlined as penalities in the statute, and neither were draft card burning nor recruitment interference specified as crimes. As was pointed out however, Hershey had long supported induction as an alternative to prosecution for draft offenders, and such a philosophy had not been explicitly rejected by prior administrations and courts. The Johnson administration, however, was under fire for its involvement in the Southeast Asian war at the time of the incident, and some segments of the public had grown more sensitive to the rights and limits of dissent. Hershey's policy attempt might have succeeded in calmer times (although such times might not have produced the dissent which occasioned the directive). But since issues involving freedom of dissent were in serious contention at the time, and since significant public opposition to the draft had been mobilized, the policy was doomed. It was not only the technical illegality of the policy that defeated it, but as well, the larger political context within which the law had to be administered.

Hershey may have misread or underestimated both the level of general opposition to the war and the specific opposition to the draft, opposition which could be organized around what appeared to be an autocratic, unilateral, and vindictive public policy. His actions appeared to many as violating all semblance of democratic policy making, and the order itself raised a threat to constitutional protections of free speech. In answer to his critics, Hershey contended that innocence and guilt could be determined by local boards, that trials were not necessary, and that draft deferments were mere privileges. These statements immediately raised questions about the democratic myth of due process, which turns on questions of jury trial, legal representation, presumed innocence, and similar factors. If dissent had not been a public issue at the time, the policy might have succeeded. But once issues involving freedom of speech and due process were publicly brought to bear on the General, he was lost. Because of implied threats to free speech, the Johnson administration could not hope publicly to support Hershey in his policy, even though it may have been sympathetic to his efforts. When criticism was launched against the policy, Hershey found himself isolated from effective political support. Had he sought official government support before issuing the order, he might have weathered the crisis and retained some measure of credibility. But he was caught outside of an effective coalition and had to absorb singly all criticism raised against him, including that raised by the administration he was supposed to have represented. The same was true of congressional opinion. With no prior official support, Hershey was not later in a position to gain approval for his actions once such democratic ideals as free speech were brought into play.

It is possible also that General Hershey's successes of twenty-five or so years, during which he had received congressional, judicial, and presidential support for his administration of the draft system, had lulled him into a false sense of security. Perhaps he believed that he had more allies than later results proved him to have and that his membership in a coalition that had sustained him in the past would hold firm as well in the controversy at hand. It is quite true that some coalitions in American politics are remarkably stable, but it is also the case that their durability requires continual testing and that some of the less basic ones can be transitory indeed. Precisely why Hershey failed actively to enlist prior support for his policy is hard to say. But the unchallenged power he had exercised in the past may well have had something to do with it. When all or most parties to the dominant ruling coalition in America choose to ignore democratic values, then a public challenge to the coalition is extraordinarily difficult to mount. But if some elements of the coalition seek to invoke a democratic value such as free speech, perhaps in order to defend its public action on other questions or issues, then the myth is likely to prevail. The Johnson administration, hard pressed to maintain a semblance of public support for an intensely unpopular war, was hesitant to provide its critics with still further issues upon which to base a challenge to the very legitimacy of the government.

Another factor that may have contributed to Hershey's failure was his personality. He was far from being a warm and engaging public personality and, in the face of criticism, was unable to respond in a manner that might have earned him significant public support. His curt and harsh reactions to his critics only added to his already adverse public image, one that had been created by the initial publicity on the incident. The vindictive nature of the original directive was borne out in subsequent public statements made by the

General. Large portions of the public expect bureaucrats to conform to a set of expectations which turn on disinterestedness, neutrality in the face of controversy, even-handedness. It was not, apparently, in General Hershey's nature to play such a role. He was a man of staunch and decided opinions which he was frank to reveal and defend. He was an overt partisan in a social role that required an emphasis upon the reconciliation of contentious values. Hershey was a bureaucrat whose age and personality were liabilities in a position as sensitive as his became in a time of severe crisis. The democratic myths were invoked and Hershey failed to assess correctly his position within these new realities. Adverse publicity presented him as an insensitive bureaucrat who was attempting to curb free speech, and he was insufficiently flexible in his policy stance to counter such charges.

An important question to be asked now concerns the implications of this particular case for other unilaterally-developed public policies. Quite obviously, a good deal of such policy is made daily so it is useful to note at the outset that this method of policy making can be successful. But in order for such policy to succeed, it must conform to certain unwritten rules.

The public has limited access to most processes of policy making, even less to policy which originates within the public bureaucracy, and less still to the type of "one-man" policy outlined in this case. For the most part, indeed, various publics and elites are willing, often anxious, to allow bureaucrats to exercise their expertise with relatively little interference. As long as the requirements of bureaucratic or "invisible" policy making are tolerable, and no crises arise, the public is content. But when a bureaucrat is brought to public attention for initiating an unpopular policy, as was Hershey, he must be prepared to defend himself if he is to survive as a public man. If he has been careful to monitor the state of the coalitions of which he invariably is a part, or if he can move quickly to mobilize important sources of political power, he may weather the crisis. On the other hand, if he has wandered too far from the central myths of his society and forgotten the dangers of political isolation, a crisis can mean personal disaster and failure for the policy.

Most bureaucrats in a position to shape policy in the manner of Hershey have influence over a narrow and specialized segment of society. Such individuals can make important policy decisions without public debate as long as they avoid precipitating a public crisis. Publicity of any type, but particularly adverse publicity, can be a threat to nonvoting bureaucratically-based policy. And once the attention of significant political elements is drawn to the fact that bureaucrats have in some important way violated the game of democracy, trouble arises.

Success in these sorts of policy decisions, then, lies in dealing with a narrow, technical segment of society which understands the realities of the bureaucrat's job in light of existing democratic myths. Exposure to the public should be avoided by the prudent self-interested bureaucrat whenever possible and, above all, proof of public approval and support for a proposed policy must be kept ready at all times. The community may allow itself to be deceived about its access to public policy as long as it is to some extent content with the government. But should public discontent be generated by an adverse policy, or by a policy which can be made to seem undemocratic, then sections of the public are quick to invoke the myths of democracy and to demand justifiation for the bureaucrat's actions.

24
The Seditious Plot Thickens

Art Buchwald

Everybody thinks that the Democratic and Republican conventions and the November election decide who is going to run the country.

I hate to be the one to throw cold water on this idea, but neither the President of the United States nor Congress can really do much to change anything.

The guy who runs this country is Plotkin. He is neither elected by the American people nor does he have to answer to them.

Plotkin, and the thousands like him, are civil servants averaging somewhere around $20,000 a year. They are stashed away in large brick and glass buildings all over Washington, Maryland and Virginia, and no matter what Congress or the President decides, they are the people in charge.

Let us say that the President wants a pothole reform bill. He sends it up to Congress where, after two years, it is passed. The President signs it and everyone in the United States believes it is the law of the land.

Except Plotkin.

Plotkin gets the bill and examines it. The wording, after the lobbyists get through with it, is of course, vague. What kind of potholes does the law cover? How much money should be spent to fill each pothole? Should the work be contracted to private industry or to the Army Corps of Engineers? Was it Congress' intent to deal with all potholes or just those on federal property? And, finally, what constitutes a pothole in the first place?

Plotkin, who has been a civil servant for 20 years, knows if he takes any action on his own, he could be criticized and he could blot his copy book.

So he calls a meeting of all his department heads and asks them to write him memoranda on the best way to administer the pothole bill. He tells them it is a matter of urgency and he wants to hear from everybody in six months.

From the *Los Angeles Times*, August 26, 1976. Copyright 1976 Los Angeles Times Syndicate. Reprinted with permission of author.
Art Buchwald is a syndicated columnist writing from Washington.

Six months later the people under Plotkin all submit memoranda. A majority of them suggest that a study be made of potholes by a commission made up of engineering experts from companies, universities and government that will report back to the bureau in a year.

Plotkin likes the idea and approves it. But to play it safe he also hires his own experts to check out the report of the commission. This means larger office space and Plotkin decides to move the bureau to a new building. The move requires tremendous logistics, but also causes fierce competition among all of Plotkin's subordinates as to where their offices will be situated, as well as carpeting, furniture and the location of the water cooler.

There is so much controversy over the new quarters that Plotkin hasn't had too much time to worry about the potholes.

Finally the move is made, new people are hired and everyone settles down to the task of administering the pothole bill. The outside commission has submitted its report, which is circulated throughout the bureau for comments.

The comments are all negative and it is decided to scrap the commission's report. The fear of most of the people in Plotkin's office is that, if they accept the recommendations of the commission, they would have to put them into action. If they turn them down, they'll have to come up with their own, which would mean expanding the bureau, thus guaranteeing everyone a promotion to the next civil service grade.

By this time Congress and the President have forgotten they even passed a pothole bill. But one day the President is driving on U.S. Highway 95 and he hits a pothole. His head bumps the ceiling of the limousine and an AP photographer gets a picture of it. This makes the President very mad and he says to his aide, "Whatever happened to the pothole bill I signed?"

That night Plotkin gets a call from the White House and the aide says, "The President wants a progress report on what you're doing about the potholes in this country."

"We're working on a report right now," Plotkin assures him. "But just because the President signs a bill doesn't mean he can expect results overnight."

25

PERSONALITY PROFILE

Vietnam Cover-Up: Playing War with Numbers

Sam Adams

In late 1965, well after the United States had committed ground troops to Vietnam, the CIA assigned me to study the Vietcong. Despite the almost 200,000 American troops and the advanced state of warfare in South Vietnam, I was the first intelligence analyst in Washington to be given the full-time job of researching our South Vietnamese enemies. Incredible as it now seems, I remained the only analyst with this assignment until just before the Tet offensive of 1968.

At CIA headquarters in 1965 nobody was studying the enemy systematically, the principal effort being geared to a daily publication called the "Sitrep" (Vietnam Situation Report), which concerned itself with news about the activities of South Vietnamese politicians and the location of Vietcong units. The Sitrep analysts used the latest cables from Saigon, and tended to neglect information that didn't fit their objectives. The Johnson Administration was already wondering how long the Vietcong could stick it out, and since this seemed too complicated a question for the Sitrep to answer, the CIA's research department assigned it to me. I was told to find out the state of enemy morale.

Good news and bad news

I looked upon the new job as something of a promotion. Although I had graduated from Harvard in 1955, I didn't join the Agency until 1963, and I had been fortunate in my first assignment as an analyst of the Congo rebellion. My daily and weekly reports earned the praise of my superiors, and the Vietcong study was given to me by way of reward, encouraging me in my ambition to make a career within the CIA.

Without guidance and not knowing what else to do, I began to tinker with the VC defector statistics, trying to figure out such things as where the defectors came from, what jobs they had, and why they had wanted to quit. In short order I read through the collection of weekly reports, and so I asked for a ticket to Vietnam to see what other evidence was available over there. In mid-January 1966, I arrived in Saigon to take up a desk in the U.S. Embassy. After a couple of weeks, the CIA station chief (everyone called him "Jorgy") heard I was in the building adding and subtracting the number of defectors. He called me into his office. "Those statistics aren't worth a damn," he said. "No numbers in Vietnam are, and, besides, you'll never learn anything sitting around Saigon." He told me I ought to go to the field and start reading captured documents. I followed Jorgy's advice.

The captured documents suggested a phenomenon that seemed incredible to me. Not only were the VC taking extremely heavy casualties, but large numbers of them were deserting. I got together two sets of captured papers concerning desertion. The first set consisted of enemy unit rosters, which would say, for example, that in a certain seventy-seven-man outfit, only sixty men were "present for duty." Of the seventeen absent, two were down with malaria, two were at training school, and thirteen had deserted. The other documents were directives from various VC headquarters telling subordinates to do something about the growing desertion rate. "Christ Almighty," they all seemed to say. "These AWOLs are getting out of hand. Far too many of our boys are going over the hill."

I soon collected a respectable stack of rosters, some of them from large units, and I began to extrapolate. I set up an equation which went like this: if A, B, and C units (the ones for which I had documents) had so many deserters in such and such a period of time, then the number of deserters per year for the whole VC Army was X. No matter how I arranged the equation, X always turned out to be a very big number. I could never get it below 50,000. Once I even got it up to 100,000.

The significance of this finding in 1966 was immense. At that time our official estimate of the strength of the enemy was 270,000. We were killing, capturing, and wounding VC at a rate of almost 150,000 a year. If to these casualties you added 50,000 to 100,000 deserters—well, it was hard to see how a 270,000-man army could last more than a year or two longer.

I returned in May to tell everyone the good news. No one at CIA headquarters had paid much attention to VC deserters because captured documents were almost entirely neglected. The finding created a big stir. Adm. William F. Raborn, Jr., then director of the CIA, called me in to brief him and his deputies about the Vietcong's AWOL problem. Right after the briefing, I was told that the Agency's chief of research, R. Jack Smith, had called me "*the* outstanding analyst" in the research directorate.

But there were also skeptics, particularly among the CIA's old Vietnam hands, who had long since learned that good news was often illusory. To be on the safe side, the Agency formed what was called a "Vietcong morale team" and sent it to Saigon to see if the news was really true. The team consisted of myself, acting as a "consultant," and four Agency psychiatrists, who presumably understood things like morale.

The psychiatrists had no better idea than I'd had, when I started out, how to plumb the Vietcong mind. One of the psychiatrists said, "We'll never get Ho Chi Minh to lie still on a leather couch, so we better think up something else quick." They decided to ask the CIA men in the provinces what *they* thought abut enemy morale. After a month or so of doing this, the psychiatrists went back to Washington convinced that, by and large, Vietcong spirits were in good shape. I went back with suitcases full of captured documents that supported my thesis about the Vietcong desertion rate.

But I was getting uneasy. I trusted the opinion of the CIA men in the field who had told the psychiatrists of the Vietcong's resilience. The South Vietnamese government was in one of its periodic states of collapse, and somehow it seemed unlikely that the Vietcong would be falling apart at the same time. I began to suspect that something was wrong with my prediction that the VC were headed for imminent trouble. On reexamining the logic that had led me to the prediction, I saw that it was based on three main premises. Premise number one was that the Vietcong were suffering very heavy casualties. Although I'd heard all the stories about exaggerated reporting, I tended not to believe them, because the heavy losses were also reflected in the documents. Premise two was my finding that the enemy army had a high desertion rate. Again, I believed the documents. Premise three was that both the casualties and the deserters came out of an enemy force of 270,000. An old Vietnam hand, George Allen, had already told me that this number was suspect.

In July, I went to my supervisor and told him I thought there might be something radically wrong with our estimate of enemy strength, or, in military jargon, the order of battle. "Maybe the 270,000 number is too low," I said. "Can I take a closer look at it?" He said it was okay with him just so long as I handed in an occasional item for the Sitrep. This seemed fair enough, and so I began to put together a file of captured documents.

The documents in those days were arranged in "bulletins," and by mid-August I had collected more than 600 of them. Each bulletin contained several sheets of paper with summaries in English of the information in the papers taken by American miltary units. On the afternoon of August 19, 1966, a Friday, Bulletin 689 reached my desk on the CIA's fifth floor. It contained a report put out by the Vietcong headquarters in Binh Dinh province, to the effect that the guerrilla-militia in the province numbered just over 50,000. I looked for our own intelligence figures for Binh Dinh in the order of battle and found the number 4,500.

"My God," I thought, "that's not even a tenth of what the VC say."

In a state of nervous excitement, I began searching through my file of bulletins for other discrepancies. Almost the next document I looked at, the one for Phu Yen province, showed 11,000 guerrilla-militia. In the official order of battle we had listed 1,400, an eighth of the Vietcong estimate. I almost shouted from my desk, "There goes the whole damn order of battle!"

Unable to contain my excitement, I began walking around the office, telling anybody who would listen about the enormity of the oversight and the implications of it for our conduct of the war. That weekend I returned to the office, and on both Saturday and Sunday I searched through the entire collection of 600-odd bulletins and found further proof of a gross underestimate of the strength of the enemy we had been fighting for almost two years. When I arrived in the office on Monday a colleague of mine brought me a document of a year earlier which he thought might interest me. It was from Vietcong headquarters in South Vietnam, and it showed that in early 1965 the VC had about 200,000 guerrilla-militia in the south, and that they were planning to build up to 300,000 by the end of the year. Once again, I checked the official order of battle. It listed a figure of exactly 103,573 guerrilla-militia—in other words, half as many as the Vietcong said they had in early 1965, and a third as many as they planned to have by 1966.[1]

No official comment

That afternoon, August 22, I wrote a memorandum suggesting that the overall order of battle estimate of 270,000 might be 200,000 men too low. Supporting it with references to numerous bulletins, I sent it up to the seventh floor, and then waited anxiously for the response. I imagined all kinds of sudden and dramatic telephone calls. "Mr. Adams, come brief the director." "The President's got to be told about this, and you'd better be able to defend those numbers." I wasn't sure what would happen, but I was sure it would be significant, because I knew this was the biggest intelligence find of the war—by far. It was important because the planners running the war in those days used statistics as a basis for everything they did, and the most important figure of all was the size of the enemy army—that order of battle number, 270,000. All our other intelligence estimates were tied to the order of battle: how much rice the VC ate, how much ammunition they shot off, and so forth. If the Vietcong Army suddenly doubled in size, our whole statistical system would collapse. We'd be fighting a war twice as big as the one we thought we were fighting. We already had about 350,000 soldiers in Vietnam, and everyone was talking about "force ratios." Some experts maintained that in a guerrilla war our side had to outnumber the enemy by a ratio of 10 to 1; others said 5 to 1; the most optimistic said 3 to 1. But even if we used the 3 to 1 ratio, the addition of 200,000 men to the enemy order of battle meant that somebody had to find an extra 600,000 troops for our side. This would put President Johnson in a very tight fix—either quit the war or send more soldiers. Once he was informed of the actual enemy strength, it seemed inconceivable that he could continue with the existing force levels. I envisioned the President calling the director on the carpet, asking him why this information hadn't been found out before.

Nothing happened. No phone calls from anybody. On Wednesday I still thought there must have been some terrible mistake; on Thursday I thought the news might have been so important that people were still trying to decide what to do with it. Instead, on Friday, the memorandum dropped back in my in-box. There was no comment on it at all—no request for amplification , no question about my numbers, nothing, just a routine slip attached showing that the entire CIA hierarchy had read it.

I was aghast. Here I had come up with 200,000 additional enemy troops, and the CIA hadn't even bothered to ask me about it, let alone tell anybody else. I got rather angry and wrote a second memorandum, attaching even more references to other documents. Among these was a report from the Vietcong high command showing that the VC controlled not 3 million people (as in our official estimate) but 6 million (their estimate). I thought that this helped to explain the origins of the extra 200,000 guerrilla-militia, and also that it was an extraordinary piece of news in its own right. A memorandum from my office—the office of Current Intelligence—ordinarily would be read, edited, and distributed within a few days to the White House, the Pentagon, and the State Department. It's a routine procedure, but once again I found myself sitting around waiting for a response, getting angrier and angrier. After about a week I went up to the seventh floor to find out what had happened to my memo. I found it in a safe, in a manila folder marked "Indefinite Hold."

I went back down to the fifth floor, and wrote still another memo, referencing even more documents. This time I didn't send it up, as I had the others, through regular channels. Instead, I carried it upstairs with the intention of giving it to somebody who would comment on it. When I reached the office of the Asia-Africa area chief, Waldo Duberstein, he looked at me and said: "It's that Goddamn memo again. Adams, stop being such a prima donna." In the next office, an official said that the order of battle was General Westmoreland's concern, and we had no business intruding. This made me even angrier. "We're all in the same government," I said. "If there's discrepancy this big, it doesn't matter who points it out. This is no joke. We're in a war with these guys." My remarks were dismissed as rhetorical, bombastic, and irrelevant.

On the ninth of September, eighteen days after I'd written the first memo, the CIA agreed to let a version of it out of the building, but with very strange restrictions. It was to be called a "draft working paper," meaning that it lacked official status; it was issued in only 25 copies, instead of the usual run of over 200; it could go to "working-level types" only—analysts and staff people—but not to anyone in a policy-making position—to no one, for example, on the National Security Council. One copy went to Saigon, care of Westmoreland's Order of Battle Section, carried by an official who worked in the Pentagon for the Defense Intelligence Agency.

By this time I was so angry and exhausted that I decided to take two weeks off to simmer down. This was useless. I spent the whole vacation thinking about the order of battle. When I returned to the Agency, I found that it came out monthly and was divided into four parts, as follows:

Communist regulars	About 110,000
	(it varied by month)
Guerrilla-militia	Exactly 103,573
Service troops	Exactly 18,553
Political cadres	Exactly 39,175
	That is 271,301
	or about 270,000

The only category that ever changed was "Communist regulars" (uniformed soldiers in the Vietcong Army). In the last two years, this figure had more than doubled. The numbers for the other three categories had remained precisely the same, even to the last digit. There was only one conclusion: no one had even looked at them! I decided to do so right away, and to find out where the numbers came from and whom they were describing.

I began by collecting more documents on the guerrilla-militia. These were "the soldiers in black pajamas" the press kept talking about; lightly armed in some areas, armed to the teeth in others, they planted most of the VC's mines and booby traps. This was important, I discovered, because in the Da Nang area, for example, mines and booby traps caused about two-thirds of all the casualties suffered by U.S. Marines.

I also found where the number 103,573 came from. The South Vietnamese had thought it up in 1964; American Intelligence had accepted it without question, and hadn't checked it since. "Can you believe it?" I said to a fellow analyst. "Here we are in the middle of a guerrilla war, and we haven't even bothered to count the number of guerrillas."

The service troops were harder to locate. The order of battle made it clear that these VC soldiers were comparable to specialists in the American Army—ordnance sergeants, quartermasters, medics, engineers, and so forth. But despite repeated phone calls to the Pentagon, to U.S. Army headquarters, and to the office of the Joint Chiefs of Staff, I couldn't find anyone who knew where or when we'd hit upon the number 18,553. Again I began collecting VC documents, and within a week or so had come to the astonishing conclusion that our official estimate for service troops was at least two years old and five times too low—it should not have been 18,553, but more like 100,000. In the process I discovered a whole new category of soldiers known as "assault youths" who weren't in the order of battle at all.

I also drew a blank at the Pentagon regarding political cadres, so I started asking CIA analysts who these cadres might be. One analyst said they belonged to something called the "infrastructure," but he wasn't quite sure what it was. Finally, George Allen, who seemed to know more about the VC than anyone else, said the "infrastructure" included Communist party members and armed police and people like that, and that there was a study around which showed how the 39,175 number had been arrived at. I eventually found a copy on a shelf in the CIA archives. Unopened, it had never been looked at before. The study had been published in Saigon in 1965, and one glance showed it was full of holes. Among other things, it left out all the VC cadres serving in the countryside—where most of them were.

By December 1966 I had concluded that the number of Vietcong in South Vietnam, instead of being 270,000, was more like 600,000, or over twice the official estimate.[2] The higher number made many things about the Vietnam war fall into place. It explained, for instance, how the Vietcong Army could have so many deserters and casualties and still remain effective.

Nobody listens

Mind you, during all this time I didn't keep this information secret—just the opposite. I not only told everyone in the Agency who'd listen, I also wrote a continuous sequence of memorandums, none of which provoked the least response. I'd write a memo, document it with footnotes, and send it up to the seventh floor. A week would pass, and then the paper would return to my in-box: no comment, only the same old buck slip showing that everyone upstairs had read it.

By this time I was so angry and so discouraged with the research director-ate that I began looking for another job within the CIA, preferably in a section that had some use for real numbers. I still believed that all this indifference to unwelcome information afflicted only part of the bureaucracy, that it was not something characteristic of the entire Agency. Through George Allen I met George Carver, a man on the staff of Richard Helms, the new CIA director, who had the title "special assistant for Vietnamese affairs." Carver told me that I was "on the right track" with the numbers, and he seemed an independent-minded man who could circumvent the bureaucratic timidities of the research directorate. At the time I had great hopes of Carver because, partly as a result of his efforts, word of my memorandums had reached the White House. Cables were passing back and forth between Saigon and Washington, and it had become fairly common knowledge that something was very wrong with the enemy strength estimates.

In mid-January 1967, Gen. Earle Wheeler, chairman of the Joint Chiefs of Staff, called for an order-of-battle conference to be held in Honolulu. The idea was to assemble all the analysts from the military, the CIA, and the Defense Intelligence Agency in the hope that they might reach a consensus on the numbers. I went to Honolulu as part of the CIA delegation. I didn't trust the military and, frankly, I expected them to pull a fast one and lie about the numbers. What happened instead was that the head of Westmoreland's Order of Battle Section, Col. Gains B. Hawkins, got up right at the beginning of the conference and said, "You know, there's a lot more of these little bastards out there than we thought there were." He and his analysts then raised the estimate of enemy strength in each category of the order of battle; instead of the 103,573 guerrilla-militia, for example, they'd come up with 198,000. Hawkins's remarks were unofficial, but nevertheless, I figured, "the fight's over. They're reading the same documents that I am, and everybody's beginning to use real numbers."

I couldn't have been more wrong.

After a study trip to Vietnam, I returned to Washington in May 1967, to find a new CIA report to Secretary of Defense Robert McNamara called something like "Whither Vietnam?" Its section on the Vietcong Army listed all the discredited official figures, adding up to 270,000. Dumbfounded, I rushed into George Carver's office and got permission to correct the numbers. Instead of my own total of 600,000, I used 500,000, which was more in line with what

Colonel Hawkins had said in Honolulu. Even so, one of the chief deputies of the research directorate, Drexel Godfrey, called me up to say that the directorate couldn't use 500,000 because "it wasn't official." I said: "That's the silliest thing I've ever heard. We're going to use real numbers for a change." Much to my satisfaction and relief, George Carver supported my figures. For the first time in the history of the Vietnam war a CIA paper challenging the previous estimates went directly to McNamara. Once again I said to myself: "The battle's won; virtue triumphs." Once again, I was wrong.

Soon after, I attended the annual meeting of the Board of National Estimates on Vietnam. Held in a windowless room on the CIA's seventh floor, a room furnished with leather chairs, blackboards, maps, and a large conference table, the meeting comprised the whole of the intelligence community, about forty people representing the CIA, the Defense Intelligence Agency, the Army, the Navy, the Air Force, and the State Department. Ordinarily the meeting lasted about a week, its purpose being to come to a community-wide agreement about the progress of the war. This particular consensus required the better part of six months.

The procedure of these estimates requires the CIA to submit the first draft, and then everyone else argues his group's position. If one of the services violently disagrees, it is allowed to take exception in a footnote to the report. The CIA's first draft used the same 500,000 number that had gone to McNamara in May. None of us expected what followed.

George Fowler from DIA, the same man who'd carried my guerrilla memo to Saigon in September 1966, got up and explained he was speaking for the entire military. "Gentlemen, we cannot agree to this estimate as currently written. What we object to are the numbers. We feel we should continue with the official order of battle." I almost fell off my chair. The official OB figure at that time, June 1967, was still 270,000, with all the old components, including 103,573 guerrilla-militia.

In disbelief I hurried downstairs to tell my boss, George Carver, of the deception. He was reassuring. "Now, Sam," he said, "don't you worry. It's time to bite the bullet. You go on back up there and do the best you can." For the next two-and-a-half months, armed with stacks of documents, I argued with the military over the numbers. By the end of August, they no longer insisted on the official order of battle figures, but would not raise them above 300,000. The CIA numbers remained at about 500,000. The meetings recessed for a few weeks at the end of the month, and I left Washington with my wife, Eleanor, to visit her parents in Alabama. No sooner had we arrived at their house when the phone rang. It was George Carver. "Sam, come back up. We're going to Saigon to thrash out the numbers."

I was a little cynical. "We won't sell out, will we?"

"No, no, we're going to bite the bullet," he said.

Army estimate

We went to Saigon in early September to yet another order-of-battle meeting, this one convened in the austere conference room in Westmoreland's headquarters. Among the officers supporting Westmoreland were Gen. Philip Davidson, head of intelligence (the military calls it G-2); General Sidle, head of press relations ("What the dickens is he doing at an OB conference?" I thought); Colonel Morris, one of Davidson's aides; Col. Danny Graham, head of the G-2 Estimates Staff; and of course, Col. Gains B. Hawkins, chief of the G-2 Order of Battle Section. There were also numerous lieutenant colonels, majors, and captains, all equipped with maps, charts, files, and pointers.

The military dominated the first day of the conference. A major gave a lecture on the VC's low morale. I kept my mouth shut on the subject, even though I knew their documents showed a dwindling VC desertion rate. Another officer gave a talk full of complicated statistics which proved the Vietcong were running out of men. It was based on something called the cross-over memo which had been put together by Colonel Graham's staff. On the second day we got down to business—the numbers.

It was suspicious from the start. Every time I'd argue one category up, the military would drop another category down by the same amount. Then there was the little piece of paper put on everybody's desk saying that the military would agree to count more of one type of VC if we'd agree to eliminate another type of VC. Finally, there was the argument over a subcategory called the district-level service troops.

I stood up to present the CIA's case. I said that I had estimated that there were about seventy-five service soldiers in each of the VC's districts, explaining that I had averaged the numbers in a sample of twenty-eight documents. I briefly reviewed the evidence and asked whether there were any questions.

"I have a question," said General Davidson. "You mean to tell me that you only have twenty-eight documents?"

"Yes sir," I said. "That's all I could find."

"Well, I've been in the intelligence business for many years, and if you're trying to sell me a number on the basis of that small a sample, you might as well pack up and go home." As I resumed my seat, Davidson's aide, Colonel Morris, turned around and said, "Adams, you're full of shit."

A lieutenant colonel then got up to present the military's side of the case. He had counted about twenty service soldiers per district, he said, and then he went on to describe how a district was organized. When he asked for questions, I said, "How many documents are in your sample?"

He looked as if somebody had kicked him in the stomach. Instead of answering the question, he repeated his description of how the VC organized a district.

Then George Carver interrupted him. "Come, come, Colonel," he said. "You're not answering the question. General Davidson has just taken Mr. Adams to task for having only twenty-eight documents in his sample. It's a perfectly legitimate question. How many have you in yours?"

In a very low voice, the lieutenant colonel said, "One." I looked over at General Davidson and Colonel Morris to see whether they'd denounce the lieutenant colonel for having such a small sample. Both of them were looking at the ceiling.

"Colonel," I continued, "may I see your document?" He didn't have it, he said, and, besides, it wasn't a document, it was a POW report.

Well, I asked, could he please try and remember who the twenty service soldiers were? He ticked them off. I kept count. The total was forty.

"Colonel," I said, "you have forty soldiers here, not twenty. How did you get from forty to twenty?"

"We scaled down the evidence," he replied.

"Scaled down the evidence?"

"Yes," he said. "We cut out the hangers-on."

"And how do you determine what a hanger-on is?"

"Civilians, for example."

Now, I knew that civilians sometimes worked alongside VC service troops, but normally the rosters listed them separately. So I waited until the next coffee break to ask Colonel Hawkins how he'd "scale down" the service troops in a document I had. It concerned Long Dat District in the southern half of South Vietnam, and its 111 service troops were broken down by components. We went over each one. Of the twenty in the medical component, Hawkins would count three, of the twelve in the ordnance section, he'd count two, and so forth, until Long Dat's 111 service soldiers were down to just over forty. There was no indication in the document that any of those dropped were civilians.

As we were driving back from the conference that day, an Army officer in the car with us explained what the real trouble was: "You know, our basic problem is that we've been told to keep our numbers under 300,000."

Later, after retiring from the Army, Colonel Hawkins confirmed that this was basically the case. At the start of the conference, he'd been told to stay below a certain number. He could no longer remember what it was, but he recalled that the person who gave it to him was Colonel Morris, the officer who had told me I was "full of shit."

The Saigon conference was in its third day, when we received a cable from Helms that, for all its euphemisms, gave us no choice but to accept the military's numbers. We did so, and the conference concluded that the size of the Vietcong force in South Vietnam was 299,000. We accomplished this by simply marching certain categories of Vietcong out of the order of battle, and by using the military's "scaled-down" numbers.

I left the conference extremely angry. Another member of the CIA contingent, William Hyland (now head of intelligence at the Department of State), tried to explain. "Sam, don't take it so hard. You know what the political climate is. If you think they'd accept the higher numbers, you're living in a dream world." Shortly after the conference ended, another category was frog-marched out of the estimate, which dropped from 299,000 to 248,000.

I returned to Washington, and in October I went once again in front of the Board of National Estimates, by this time reduced to only its CIA members. I told them exactly what had happened at the conference—how the number had been scaled down, which types of Vietcong had left the order of battle, and even about the affair of Long Dat District. They were sympathetic.

"Sam, it makes my blood boil to see the military cooking the books," one of the board members said. Another asked, "Sam, have we gone beyond the bounds of reasonable dishonesty?" And I said, "Sir, we went past them last August." Nonetheless, the board sent the estimate forward for the director's signature, with the numbers unchanged. I was told there was no other choice because Helms had committed the CIA to the military's numbers.

"But that's crazy," I said. "The numbers were faked." I made one last try. My memorandum was nine pages long. The first eight pages told how the numbers had got that way. The ninth page accused the military of lying. If we accepted their numbers, I argued, we would not only be dishonest and cowardly, we would be stupid. I handed the memo to George Carver to give to the director, and sent copies to everyone I could think of in the research branch. Although I was the only CIA analyst working on the subject at the time, nobody replied. Two days later Helms signed the estimate, along with its doctored numbers.

That was that. I went into Carver's office and quit Helms's staff. He looked embarrassed when I told him why I was doing so, but he said there was nothing he could do. I thanked him for all he had done in the earlier part of the year and for his attempt at trying to deal with real rather than imaginary numbers. I thought of leaving the CIA, but I still retained some faith in the Agency, and I knew that I was the only person in the government arguing for higher numbers with accurate evidence. I told Carver that the research directorate had formed a VC branch, in which, I said, I hoped to find somebody who would listen to me.

Facing facts

In November General Westmoreland returned to Washington and held a press conference. "The enemy is running out of men," he said. He based this on the fabricated numbers, and on Colonel Graham's crossover memo. In early December, the CIA sent McNamara another "Whither Vietnam?" memo. It had the doctored numbers, but this time I was forbidden to change them. It was the same story with Helms's New Year briefing to Congress. Wrong numbers, no changes allowed. When I heard that Colonel Hawkins, whom I still liked and admired, had been reassigned to Fort Holabird in Baltimore, I went to see him to find out what he really thought about the order of battle. "Those were the worst three months in my life," he said, referring to July, August, and September, and he offered to do anything he could to help. When he had been asked to lower the estimates, he said, he had retained as many of the frontline VC troops as possible. For several hours we went over the order of battle. We had few disagreements, but I began to see for the first time that the Communist regulars, the only category I'd never looked at, were also seriously understated—perhaps by as many as 50,000 men. No one was interested, because adding 50,000 troops would have forced a reopening of the issue of numbers, which everyone thought was settled. On January 29, 1968, I began the laborious job of transferring my files from Carver's office to the newly formed Vietcong branch.

The next day the VC launched the Tet offensive. Carver's office was chaos. There were so many separate attacks that someone was assigned full time to stick red pins in the map of South Vietnam just to keep track of them. Within a week's time it was clear that the scale of the Tet offensive was the biggest surprise to American intelligence since Pearl Harbor. As I read the cables coming in, I experienced both anger and a sort of grim satisfaction. There was just no way they could have pulled it off with only 248,000 men, and the cables were beginning to show which units had taken part. Many had never been in the order of battle at all; others had been taken out or scaled down. I made a collection of these units, which I showed Carver. Two weeks later, the CIA agreed to re-open the order-of-battle controversy.

Suddenly I was asked to revise and extend the memorandums that I had been attempting to submit for the past eighteen months. People began to congratulate me, to slap me on the back and say what a fine intelligence analyst I was. The Agency's chief of research, R. Jack Smith, who had once called me "*the* outstanding analyst" in the CIA but who had ignored all my reporting on the Vietcong, came down from the seventh floor to shake my hand. "We're glad to have you back," he said. "You know more about Vietnam than you did about the Congo." All of this disgusted me, and I accepted the compliments without comment. What was the purpose of intelligence, I thought, if not to warn people, to tell them what to expect? As many as 10,000 American soldiers had been killed in the Tet offensive because the generals had played politics with the numbers, and here I was being congratulated by the people who had agreed to the fiction.

In February the Agency accepted my analysis, and in April another order-of-battle conference was convened at CIA headquarters. Westmoreland's delegation, headed by Colonel Graham (now a lieutenant general and head of the Defense Intelligence Agency) continued to argue for the lower numbers. But from that point forward the White House stopped using the military estimate and relied on the CIA estimate of 600,000 Vietcong.

All along I had wondered whether the White House had had anything to do with fixing the estimates. The military wanted to keep them low in order to display the "light at the end of the tunnel," but it had long since occurred to me that maybe the generals were under pressure from the politicians. Carver had told me a number of times that he had mentioned my OB figures to Walt Rostow of the White House. But even now I don't know whether Rostow ordered the falsification, or whether he was merely reluctant to face unpleasant facts. Accepting the higher numbers forced the same old decision: pack up or send a lot more troops.

On the evening of March 31, the question of the White House role became, in a way, irrelevant. President Johnson made his announcement that he wasn't going to run again. Whoever the next President was, I felt, needed to be told about the sorry state of American intelligence so that he could do something about it. The next morning, April 1, I went to the CIA inspector general's office and said: "Gentlemen, I've come here to file a complaint, and it involves both the research department and the director. I want to make sure that the next administration finds out what's gone on down here." On May 28 I filed formal charges and asked that they be sent to "appropriate members of the White House staff" and to the President's Foreign Intelligence Advisory Board. I also requested an investigation by the CIA inspector general. Helms responded by telling the inspector general to start an investigation. This took two months. The director then appointed a high-level review board to go over the inspector general's report. The review board was on its way to taking another two months when I went to the general counsel's office and talked to a Mr. Ueberhorst. I said, "Mr. Ueberhorst, I wrote a report for the White House about three months ago complaining about the CIA management, and I've been getting the runaround ever since. What I want is some legal advice. Would I be breaking any laws if I took my memo and carried it over to the White House myself?" A few days later, on September 20, 1968, the executive director of the CIA, the number-three man in the hierarchy, called me to his office: "Mr. Adams, we think well of you, but Mr. Helms says he doesn't want your memo to leave the building." I took notes of the conversation, so my reproduction of it is almost verbatim. "This is not a legal problem but a practical one of your future within the CIA," I was told. "Because if you take that memo to the White House, it will be at your own peril, and even if you get what you want by doing so, your usefulness to the Agency will thereafter be nil." The executive director carried on this conversation for thirty-five minutes. I copied it all out until he said, "Do you have anything to say, Mr. Adams?" "Yes sir," I said, "I think I'll take this right on over to the White House, and please tell the director of my intention." I wrote a memorandum of the conversation, and sent it back up to the executive director's office with a covering letter saying, "I hope I'm quoting you correctly; please tell me if I'm not."

A short while later he called me back to his office and said, "I'm afraid there's been a misunderstanding, because the last thing in the world the director wanted to do was threaten. He has decided that this thing can go forward."

I waited until after the Presidential election. Nixon won, and the next day I called the seventh floor to ask if it was now okay to send on my memo to the White House. On November 8, 1968, Mr. Helms summoned me to his office. The first thing he said to me was "Don't take notes." To the best of my recollection, the conversation then proceeded along the following lines. He asked what was bothering me; did I think my supervisors were treating me unfairly, or weren't they promoting me fast enough? No, I said. My problem was that he caved in on the numbers right before Tet. I enlarged on the theme for about ten minutes. He listened without expression, and when I was done he asked what I would have had him do—take on the whole military? I said, that under the circumstances, that was the only thing he could have done; the military's numbers were faked. He then told me that I didn't know what things were like, that we could have told the White House that there were a million more Vietcong out there, and it wouldn't have made the slightest bit of difference in our policy. I said that we weren't the ones to decide about policy; all we should do was to send up the right numbers and let them worry. He asked me who I wanted to see, and I said that I had requested appropriate members of the White House staff and the President's Foreign Intelligence Advisory Board in my memo, but, frankly, I didn't know who the appropriate members were. He asked whether Gen. Maxwell Taylor and Walt Rostow would be all right. I told him that was not only acceptable, it was generous, and he said he would arrange the appointments for me.

With that I was sent around to see the deputy directors. The chief of research, R. Jack Smith, asked me what the matter was, and I told him the same things I had told Helms. The Vietnam war, he said, was an extraordinarily complex affair, and the size of the enemy army was only—his exact words—"a small but significant byway of the problem." His deputy, Edward Procter, now the CIA's chief of research, remarked, "Mr. Adams, the real problem is you. You ought to look into yourself."

Permission denied

After making these rounds, I wrote letters to Rostow and Taylor, telling them who I was and asking that they include a member of Nixon's staff in any talks we had about the CIA's shortcomings. I forwarded the letters, through channels, to the director's office, asking his permission to send them on. Permission was denied, and that was the last I ever heard about meeting with Mr. Rostow and General Taylor.

In early December I did manage to see the executive secretary of the President's Foreign Intelligence Advisory Board, J. Patrick Coyne. He told me that a few days earlier Helms had sent over my memo, that some members of PFIAB had read it, and that they were asking me to enlarge on my views and to make any recommendations I thought were in order. Coyne encouraged me to write a full report, and in the following weeks I put together a thirty-five-page paper explaining why I had brought charges. A few days after Nixon's inauguration, in January 1969, I sent the paper to Helms's office with a request for permission to send it to the White House. Permission was denied in a letter from the deputy director, Adm. Rufus Taylor, who informed me that the CIA was a team, and that if I didn't want to accept the team's decision, then I should resign.

There I was—with nobody from Nixon's staff having heard of any of this. It was far from clear whether Nixon intended to retain the President's Foreign Intelligence Advisory Board. J. Patrick Coyne said he didn't know. He also said he didn't intend to press for the release of the thirty-five page report. I thought I had been had.

For the first time in my career, I decided to leave official channels. This had never occurred to me before, not even when Helms had authorized the doctored numbers in the month before Tet. I had met a man named John Court, a member of the incoming staff of the National Security Council, and through him I hoped for a measure of redress. I gave him my memorandum and explained its import—including Westmoreland's deceptions before Tet—and asked him to pass it around so that at least the new administration might know what had gone on at the CIA and could take any action it thought necessary. Three weeks later Court told me that the memo had gotten around, all right, but the decision had been made not to do anything about it.

So I gave up. If the White House wasn't interested, there didn't seem to be any other place I could go. I felt I'd done as much as I possibly could do, and that was that.

Once again I thought about quitting the Agency. But again I decided not to, even though my career was pretty much in ruins. Not only had the deputy director just suggested that I resign, but I was now working under all kinds of new restrictions. I was no longer permitted to go to Vietnam. After the order-of-battle conference in Saigon in September 1967, Westmoreland's headquarters had informed the CIA station chief that I was persona non grata, and that they didn't want me on any military installations throughout the country. In CIA headquarters I was more or less confined to quarters, since I was no longer asked to attend any meetings at which outsiders were present. I was even told to cut back on the lectures I was giving about the VC to CIA case officers bound for Vietnam.[3]

I suppose what kept me from quitting this time was that I loved the job. The numbers business was going along fairly well, or so I thought, and I was becoming increasingly fascinated with what struck me as another disturbing question. Why was it that the Vietcong always seemed to know what we were up to, while we could never find out about them except through captured documents? At the time of the Tet offensive, for example, the CIA had only a single agent in the enemy's midst, and he was low-level.

At about this time, Robert Klein joined the VC branch. He had just graduated from college, and I thought him one of the brightest and most delightful people I had ever met. We began batting back and forth the question of why the VC always knew what was going to happen next. Having written a study on the Vietcong secret police in 1967, I already knew that the Communists had a fairly large and sophisticated espionage system. But I had no idea *how* large, and, besides, there were several other enemy organizations in addition to the secret police that had infiltrated the Saigon government. Klein and I began to sort them out. The biggest one, we found, was called the Military Proselytizing Directorate, which concentrated on recruiting agents in the South Vietnamese Army and National Police. By May 1969 we felt things were beginning to fall into place, but we still hadn't answered the fundamental question of how many agents the VC had in the South Vietnamese government. I decided to do the obvious thing, which was to start looking in the captured documents for references to spies. Klein and I each got a big stack of documents, and we began going through them, one by one. Within two weeks we had references to more than 1,000 VC agents. "Jesus Christ!" I said to Klein. "A thousand agents! And before Tet the CIA only had one." Furthermore, it was clear from the documents that the thousand we'd found were only the top of a very big iceberg.

Right away I went off to tell everybody the bad news. I had begun to take a perverse pleasure in my role as the man in opposition at the Agency. The first person I spoke to was the head of the Vietnam branch of the CIA Clandestine Services. I said, "Hey, a guy called Klein and I just turned up references to over 1,000 VC agents, and from the looks of the documents the overall number might run into the tens of thousands." He said, "For God's sake, don't open that Pandora's box. We have enough troubles as it is."

The next place I tried to reach was the Board of National Estimates, which was just convening its annual meeting on the Vietnam draft. Because of the trouble I'd made the year before, and because the meeting included outsiders, I wasn't allowed to attend. By now, Klein and I had come to the very tentative conclusion, based mostly on extrapolations from documents, that the Military Proselytizing Directorate alone had 20,000 agents in the South Vietnamese Army and government. This made it by far the biggest agent network in the history of espionage, and I was curious to know whether this was known in Saigon. I prompted a friend of mine to ask the CIA's Saigon station chief—back in Washington to give another briefing I wasn't allowed to attend—just how many Vietcong agents there were in the South Vietnamese Army. The station chief (a new one; Jorgy had long since moved) was taken aback at the question. He'd never considered it before. He said, "Well, the South Vietnamese Military Security Service has about 300 suspects under consideration. I think that about covers it." If Klein and I were anywhere near right with our estimate of 20,000, that made the station chief's figure too low by at least 6,000 percent.

New discoveries

Deciding that we didn't yet know enough to make an issue of the matter, Klein and I went back to plugging the documents. The more we read, the wilder the story became. With a great deal of help from the CIA counterintelligence staff, we eventually found that Vietcong agents were running the government's National Police in the northern part of the country, that for many years the VC had controlled the counterintelligence branch of the South Vietnamese Military Security Service (which may explain why the station chief's estimate was so low), and that in several areas of Vietnam, the VC were in charge of our own Phoenix Program. Scarcely a day passed without a new discovery. The most dramatic of them concerned a Vietcong agent posing as a South Vietnamese ordnance sergeant in Da Nang. The document said that the agent had been responsible for setting off explosions at the American air base in April 1969, and destroying 40,000 tons of ammunition worth $100 million.

The explosions were so big that they attracted a Congressional investigation, but the military managed to pass them off as having been started accidentally by a grass fire.

The problem with all these reports was not that they were hidden, but that they'd never been gathered and analyzed before in a systematic manner. Although CIA men in the field were aware of VC agents, Washington had failed to study the extent of the Vietcong network.

This is exactly what Klein and I attempted in the fall of 1969. By this time we had concluded that the total number of VC agents in the South Vietnamese Army and government was in the neighborhood of 30,000. While we admitted that the agents were a mixed bag—most of them were low-level personnel hedging their bets—we nonetheless arrived at an extremely bleak overall conclusion. That was that the agents were so numerous, so easy to recruit, and so hard to catch that their existence "called into question the basic loyalty of the South Vietnamese goverment and armed forces." This, in turn, brought up questions about the ultimate chances for success of our new policy of turning the war over to the Vietnamese.

In late November Klein and I had just about finished the first draft of our study when we were told that *under no circumstances* was it to leave CIA headquarters, and that, specifically, it shouldn't go to John Court of the White House staff. Meanwhile, however, I had called Court a number of times, telling him that the study existed, and that it suggested that Vietnamization probably wouldn't work. For the next two-and-a-half months, Court called the CIA front office asking for a draft of our memo on agents. Each time he was turned down.

Finally, in mid-February 1970, Court came over to the VC branch, and asked if he could have a copy of the agent memorandum. I told him he couldn't, but that I supposed it was okay if he looked at it at a nearby desk. By closing time Court had disappeared, along with the memo. I phoned him the next morning at the Executive Office Building and asked him if he had it. "Yes, I took it. Is that okay?" he said. It wasn't okay, and shortly after informing my superiors I received a letter of reprimand for releasing the memo to an "outsider." (Court, who worked for the White House, was the "outsider.") All copies of the study within the CIA—several were around being reviewed— were recalled to the Vietcong branch and put in a safe. Klein was removed from working on agents, and told that if he didn't "shape up," he'd be fired.

The research department and perhaps even Helms (I don't know) apparently were appalled by the agent's memo reaching the White House. It was embarrassing for the CIA, since we'd never let anything like that out before. To suddenly say, oh, by the way, our ally, the South Vietnamese government, is crawling with spies, might lead someone to think that maybe the Agency should have noticed them sooner. We'd been in the war, after all, for almost six years.

Court later wrote a précis of the memo and gave it to Kissinger. Kissinger gave it to Nixon. Shortly thereafter, the White House sent a directive to Helms which said, in effect: "Okay, Helms, get that damn agent paper out of the safe drawer." Some months later, the Agency coughed it up, almost intact.

Meanwhile, Klein quit. I tried to talk him out of it, but he decided to go to graduate school. He did so in September 1970, but not before leaving a letter of resignation with the CIA inspector general. Klein's letter told the complete story of the agent study, concluding with his opinion that the White House would never have learned about the Communist spies had it not been for John Court's sticky fingers.

By now my fortunes had sunk to a low ebb. For the first time in seven years, I was given an unfavorable fitness report. I was rated "marginal" at conducting research; I had lost my "balance and objectivity" on the war, and worst of all, I was the cause of the "discontent leading to the recent resignation" of Klein. For these shortcomings I was being reassigned to a position where I would be "less directly involved in research on the war." This meant I had to leave the Vietcong branch and join a small historical staff, where I was to take up the relatively innocuous job of writing a history of the Cambodian rebels.

Once again, I considered resigning from the CIA, but the job still had me hooked, and ever since the coup that deposed Sihanouk in March 1970 I had been wondering what was going on in Cambodia. Within a few weeks of that coup, the Communist army had begun to disappear from the southern half of South Vietnam for service next door, and I was curious to find out what it was up to. When I reported to the historical staff, I began, as usual, to collect documents. This was my main occupation for almost the next five months. I knew so little about Cambodia that I was fairly indiscriminate, and therefore grabbed just about everything I could find. By late April 1971, I had gathered several thousand reports, and had divided them into broad categories, such as "military" and "political." In early May, I began to go through the "military" reports.

One of the first of these was an interrogation report of a Vietcong staff officer who had surrendered in Cambodia in late 1970. The staff officer said he belonged to a Cambodian Communist regional command with a code name I'd never heard of: C-40. Apparently C-40 had several units attached to it, including regiments, and I'd never heard of any of these, either. And, it seemed, the units were mostly composed of Khmers, of whom C-40 had a total of 18,000. Now that appeared to me to be an awful lot of Khmer soldiers just for one area, so I decided to check it against our Cambodian order of battle. Within a month I made a startling discovery: there was *no* order of battle. All I could find was a little sheet of paper estimating the size of the Khmer Communist Army at 5,000 to 10,000 men. This sheet of paper, with exactly the same numbers, had been kicking around since early 1970.

It was the same story as our Vietcong estimate of 1966, only worse. In Vietnam we had neglected to look at three of the four parts of the Vietcong Army; in Cambodia we hadn't looked at the Khmer Communist Army at all. It later turned out that the 5,000-to-10,000 figure was based on numbers put together by a sergeant in the Royal Cambodian Army in 1969.

From then on, it was easy. Right in the same room with me was every single intelligence report on the Khmer rebels that had ever come in. Straightaway I found what the VC Army had been doing in Cambodia since Sihanouk's fall: it had put together the largest and best advisory structure in the Indochina war. Within two weeks I had discovered thirteen regiments, several dozen battalions, and a great many companies and platoons. Using exactly the same methods that I'd used on the Vietcong estimate before Tet (only now the methods were more refined), I came to the conclusion that the size of the Cambodian Communist Army was not 5,000 to 10,000 but more like 100,000 to 150,000. In other words, the U.S. government's official estimate was between ten and thirty times too low.

My memo was ready in early June, and this time I gave a copy to John Court of the White House the day before I turned it in at the Agency. This proved to have been a wise move, because when I turned it in I was told, "Under no circumstances does this go out of the room." It was the best order-of-battle paper I'd ever done. It had about 120 footnotes, referencing about twice that many intelligence reports, and it was solid as a rock.

A week later I was taken off the Khmer Communist Army and forbidden to work on numbers anymore. A junior analyst began reworking my memo with instructions to hold the figure below 30,000. The analyst puzzled over this for several months, and at last settled on the same method the military had used in lowering the Vietcong estimate before Tet. He marched two whole categories out of the order of battle and "scaled down" what was left. In November 1971, he wrote up a memo placing the size of the Khmer Communst Army at 15,000 to 30,000 men. The CIA published the memo, and that number became the U.S. government's official estimate.

More distortions

The present official estimate of the Khmer rebels—65,000—derives from the earlier one. It is just as absurd. Until very recently the Royal Cambodian Army was estimated at over 200,000 men. We are therefore asked to believe that the insurgents, who control four-fifths of Cambodia's land and most of its people, are outnumbered by the ratio of 3 to 1. In fact, if we count *all* the rebel soldiers, including those dropped or omitted from the official estimate, the Khmer Rebel Army is probably larger than the government's—perhaps by a considerable margin.

The trouble with this kind of underestimate is not simply a miscalculation of numbers. It also distorts the meaning of the war. In Cambodia, as in the rest of Southeast Asia, the struggle is for allegiance, and the severest test of loyalty has to do with who can persuade the largest number of peasants to pick up a gun. When American intelligence downgrades the strength of the enemy army, it ignores the Communist success at organizing and recruiting people. This is why the Communists call the struggle a "people's war" and why the government found it difficult to understand.

I spent the rest of 1971 and a large part of 1972 trying to get the CIA to raise the Cambodian estimate. It was useless. The Agency was busy with other matters, and I became increasingly discouraged. The Cambodian affair seemed to me to be a repeat of the Vietnam one, the same people made the same mistakes, in precisely the same ways, and everybody was allowed to conceal his duplicity. In the fall of 1972 I decided to make one last attempt at bringing the shoddiness of American intelligence to the attention of someone, anyone who could do anything about it.

Between October 1972 and January 1973 I approached the U.S. Army inspector general, the CIA inspector general, and the Congress—all to no avail. To the Army inspector general I delivered a memorandum setting forth the details of what had happened to the VC estimate before Tet. I mentioned the possibility of General Westmoreland's complicity, which might have implicated him in three violations of the Uniform Code of Military Justice. The memorandum asked for an investigation, but the inspector general explained that I was in the wrong jurisdiction. Of the CIA inspector general I requested an investigation of the Cambodian estimates, but he adopted the device of neglecting to answer his mail, and no inquiry took place. In a last desperate measure—desperate because my friends at the CIA assured me that Congressional watchdog committees were a joke—I even appealed to Congress. To committees in both the House and Senate that watch over the CIA I sent a thirteen-page memorandum with names, dates, numbers, and a sequence of events. A staff assistant to the Senate Armed Services Committee thought it an interesting document, but he doubted that the Intelligence Subcommittee would take it up because it hadn't met in over a year and a half. Lucien Nedzi, the chief superintendent of the CIA in the House, also thought the document "pertinent," but he observed that the forthcoming elections obliged him to concern himself primarily with the question of busing. When I telephoned his office in late November, after the elections had come and gone, his administrative assistant told me, in effect, "Don't call us; we'll call you."

By mid-January 1973 I had reached the end of the road. I happened to read a newspaper account of Daniel Ellsberg's trial in Los Angeles, and I noticed that the government was alleging that Ellsberg had injured the national security by releasing estimates of the enemy force in Vietnam. I looked, and damned if they weren't from the same order of battle which the military had doctored back in 1967. Imagine! Hanging a man for leaking faked numbers! In late February I went to Los Angeles to testify at the trial and told the story of how the numbers got to be so wrong. When I returned to Washington in March, the CIA once again threatened to fire me. I complained, and, as usual, the Agency backed own. After a decent interval, I quit.

One last word. Some day, when everybody has returned to his senses, I hope to go back to the CIA as an analyst. I like the work.

Notes

1. A document was later captured which showed the Vietcong not only reached but exceeded their quota. Dated April 1966, it put the number of guerrilla-militia at 330,000.

2. This was broken down as follows: Communist regulars, about 100,000; guerrilla-militia, about 300,000; service troops, about 100,000; political cadres, about 100,000.

3. In mid-1968 I had discovered that Agency officers sent to Vietnam received a total of only one hour's instruction on the organization and methods of operation of the Vietcong. Disturbed that they should be sent up against so formidable a foe with so little training, I had by the end of the year increased the hours from one to twenty-four. I gave most of the lectures myself.

The Moral of the Tale

Readers interested in the question of integrity in American government might take note of three successful bureaucrats mentioned in this chronicle. All of them acknowledged or abetted the counterfeiting of military intelligence, and all of them have risen to high places within their respective apparats. Lt. Gen. Daniel Graham, who helped to lower the U.S. Army's estimate of Vietcong strength, is now the head of the Defense Intelligence Agency; Edward Procter, who steadfastly ignored accurate intelligence, is now chief of the CIA research directorate; and William Hyland, who conceded the impossibility of contesting a political fiction, is now the head of State Department Intelligence. Their collective docility might also interest readers concerned with questions of national security.

26
MBO goes to work in the public sector

Rodney H. Brady

The nation's largest organization in terms of spending power—the United States Department of Health, Education, and Welfare (HEW)—has been called unmanageable. It may have been at one time, but an important step toward making HEW more manageable has been the development and implementation of one of the most far-reaching management by objectives (MBO) systems in operation anywhere.

Reprinted by permission,*Harvard Business Review,* March-April 1973. Copyright © 1973 by the President and Fellows of Harvard College; all rights reserved.
Rodney Brady was Assistant Secretary for Administration and Management at HEW from 1970 to 1972. He left that post to return to private industry.

Although MBO is a familiar management tool in the private business sector, it had been used sparingly in the public sector prior to being introduced at HEW. The department turned to MBO as a means of coping with a veritable explosion in the size and scope of its operations. HEW's budget authority for the 1973 fiscal year is $87 billion—an increase of 70% over its budget of just four years ago, and the first civilian-agency budget in modern U.S. history to eclipse that of the Department of Defense. More than one third of all the money dispensed by the federal government this fiscal year will flow through HEW.

Prior to becoming the chief administrative and management officer of HEW in late 1970, I had been a senior executive and a management consultant in the private business sector and had discovered firsthand the value of MBO as an effective tool for managing large, complex organizations. However, the imponderable question facing me and my staff as we sought to implement a departmentwide MBO system at HEW was whether this method of management, believed by many to depend on the discipline of a profit and loss statement for successful operation, could be adapted to an organization that must ultimately measure success in terms of improving the quality of life.

Now, after over two years of experience with MBO, we have learned not only that this technique will indeed work at HEW but also that it has applicability to other large, public-sector organizations. It is the objective of this article to (a) explain some major differences in introducing MBO to a public, as opposed to a private, sector organization; (b) briefly describe the MBO approach that has evolved at HEW and summarize the lessons we have learned in applying it; and (c) provide guidelines for other public-and private-sector organizations that may wish to adopt this management tool.

Private & public MBO

In 1954, Peter F. Drucker gave form to the concept of MBO in his book, *The Practice of Management.*[1] Ten years later, in giving the concept substance, he could still complain that "the foundation for systematic, purposeful performance of the specific task and function of business enterprise is . . . still missing."[2] Today, however, MBO is installed in numerous private companies and its premises are familiar to many business managers.[3] The strength of these premises lies in their simplicity.

◆The clearer the idea of what one wants to accomplish, the greater the chances of accomplishing it.

◆Real progress can only be measured in relation to what one is trying to make progress toward.

In other words, if one knows where he is going, he finds it easier to get there, he can get there faster, and he will know it when he arrives.

Although the premises of MBO have been tested and proven in the private sector, it has taken the public sector considerably longer to effectively incorporate them. Executives in the federal government have long grasped the *need* for more effective management, but for the most part they have failed to develop and implement systems such as MBO. This is one reason why they are so often frustrated in their attempts to manage large federal departments.

As John Gardner, who spent three years at the helm of HEW, put it: "When you figure out how to hold a middle-level bureaucrat accountable, it'll be comparable to landing on the moon."[4]

Similarly, Senator Abraham Ribicoff, HEW Secretary in 1961, remarked that "no matter how brilliant he is, no Secretary can handle the job with distinction because of the enormity of the task of managing billions of dollars worth of programs spanning the wide range of social needs in the United States."[5]

Former Secretary Ribicoff would have been quite correct if he had added that no Secretary can manage HEW with distinction unless he is given the management tools required to do the job. I am convinced that MBO is foremost among these tools. But before it can be used effectively, some problems that are unique to the public sector must be overcome. These include (a) defining objectives, (b) measuring benefits, and (c) the operating cycle.

The objectives problem

In the private-sector organization, the primary objective traditionally has been defined by the stockholders and board of directors as maximizing return on investment. This main objective is often supplemented by subobjectives such as rate of growth, development of new products, provisions for executive succession, and contributions to society.[6] Except for the latter (and even that to a large extent), all of these subobjectives focus directly on the primary goal of maximizing return on investment. It is possible, therefore, to translate the overall objective and each of its subobjectives into consistent, measurable, and mathematically relatable components. Thus, a single management system can be implemented throughout the enterprise to create a model of goal congruence.

In the public-sector organization, however, there is no such single return-on-investment objective to which subobjectives can easily be tied. Unanimity on an overall objective for HEW, for example, does not exist among the 209 million Americans who are the department's "stockholders" as well as its "customers." Nor is such agreement to be found among those who cast the proxy votes for these stockholders—the decision makers in the legislative and executive branches, and even the judicial branch, of the federal government.

Moreover, on the rare occasions when these parties agree on subobjectives for HEW, the subobjectives are usually nebulous, difficult to measure, and lacking in the summing qualities that characterize the return-on-investment subobjectives common to the private sector.

The benefits problem

Measuring cost/benefits in the public sector is also more difficult than in private industry. One can calculate the dollar cost of teaching a disadvantaged child to read, for example, but how does one measure the "profitability" of this service to society? There is no single criterion for success when the benefit gained is in terms of newly unleashed human potential.

Although the department is continuing to seek ways to measure a dollar's effectiveness in, say, rehabilitating handicapped workers or reducing juvenile delinquency, such measurement is still a very rough science. In most cases, it will be years before the real benefits toward which these objectives are aimed can be evaluated effectively.

The operating-cycle problem

A necessarily short operating cycle is another limiting factor when introducing MBO into a public-sector organization. Although federal agencies like HEW have their own long-range goals, these goals are more likely to be upset than those in private industry. There are three reasons for this:

1. Federal agencies are budgeted annually in a complex process that too frequently is unpredictable.

2. A high rate of turnover among top-level, decision-making personnel is characteristic of the federal government.

3. Objectives set by public-sector managers in today's political setting will likely be deemed inadequate in tomorrow's political setting.

The MBO process in HEW is based on a one-year operating cycle—the federal fiscal year. Even given this relatively short time frame, the department's objectives for the year are subject to change, based on new or altered legislative mandates and/or new executive initiatives.

Yet, despite these not unexpected difficulties in establishing objectives and the allied difficulties of measuring progress toward their achievement, MBO has proved to be extremely helpful in managing the affairs of HEW. In the next section, I shall discuss how MBO actually operates in the department; but first, a closer look at HEW may help explain why a rigorous, formalized management system is essential if such a large, politically sensitive organization is to be managed effectively. Accordingly, the HEW structure and mission are described in the ruled insert.

The structure and the mission of HEW

HEW is charged with the responsibility for administering federal programs in the fields of health, education income security, and social services. The department has over 100,000 employees; and it administers some 300 programs, ranging from cancer research to vocational education to family planning. Owing in part to the shift of national priorities away from defense spending and toward human-resources spending, HEW has recently been caught in a stream of national debate. It has been forced to operate in an atmosphere characterized by such highly political issues as school desegregation, busing, and welfare reform.

HEW is divided into seven major agencies and ten regional offices located across the country from Boston to Seattle. The staff of the Office of the Secretary provides advice to the Secretary as well as centralized support to the agencies and regional offices. The seven agencies and their basic missions are:

1. *National Institutes of Health* (NIH), which conducts and sponsors biomedical research and health-education programs.

2. *Health Services and Mental Health Administration* (HSMHA), which provides and sponsors health services, and conducts and sponsors research in the field of mental health.

3. *Food and Drug Administration* (FDA), which is a regulatory agency charged with ensuring that food, drugs, and other substances and devices utilized by consumers are safe and effective.

4. *Office of Education* (OE), which promotes the establishment of an effective and efficient educational system throughout the nation.

5. *Social Security Administration* (SSA), which operates the nation's system of social insurance through receiving contributions, processing claims, and making payments to beneficiaries; it also administers the Medicare program.

6. *Social and Rehabilitation Service* (SRS), which manages the federal social service and assistance payments programs.

7. *Office of Child Development* (OCD), which acts as an advocate for children and coordinates federal programs specifically aimed at children. youth, and their families.

While each of these agencies administers assigned programs, many of these programs require the cooperation of two or more agencies. For example, drug abuse prevention requires significant participation by nearly every agency.

The ten regional offices, and the field staffs of each of the agencies, oversee the delivery of services at the local level and maintain close contact with states, local governments, and grantees receiving funds from HEW. In this regard, it is important to note that less than 10% of HEW's money is spent on direct operations. More than 90% goes to Social Security beneficiaries or is dispersed to some 40,000 grantees, including state and local governments and educational or other non-profit institutions.

Application at HEW

Before MBO was introduced, the HEW operating cycle failed in several ways to systematically control the implementation of policy and budget decisions. For example:

◆ There was no adequate provision for stating program objectives that were based on specific, measurable results. Consequently, program success often was measured on the wrong criteria (e.g., the number of grants awarded rather than the number of people served or problems solved).

◆ There was no effective formal mechanism to ensure a continuing dialogue, throughout the operating cycle, between policy makers and program managers regarding the problems and successes encountered during the implementation phase. Consequently, there was both a lack of information for policy developers and a lack of guidance for managers.

Exhibit I. Comparison of HEW operating cycles

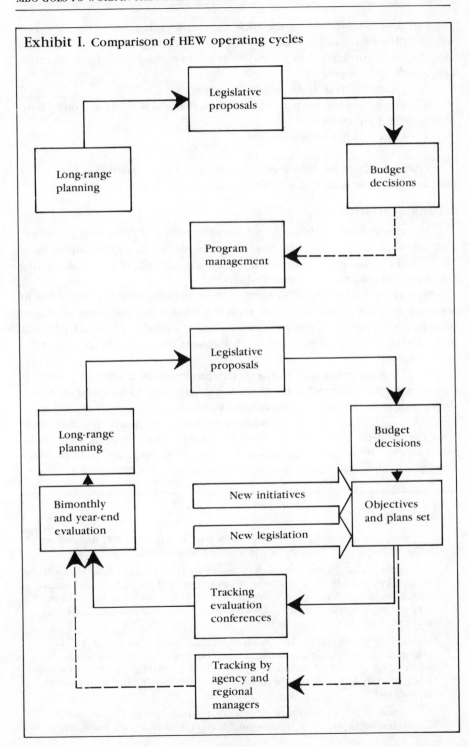

Part A of *Exhibit I* shows the HEW operating cycle prior to the introduction of MBO; Part B of the exhibit shows the operating cycle after MBO was introduced. Accordingly, when the system was implemented at HEW, its major operational goals were:

- To identify clear, measurable objectives.
- To monitor progress toward objectives that had been agreed on by both managers and policy makers.
- To effectively evaluate results.

Later I shall discuss how well the system met these goals. But first, let us take a closer look at how it actually works.

Setting objectives

The annual MBO cycle begins when the department formulates its budget and makes the key resource and fund-allocation decisions for the coming fiscal year. Program managers are urged to accompany each request for funds with a list of measurable, results-oriented objectives.

By linking fund requests to the specific results the funds are intended to accomplish, HEW seeks to avoid awarding money on the basis of vague, projected activities. As mentioned earlier, this is a particularly acute problem in the public sector. To overcome it, HEW has instituted a six-stage, objective-setting procedure:

1. The Secretary employs the initial proposals as a starting point. He determines specifically what he wants the department to accomplish during the coming year and how the department's short-range goals will contribute to long-range objectives. He works closely with agency heads to refine their objectives and their requests for funds in the light of these goals. (The ruled insert below contains a typical dialogue between the Secretary and one of his managers as they attempt to formulate a results-oriented objective.)

An objective-setting meeting at HEW

Here is a typical dialogue between former Secretary Elliot L. Richardson HEW and an agency head as they formulated an objective.

Agency head: One of our agency's most important initiatives this year will be to focus our efforts in the area of alcoholism and to treat an additional 10,000 alcoholics. Given last year's funding of 41 alcoholism treatment centers and the direction of other resources at the state and local level, we feel that this is an achievable objective.

Secretary: Are these 41 centers operating independently or are they linked to other service organizations in their communities? In other words, are we treating the whole problem of alcoholism, including its employment, mental health and welfare aspects, or are we just treating the *symptoms* of alcoholism?

Agency head: A program requirement for getting funds is that the services involved must be linked in an integrated fashion with these other resources.

> *Secretary:* I am not interested in just looking at the number of alcoholics that are treated. Our goal ought to be the actual rehabilitation of these patients. Do you have data to enable you to restate the objective in terms of that goal?
>
> *Agency head:* As a matter of fact, Mr. Secretary, we have developed a management information and evaluation system in which each grantee will be providing quarterly data on the number of alcoholics treated, as well as on the number of alcoholics who are actually rehabilitated.
>
> *Secretary:* How do you define "rehabilitated"?
>
> *Agency head:* If they are gainfully employed one year after treatment, we regard them as being rehabilitated.
>
> *Secretary:* Please revise this objective, then, to enable us to track progress on how effective these programs really are in treating the disease of alcoholism and in rehabilitating alcoholics.

2. The staff of the Secretary draws up the department's budget and then forwards it to the President and Congress for action.

3. The Secretary, who has determined priorities during the budgeting process, then formalizes them in a document that provides planning guidance to agency heads and regional managers.

4. These executives then review and alter their preliminary objectives to conform to changed budget priorities and overall department goals, typically selecting eight to ten objectives that represent the most important results expected of their respective programs.

5. Just prior to the start of the fiscal year, agency heads and regional managers submit these objectives, along with outlines of milestones that must be reached and resources that must be expended for their accomplishment, to the Office of the Secretary, where they are given careful analysis by his staff.

6. From this list of objectives, the Secretary selects those he will personally track. He also has the option of adding other objectives to the department's list (either at the start of the cycle or during the year), depending on his perception of HEW's changing mandate, the passage of new legislation, executive initiative, or other developments that affect the department's role.

Obviously, the Secretary cannot personally track all objectives. Many are tracked on a continuing basis by HEW agency leaders and managers at several organizational levels. In addition to the 70 objectives personally tracked by the Secretary last year, HEW agency heads and regional directors tracked approximately 300 objectives, and agency bureaus tracked about 1,500.

Monitoring progress

The Office of the Secretary and the staff workers in each agency monitor progress in meeting objectives. The ongoing review process is facilitated by milestone charts that are prepared for each objective.

Of course, interim progress cannot always be expressed in terms of the final result. Yet by carefully selecting intermediate milestones that logic says must be achieved to accomplish the end result, one can in effect measure interim progress.

For example, one objective of the Health Services and Mental Health Administration (HSMHA) during 1971 was to increase the capacity of institutions receiving HSMHA support to provide family planning services for an additional 800,000 low-income patients. *Exhibit II* shows a detailed plan, including eight major milestones, that was outlined for accomplishing this objective. This was the status of the objective in October of 1971; since then, the other milestones have been reached and the objective has been completed.

The progress of objectives that are narrower in scope can usually be expressed more readily throughout the year in terms of final results. An example is the section of a HSMHA objective which called for providing immunizations to 8 million children. It was relatively easy to determine how many immunizations had been completed as the year progressed and to know by the end of the year that the objective had, in fact, been met.

Management conferences: Managers are encouraged to maintain close contact with the Office of the Secretary and to seek advice or assistance in meeting their goals. In addition to this informal dialogue, the Secretary holds a bimonthly management conference with each agency head and regional direc-

---

Exhibit II. Operating plan for HSMHA family planning objective

Resources committed: $88,815,000

	COMPLETION DATE					
MILESTONES	JULY AUG.	SEPT. OCT.	NOV. DEC.	JAN. FEB.	MAR. APR.	MAY JUNE
1. Expand and transfer OEO projects to increase capacity by 25,000 patients		★				
2. Establish regional coordinating councils		★				
3. Fund new projects, expand and transfer projects to increase capacity by 200,000 patients			●			
4. Report to Congress on five-year plan				●		
5. Fund new projects, expand and transfer projects to increase capacity by 250,000 patients					●	
6. Develop evaluation strategy for fiscal year 1973						●
7. Fund new projects, expand and transfer projects to increase capacity by 325,000 patients						●
8. Prepare final report						●

Health Priority — Family planning objective

KEY
★ COMPLETED
● NOT COMPLETED

tor. These conferences, which are also attended by principal staff aides, are the keystone to the success of the entire MBO system.

It has been charged that the typical MBO system, characterized by such periodic appraisals, "perpetuates and intensifies hostility, resentment, and distrust between a manager and subordinates."[7] This may be the case in some instances, but it does not have to be. At HEW, for example, a publication entitled *Focus* is distributed to managers who are, or will be, participating in the bimonthly review conferences. It emphasizes that these are not "knuckle-rapping sessions" and states:

"They are undertaken with the understanding that circumstances change; that, given the best will, spirit, and effort possible, *the things we do,* unfortunately, do not always *produce the results* intelligent men predict of them."[8]

Ten days prior to each management conference, an agency head or regional director submits to the Secretary a status report and evaluation on all objectives for which he is responsible. If a milestone has been accomplished on time and no problems are anticipated with future steps, the manager simply fills in the triangle representing the completion date of schedule milestones (see *Exhibit II*). If, however, a milestone has not been completed on schedule or a future milestone is not likely to be completed on schedule, the agency head or regional director indicates the anticipated completion deadline by adding a triangle in the column which corresponds to the new planned month of accomplishment.

Managers also submit an evaluation of the status of each objective. This is based on a three-level classification system:

1. Satisfactory—no problem exists, nor is any anticipated, that will hinder the accomplishment of the objective on schedule.

2. Minor problem—although there is a problem, it does not presently jeopardize accomplishment of the objective.

3. Major problem—there is a distinct possibility that the objective will not be achieved in the absence of major corrective action.

The conference provides a dialogue between the Secretary and the manager, giving them a joint opportunity to identify and resolve management problems. Its agenda, planned jointly by the Secretary and the manager, centers on the objectives of the manager's agency. However, the conference is also used to familiarize both parties with changes inside or outside the agency that will affect its work. Even the objectives themselves may be changed to conform to new initiatives, thus resulting in a dynamic rather than a static process.

This ability to quickly change directions, even to the point of abandoning or drastically altering prior objectives, is a must in the public sector. Contrast this with the following statement on objectives by the former chairman of the board of Avis: "Once . . . objectives are agreed on, the leader must be merciless on himself and on his people. If an idea that pops into his head or out of their mouths is outside the objectives of the company, he kills it without a trial."[9]

Following each management conference, a detailed report is provided to the Secretary and other key participants. The report outlines the discussion items, decisions, and specific assignments. The status of each assignment is then reviewed at each succeeding conference until the action is completed.

Evaluating results

In addition to the bimonthly reports just described, each manager submits a year-end evaluation to the Office of the Secretary which describes successes and failures in meeting objectives. The annual report details such things as revisions of objectives during the year, reasons for failure in fulfilling any objective, and steps taken to ensure that the same problems will not arise again. These evaluations are used in the long-range planning process to help make the department's future objectives more realistic as well as to help obviate potential problems.

Problems along the way

The cliché that old ways are not easily changed is particularly apt in the federal bureaucracy. This is true for a number of reasons, most of which are inherent in the nature of a system governed by a mixture of politically appointed personnel and professional personnel. In theory, the latter are subject to the policy decisions of the former. In reality, it is no secret that this is not always the case. Presidents and heads of departments come and go; yet the bureaucracy remains behind to keep the wheels of government turning.

The primary constraint to the success of MBO at HEW has been an attitude on the part of some managers that the regular attention required of them by such a system is either (a) not consistent with their roles or (b) not as effective a way to manage as some other approach. Some managers have viewed their roles as principally involving policy making, development of legislation, and defense of their budget requests. The intricacies of formalized management planning and control have taken a secondary role to these other functions. Too often, top-level managers have become preoccupied with handling crises in their agencies and have dealt with management issues on an ad hoc, rather than on an anticipatory, results-oriented basis.

Ironically, the fact that MBO gives managers access to the highest level of the department has been a hindrance, as well as a help, in gaining acceptance of the system. A common belief among managers in organizations of all types is that you have somehow failed if you have to bring your problems to the head of the organization. Thus, at HEW, some managers have proposed only those areas for control under MBO which would not prove a source of embarrassment in face-to-face dialogue at management conferences.

A related problem has been getting managers not only to adequately define problem areas but also to "stretch" in setting their objectives in those areas. In some cases, managers have established easily achievable objectives whose accomplishment is almost a foregone conclusion. Last year, for example, one HEW agency set a goal of decreasing by 2% the number of persons, in

13 selected geographical areas, who would need rehabilitative assistance of a certain type. By the end of the year, the goal had not only been met but had been exceeded ten times over.

Old ways can, however, be changed, as long as one can demonstrate good reasons for such change. Department leaders are satisfied that, in spite of the aforementioned obstacles, MBO has taken hold and is being genuinely accepted throughout the department.

Benefits of the system

Although HEW still has significant problems, measurable results to date document some substantial benefits from the three-year-old MBO system. For example:

☐ During fiscal year 1972, the Food and Drug Administration (FDA) determined that, within existing resources, it would attempt to increase by 50% the number of import products inspected. This objective was met despite the delay and disruption to shipping caused by the Eastern Seaboard dock strike.

☐ In fiscal year 1971, the first full year of MBO in operation in the department, an objective of a program run by the Social and Rehabilitation Service (SRS) was to train and place 35,000 welfare recipients in meaningful jobs. SRS faced the need to convince the state agencies, which are the conduits for rehabilitation funds, that such concentration on public assistance recipients was warranted. It also faced the fact that the rehabilitation of welfare recipients is not an easy task. By establishing a results-oriented objective, carefully planning for its accomplishment, and communicating it to all levels of government, SRS actually exceeded its goal. It trained more than 40,000 welfare recipients and offered them a productive future by taking them off welfare rolls and putting them on payrolls.

Moreover, the rehabilitation objective in fiscal year 1973 is to move from a level of approximately 50,000 recipients per year to a level of 69,000. This planned 38% increase is approximately double the normally expected figure based on projected historical trend lines. Further, the department plans to achieve this objective with only a 14% increase in resources.

In addition to the short-term benefits from HEW's adaptation of MBO, there have been improvements in overall management. A key role the Secretary plays in regular management conferences is to ensure that the department is responding on an integrated basis to social problems, which rarely cut cleanly along jurisdictional lines of public agencies. In particular, he can use the conferences to communicate successes and problems identified elsewhere in HEW that have relevance to conferees.

For example, in its initial presentation of proposed fiscal year 1973 objectives, the Office of Child Development (OCD) indicated it would establish a new category of day care worker. The new position, to be called "child development associate," will be filled by competent individuals who do not have special education or college degrees but who, nonetheless, are able to work well with children. The Secretary was able to receive assurances that this objective would be developed in such a way that it would provide a basis for similar categories of workers in other HEW programs.

Conclusion

MBO as a concept is simple—deceptively so. It is much easier to explain this technique than it is to introduce it to an organization, especially one as complex as HEW. Although the department is now in its third year of utilizing MBO as a primary management device, it is still building toward achieving a fully institutionalized, short-term management and control system that is used by all of its key managers.

Many lessons have been gleaned from HEW's experience with MBO that both add to the knowledge of the concept as used in the public sector and reinforce lessons already learned in the private sector. I shall conclude this discussion by grouping the lessons we have learned into four broad categories.

1. Differences in public-sector approach:

◆ While effective objectives can be established in public sector organizations, the process of developing the objectives is often more complex and requires broader coordination and participation of interested parties than in the private sector.

◆ Objectives in the public sector must take a different form from those in the private sector. In the former, the objectives must usually be stated in terms of interim results; in the latter, objectives can normally be stated in terms of the ultimate objective of "return on investment."

◆ Although progress toward achieving many public sector objectives is difficult to measure, few meaningful objectives are beyond effective measurement. Through utilization of milestone charts, which document accomplishments to be achieved by established dates, progress toward achieving almost any objective can be measured.

2. Role of the top executive:

◆ A chief executive officer who has both the will and the capacity to manage is essential to the effective utilization of an MBO system.

◆ MBO must be tailored to the chief executive's style of managing. One leader might take a decisive role in the operation of the system, while another leader might well have a different style of operating. Resistance to modifying the system to fit the style can destroy the MBO process.

◆ The chief executive officer must communicate clearly to other organizational components what he feels the general goals and priorities of the organization ought to be. Without such guidance, the subordinates' development of initial objectives for submission to the boss tends to be wasteful and counterproductive.

◆ The chief executive's attitude affects the spirit in which the system functions, and it will determine whether MBO encourages the defining and solving of problems or the hiding of problems. If MBO is perceived by a chief executive as a problem-solving and goal-reaching device (rather than as an opportunity to point an accusing finger at one of his subordinates), the subordinates themselves are likely to take this view.

3. *Managerial relationships:*

◆ The establishment of objectives must be a cooperative venture between subordinate and superior. Moreover, unless both parties feel that the objective is important, challenging, and achievable, even cooperative activity will become only a meaningless exercise.

◆ Managers must be persuaded that the primary function of MBO is to enable them to manage more effectively, *not* to use the management conference to reach the ear of the chief executive on random issues of particular momentary interest to the manager.

◆ To be effective, the MBO system must operate on a line manager-to-subordinate basis, not on a staff-to-staff basis. Although staff assistance is essential to keep the system functioning, staff must serve as a facilitator of the system and not its operator. To operate otherwise invites confusion in lines of authority and causes a breakdown in accountability.

◆ Unless the superior and subordinate have regular face-to-face reviews of interim progress, the importance of the system begins to be questioned, there is danger of misunderstanding, and much of the motivational value of the system is lost. Prior to such interim review meetings, it is essential that the superior's staff prepare him to ask the right questions and to avoid being "snowed" by the subordinate.

4. *General strategy considerations:*

◆ It is important to receive a detailed plan for accomplishing an objective at the same time the objective itself is submitted for approval. Otherwise, proposed objectives too often will not be well thought out in advance, and the possibility for eventual success will ultimately be decreased.

◆ A middle ground must be found between holding personnel too rigidly to their objectives and allowing them to alter the objectives at will. HEW's method has been to (a) have the Secretary himself approve all proposed changes and (b) ensure that such changes are evaluated in each agency's annual performance report.

◆ If an organization is consistently accomplishing 100% of its objectives, there is probably reason for concern rather than celebration. Objectives are not really effective unless an organization must "stretch" to reach them. During the last fiscal year, for example, approximately one fourth of HEW's objectives were only partially achieved and another one eighth fell far short of expectation. This is probably not an unhealthy balance.

◆ It is a mistake to try to make MBO so systematic and rigid that it precludes discussion of important matters not contained in formalized objectives. In fact, MBO should be expected to trigger ad hoc discussions of matters that are not included in stated objectives but are nonetheless vital to the success of the organization.

◆ MBO is perhaps better perceived as a muscle than as merely a tool. The more it is used, the stronger and more necessary it becomes. However, if MBO is merely a management system on paper and is not allowed to be exercised as an integral part of running an organization, it will atrophy and become useless.

Notes

1. New York, Harper & Row, 1954.
2. Peter F. Drucker, *Managing for Results* (New York, Harper & Row, 1964), Introduction, p.x.
3. For more detail on both the theory behind MBO and its practical application in private companies, see "Managing by—and with—Objectives," *The Conference Board Record* (1968). Also see John B. Lasagna, "Make Your MBO Pragmatic," HBR November-December 1971, p. 64.
4. Quoted in Robert Sherrill, "The Hatchetman and the Hatchetmyth," *Potomac* (Sunday Supplement to the Washington Post), February 6, 1972, pp. 13, 26.
5. Quoted in Robert Sherrill, "The Real Robert Finch Stands Up," *The New York Times Magazine,* July 5, 1970, p. 19.
6. For a discussion of social contributions in the private sector, see Raymond A. Bauer and Dan H. Fenn, Jr., "What *Is* a Corporate Social Audit?" HBR January-February 1973, p. 37.
7. Harry Levinson, "Management by Whose Objectives?" HBR July-August 1970, p. 125.
8. Department of Health, Education and Welfare, March 1972, Introduction, p. x.
9. See Robert Townsend, *Up The Organization* (New York, Alfred A. Knopf, Inc., 1970), p. 130.

27
Management
vs. Man

August Heckscher

A mong the less attractive things that can be said about the age we live in, is that it is the Age of the Managers. Call it the Age of Permissiveness, or the Age of Waste, or any other sort of age you wish: I shall find some good in it and defend my own times cheerfully. But my heart sinks when I am told that the managers are in control. I fear they may indeed be, and I see only the darkest consequences.

I was a manager once myself. I was called from my role as observer and critic to take charge of a vast "metropolitan" park system. At first it seemed a most delightful change. It was obviously so much easier to act than it had been to think. One told other people what to do, and was pleased that they, more or less, did it.

I soon discovered, however, that being a manager meant acting in a particular way. No longer could I plan merely to make the parks more beautiful, or more enjoyable or even more safe; I had to make them more *productive*. Soon I was being asked to make each area and each facility justify itself in such terms as the number of people that visited it, or the number of dollars it brought to the city through such diversions as restaurants or paid amusements. Cold numbers, measurable indices, were to be given more weight than sentiment, service, or tradition.

One of the pleasant institutions of the older system was the park man who presided at each park. He cleaned the place in a leisurely fashion, got to know the kids in the neighborhood, encouraged them in the better forms of recreation. By his presence—which was not necessarily fierce or inhospitable—he kept off the vandals. But being a manager I saw it would be more efficient if two or three men were assigned to a small truck, and kept in constant motion visiting and cleaning as many as a dozen parks a day. A brilliant managerial innovation it was; but in human terms I am afraid it never really worked. The parks became less friendly places; recreation declined and vandalism mounted.

Well, I reformed my ways, and in due course went back to trying to understand the world rather than to manage it—among other things becoming a scribbler of such small articles as these. But beware! The managers are on the loose and they ride mankind. Nobody but a manager could be in charge of the subway system in New York where there are fewer and fewer trains, arriving at increasingly infrequent intervals, and all of them more crowded. I can see the managerial genius at work, figuring ways in which a lesser number of trainmen could transport a larger number of passengers—with standards of comfort and convenience totally discarded.

No one but a manager, again, could be in charge of our modern supermarkets. The old grocery store, with its helpful clerks, its willingness to give credit and to make deliveries, has given way under the drive for efficiency to these mindless emporia where merely trying to pay for what one has oneself taken off the shelf becomes a time-consuming ordeal. And it is the managerial mind, surely, that at the local bank figures out the way to make every line longer by simply closing down a few windows.

Evidence that the same standards are being applied to the so-called amusement parks should hardly come as a surprise. According to the latest issue of *Fortune* magazine it has been discovered that the average guest spends up to three out of a total eight-hour visit just walking, standing, and watching. I would have supposed these were excellent ways of finding amusement. But to the manager's mind, *Fortune* tells us, they are deplorable. It becomes essential "to keep chipping away at those unproductive hours by offering more and better spending opportunities." Unhappy mortals that we are, whose lives can be called productive only when we are responding to "spending opportunities."

The object of management, I have concluded, is to put an ever larger cost on the consumer and less upon the system. It is to share the work, to shift the burden, to change the priorities. Let the customer beware; let *him* carry the goods; let *him* wait endlessly and uninformed for the bus that never seems to come. If management cared a fig for the human being, would it not long ago have found ways of seeing that the bus, when it does come, is not one of a troop; or have eased the nervous tension of men and women by posting the number of minutes before the next subway train arrives?

Topic Six

Budgets and Program Evaluation:
On the Road to Accountability

Introduction

The use of budgets as a managerial tool has changed markedly over the past twenty-five years and, as a result, they have become increasingly important to public administrators in all phases of their responsibilities. Budgets were once considered to be little more than documents showing sums of money to be spent for particular purposes in a given period of time. Budgeting, or the process of creating the budget, was treated as an isolated administrative duty, and the significant relationship between budgeting and other managerial functions was not fully recognized. In brief, the primary concern and purpose of budgets were to ensure that money was being spent only for what had been approved. This accounting approach to budgets gave little attention to the human aspects of administration, and it greatly underestimated the broader role that budgets could serve for administrators.

Most contemporary administrators view budgets not only as fiscal statements describing the revenues and expenditures of an agency, but also as mechanisms for planning, managing and, most recently, evaluating all the activities of an organization. In Topic Six we examine some ways that budgets have been used by administrators to perform these administrative functions and see how different types of budgets have given new responsibilities to administrators. Particular attention is paid to two themes: (1) the conflict between the technical approaches to and the political realities of budgeting and (2) the greater use of budgets as program evaluation tools with the implication of this for public administration. Budgeting and evaluation in recent years have been generally accepted as parts of the same process by public administrators and elected officials. This is the way they should be considered, and for this reason, these two administrative functions are placed together in this Topic. Furthermore, budgeting and program evaluation are closely allied with accountability. This relationship is discussed at the conclusion of this Introduction, thereby linking the final Topic with a concept that has appeared throughout the book.

Changing Trends in the Use of Budgets

Allen Schick identified three distinct purposes for which budgets have been used: control, management, and planning. These purposes correspond to three historical periods in this century during which certain types of budgets were dominant.[1] We are currently in a fourth period, and budgets now are used for evaluation purposes. It should be noted that although within each of the four periods a dominant type is found, every succeeding period continued to employ some of the previous budget techniques. Before looking at how these have changed, a few general comments on budgets are appropriate.

A budget "is a plan to spend a sum of money for various purposes, which takes into account competitive claims as to how to spend that money. The process of budgeting is a process of compromising among competing values over how funds should be expended."[2] At its simplest, a budget is a plan for spending money based upon certain anticipated revenues. Most people use some budgetary process whether or not they call it that. It is a matter of making decisions about priorities—reconciling needs and desires for certain goods and services with the ability to pay for them.

Budgets are also political in content. As a political statement, a budget indicates a government's ranking of many activities. It tells us about the relative strengths of competing groups, and it suggests the direction in which the government and the public intend to go in the near future. As more and more groups in society become politically organized, the number of claims on government's financial resources increases. This has been a major factor in the growth of government at all levels during the past decade, and it has contributed to the use of budgets as evaluation tools in order to restrict some governmental spending.

The first period described by Schick emphasized the control function. From about 1900 to the middle of the 1930s line-item budgets were most widely used. They featured a detailed accounting of every item that had been appropriated, and they gave legislative bodies maximum control over administrators. One characteristic of a strict line-item budget was that no expenditure (item) approved by the legislature could be changed subsequently by an agency administrator without authorization from the legislature. This in effect meant going back through the budgetary process for that one item. Administrators, therefore, found themselves with no discretion or flexibility in the management of their agency's resources. If money had been allocated for a particular piece of equipment or program, administrators were required to spend that amount even though conditions changed after the original appropriation and the money might better be spent for another purpose. Administrators could try to persuade the legislature to approve spending for another item, but that might take considerable time away from other administrative responsibilities.

An additional problem was often created for administrators if, for one reason or another, their agency failed to spend all the money that had been allocated. Should this happen, even if there were justifiable reasons, the agency could expect to be penalized in the next budget. Legislators would rationalize that the organization's requests must have been inflated since it had not spent all that was given to it the last fiscal year. Line item budgets, therefore, did not reward administrators who cut expenses in a program or who tried to be flexible when circumstances suggested.

Another feature of this control period was the establishment of central budgeting offices. At the federal level, in 1921 the Budgeting and Accounting Act created the Bureau of the Budget which has since become the Office of Management and Budget (OMB). The intent of these types of organizations was to funnel budget requests from all executive departments into a central clearinghouse. This was to ensure that a check could be made more easily on the requests for both money and expenditures once they had been approved. State and local governments have also established similar budget control offices for the same reasons.

There were several consequences for administrators during this control period with its heavy reliance on line-item budgets. Legislators and the public did know exactly how much money was being spent for every item in an agency's budget. Legislators felt confident that they were protecting the public purse by keeping a tight control on expenditures and administrators charged with administering programs. In all of this, there was an implied attitude by legislators that administrators could not be trusted entirely. Line-item budgets favored those managers who would "go by the book," meaning they would follow precisely a budget with a detailed accounting procedure.

The advantage of a line-item budget—tight control—is also part of its limitation. A line-item budget tells administrators how much money is being spent for each item, but not whether this money is being expended wisely. Evaluation is not an intended purpose of a line-item budget, and so the individual expenditures are not related to each other or to the agency's goals or programs. Hence, about all a line-item budget indicates is the total dollar amount being spent, but it does not say what collective purpose the items are intended to serve.

The second budgetary period attempted to correct this deficiency of line-item budgets. Schick points out that "management" and not control became the purpose of budgets from the mid 1930s until the late 1950s. Performance or program budgets were the new types, and they were designed to answer the question of how well (efficiently) programs were being administered. In this period, therefore, we see the beginnings of budgets as evaluation devices.

Performance budgets are constructed so that all the individual expenditures (the former line-items) are collected and arranged into the functions, activities and projects that the organization is to perform. Instead of looking at a string of separate expense items, administrators with a performance budget can see how all of these relate to the larger purposes of the agency. A relationship is established between expenditures and what they are intended to accomplish. Administrators and legislators are then in a position to assess the value—not just the cost—of particular expenditures.

In this second period administrators were given much more personal responsibility for their organization's budget. While they had to meet a rigid objective, "be efficient," they were given some discretion in the use of appropriated resources. Administrators were seen as managers and not clerks. Legislators began to differentiate the role they had from that of the administrators, and as a consequence, this period had a different orientation from its predecessor.

Despite the improvement over line-item budgets, performance budgets still had a major limitation. They evaluated what was being done by an organization, but did not ask the more basic question: should the particular program have been implemented in the first place? A performance budget only assessed the program that had been determined as the one the agency could administer. There was always the possibility that even though the program was being run efficiently, it was not the best one to meet the agency's goals. As a result, money was wasted. In short, performance budgets did not select the "best" program from among all the possibilities. It only assessed what was already in existence. It was not until the next period that budgets were used to make initial program selections.

The third budget period according to Schick emphasized "planning," and it began in the late 1950s and lasted for about ten years. The budget process used during this time was Planning, Programming, Budgeting System (PPBS). As its name indicates, there were three parts to PPBS. The overall purpose was to create greater "rationality" in the budgeting process by first requiring administrators to plan long-range (several years) organizational goals, then to establish programs to attain those goals, and finally to budget specific projects within those programs to make them effective. The assumption behind PPBS was that the search for and selection of goals, programs and projects could be quantified. By identifying all the possible alternatives in each category, administrators would then apply cost-benefit analyses to each one. The alternative that showed the most benefits for a given cost (or a predetermined benefit for the least cost) would be the best, the most rational choice. In several ways, PPBS was not much more than a complicated application of the rational decisionmaking model which was discussed in Topic Five.

Under PPBS, administrators were involved with evaluation at virtually every step of the budgetary process. A great deal of managerial responsibility flowed to top administrators as compared to their situation when performance budgeting was used. For example, performance budgeting was applied to a program after the legislature had determined which one the agency should implement. In contrast to this procedure, with PPBS the selection of organizational goals, programs or projects was not made until after much of the PPBS process had been completed by the administrators themselves. Therefore, PPBS gave administrators much discretion and authority, but that ultimately led to its downfall.

In general, many of the limitations of PPBS had also been found in the rational decisionmaking model. It was extremely difficult, some said impossible, for administrators to identify and then to quantify all possible goals, programs and projects. As one might expect, trying to place an accurate (and agreed upon) dollar amount on the costs and benefits of social programs was an immense challenge. How does an administrator determine if a park is worth more or less than a library? What kinds of costs and benefits are to be measured?

PPBS also ignored three political considerations and these undermined its usefulness and credibility. Elected officials suspected, and they were right to a degree, that their control over many key policy decisions had been usurped by the PPBS administrators. Legislators believed that they were not receiving all the information they needed and that they had no way to evaluate the data. PPBS put administrators in positions of great authority, for they controlled much of the debate through their computer-simulation models which turned out the analyses of the various alternatives. In one sense, PPBS tended to reverse the role of legislators and administrators. The legislature was placed in the uncomfortable position of having to look to the bureaucracy for policy options and information, and this was not acceptable to most legislators.

Another political problem with PPBS was that many of the planning projections of the organizations were for periods of five to seven years or longer. Legislators, however, tended to think and work within the shorter spans of their own terms in office or the time until the next elections.

The third political consideration which PPBS ignored was the political importance of individual politicians and groups. The most "rational" or "cost-effective" program according to PPBS might not be the most politically feasible if it failed to reflect the political strength of legislators or constituencies. All the charts and computer printout data could never convince an elected official that political realities or values should be neglected. Yet, in a fundamental way, PPBS was premised on the fact that variables of this kind should be disregarded when people made and evaluated public policies.

By the end of the 1960s many legislators became disenchanted with PPBS, and it was phased out in many places, especially in the federal government. There was a return to performance budgeting and Management by Objectives. The effort by the advocates of PPBS, however, to bring planning and rationality to the budget process should not be underestimated. It did make people aware of the need to evaluate critically various policy and program alternatives, and it did employ techniques such as cost-benefit analyses that are still used for assessing the relative merits of choices.

The fourth period of budgeting which has emerged the past few years has emphasized the evaluation of existing programs instead of analyzing a variety of alternative ones. The budget method being used is called Zero-Based Budgeting (ZBB). This is a system which requires all spending for an entire program or agency to be justified from zero each year. For years, budgets were constructed on the principle of "incrementalism," which meant that the next year's budget began at or near the funding level of the last year's budget. If an agency was working with a budget of $30 million, it could expect that the next year's total would be at least that amount. ZBB challenges that entire incremental procedure. It does not assume that just because a program was necessary last year and received so much money, it is automatically entitled to that amount this year. In fact, ZBB questions the very existence of the need for the program at any funding level.

Selection 28, "The Tale of How One Agency Used ZBB—and Lived to Tell About It," shows the experience of the Environmental Protection Agency (EPA) as it used ZBB. The case summarizes many of the advantages and disadvantages of this budgeting technique, and these need not be discussed here. In general, the proponents of ZBB, including President Carter who introduced it to Georgia when he was Governor, contend that ZBB demands that administrators at all levels of an organization develop a close working knowledge of their agency and its activities. ZBB and its procedures, such as the ranking process, enable administrators to manage more efficiently because they soon learn which programs are worth keeping and which are duplicates and ineffective. ZBB therefore must depend greatly upon administrators throughout the agency who are able and willing to make difficult decisions about allocating funds and people.

There are two general criticisms of ZBB. The administrative complaint heard most frequently is that a great amount of time is required to prepare a zero-based budget. As the EPA experience indicates, this is a valid point, although proponents of ZBB believe that once the process becomes more familiar, the time required of administrators will decrease. The second limitation of ZBB is the all-too-familiar one that we encountered with the rational decisionmaking model and PPBS: ZBB does not take into consideration political factors when ranking programs and deciding which ones to eliminate.

Selection 29, "Zero-Based Budgeting Comes to Washington," focuses on some of these political realities. This satire illustrates how agency administrators are averse to cooperating with any budget system that can be used to cut their funding. Even if an organization were willing to admit that some of its programs should be reduced, there usually is a constituency ready to fight that cut. Groups outside an agency can be important allies to administrators in the struggle to defend or expand budgets for particular programs.

The discussion of these four periods in budgeting—control, management, planning, and evaluation—has shown the changes in the ways budgets have been used and the different responsibilities that administrators have had to assume. Despite all the advancements in the technical aspects of budgeting, political interests continue to be the fundamental influence in the process. This will be even more evident in the next section.

Budget Strategies and the Political Process

Selection 30 by Aaron Wildavsky is a collection of excerpts on various strategies that administrators can follow to obtain legislative funds. The examples are from the U.S. Congress, but the same procedures apply to other legislatures as well. These show the very personal side of the budgetary process. Legislators tend to focus on questions of individual or political interest which are not always the most vital to the agency. Several of the descriptions from Selection 30 suggest that purely "rational" budgets are disregarded by elected officials because they are politically irrelevant. The selection also illustrates some of the rituals that have evolved in budget hearings between administrators and legislators. These can be as important as the actual preparation of the budget document itself.

If an agency does not have sufficient funds with which to operate, its programs will not be successful no matter how well conceived they were. Lack of money can adversely affect an agency including the morale of its employees. Selection 31, "National Bureau of Standards: A Fall from Grace," illustrates this point. In the past few years, this organization has been given additional responsibilities by Congress without corresponding increases in its budgets. As a consequence, the National Bureau of Standards (NBS) has suffered severe cutbacks in personnel and other resources needed to perform these assignments. A major cause for its budget problems has been its lack of a strong constituency and political support. NBS performs vital work, but few people are aware of it. Further, NBS has not had continuous top leadership, and its relationships with other governmental agencies, especially OMB, have not been salutary.

In the case of NBS, it appears that its employees are at the mercy of Congress. However, there are situations when administrators may find the means to launch a budgetary counter-attack and convince Congress to reconsider some cuts. An incident several years ago within another agency is one such instance.

Congress cut the National Park Service budget over the warnings of Park administrators that severe program reductions would result. When the budget cuts became a reality, top administrators immediately retaliated by drastically curtailing the elevator service for the Washington Monument during the height of the tourist season. This resulted in long lines of impatient visitors, and the public outcry was such that Congress quickly restored funds to the Park Service before other popular programs could be eliminated.

The Office of Management and Budget

In 1970 by an executive order of the President, the Office of Management and Budget (OMB) was created to replace the Bureau of the Budget which had been in existence since 1921. OMB's primary purpose is to help the President prepare the budget. The director of the OMB is appointed by the President with Senate confirmation. OMB acts as a clearinghouse for all executive department budget requests, and it conducts its own fiscal analyses throughout the year.

About eighteen months before the new fiscal year is to begin (October 1 for the federal government), OMB requests that all agencies submit to it their proposals for spending. OMB examines these and confers with agency administrators. After analyzing these requests, it makes its own recommendations. At the same time, the President is developing a budget outline in terms of spending priorities, estimated revenues and a general fiscal policy. After OMB sends its proposals to the President and the President weighs other opinions and evidence, a final budget is drafted and submitted to Congress.

OMB's functions continue after the budget has been prepared and passed. It monitors executive programs that are in operation, and it often appears before Congress in committee hearings. OMB is obviously a central agency in the federal bureaucracy, and the President must have a great deal of confidence in its competency. Selection 32 is a personality profile of James McIntyre, the director of OMB. It points to the importance of personal relationships between the President and the head of an agency like the OMB. The selection also contrasts the administrative styles of McIntyre with that of his predecessor, Bert Lance. It is too soon to determine which approach—that of a technician or a salesman—is more effective in administering OMB, but there appear to be enough differences that some comparisons can be made at a later date.

Program Evaluation

One of the most difficult problems in public administration is determining how well a program is doing in relation to what it was intended to accomplish. Because many public administrators have paid little attention to this question until recently, the technology to measure programs is comparatively new and primitive. Today people are much more aware of the need for evaluation and of the kinds of problems that must be overcome.

Government encounters special problems not found in the private sector when evaluating many of its programs. First, there is often disagreement over the meaning of the goals of a governmental program. They are stated in vague terms so that the many political factions supporting the program can claim some influence in the final political product.In addition to disagreement on the goals and their meaning, the determination of whether or not the goals actually have been reached is sometimes more a matter of personal judgement than precise measurement. By contrast, private organizations have profit as their primary goal and this can be determined relatively easily through accounting practices. Business corporations are likely to have several subgoals, and of course the battle over these, as well as the debate about how to achieve a profit, may be as intense as any in public administration. Yet there is at all times an overriding objective by which all private organizational action can be measured and evaluated.

Another limitation government has in evaluating programs is the absence of "market signals" to tell it how the public is reacting to what government is doing. It is particularly true that when government has a monopoly of a service, it lacks indicators of consumer satisfaction and demand patterns. Few opportunities are offered the public to express direct opinions on specific governmental programs. Elections usually are dominated by the personalities of candidates and, according to a number of political behavior studies, tell us very little about the policy preferences of voters. In contrast, business corporations are able to obtain consumer reactions quickly to their products or services. They do not have to wait long to get a response to what they are doing. In effect, business is being constantly evaluated in the marketplace.

Selection 33, "Evaluating a Program's Success or Failure. . ." by Joel Havemann, examines three fundamental conditions which must be met by public administrators when evaluating programs: 1) the goals and purposes of the program must be stated clearly; 2) techniques must be available to measure the results of the program; 3) a cause and effect relationship must be established between the program and the results that appear. This selection provides several illustrations of the methodological and political obstacles peculiar to program evaluation.

A more detailed analysis of the problems of evaluation is found in Jack McCurdy's "Education Programs Getting Critical Look," (Selection 34). The California Legislature has been attempting to assess special education programs and, as a result, they have been faced with a wide range of issues. These have included identifying who should be the evaluators, what should be the measurement indices, and how the ethical questions which have been raised should be handled.

Evaluation and Accountability

We have seen in this Topic that budgeting is related to evaluation and evaluation is coupled with performance standards. All of these are linked to accountability. As there is more public demand for evaluating governmental programs, this will inevitably lead to a greater focus on accountability— determining who is responsible for what government is doing.

A variety of techniques to make public employees accountable have been mentioned throughout this book. These have ranged from laws governing personal behavior to attempts at reorganization to management practices such as MBO, PPBS and ZBB. Some governmental jurisdictions are currently using "sunshine" laws which require public employees to conduct the public's business in the open. (Employees must keep logs of all their official business contacts, and meetings, with a few exceptions, must be open to the public). Most recently, proposals for increasing accountability have suggested making greater use of the courts. The public would be able to sue public administrators and to collect damages for incompetent administrative performance.

A word of caution, however, should be made at this point. Too much emphasis on accountability can have a chilling effect on public employees. Just as we saw that too much citizen participation in decisionmaking can diffuse the accountability of the professional administrator, so can initiative be stifled if every act of a public employee is under intense scrutiny. There must be room for governmental employees to take reasonable risks and to make human errors without fear of punishment.

If individuals in and out of the governmental bureaucracies are performing well their respective functions, then government and the public are on the road to accountability. The formal institutional arrangements that have been discussed in this book can be useful in upgrading the day-to-day functioning of government. Yet, virtually all of the selections have shown how much more important are individual attitudes in improving its quality. Mechanisms may make government efficient, but it is the individuals who make it responsive.

Public administrators who are aware of the human elements and recognize their relationship to the administrative process will be much more capable public servants than those who are strictly technicians. Public administrators, as this book has emphasized, should be aware of the importance to public administration of the attitudes, values and behaviors of individuals—not only of those with whom they work, but also of those for whom they work.

Notes

1. Allen Schick, "The Road to PPB: The Stages of Budget Reform," *Public Administration Review*, December 1966, Vol. 26 No. 4, pp. 243-258.
2. William L. Morrow, *Public Administration: Politics and the Political System* (New York: Random House, 1975), p.209.

28
The Tale of How One Agency Used ZBB— and Lived to Tell About It
Joel Havemann

L ast fall, when President Carter was promoting the virtues of zero-base budgeting, he told a Cabinet meeting that one agency in particular was making excellent use of the new budgeting technique. The Environmental Protection Agency, he said, was the best in the government.

That is a view that encounters little opposition at EPA, where the bureaucracy worked long and hard to put one of the President's favorite good government tools into practice. EPA officials can point to a variety of ways in which zero-base budgeting enabled them to improve their fiscal 1979 budget.

On the other hand, zero-base budgeting did not work perfectly at EPA, and it certainly did not produce revolutionary change in EPA budget decisions. "If

---

From the *National Journal*, February 18, 1978, pp. 265-269. Copyright 1978 by National Journal. Reprinted with permission.
Joel Havemann is Deputy Editor of the *National Journal*.

we did the best job in the government," said one EPA budget official, "I'd hate to see what the rest of the government did."

Using zero-base budgeting, EPA was better able to coordinate its plans to combat air pollution, water pollution and other environmental evils it is dedicated to controlling. Responsibility for each of these programs is split among EPA's divisions; zero-base budgeting enabled the agency to cut through its organizational barriers and achieve coherent planning.

Despite its name, zero-base budgeting did not allow EPA to build its 1979 budget from zero. But it made the agency examine the consequences of deep cuts, usually of 25 per cent, in each of its programs. Most of the cuts will not become reality—but some will.

The system forced EPA, whose budget is not growing as fast as the new responsibilities assigned it by Congress, to decide which of its programs were more important. Thus EPA decided to cut its noise program, even though the program generally is regarded within EPA as too small to begin with. At the same time, EPA budgeted considerable new resources for its newer safe drinking water program.

EPA drew raves from the Office of Management and Budget (OMB) for its use of zero-base budgeting. "We came out with a very clear understanding of EPA's priorities," said associate OMB director Eliot R. Cutler, who heads the OMB division that reviews the EPA budget.

The feeling was not mutual. Many EPA officials complained that despite the new system, OMB reviewed their budget in the same old way, unfairly reducing EPA's spending estimates and overturning its priorities.

William Drayton Jr., EPA's assistant administrator for planning and management, criticized OMB for not explicitly setting priorities among similar programs of different agencies. OMB is planning a cross-agency ranking of programs next year.

The budget finally approved for EPA provided $1.13 billion for 10,840 employees and another $4.5 billion for sewer grants. OMB initially cut EPA's request (excluding sewer grants) by about 11 per cent, but it reduced the cut to 8 per cent after EPA appealed.

Zero-base budgeting drew EPA's program managers deeply into the business of preparing the 1979 budget. From the lowest levels to administrator Douglas M. Costle, program officials made decisions about the goals they intended to accomplish and the resources they would need to accomplish them.

"If you wanted to see a bureaucracy really working, this was it," said Clifford J. Parker, director of EPA's program analysis division under Drayton.

As useful as zero-base budgeting was, many EPA officials recognize that it is not the ultimate tool for managing their agency. Victor Kimm, who runs the safe drinking water program, said no system can substitute for good judgment and sound policy decisions. And Parker added, "No system will accomplish all of the things we expect this one to accomplish."

The EPA Style

Except for a few twists, the Environmental Protection Agency's approach to zero-base budgeting paralleled that of most of the other departments and agencies. EPA did nothing dramatically different; it just did it better.

The first task was the identification of the programs from which the budget would be built. That presented no great problem, because EPA's budget, unlike those of some other parts of the government, already had been based on agency programs. For budgetary purposes, preparation of clean drinking water standards became one program; enforcement of regulations against noise, another.

EPA program managers were asked to describe how they would operate their programs with 25 per cent cuts from their 1978 budgets. Then the managers had to explain what they would do with budgetary increments that would restore the program to 90 and 100 per cent of its current level and increase it to 110 per cent and beyond.

At each level, program managers had to spell out the accomplishments they expected to achieve. Cutler said EPA did a particularly good job of relating expected accomplishments to costs.

The program levels became the building blocks of EPA's zero-base budget. Each of the agency's six assistant administrators had to list his program levels in order of importance.

In addition, special task forces were assigned to rank all the programs related to a particular goal, such as noise control or safe drinking water. This step was crucial, because responsibility for related EPA programs in most cases is scattered among the agency's six assistant administrators.

In this fashion, most EPA programs were ranked twice, once with other related programs and once with other programs in the jurisdiction of the same assistant administrator. The two sets of priority lists were sent to EPA's assistant administrators, who met as a group to consolidate the preliminary rankings into a giant ranking of all EPA programs.

Excluded from the EPA ranking was the agency's biggest program—grants to local governments for sewer construction. Carter already had committed himself to $4.5 billion a year for this program, which constitutes more than 80 per cent of EPA's budget. But the EPA personnel who administer the sewer grants were included in the ranking, among the more than 10,000 staffers who operate EPA's pollution control programs.

Altogether, the assistant administrators ranked 550 program levels for 96 programs. Costle reviewed their ranking, made some changes, and decided that the EPA budget request should total $1.22 billion (not counting sewer grants) for 11,496 employees.

Direct Impact

As a technique to improve decision making, zero-base budgeting (ZBB) is not necessarily supposed to push an agency's budget either up or down. But at

EPA, the new process clearly affected the shape, if not the over-all size, of the agency's budget.

National Journal looked closely at EPA's noise and safe drinking water programs, two of the smaller components of the EPA budget. Zero-base budgeting almost surely was responsible for a cut in the noise budget, and it probably facilitated an increase in the safe drinking water budget.

As it began preparing its 1979 budget, EPA found itself required to enforce several new laws, including those regulating toxic substances and drinking water. But since it did not expect to receive a proportionate increase in its budget, it was aware that some resources would have to be transferred from old programs to new ones.

Noise control is one of EPA's old programs. Although Congress and the General Accounting Office (GAO) criticized the agency last year for spending too little to control noise, EPA recommended a further cut, from 101 employees to 95, in 1979.

Charles L. Elkins, director of the noise control program, complained that without zero-base budgeting, the program probably would have gained rather than lost. The new process, he said, forced EPA to allocate every dollar where it would do the most good, and it became clear that some of the noise dollars could be put to better use in the programs where recent legislation required expansion.

But Elkins said the objectivity of zero-base budgeting was a mixed blessing. From a political standpoint, he said, the decision to cut the noise program made little sense. The reduction of only six persons is practically negligible in an agency of 10,000, he said, but is sure to bring criticism from a Congress that feels the noise program already is too small.

"The ZBB process," Elkins wrote in a June 20 memo, "does not sufficiently raise to the attention of this agency's management the need to make a more adequate commitment of resources to a program whose statutory mandate has never been adequately funded and where the agency has received severe criticism for its previous performance."

In the fall, Costle drafted a letter to OMB asking for 20 more positions for the noise program and more funds for the radiation program, which also suffered under zero-base budgeting. "In my effort to adhere to the Administration's need for rigorous budget stringency, I believe our zero-based review, in trying to balance and prioritize all agency activities, placed the noise and radiation programs at a disadvantage in order to bolster other programs having more pressing major public health responsibilities," Costle wrote in the letter.

But he never sent the letter. Choosing to live with the consequences of zero-base budgeting, he decided that it would be inconsistent to ask for more funds for programs that ranked low on the agency's list of priorities.

Unlike the noise program staff, the officials who operate the safe drinking water program found that zero-base budgeting provided a means of emphasizing the importance of their program.

"Usually it's difficult for a new program to gain the attention of the top policy makers," said James H. McDermott, chairman of the team that put together the zero-base budget for the safe drinking water program. But with zero-base budgeting, the program was granted an increase by OMB from 334 employees this year to 500 in 1979. Even that did not satisfy EPA, which appealed for 76 more employees—and got 55 of them.

Joan K. Barnes, the program analyst on Parker's staff who worked with the safe drinking water team, said zero-base budgeting allowed EPA to decide that the need to ensure the safety of public water systems was more pressing than the need to control contamination of underground water supplies. The team did not find the latter activity to be unimportant she said, but it determined that EPA probably could not afford it.

Getting Together

Beyond its direct impact on the shape of the EPA budget, zero-base budgeting improved the way in which EPA is managed. Most notably, it brought together EPA officials assigned to related tasks but separated by the agency's curious organizational structure.

When EPA was formed in 1971, it consolidated the air pollution program operated by the Health, Education and Welfare Department and the water pollution program of the Interior Department. To break up the old empires and make them more responsive to the new EPA administrator, the agency's organizers removed the enforcement and the research and development offices from the air and water pollution programs and placed them in the domain of EPA-wide enforcement and R & D offices.

Zero-base budgeting cut through EPA's organizational structure. The teams assigned to prepare the budgets for each of the agency's anti-pollution programs made it possible for the agency to coordinate its plans for new regulations, enforcement and R & D.

Take the safe drinking water team. Leonard A. Miller, the Office of Enforcement's representative on that team, said zero-base budgeting forced EPA to prepare a balanced plan for conducting research, writing standards and enforcing regulations.

"It's easy in government to view your activity as the be-all and end-all," he said. "Zero-base budgeting let us get away from that."

Coordination is particularly important for EPA's drinking water program. Before the agency can grant a variance to its safe drinking water standards, the Office of Enforcement must set up public hearings and handle a variety of other administrative chores. But the decision to grant the variance comes from the separate Office of Water Supply.

Zero-base budgeting forced these two offices to plan for the same number of variances. Gary N. Dietrich, director of management and operations for the Office of Water and Hazardous Materials, the parent body of the Office of Water Supply, said such planning had not occurred in the past.

Victor Kimm, the Office of Water Supply director, said he found himself in the unaccustomed position of supporting a budget increase for water supply enforcement. In the past, Kimm said, his office and the Office of Enforcement would have been competing for pieces of the water supply budget. But this year, he said, the two offices cooperated to plan a balanced program.

Similarly, the noise control program probably benefited from coordination of the efforts to prepare noise control standards and to enforce them. Elkins found the cooperation among various EPA staff members responsible for the noise control program to be a "rewarding experience." Another staff member associated with the noise program said, "Zero-base budgeting really got people working together."

Some EPA officials found it surprising that a new budgeting system was necessary to force coordination of the EPA bureaucracy. Herbert Myers, the program analyst from Parker's staff who was assigned to the noise control team, said, "I don't think you should have to go through ZBB to know you need people to enforce the regulations that the abatement and control people put out."

Getting Involved

For better or worse, zero-base budgeting forced EPA program managers to put much more effort into budget preparation than ever before. Throughout the agency, program managers said they found huge chunks of their time consumed by the budget.

This proved useful to the assistant administrators, who were brand new to EPA when the budget season reached peak intensity last summer. Zero-base budgeting provided them with a crash course in the activities of their new organization.

Responsibility for budget preparation filtered well down into the program offices. Many low-level managers joined in the effort to define the jobs they could accomplish if their budgets were cut, held even or increased.

"The staff four and five levels down had to struggle with setting priorities," said Drayton. "This democratization gave the process legitimacy and made it seem less conspiratorial."

In particular, zero-base budgeting gave EPA managers a chance to participate in a necessary but unpleasant task—identifying possible cuts in their own budgets. In the past, said Dietrich, EPA's program offices proposed only budget increases, never budget cuts. When cuts were in order, they were made by the Office of Planning and Management.

Unfortunately, Dietrich said, the Office of Planning and Management often lacked the expertise to make the cuts that would do the least damage to the programs. Zero-base budgeting, by requiring the program offices to spell out what they would do if their budgets were reduced to 75 per cent or 90 per cent of their current levels, shifted the job of identifying budget cuts to those offices.

If zero-base budgeting meant more involvement for program managers, it also meant more work—a lot more work. "It was 12-hour days, six or seven days a week," said Dietrich. "It does take its toll."

The workload reached its peak in the summer, when the assistant administrators spent the better part of every day for three weeks on the effort to list all of EPA's programs in priority order. The final session began early one Thursday morning and ended at about 11 p.m. More than one EPA staff member celebrated so much when that session was over they were in no condition to go to work the following day.

One EPA staff member, who asked not to be identified, warned of the danger that the staff would get so absorbed by the budget that it would forget about the environment. "We spent so much time on the budget," he said, "that a lot of other things slipped."

'Minimum' Programs

Traditionally, each year's federal budget is built on the last one, with program managers seeking changes—usually increases—from their current levels of activity.

At EPA, zero-base budgeting meant that the 1979 budget was built not from the 1978 budget but from the "minimum" levels at which the agency's programs could operate.

OMB instructed EPA and the other departments and agencies to define minimum levels as those below which programs would serve no useful purpose. For some programs, that might mean levels far below current levels; for others, it might mean current levels.

EPA, like many other departments and agencies, found it could not operate according to OMB's definition. Parker said that for many EPA programs, there is no clear level below which the programs would be useless. So Parker's office arbitrarily defined minimum levels to be 50 per cent to 75 per cent of current levels. Most program managers chose not to go below 75 per cent.

But even OMB did not object strenuously when most of EPA changed the OMB definition of minimum program levels. "It would be ideal," said Cutler, "if you really went at it from zero and worked up from there." But, he added, 75 per cent of current spending was low enough to identify nearly all realistic spending cuts.

EPA program managers were required to spell out how they would spend their funds if they were held to 75 per cent of their current budgets. Then they had to do the same for spending increments that would restore their budgets to current levels and beyond.

The first increment, when added to the minimum level, had to leave the program at 90 per cent of its current level. The second had to restore it to its current level. Subsequent increments were to increase the program by 10 per cent and more.

For many program managers, identifying minimum program levels seemed less painful than spelling out possible spending cuts. In fact, of course, a 75 per cent minimum level is no different from a 25 per cent cut—but it seemed different. Dietrich found it "psychologically more acceptable" to think in terms of increasing a minimum program rather than cutting a current program.

Elkins, who runs the noise control program, said his team might not have been able to force itself to identify ways to cut such a small program. Even as it was, he said, "our most difficult question was how we could get along with fewer resources."

Ranking

The minimum program levels and program increments found their way into two kinds of preliminary lists of EPA programs. Teams of agency officials ranked related programs in 13 categories of activity, from air pollution control to water quality control. At the same time, the six assistant EPA administrators were supposed to draw up priority lists of programs in their domains— although the Office of Water and Hazardous Materials prepared no ranking of its diverse programs.

Then came the awesome task of consolidating the preliminary rankings into a single list of all 550 EPA program levels in order of importance. It fell to EPA's six assistant administrators, none of whom had been at the agency for more than a few months, and to a single deputy regional administrator.

Drayton, one of the six assistant administrators, said he and his colleagues were united by "a common level of ignorance." Elkins, who presented the ranking of the noise control programs to the assistant administrators, said no group of seven individuals, no matter how experienced, could grasp all the complexities of all EPA programs.

McDermott, as chairman of the safe drinking water team, made the first of 13 presentations to the assistant administrators by the various teams. He was told he would have no more than an hour to make his presentation and answer questions.

"Two and a half hours later, I got out of there," he said. "They were new to the business, and they asked one hell of a lot of questions."

After the presentations by the teams, a group of staff members representing each of the assistant administrators prepared a first draft of an EPA-wide ranking, based on four spheres of activity that Costle said he wanted to emphasize. They were protecting public health, enforcing the law, encouraging state and local governments to assume responsibility for the environment and promoting management and regulatory reform.

To make the ranking process more manageable, the staff group divided all of EPA's minimum program levels and program increments into three piles.

In the first pile, which totaled 90 per cent of this year's EPA budget, went all the activities that seemed essential to the continued functioning of the agency, with the items in the pile simply grouped according to program—air pollution first, water pollution second, and so on. There was no effort to set priorities among them.

In the third pile went all the items that EPA did not expect to be approved in its 1979 budget. Again, these items simply were listed according to program.

The middle pile absorbed most of the assistant administrators' attention. It included 148 program increments, not important enough to become part of EPA's budget request automatically, but of sufficient merit to receive careful consideration for inclusion in the agency's budget. The 148 increments, if made part of the 1979 EPA budget, would bring the total 8 per cent beyond the 1978 level.

By consolidating similar program increments, the EPA staff reduced the number of items under careful scrutiny from 148 to 62. Even so, the items were as small as $120,000 for four employees.

The assistant administrators ranked these 62 items in order of importance. But in the end, the EPA budget request included all but six of the items.

The ranking prepared by the assistant administrators went to Costle for review and revision. On the Sept. 15 deadline, Costle sent his 1979 budget request on to OMB, calling it "the product of an exhaustive and highly successful agency-wide ZBB review."

After the zero-base budgeting exercise was over, EPA decided to add supplemental requests that left its entire budget submission nearly 17 per cent greater than its 1978 budget.

OMB Review

As a result of its painstaking budget process, EPA submitted to OMB a budget request supported by volumes of detailed justification. OMB replied in kind, subjecting the EPA request to an unusually thorough review before cutting it by about 10 per cent.

The OMB review was cause for concern among many EPA officials. "OMB's tops-down approach to budgeting is incompatible with successfully introducing a bottoms-up approach in the agencies," Drayton said.

Drayton urged OMB to challenge EPA's cost estimates early in the process, so that the agency could get down to the more serious business of setting priorities without being sidetracked by technical matters. Parker added that OMB's challenges of EPA cost estimates sometimes reached down to minor EPA activities, where he said the agency is in a better position than OMB to estimate resource requirements.

Cutler, who heads the OMB division that reviewed EPA's budget request, replied that one of OMB's jobs is to challenge agency budget estimates. "It's not unreasonable," he said, "to expect an agency to be relatively generous in its resource estimates."

Parker also questioned whether OMB had a right to overturn EPA's priorities as often as it did. He conceded that OMB should make political judgments that the agency might have overlooked; thus OMB acted properly when it added to EPA's budget request a clean lakes program supported by Vice President Walter F. Mondale.

But Parker said many of OMB's priority-related decisions seemed little more than substitutions of OMB's judgments for EPA's. At the same time, he noted that many of OMB's judgments were advisory, not mandatory; OMB consulted with EPA before juggling the agency's priorities. Cutler added that the President expected OMB to analyze department and agency priorities to make sure they are consistent with his own.

Beyond the question of EPA priorities, Drayton said OMB should rank similar programs administered by different agencies. Because of overlapping responsibilities of departments and agencies, he said, such an effort could result in considerable efficiencies and savings. "If we need to set priorities within agencies," he said, "God knows we need to do it between agencies."

The OMB review of the EPA budget request left the agency with 846 fewer positions than it had requested. EPA appealed to OMB to restore 405. Cutler was able to settle most of the appeals on his own authority, agreeing to let EPA have 190 of the positions.

The appeals process concluded the work of preparing the Administration's budget. The next step will be up to Congress.

29
Zero-Based Budgeting Comes to Washington
James Q. Wilson

You remember ZBB — that government reform candidate Jimmy Carter promised. Here's how it will work.

Charles Pettypoint, the newly-installed efficiency expert in the White House, was eager to see at firsthand how Zero-Based Budgeting was working. He decided to drop in on an agency getting ready to use it, and selected the National Park Service in the Department of the Interior.

He arrived to find the entire senior staff of the Park Service seated around a big table. The Director seemed pleased to have so distinguished a visitor, and asked Mr. Pettypoint to explain ZBB to his aides.

"Well, the idea is to get the most out of the taxpayer's dollar by making sure that every cent we spend is justified."

Everybody around the table nodded. "Hear, hear," one said.

"What we do," Pettypoint continued, "is to assume that the agency — in this case, the Park Service — has no money at all and then. . ."

Murmurs of outraged disbelief erupted, but the Director silenced the room with a firm glare.

"As I was saying," Pettypoint went on, somewhat stiffly, "we then ask the Park Service to justify each dollar of its budget and every activity it carries out.

From *The American Spectator,* February, 1977, p. 5. Copyright 1977, The American Spectator, Bloomington, Indiana 47401. Reprinted with permission.
James Wilson is Shattuck Professor of Government, Harvard University

You will have to show us how much of your product or service you can produce for a given amount of money."

Only after a pin dropped noisily to the floor did everyone realize how quiet the room had become. Two older Park officials had turned pale, and the hands of another began to shake uncontrollably.

"Justify *everything?*" the Director asked.

"Everything," Pettypoint replied.

"This year?"

"This year: In fact, within the next three months."

A long pause.

"Men," the Director finally said, "I think we ought to cooperate 100 percent with this splendid idea."

"Sir, you can't be serious. . ." An aide started to rise, but was waved back to his seat by the Director.

"Of course I am serious. Mr. Pettypoint is serious. The President of the United States is serious. We will all be serious."

"Here is what we will do," the Director continued. "Smith, you tell Senator Henry Jackson, the chairman of the Interior Committee, that we are considering what would happen if we closed all the national parks."

"Even those in the state of Washington?"Smith asked incredulously.

"Especially those in Washington," the Director replied. "But stress to the Senator that it is just a mental experiment, a planning exercise. We probably won't *really* close any of the parks in his state."

Suddenly, a beatific expression of sudden enlightenment spread across Smith's face. "Gotcha, chief."

"Gorstwinkle, I want you to get right to work on making up a list of national parks in the order of their importance, so we will know which ones to leave open if we can't reopen all of them," the Director said.

Gorstwinkle started to giggle uncontrollably: "Right away. Of course, I won't be able to keep the list secret, chief. You know, Freedom of Information and all that. . . ." He broke up in laughter.

"I understand," the Director replied, allowing a thin smile to crease his stern features. "Nothing's ever secret any more. I suppose the Sierra Club is bound to find out that we are thinking of closing Yellowstone."

"The Audubon Society will suspect that we might be cutting back on bird sanctuaries," someone remarked.

"Wait until the Daughters of the American Revolution finds out that we are. . ." the speaker gasped for breath, as he shook convulsively with laughter, "that we are analyzing whether it makes sense to leave Independence Hall open!"

Howls rang through the room. One man staggered to the drinking fountain, and another had to loosen his tie to avoid choking.

Pettypoint bristled. "You are not looking at this constructively."

"Oh, but we are, Mr. Pettypoint," the Director replied. "I firmly believe that, as a result of this ZBB exercise, the public will realize that we need more money for more parks."

"But that isn't the purpose," Pettypoint rejoined.

"Isn't it?" the Director asked innocently.

Smith, wiping his eyes, shouted: "Hey, Pettypoint, did you know that some of those women in the Garden Club can hit a moving White House staffer at twenty paces with a potted geranium?" He collapsed back in his chair, overcome with hilarity.

Crestfallen, Pettypoint said plaintively, "Well, maybe the Park Service is not the place to begin. I suppose ZBB would work best applied to a program that didn't have this kind of organized public support."

The Director stared at him for a long moment.

"Name one."

30
Budgetary Strategies

Aaron Wildavsky

[*Editor's Note: This selection consists of excerpts from Chapter 3, "Strategies," from* The Politics of the Budgetary Process. *Wildavsky defines budgetary strategies as "actions by governmental agencies intended to maintain or increase the amount of money available to them." (p. 63). The following are examples of various strategies that administrators can pursue.*

The first group of strategies is designed to gain the confidence of other governmental officials.]

RESULTS

Confidence rests to some extent on showing the Budget Bureau and Congress that the programs are worthwhile because they lead to useful results. The word "results" in this context has at least two meanings, which must be disentangled. In one sense it means that some people feel they are being served. In a second sense it means that the activity accomplishes its intended purposes. This sense of "result" itself involves a basic distinction. There are programs that involve a product or a service that is concrete, such as an airplane, and others that involve activities that resist measurement, such as propaganda abroad. The demonstration of results differs in both cases, as do the strategies employed.

Excerpted from Aaron Wildavsky, *The Politics of the Budgetary Process,* 2nd Edition, pp. 90-114.
Copyright © 1964, 1974 by Little, Brown and Company (Inc.). Reprinted by permission.
Aaron Wildavsky is a professor of political science. He is at the Russell Sage Foundation in New York.

SERVE AN APPRECIATIVE CLIENTELE. The best kind of result is one that provides services to a large and strategically placed clientele, which brings its satisfaction to the attention of decision makers. (The clientele may be producers of services, as in the case of defense contractors.) The kinds of strategies involved have been discussed under "clientele," and we shall go on to others in which the second sense of "result" is implicated.

IT WORKS: THE PROBLEM OF CRITERIA. Outside of overwhelming public support, there is nothing that demonstrates results better than tangible accomplishment. The Polaris does fire and hit a target with reasonable accuracy; a nuclear submarine actually operates; a range-reseeding project makes the grass grow again. Interpretation of accomplishments as being worthwhile depends on finding criteria and on how tough these criteria are permitted to be. The Nike-Zeus missile may be fine if it is only supposed to knock down a few missiles or half of an enemy's missiles; it may be utterly inadequate if the criterion is raised to all missiles or most missiles or is changed to include avoidance of decoys. There is great temptation to devise a criterion that will enable a project's supporters to say that it works. At the same time, opponents of a project may unfairly propose criteria that cannot be met. And there are times when men reasonably disagree over criteria because no one knows what will happen. We hope and pray to avoid nuclear war. But if it comes, what criteria should a civil defense program have to meet? If one argues that it must save everyone, then no program can show results. Suppose, however, that one is willing to accept much less—say half or a third or a fifth of the population. Then everything depends on estimates which can surely be improved upon but which nobody can really claim to be reliable as to likely levels of attack, patterns of wind and radiation, and a multitude of other factors. . . .

AVOID TOO GOOD RESULTS. The danger of claiming superb accomplishments is that Congress and the Budget Bureau may reward the agency by ending the program. "Why would you need five more people in the supervisory unit?" John Rooney inquired of the Justice Department, "Since you are doing so well, as we have heard for fifteen minutes, you surely do not need any more supervision." However good it may be said that results are, it is advisable to put equal stress on what remains to be done. "Progress has been realized in the past," the Civil Defense agency asserted, "but we cannot permit these past accomplishments to lull us into a false sense of security."

Now we turn to strategies pursued by agencies that do not produce tangible items that are easy to measure. . . .

IT CAN'T BE MEASURED. The USIA lacks confidence partly because it is particularly vulnerable to a line of attack based on the lack of results. "I have been on this committee now for twenty years," Senator Ellender told the agency, "and I have not seen any results from the money we have expended." A USIA official could only say that ". . . It would be very good to have a fine and exact measure of total results. We just don't have it. We will never get it. . . ." When an affluent agency that has confidence runs into this kind of difficulty the approach is quite different. "I wish," Representative Fogarty said, "that you would supply the committee with a list of things that the National Institutes of Health have accomplished. . . because we are being continually reminded that we are appropriating a lot of money for research and nothing ever comes of it." The best response is a scientific breakthrough, when a disease is brought under control.

TOMORROW AND TOMORROW. If there are no results today, they can always be promised for some remote future.
Representative Kirwan: Can you give us a few recent results of your research?
Bureau of Mines: (Reads a prepared statement.)
Representative Kirwan: . . . that is something that you are going to undertake, is it not?
Bureau of Mines: It is something that is underway.
Representative Kirwan: But there are no results. . .
Bureau of Mines: That is correct. There have been no immediate results by industry at the present time but as the program proceeds, new findings are made continually which will lead to further research on the subject.
Representative Kirwan: . . . Were there any results. . . ?
This program's estimate was cut by $150,000 by the committee.

STATISTICS. Research of all kinds is a complicated subject because the results are difficult to measure and there is always hope that something good will turn up. Since significant results are not easily demonstrable, the advocates of a research program may resort to presenting a procession of figures that may or may not have any relevance. Take a look at a doctor's testimony:

To mention just a few of the research contributions . . . merely as being indicative of progress. There have been . . . 2,800 compounds tested which have some tumor-damaging properties. Four hundred of these have proved to be very interesting and, narrowing these down, twelve of them have been found to have very, very interesting possibilities in the future treatment of cancer.
Is this research valuable? No one can tell from this presentation.

STRETCHING THINGS. Should results directly germane to the agency's program not be forthcoming, it is always possible to stretch things a little. A claim like the one by the Weather Bureau that follows is not only difficult to prove; it is virtually impossible to disprove.

Representative Rooney: (Do you take) editorial credit for the sentence near the top of page two: "Guidance to motorists regarding the use of antifreeze is estimated to be worth $50 million per year"? . . . How do you arrive at that figure?

Weather Bureau Official: Total value of motor vehicles is of the order of billions. . . . Some $3 billion is the estimated value of all automotive equipment in the United States. . . . It does not take a very high percentage of motor blocks in terms of the millions of motor vehicles that are to be protected, to roll up a total of $50 million a year preventable loss. That figure has been very carefully arrived at.

AVOID EXTREME CLAIMS THAT CAN BE TESTED. There are times when a desire to show direct results boomerangs because of the very absurdity of the claim. Such is the unhappy tale of the State Department official who refused to admit that a Chinese language program would necessarily have a deferred pay off in view of the fact that we had no formal diplomatic relations with Communist China and the number of men we could send to Formosa was limited.

Representative Rooney: I find a gentleman here, an FSO-6. He got an A in Chinese and you assigned him to London.
Mr. X: Yes, sir. That officer will have opportunities in London — not as many as he would have in Hong Kong, for example —
Representative Rooney: What will he do? Spend his time in Chinatown?
Mr. X: No, sir. There will be opportunities in dealing with officers in the British Foreign Office who are concerned with Far Eastern affairs. . . .
Representative Rooney: So instead of speaking English to one another, they will sit in the London office and talk Chinese?
Mr. X: Yes, sir.
Representative Rooney: Is that not fantastic?
Mr. X: No, sir. They are anxious to keep up their practice. . . .
Representative Rooney: They go out to Chinese restaurants and have chop suey together?
Mr. X: Yes, sir.
Representative Rooney: And that is all at the expense of the American taxpayer?. . . .

[Editor's Note: Several different strategies arise because most budgets are incremental in nature. Administrators must protect their base (current funding level) in order to begin next year's budget discussions from an advantageous position. The following examples illustrate strategies designed to defend an agency's base.]

Defending the Base: Guarding Against Cuts in the Old Programs

CUT THE POPULAR PROGRAM. No one should assume that most agencies engage in perpetual feasting. There is always the specter of cuts. A major strategy in resisting cuts is to make them in such a way that they have to be put back. Rather than cut the national office's administrative expenses, for instance, an agency might cut down on the handling of applications from citizens with full realization that the ensuing discontent would be bound to get back to

Congressmen, who would have to restore the funds. When the National Institutes of Health wanted to get funds for a new, struggling institute such as one devoted to dental research, it would cut one or all of the popular institutes. The committee would be upset that heart, cancer, or mental health had been cut and would replace the funds. The same strategy was used in transferring funds from the popular research to the unpopular operating expenses category.

CUT THE LESS-VISIBLE ITEMS. Counter-strategies are available to legislators. Many Congressmen feel a need to cut an agency's requests somewhere. Yet the same Congressman may be sympathetic to the agency's program or feel obliged to support it because people in his constituency are thought to want it. Where, then, can the cuts be made? In those places which do not appear to directly involve program activities. The department office or general administrative expenses, for example, may be cut without appearing to affect any specific desirable program. And this fits in well with a general suspicion current in society that the bureaucrats are wasteful. Housekeeping activities may also suffer since it often appears that they can be put off for another year and they do not seem directly connected with programs. The result may be that deferred maintenance may turn out to be much more expensive in the end. But cutting here enables the Congressman to meet conflicting pressures for the time being.

Promotional activities, non-tangible items, are also difficult to support. Unless the appropriations committee members trust the agency officials more than it ordinarily happens, they will inevitably be suspicious of items that resist measurement and concrete demonstration of accomplishment. Here, again, is a place to cut where the bureaucracy can be chastised and where powerful interest group support is likely to be lacking.

ALL OR NOTHING. The tactic is to assert that if a cut is made the entire program will have to be scrapped. "Reducing the fund to $50,000 would reduce it too much for us to carry forward the work. We have to request the restoration. . . " said the Bureau of Mines. The danger is that Congress may take the hint and cut out the whole program. So this strategy must be employed with care in connection with a program that is most unlikely to be abolished.

SQUEEZED TO THE WALL. "It so happens," the Fish and Wildlife Service told the Senate Committee, that our budget is so tight that we have no provision at all for any leeway in this amount. This will simply result in a lower level of production at our fish hatcheries."

ALTER THE FORM. We have seen that appearance counts for a great deal and that a program viewed and calculated in one light may be more attractive than when viewed in another. The form of the budget, therefore, may become crucial in determining the budgetary outcomes. Suppose that an agency has strong clientele backing for individual projects. It is likely to gain by presenting them separately so that any cut may be readily identified and support may be easily mobilized. Lumping a large number of items together may facilitate cuts on an across-the-board basis. Items lacking support, on the other hand, may do better by being placed in large categories. A program budget may help raise appropriations by focusing attention on favored aspects of an agency's activities while burying others. The opposite result is also possible and an agency may object to presenting its budget in categories that do not show it off to best advantage.

SHIFT THE BLAME. A widespread strategy is to get the other party to make the difficult decisions of cutting down on requests, thus shifting the onus for the cuts. If he has to take the blame he may not be willing to make the cut. In many bureaus it is the practice to submit initial requests to the agency head or budget officer that are considerably above expectations for support either in the Executive Branch or Congress. By including many good projects the bureau hopes to compel the department head to make the difficult choice of which ones are to be excluded. As a counter-strategy, the agency head may set down a ceiling and insist that the subdivision decide which of its desired projects are to be included. Both the agency head and the subdivision may be restrained, however, by their desire not to come in so high or so low that they risk loss of confidence by others.

Everyone knows that many agencies raise their budgetary requests (among other reasons) in order to show their supporting interests that they are working hard but are being thwarted by the Administration. So the Budget Bureau is disposed to cut. The most frustrating aspect of this activity is that when an agency's budget is squeezed it is often not the "wasteful" things that come out; priorities within the agency and Congress vary greatly and the legendary obsolete munitions factory may survive long after more essential activities have disappeared. Thus the Budget Bureau may be caught between its desire to make the agency responsible for cuts and the need to insist that they be made in certain places rather than others.

After reviewing their program, agency officials often find that they have many programs in which they believe and which cost more than they think the Budget Bureau will allow. Rather than choose the priorities themselves, the officials may try to get the Bureau to do the paring on the very best items. In this way they maintain their reputation for submitting only first-class programs and let the Budget Bureau take the blame for denying some of them. When clientele groups complain, the agency can always say that it tried but the Budget Bureau turned it down. . . .

[*Editor's Note: A final set of strategies is designed to broaden existing agency activities or to add new programs without giving the appearance that an organization is expanding dramatically or that its requests deviate very much from past allocations.*]

Expanding the Base: Adding New Programs

THE WEDGE OR THE CAMEL'S NOSE. A large program may be begun by an apparently insignificant sum. The agency then claims that (1) this has become part of its base and that (2) it would be terrible to lose the money already spent by not going ahead and finishing the job. As Representative Rooney observed, "This may be only $250 but this is the camel's nose. These things never get out of a budget. They manage to stay and grow." It was for a long time common practice for agencies to submit a request for a relatively small sum to begin a project without showing its full cost over a period of years. Congress has sought to counter this strategy by passing legislation requiring a total estimate for a project before any part can be authorized. But estimates are subject to change and a small sum one year rarely seems imposing even if a larger amount is postulated for the future. . . .

An agency may engage in wedging by requesting a small sum for research and using it to justify the feasibility of a big new project. The agency may borrow some personnel and equipment, use a few people part time in order to develop a program, and then tease Congress and the Budget Bureau with an established operation that has generated support for its continuance. A change in the wording of authorization legislation may then be sought so that the agency does not appear to be building empires.

The desire of budget officials to keep items in the budget, even if they are small and underfinanced, is readily explained once it is understood that they may one day serve to launch full-blown programs when conditions are more favorable. Research projects are often not terminated when they have proven successful or have failed; a small item concerning applicability of the research is kept in the budget so that if the agency wishes to resume it has a foot in the door, and if it wishes to begin a new project that may be connected with the old one.

JUST FOR NOW. "Is there anything more permanent than a temporary agency of the Government?" Representative Phillips wanted to know. His colleague, Mr. Thomas, spoke with some asperity of a temporary activity that had begun four years ago. "Of course, [the agency] said it would take them about two years to clear it up and then they would be off the payroll. Since then I think you have added 30 to this group." A temporary adjustment to a passing situation results in an emergency appropriation for a fixed period, which turns out to be a permanent expenditure.

SO SMALL. When an increase is presented as one, a firstline of defense is to say that it is so small as to be eminently justifiable or, if not, then certainly not worth bothering about. Here, as elsewhere, much depends on the basis of comparison. Administrator Petersen was fond of comparing the "negligible" costs of Civil Defense with the "outrageous" advertising costs of a certain beer. "The costs of the investigations that we make," the Fish and Wildlife Service asserted, "are tiny in relation to the total project costs of the engineering agencies. Normally, they can be accomplished for a few thousand dollars on a project that cost millions . . . ." A more extreme example was furnished by Representative Siemanski who defended the Narcotics Bureau by asserting that it would cost $279 million to run for one hundred years. "Stack that against the two billion cargo that vanished in 1950 and the issue is clear. In 100 years, at 500 tons a year, opium runners at present prices would net 200 billion."

This strategy is also meant to suggest that a particular item or class of items is too insignificant to warrant study. A Justice Department Official spoke of "a net increase of $162,000 made up of a number of small items. I question seriously whether the committee wants to spend time on them, they are so small." He was wrong. But it is impossible to go into everything and the way in which the agency presents its budget, the kinds of emphasis it gives, the comparisons it suggests, may serve to direct attention to and from various objects. A miscellaneous category is unlikely to excite anyone's imagination. Every once in a while a Congressman will say, "Give us a breakdown here of 'other objects,' $2,264,000," as happened to the Weather Bureau in 1961.

31
National Bureau of Standards:
A Fall from Grace

G. B. Kolata

Most government agencies complain that their budgets have not kept pace with inflation and increasing demands for services. But officials at the National Bureau of Standards (NBS) say they have been hit harder than most—a view that is confirmed by a statutory Visiting Committee, appointed by the Secretary of Commerce, and by staff members of the Senate Commerce Committee. The Visiting Committee goes so far as to say that "NBS current resources are inadequate or nonexistent in a number of research areas that have been identified as critical to national needs."

Malaise pervades NBS at its headquarters in Gaithersburg, Maryland—a suburb of Washington, D.C. Officials and laboratory scientists there see a pattern of declining performance and capability that began 10 years ago and picked up speed within the past 5 years as the bureau was loaded with new responsibilities that draw heavily on its allotted money and personnel. The causes of this situation are complex and involve a chain of government officials that stretches from NBS to the Department of Commerce (under whose aegis NBS falls) to the Office of Management and Budget (OMB), and includes members of Congress and even the President.

In recent years, Congress has made increasing demands on the technical expertise at NBS. It has passed 15 laws since 1965 giving the bureau new assignments. But during that time NBS has had a constant budget despite inflation and has had to reduce the number of its employees from 3163 permanent full-time workers to 3055. The result, say NBS administrators, is that the bureau is no longer able to fulfill its functions. The scientific reputation of NBS is also deteriorating. Morale is low and the best young researchers

From *Science*, Vol. 197, pp. 968-970, 2 September 1977. Copyright 1977 by the American Association for the Advancement of Science. Reprinted with permission.
G. B. Kolata is a reporter for *Science*.

are no longer interested in working there. What was once a first-rate research institution is now in some danger of becoming a job shop.

The work of NBS is seldom in the news, and its mandated responsibility for developing and maintaining a large array of measurement standards hardly excites the imagination. But many of these standards are crucial to regulatory agencies, to consumers, and to businesses and industries. For example, the bureau recently established a calibration service for diagnostic x-ray units to help prevent the public from being overexposed to x-rays. It develops standards for measuring pollutants in air and water, thus ensuring that regulators measure pollutants in the same way as the industries they regulate. It issued a standard establishing safety requirements for toys. It helps industries calibrate gage blocks, which are used to check on the accuracy of measurements.

Some of NBS's work involves problems whose solutions require long-term research. One such problem is to devise means of measuring amounts of radioactivity in nuclear fuels at various stages of processing. This is necessary to provide a basis for accountability for nuclear materials. According to Arthur McCoubrey, director of the Institute for Basic Standards at NBS, these measurements "go beyond the existing state of the art," and NBS will require several years of research to come up with the necessary techniques. In the meantime, says McCoubrey, problems of tracing the more than 4 tons of nuclear fuel that have disappeared from laboratories and factories over the past 30 years may boil down to a lack of adequate measurement methods.

John Hoffman, director of NBS's Institute for Materials Research, cites several examples of deteriorating capabilities in his institute and in NBS as a whole. He reports that the bureau was recently required to develop standards for the use of recycled oil, which requires the testing of recycled oil in engines. The NBS, however, has no wear and lubrication scientists. Competence in electrochemistry (which is important for studies of water pollution and corrosion) is declining or lost, as is strength in alloy physics (which is needed to develop safe and effective substitutes for increasingly scarce and expensive materials, such as dental gold.).

Technicians, according to Hoffman, are "an endangered species" at the bureau. Out of a total of about 2600 employees at Gaithersburg, only 10 or 15 are technicians. Highly trained Ph.D.'s now must do routine technical work and some have left NBS because of this. Productivity is also diminished and staff morale is low owing to budget problems and personnel cutbacks. "At times I feel these morale problems related to the budget process are becoming a continuous agony," Hoffman says.

McCoubrey tells a similar story about the Institute for Basic Standards. His institute lost about 70 people out of 850 in the past year, and its budget was cut by 8 percent. It has had to terminate or greatly reduce what McCoubrey views as important programs. For example, it terminated its program on signal lighting for airports and airplane cockpits. It reduced its programs to develop means to calibrate flow instruments, which are important for measuring the flow of such things as oil and natural gas in pipelines.

McCoubrey charges that political forces require the bureau to respond to short-range problems for which answers can be found in 1 or 2 years, at the expense of long-term programs. Now, says McCoubrey, "people tend to come to NBS in order to work with a particular NBS scientist and not because NBS is a first-rate scientific institution."

The climate for research at NBS has been monitored by a committee composed of scientists and engineers at the bureau, who tell a similar story. The problem, according to Richard Deslattes who, for the past year, was chairman of the committee, is that "we are mandated to produce results only of immediate and tangible public benefit, at the cost of losing touch with the deeper and longer term benefits of rationally conceived and executed programs." He says that the message passed on to the laboratory scientists is that it is necessary to hide the best scientific work of the bureau which may not bear directly on politically popular problems. The result, he says, is that "there is a continuous sense of frustration in behalf of the NBS as an institution." Deslattes recognizes that NBS is not intended to be another Institute for Advanced Studies, but feels that there is room and a need for some excellent basic research at the bureau.

One example of "hidden" work is research on atomic and molecular data, which is directed by William Martin. Martin says he has been told informally by NBS administrators that his work is not salable to the Commerce Department and so it is buried under descriptions that make it difficult to identify. According to Martin, this work is applicable to energy research and is highly valued by physicists in universities. It could not easily be done outside NBS since it "does not lend itself to a Ph.D. thesis," being long-range and requiring tedious literature searches and the compiling of published data. Most of the people who are willing to do this sort of work, says Martin, are at NBS. But the bureau's abilities to keep these researchers are eroded by the message that their work is not salable.

The problems cited by the institute directors and laboratory scientists of NBS are confirmed by the Visiting Committee, which is required by law to report annually to the Secretary of Commerce on the condition of the bureau. The committee reports that "Shocking gaps exist in NBS's ability to carry out its basic assignment as well as the supplemental assignments that have been thrust upon the bureau." The committee points out that the amount of money devoted to basic research is now about half that devoted 10 years ago, a statement confirmed by Raymond Kammer, senior program analyst at NBS. In fiscal year 1978, $3 million is devoted to basic research out of a total of $70.4 million, Kammer says. In fiscal year 1965 nearly $7 million out of $26.5 million was devoted to basic research.

The sources of NBS's decline seem to be in various federal agencies, including NBS itself. The bureau has had four different directors in 10 years. "The NBS has been an admirable training ground for people to go on to other responsibilities," according to William O. Baker, head of Bell Laboratories in Murray Hill, New Jersey, and Chairman of the National Academy of Sciences

NBS Evaluation Panels committee. But the most pressing problem is that its current leader, Ernest Ambler, has been an "acting" director for 2 years. "I think it is an outrage," Baker says, "Ambler has done superbly but damage is inevitable, both to him and to the conduct of the bureau. He is unable to speak out or plan without being confirmed as director." As yet, there are no plans afoot to confirm Ambler or to name a successor. Some observers say it's up to Jordan Baruch, the new Assistant Secretary for Science and Technology at the Department of Commerce, to initiate confirmation hearings. Baruch, however, evades the question of confirming a director, saying the responsibility is in President Carter's hands.

Another source of NBS's problems is the Commerce Department, which the Visiting Committee accuses of having a "laissez-faire attitude." This analysis is confirmed by Elsa Porter, the new Assistant Secretary for Administration at Commerce. The Commerce Department, like the NBS, has had a rapid succession of leaders. "For the past 8 years, no Secretary of Commerce came in with the idea that he would stay around and improve the situation," she says. There were five secretaries during that period, which resulted in "an absence of sustained leadership" and subsequent internal problems at Commerce.

The Department of Commerce is responsible for presenting to OMB the bureau's case for more funds. The OMB, however, has blundered in its relations with NBS and contributed to the problems, according to the Visiting Committee. For example, the committee says that Congress gave NBS the task of prescribing tests of energy use or energy efficiency of household products. Although OMB approved this project, it told NBS to obtain funds from the Federal Energy Administration (FEA). Then OMB took the money for this project away from FEA. Joyce Walker, Deputy Assistant Director for Economics and Government at OMB, says that OMB took money away from FEA because of congressional directives.

Another example cited by the Visiting Committee of how OMB exacerbated NBS's problems concerns the Resource Conservation and Recovery Act of 1976. Congress gave NBS a deadline of 2 years to develop guidelines for the specifications for materials recovered from wastes. But OMB has denied NBS any funds for this project. Walker explains, however, that NBS is to work with both the Environmental Protection Agency and the Department of the Interior on this project. The OMB has denied funds to all three agencies until they come up with a plan that ensures that they will not duplicate each other's work.

Some observers say the source of these difficulties with OMB may be the channels through which the bureau's budget is reviewed. Most of the government's science and technology agencies have their budgets reviewed together by analysts familiar with scientific issues, many of whom were brought in by Hugh Loweth, Deputy Associate Director for Energy and Science. The NBS budget, on the other hand, is reviewed in the economics and general government area of OMB. The Visiting Committee states that "the people from OMB responsible for oversight of NBS are nontechnical people and have little understanding of the relevance of this highly technical work." Ambler says circumspectly, "I would think that the most logical way to review the NBS budget would be to compare it to other science and technology budgets."

Administrators at OMB, however, say that it is neither possible nor necessarily desirable to have scientifically trained people review NBS's budget. Loweth points out that there is no single technical area that predominates in NBS's research, so it is not clear just what sort of scientists would be appropriate to review the bureau's budget. Moreover, NBS is a small agency compared to such agencies as the National Aeronautics and Space Administration, whose budget is reviewed by Loweth's technical staff, and it would be hard to justify bringing in technical people to review NBS's budget. Walker believes that it is entirely appropriate that OMB be peopled with generalists rather than specialists. Specialists, she says, may tend to be advocates of various programs and strong advocates are not necessarily desirable people to help divide up a limited amount of money.

Administrators Not Convinced

Administrators at OMB are not completely convinced that NBS's plight is so dire. Walker explains that, because NBS feels itself to be very important, it doesn't realize that the private sector could do some tasks equally well and that some tasks could be turned over to other agencies. Unfortunately, she says, OMB must give agencies less money than they could profitably use. The OMB wants to encourage NBS to monitor itself, to determine which of its programs could be dropped in order to make best use of limited funds.

Despite the current tales of woe of NBS, many observers have not given up hope that the situation may change. Even the Visiting Committee says that the bureau's decline is not irreversible and that good management and firm support for NBS at the Commerce Department can yet allow the bureau to regain its scientific reputation. Deslattes, reporting the scientists' view at NBS, says that there remains among the NBS staff a cadre with "deep reserves of intellect and culture within their disciplines." He concludes that changes in the way research at NBS is administered can renew the bureau's scientific vigor.

Administrators at NBS are pinning many of their hopes for change on Baruch, being encouraged by what they say was an unprecedented visit to the bureau on 26 July. During that visit, Baruch invited NBS managers to help him decide on the future role of NBS as a scientific and technical resource. He seems to have favorably impressed NBS administrators and convinced them of his sincerity.

Although the Visiting Committee suggested that NBS declare a moratorium on new assignments not directly funded by Congress, Baruch believes the bureau cannot abrogate its responsibilities in the face of decreasing funds—a laudable goal but one that is difficult, at the very least, to achieve. He indicates that NBS must maintain its classical role of "technologist of last resort," but wants the price paid for reprogramming made clear. "Congress and the Executive are reasonable. They know you can't get something for nothing," he says.

Porter is also concerned about the decline of NBS and hopes the situation will change as the bureau becomes more visible at Commerce. She and her associates are now trying to link the various programs at Commerce together. They are setting up weekly meetings of key program managers, for example. As a result of this increased communication, she predicts that "other parts of Commerce will appreciate NBS in a much deeper way."

Still another hint that NBS may be rescued comes from increased interest in the bureau in Congress. Members of the Senate Commerce Committee staff say they cannot remember when hearings on NBS were last held. Now, the committee "has a real commitment to look at NBS" and considers the status of the bureau to be one of the most important issues to be dealt with. As evidence of this concern, the committee plans to hold hearings on NBS in the near future, but they cannot estimate when the hearings will take place or specify what the hearings will accomplish.

It is still too early to say whether any of these professed plans to rescue NBS will be successful. But the fact that the bureau is receiving increased attention is, in itself, evidence to optimists that its decline may yet be halted and even reversed.

| PERSONALITY PROFILE |

32
The Man Who Shapes
the Federal Budget

When James Talmadge McIntyre, Jr., was appointed director of the Office of Management and Budget a few weeks ago, there was a lot of speculation about how he would operate.

A short, soft-spoken, low-key man, Mr. McIntyre had nothing like the stature in the Washington scene that his predecessor, Bert Lance, had enjoyed.

To Mr. McIntyre, however, there was no question of his being big enough for the job.

The 37-year-old lawyer from Georgia has a Texas-size confidence in his ability to oversee the management of the federal government's executive branch in the way that President Carter wants it overseen. He handled a similar job for Jimmy Carter on the state level when the President was governor of Georgia.

How will he run OMB?

"That's simple," he says with a grin. "I want to run the sharpest, brightest agency in town. And there is a tremendous amount of talent in OMB that can enable me to do it."

Congress is just now beginning to digest major handiwork of both the President and Mr. McIntyre—a federal budget bumping the half-trillion-dollar mark, the first budget wholly of the Carter administration's making.

It is also the first budget put together under the zero-base budgeting concept which the President—and Mr. McIntyre—hope ultimately will deliver to the public a balanced budget as well as more efficient government.

Mr. McIntyre, in quick, precise sentences, can inundate you with figures to support his contention that the hope will become reality.

He knows figures backward and forward, particularly the ones in this fiscal 1979 budget.

Unlike Lance

From the very beginning, the technical details of putting the budget together fell to Mr. McIntyre, who served as deputy director of OMB under Mr. Lance.

Mr. Lance, a rumpled bear of a man and the President's longtime and close personal friend, was never viewed by very many as a personification of the detail-and-figure-conscious type associated with overseers of budgets.

"Bert was a marketeer," says one close observer of OMB. "He was the guy who could sell the President's programs—zero-base budgeting, government reorganization, the big concepts.

"Jim McIntyre is the kind of guy you imagine handling the figures—the big, big figures of the government's budget."

Pushing zero-base

Mr. McIntyre doesn't pretend he has the same type of personality as Mr. Lance. But he is a lot more aggressive than most Washington pundits seem to think.

One thing he has done is to aggressively push the zero-base budgeting concept in the formulation of the new budget. In meeting after meeting with agency and department people, he preached zero-base with almost evangelical zeal.

"We got very good cooperation from everybody," he says. "Also, we didn't try to be heavy-handed. We worked with everybody to make sure they understood what we were trying to do."

He was helped, he admits, by the fact that the President himself made it clear that use of the zero-base concept was Mr. Carter's idea.

"I think that was a very important factor in the success of this program," Mr. McIntyre says softly. He doesn't have to mention the clout of a President over the bureaucracy and that a linchpin of Mr. Carter's announced goals is government reorganization.

A native of Vidalia, Ga. (pop. 9,507), Mr. McIntyre got his law degree from the University of Georgia, practiced law in Athens, Ga., and was general counsel to the Georgia Municipal Association from July, 1966, to April, 1970, when he was appointed deputy state revenue commissioner.

Jimmy Carter named him head of the Georgia Office of Planning and Budget in October, 1972, and he was reappointed to that post by Gov. George Busbee in January, 1975.

He came to Washington to serve as deputy director of OMB, at President Carter's request, in March, 1977. The Senate confirmed him unanimously.

When Bert Lance resigned last autumn after stormy congressional controversy over some of his past personal financial practices, the President gave Mr. Lance's young colleague the title of acting director. In December, as the finishing touches were being put on the budget, the President made Mr. McIntyre's new status official by announcing he was going to send his name to Congress for confirmation as the director.

Drives pickup truck

An early riser, the new OMB director gets to work by 7:30, often driving himself to downtown Washington in a pickup truck from his mini-farm in Clifton, Va.

When he isn't working in the Old Executive Office Building on weekends, he and his family raise horses, and he builds things—such as a barn. His wife, Maureen, is a veterinarian, but doesn't practice. They have three daughters.

In Washington, a city of many words but few physical actions, there is a certain aura about anyone who builds a barn himself.

OMB, too, has a certain aura, since its director is something of a general manager for government. Management supervision of agencies and departments is being emphasized more and more by the agency.

Government's heartbeat

"We are sort of a heartbeat of the government," Mr. McIntyre says. "We keep things going on a day-to-day basis on behalf of the President."

Before the President named Jim McIntyre as OMB director, there were many who thought Mr. Carter would try to get a "name" from the world of business or finance for the job.

"My betting was on Jim from the very start after Bert left," says one former Georgia state official. "You know, some Presidents don't like to talk figures and details. But Carter does. He's his own budget director in many ways. He is familiar with the details, and he liked the way Jim McIntyre did things in Georgia. He also likes the way Jim does things in Washington."

Among the things that Mr. McIntyre will try to do as OMB director is keep a lid on the growth of government and the federal budget.

He knows he isn't running the 100-yard dash.

Rome wasn't built in a day

"Government reorganization isn't going to happen in one day," he says. "It will take several years. But we have made progress already. Plans have gone to Congress for reorganizing the United States Information Agency and the State

Department's cultural affairs section. Many agencies have already done some reorganization on their own, and more is coming."

There is another whopping deficit in the new budget, and whether the dream of a balanced budget can be attained by 1981, as the President wants, depends a great deal upon the economy—and upon Congress's own spending ideas.

It also depends a great deal on the administration.

Economic manifesto

Mr. McIntyre says the economic philosophy which went into preparing the new budget and will go into future Carter budgets can be spelled out this way:

- "We should not allow the percentage of the gross national product accounted for by public spending to exceed 21 percent in the long run.

- "We should not allow federal income taxes to take an ever-increasing share of the incomes of individual taxpayers. We should cut taxes as inflation automatically increases that share.

- "We must not allow the budget deficit to become a permanent feature on the economic landscape.

- "We should move boldly to develop genuine private sector jobs—jobs with a future—for the thousands of minority and teenage workers now unemployed in our great cities."

Getting acquainted

Mr. McIntyre has been working hard to become as good a salesman for the President's programs as he is a technician.

He has been addressing business groups around the country and getting acquainted with key congressmen by calling on them.

It was no secret after Mr. Lance left that Jim McIntyre wanted the job of director. Nor was it a secret that he didn't mount any great campaign for the job, even though he was a veteran member of the Carter team and had powerful friends deep within the inner sanctum.

However, as acting director for four months, he acted like the director. Which, it turned out, suited the President just fine.

33

Evaluating a Program's Success or Failure . . . It's Much Easier Said Than Done

Joel Havemann

If the federal government were to evaluate its efforts at program evaluation, it would find that on the whole, they are a failure.

All techniques for evaluating federal programs have a common goal—to bring about changes in those programs that can be improved and to eliminate those that are beyond hope. This is a goal that federal evaluation has not met.

"There is little evidence to show that evaluation generally leads to more effective social policies or programs," the Urban Institute reported in 1974. "On the contrary, the experience to date strongly suggests that social programs have not been as effective as expected and have not improved in performance following evaluation."

Joseph S. Wholey, an author of the 1974 report and director of program evaluation studies at the Urban Institute, said in a recent interview that little has happened since 1974 to change that conclusion. The problem, he said, is not so much with the evaluators as with the programs that they are asked to evaluate.

Doing evaluation

Federal programs, especially those aimed at complex social problems, are by their nature difficult to evaluate for success or failure. Said Fernando Oaxaca, associate director for management and operations of the Office of Management and Budget (OMB): "In these kinds of programs, where there are so many factors involved, the state of the art is not very advanced."

Program objectives: Before he can determine whether a particular program is doing what was intended of it, an evaluator must identify the program's objectives. Unfortunately, legislation establishing programs often leaves program goals fuzzy.

Wholey said Congress rarely can agree on specific objectives when it enacts a new program. It is hard enough to get a majority of the House and Senate to vote for a program, Wholey said; it would be nearly impossible to get majority support for program objectives as well.

"The vaporous wish is the eloquent but elusive language of goals put forward for most federal programs," Wholey and his Urban Institute associates wrote in 1974. "Exactly what are the 'unemployability,' 'alienation,' 'dependency' and 'community tensions' some programs desire to reduce? How would

From the *National Journal,* May 22, 1976, pp. 710-711. Copyright 1976 by National Journal. Reprinted with permission.
Joel Havemann is Deputy Editor of the *National Journal.*

one know when a program crossed the line, successfully converting 'poor quality of life' into 'adequate quality of life?' "

Charles L. Schultze, President Johnson's budget director from 1965-67, cited the 1965 Elementary and Secondary Education Act (79 Stat 27) as an example of a program whose objectives were in the eye of the beholder.

"Some saw it as the beginning of a large program of federal aid to public education," Schultze, a senior fellow at the Brookings Institution, wrote in 1968. "The parochial school interests saw it as the first step in providing financial assistance for parochial school children. The third group saw it as an antipoverty measure."

The problem addressed by Wholey and Schultze is easier to identify than to solve. If Congress had to spell out precise program objectives before it could act, it might never act at all.

"Legislators often are provoked by a sense of a problem, not by some firm objective," Allen Schick, a senior specialist in American government for the Congressional Research Service (CRS), told a CRS seminar in 1975. "When legislation is controversial and objectives clash, there is a tendency to paper over differences by being vague about purposes and intent."

Cause and effect: Even when objectives can be pinned down and their attainment can be observed, it usually is difficult to determine if federal programs are responsible. In the complex environment in which most federal programs operate, relationships of cause and effect are hard to identify.

"It's extremely difficult to know if what you're doing with the dollars is having any effect," said Blair G. Ewing, director of planning and evaluation for the Law Enforcement Assistance Administration (LEAA). "It's especially difficult to know if what you see is the result of what you do."

Ewing used the example of an LEAA program aimed at increasing citizen participation in crime prevention. One result of such a program, he said, might be that more crime victims would report crimes to police. A superficial evaluation of the program would show that it forced the crime rate up, when in fact such was not the case at all.

Wholey said Congress and the executive agencies that operate programs enacted by Congress frequently do not think through the question of whether the program really is designed to treat the problem that has been identified. It is by no means clear, Wholey said, that giving money to school districts will produce pupils who read better or that training the unemployed will result in a lower unemployment rate.

Demonstration projects: Evaluation is most effective when programs are designed carefully, like experiments in a science laboratory, to prove or disprove their value. The ideal demonstration program is tested on a limited group of individuals, who can be compared with a comparable group of persons outside the program.

To date, demonstration projects have proved of limited use. If a program might be of value, it is difficult for the federal government intentionally to withhold it from some individuals. Experimental conditions turn out to be much easier to control in science labs than in cities.

In one of the first federal experiments with a social program, 725 families in New Jersey received a "negative income tax" payment for four years from a 1967 Office of Economic Opportunity grant. Their experience was compared with that of 632 similar families that had only the traditional welfare programs available to them.

"The experiment was a highly complex undertaking, and the results are ambiguous in many instances," said David N. Kershaw, senior vice president of Mathematica, Inc., the consulting firm that conducted the trial run with the negative income tax.

Kershaw said that when the experiment ended, most families that continued to need cash assistance were able to find it in other welfare programs. Many families reported that they were better off after the experiment than during it, he said.

The Urban Mass Transportation Administration (UMTA) has operated a variety of experimental programs. Ronald Kirby, director of the Urban Institute's transportation project, said UMTA has been willing to go ahead with experimental programs only if it thought the programs would be adopted in other cities. "No one had the courage to try something chancy," he said.

UMTA's Shirley Highway bus lane in Northern Virginia was successful because it was maintained after UMTA's experiment was over, Kirby said. But on the other hand, it did not add much to human knowledge about urban transportation. "The fact that buses go faster in lanes just for them was not particularly surprising," he said.

UMTA gradually undertook more daring experiments, such as the dial-a-bus program in Haddonfield, N.J., from 1972 to 1975. Kirby said this project yielded less information than it might have because of the way UMTA designed the experiment.

UMTA seems to be making progress. Kirby said a current experiment in Danville, Ill., that permits the elderly and handicapped to buy taxi tickets at reduced prices should show whether a city can use its private taxi fleet to improve transportation.

Using evaluation

Even the most carefully prepared evaluations are not necessarily useful. Sometimes, as when they are late or written in jargon, the fault lies with the evaluators. But often there is no market for evaluation; Members of Congress and agency decision makers do not want to have their preconceptions upset by facts.

Wholey said Washington is full of "evaluation studies in search of users and uses." Said Oaxaca: "There have been hundreds of millions of dollars spent on evaluations that have ended up on somebody's shelf."

Commerce Secretary Elliot L. Richardson, who set up a system of evaluation at the Health, Education and Welfare (HEW) Department while he was HEW Secretary from 1970-73, said he was pleased with the quality of some of the evaluations that HEW produced. "However," he testified to a Senate subcommittee on March 6, "the ability of even many of the successful studies to effect changes in program direction and magnitude was modest, since resulting program proposals were either ignored or submerged in rhetoric."

Timing: Many otherwise useful evaluations are completed only after decisions must be made about the programs being evaluated. "There are few concrete illustrations of well-developed and carefully executed evaluations that have been completed in time to affect either legislation or the decision-making process of policy makers," Howard E. Freeman, a sociology professor at the University of California at Los Angeles wrote in 1975.

Wholey pointed to the example of a requirement in the 1965 Elementary and Secondary Education Act that there be an evaluation of every project financed by grants to schools in poor neighborhoods. Wholey said the evaluations— 20,000 of them, at a cost of $10 million—came in the summer, but program decisions had to be made in the previous spring.

Schick said any evaluation is too late if the program evaluated already has built up strong support from the people it serves. The summer headstart program already was serving hundreds of thousands of poor children when adverse findings were released, he said, and it was too late to do much about the program's shortcomings. "Popular programs are hard to terminate," he said, "no matter what judgments flow from the evaluations."

Jargon: Evaluations can be difficult for policy makers to digest. "Program evaluators who are social scientists frequently prepare long, jargon-laded reports," the Congressional Research Service said in a 1974 report.

Schick urged evaluators to remember that their most important readers are laymen, not technical experts. Sen. Bill Brock, R-Tenn., registered the view of an interested layman in a 1975 speech. Much of the information with which Congress is bombarded, he complained, is impossible to use. "It is not a lack of information," he said. "It is a lack of comprehensible information."

Users: Evaluators are not prepared to assume full blame for the fact that much of their work never is used. Responsibility, they maintain, must be shared by the users.

The 1974 Congressional Research Service report found that federal departments and agencies often ask for the wrong information. Agency evaluation offices, according to the report, often are not in the mainstream of agency policy making.

Clark C. Abt, president of Abt Associates Inc., a regular evaluator of federal programs, said it is up to the departments and agencies to seek program information that will be useful to them. "What we cannot do with program evaluation," he told the 1975 Congressional Research Service seminar, "is get users or consumers of program evaluations to ask the right questions."

One of the prime users of evaluation should be Congress, which must decide the fate of many federal programs every year. "The Members of Congress need to know how important and valuable evaluation techniques can be," Sen. Brock said in a 1975 speech.

"The level of awareness and eagerness for this kind of information has escalated geometrically since 1969 and 1970," said Kenneth W. Hunter, associate director of the GAO's Office of Program Analysis. But Keith E. Marvin, an associate director of the same GAO office, added, "People on committee staffs who understand evaluation are sparse."

"The weak agency commitment to evaluation is reinforced by lack of congressional interest," Schick said. "Many committees function as program advocates rather than as program overseers, and Congress tends to be more oriented to prospective legislation than to past enactments."

34
Education Programs Getting Critical Look

Jack McCurdy

California taxpayers spend nearly $1 billion a year on special education programs designed to help all kinds of public school youngsters ranging from upper-middle-class "gifted" 6-year-olds to poor Hispanic teen-agers with only a limited command of English.

These programs have proliferated sharply in recent years, and in addition to the gifted and bilingual programs they deal with early childhood education, compensatory education, handicapped students, special reading instruction, free lunches, vocational training and other areas.

But as costs to run these programs continue to mount steadily, and in some cases precipitously, state policymakers are faced with a growing problem in gauging their impact.

They simply want to know if these costly programs are working. In the view of some, the answers they have been getting from the state's evaluators have not been satisfactory.

Questions have been raised about the "credibility" of the evaluation reports produced by the state Department of Education and whether the department can objectively assess the effectiveness of the programs it administers and oftentimes designs.

The difficulty in finding out if the programs work has gotten to the point where the Legislature may be ready to seek new ways to determine the results of these efforts.

From the *Los Angeles Times,* December 27, 1977. Part II, pp. 1,6. Copyright 1977 *Los Angeles Times.* Reprinted with permission.
Jack McCurdy is a *Times* education writer.

Legislators, in particular, are under increasing pressure to scrutinize closely the outcomes of such programs and to justify continued expenditures of public monies for this or that program.

"It is frustrating," said Assemblyman Gary K. Hart (D-Santa Barbara). "We (legislators) don't get the kind of clear guidance we want from evaluations of these programs."

As an outgrowth of such sentiment, a move now is under way to strip the department of this job and, in effect, turn it over to private firms which would do the evaluations under contracts with the state.

This is the recommendation of the legislative analyst's office, which contends that outside, independent contractors probably would provide more reliable evaluations and give lawmakers a better basis for judging the performance of educational programs.

But the evaluation responsibility will not be taken away from the department without a fight from Wilson Riles who, as state Superintendent of Public Instruction, heads the department.

Riles said he has confidence in the quality of the department's evaluations and objected to the implication that "somehow we are going to cover up and make something look good when it isn't."

"I frankly resent that kind of thing," he added.

However, there are indications that the Legislature will adopt the analyst's recommendations in some form during its session next year with at least the tacit support of the Brown Administration.

If this happens, the new policy would likely have several important consequences for education in California.

The Legislature might begin shifting the allocation of funds based on what the evaluations show, assuming the outside evaluations are more clear-cut than previous evaluations have been.

At present, programs typically are created by the Legislature with great expectations but subsequent evaluations never seem to resolve questions about their accomplishments. As a result, programs are rarely phased out and only infrequently changed in any substantial way.

More definitive findings could make survival of programs much tougher, resulting in termination of some programs which do not work well and reshaping of others. That could make room for other efforts which otherwise would not be launched because the funds are tied up in existing programs.

This, in turn, could mean shifting of jobs and duties for teachers and other educators in local school districts where the programs are actually run.

In short, it could mean a departure from the comfortable and relatively settled state of things which have marked involvement in these programs in the past.

But it might also lead to more effective programs and more productive results from the use of public funds.

Another consequence could be that Riles' reputation will be somewhat tarnished.

Obviously, it would reflect poorly on Riles as manager of the state's education agency if the important responsibility of evaluation of state educational programs were removed from the department's jurisdiction.

In an interview, Riles seemed unconcerned that his reputation would be damaged because of his confidence in his department's evaluation efforts.

"I don't have any fear whatsoever of anyone looking objectively and honestly at these programs," he said.

But Riles said he does oppose the wholesale removal of the responsibility from the department.

"I would not want the department to be dependent on outside evaluations for the total information and analysis (of programs) in California," he said.

"I think that would be giving up a responsibility that we have by law to some faceless individuals out there who are not accountable to anyone."

Actually, the Legislature already has started using outside contractors to do educational evaluations in addition to those routinely performed by the department.

The question now is whether all major special education programs should be evaluated solely by independent contractors, including those federal programs administered by the state.

There are 10 major state programs of this kind which cost taxpayers about $420 million annually, plus five federal programs which total about $453 million a year.

One of the first of these outside evaluations dealt with early childhood education (ECE), and more than anything else the controversy over this program and attempts to evaluate its performance have spurred consideration of a new evaluation policy.

ECE is Riles' major effort to reform California's public school system and meet public criticism that the schools are not doing a good job overall of educating youngsters.

It includes a range of innovative practices designed to raise pupil achievement, including individually designed instructional plans, smaller classes and participation of parents as classroom aides.

In 1976-77, 687,000 children or 55% of the pupils in kindergarten through third grade were enrolled in ECE classes throughout the state at a cost of $98.5 million.

The department's evaluations of ECE have said the program was producing significant achievement gains among pupils, but the test results themselves have seemed not to back up the claim.

In hopes of clarifying the picture, the Legislature ordered a $200,000 study by the UCLA Center for the Study of Evaluation, which concluded earlier this year that the ECE program made no difference in pupil achievement.

Meanwhile, the Legislature began stepping up use of outside evaluators as the UCLA report, with seemingly better documented conclusions, was favorably received among lawmakers and their aides.

The department also has had trouble meeting deadlines in submitting the evaluation reports to the Legislature and legislators in part turned to outside evaluators in order to get needed information in time to vote on whether to continue funds for various programs.

It all came to a head last spring when the Legislature ordered the analyst's office and the department to study "changes necessary to provide objective evaluations of educational programs in California on a timely basis."

The major focus was to be on the possibility of going to "independent evaluations."

The matter was assigned to the education subcommittee of the Assembly Ways and Means Committee, of which Hart is a member.

Hart said the problem is the lack of useful recommendations in the department's evaluation reports, reports which he said should help legislators in making judgments about programs.

"The bottom line for many of us who are busy is what are the recommendations?" Hart said. "What should we do to change (programs)? Some of us don't see a lot coming out as to recommendations."

The concern is that a "potential conflict of interest exists for the department to be evaluating its own programs" because of "built-in pressures" which make it difficult for the department to be critical, Hart said.

Assemblyman John Vasconcellos (D-San Jose), who heads the subcommittee, said the controversy over ECE "left us (legislators) all up in the air as to how we can assure ourselves of better information" about the programs voted on.

What also led to consideration of outside evaluations was the expansion of the number of programs and the rising overall costs during the last several years, Vasconcellos said.

"As we go into such broader program improvement, we want to be more sure we are watching what is going on and that we can be creative in improving programs as we go," he said.

Vasconcellos said he also is "concerned about the reliability of information we get" from the department.

In its report, the analyst's office concluded that "the best approach for increasing the credibility, timeliness and efficiency of education evaluations is to have the (department) contract for independent evaluations of major education programs and not conduct internal evaluations of these programs."

It recommended "ongoing (legislative) oversight" to make sure the contracts are awarded and administered properly.

The analyst estimated that costs would increase from 10% to 30% per program if outside evaluations were used, although there would be a partially offsetting saving of $750,000 in the projected rise in department evaluation costs.

Considering the benefits, the analyst indicated the higher cost would be well worth it.

In its report, the department said that "the state of the art of evaluation is such that a single and unequivocal answer cannot be made by any reputable evaluator" as far as whether a program is working or not.

Riles said, "I have come to the conclusion that you are never going to get evaluators to agree completely on how it (evaluation) is to be done, what the results are or anything else."

In other words, the department's position is evaluations cannot be definitive, and one evaluator's conclusions are as good as another's assuming they are recognized as professionally competent.

The report said the department must be intimately and completely familiar with the way a program is working in order to oversee that program and assure it runs as well as possible.

And the only way to do that is for the department to conduct the evaluations, it said.

At a recent subcommittee hearing on the matter in Sacramento, Alex Law, chief of program evaluation and research in the department, put it this way:

"We need the authority to see early problems and adjust programs. Independent evaluations are (usually) done annually and after the fact. We can do assessments during implementation (of programs) and make corrections as needed."

Hart asked why contracts could not be written to provide for this, requiring close and continual communication between the outside evaluators and department staff members.

Department lobbyist Tish Bussell conceded contracts could include such provisions, but said it would be "very difficult" to make it work.

As far as meeting legislative deadlines for evaluation reports, Law said the department staff is taxed by the limited time available to do the reports and the large number of them.

Typically, test and other data from local school districts are received in the fall by the department and must be compiled, analyzed and assembled into reports due to the Legislature by the first of the following year, he said.

Law suggested that perhaps the Legislature could forgo annual reports for every program to relieve the work load on the department staff and increase prospects that deadlines would be met.

Hart was joined by Joan Bissell of the analyst's office at the hearing in suggesting another advantage of using outside contractors.

By employing a variety of evaluators, the state would receive a wider assortment of ideas, techniques and suggestions of ways to judge the performance of programs.

Hart added that independent evaluations also could assess the performance of the department in administering programs to determine if that were a factor in the way a program worked.

Index